D1518219

European Expansion and Law

The history of European expansion overseas also includes the history of the expansion of concepts and principles of European law into the non-European world. The values and ideas it expressed have, to this day, deeply influenced indigenous societies and governments. At the same time indigenous concepts of law were "discovered" and codified by European scholars. The outcome of this was a complex and intense interaction between European and local concepts of law, which resulted in many dual legal systems in the African and Asian colonies and which is examined in this volume by prominent historians, lawyers, and legal anthropologists.

W.J. Mommsen is Professor of History at the University of Düsseldorf.

J.A. de Moor is Research Fellow at the University of Leiden.

European Expansion and Law

*The Encounter of European and Indigenous Law
in 19th- and 20th-Century Africa and Asia*

Edited by
W.J. MOMMSEN *and* J.A. DE MOOR

BERG

Oxford / New York

Distributed exclusively in the U.S. and Canada
by St. Martin's Press, New York

Published in 1992 by
Berg Publishers, Inc.
Editorial offices:
165 Taber Avenue, Providence, RI 02906, U.S.A.
150 Cowley Road, Oxford OX4 1JJ, UK

© W.J. Mommsen and J.A. de Moor

Published with support of the European Science Foundation
(Strasbourg) and the Werner-Reimers Stiftung (Bad Homburg).

British Library Cataloguing in Publication Data
European expansion and law: The encounter of
European and indigenous law in nineteenth- and
twentieth-century Africa and Asia.
I. Mommsen, W.J.   II. de Moor, J.A.
325.026

ISBN 0-85496-762-1

Library of Congress Cataloging-in-Publication Data
European expansion and law : the encounter of European and
    indigenous law in 19th- and 20th-century Africa and Asia / edited
    by W.J. Mommsen and J.A. de Moor.
        p.   cm.
    Includes bibliographical references and index.
    ISBN 0-85496-762-1
    1. Law—Asia—European influences—History. 2. Law—Africa—
European influences—History. 3. Law—Europe—History.
4. Colonies—Law and legislation. 5. Asia—Colonial influence—
History. 6. Africa—Colonial influence—History. I. Mommsen.
Wolfgang J., 1930–   . II. Moor, Jaap de.
K3376.E97   1991
349.4—dc20
[344]   91-33218
                                                                CIP

Printed and bound in Great Britain by
Billing and Sons Ltd, Worcester

Contents

Introduction

WOLFGANG J. MOMMSEN

The establishment of colonial empire in many parts of the world, and informal control in others, which began in the late fifteenth century and reached its peak in the 1890s, is today a matter of the past. Since 1947, beginning with the transfer of power in India, the European colonial empires were dismantled with surprising speed, partly under the pressure of indigenous nationalist movements, but also because the international system was no longer conducive to the maintenance of empire. Accordingly the Western powers did not consider it any longer worthwhile to retain formal imperialist control in overseas countries, for political and economic, but also for moral reasons. The United States and the USSR, the two new superpowers who dominated the world order after the Second World War, demanded the discontinuation of the older empires, although for rather different reasons. Besides, formal empire had become too costly, given the rising indigenous opposition now effectively mobilized under the banner of anti-imperialism; also, the costs of policing one's own colonial possessions in the face of growing international pressure were rising day by day. The economic rewards of formal colonial empire were thus rapidly declining, save in a few exceptional cases.

In the early 1960s decolonization was more or less completed, with but a few remnants remaining. Today formal empire, at any rate in its traditional variety, has come to an end for good. The anti-imperialist battle cries voiced by the nationalist elites who took over power have subsided. Therefore the present moment may be a good time for attempting a new colonial reckoning, rather than merely reiterating the wholesale condemnation of colonialism and imperialist rule which allegedly brutally interrupted the natural course of development of the peoples subjected to colonial rule. Instead we should analyze the impact of colonial rule upon the indigenous societies in a detached manner, by rational scholarship.

The present volume is devoted to the analysis of a special aspect of European domination during the period of colonialism and imperialism, namely the introduction of European law in many parts of the non-European world, and its consequences for the post-colonial societies which have emerged after the end of empire.

There can be no doubt that the imposition of European law and European legal procedures upon various peoples in the non-Western world was in the first place a means of establishing and extending imperial control, formal or informal. Not surprisingly, in many cases the colonial rulers displayed a massive interest in subjecting labor relations and landed property to legal norms which were in line with the European legal tradition, as this appeared to be a necessary prerequisite for economic development and profitable exploitation of these often backward regions. This being said, however, the introduction of elements of European law into indigenous societies cannot be said to have had merely a negative impact upon the colonial or semi-colonial societies, however much the colonial masters may have benefited from it in the first place. Indeed, in hindsight it may be considered perhaps one of the few positive elements of the imperialist heritage, even though this cannot serve as a justification of colonial rule. Indeed, most of the new national governments who took over power during the period of decolonization maintained, and in many cases even expanded, the elements of European law and European legal institutions which they inherited from their colonial predecessors. Only recently this legal heritage has been jeopardized, albeit indirectly, by the replacement of English or French as languages spoken in the courts and in governmental business with indigenous languages. This undermines the continuation of legal institutions of European origin, if only to some degree, as has happened for instance in Bangladesh and in the Maghrib.

The encounter between European and non-European, or, as it is usually called, customary law, is in many ways still an uncharted territory, except for the specialists in the field; its importance for the history of European expansion has not yet been generally recognized. The following studies, which deal with a wide variety of countries in time as well as in space, may provide orientation and information about recent research on this topic. They cover key regions of Africa, the Ottoman empire and the Maghrib, China and Japan, and India and Indonesia. The contributions by Jörg Fisch, "Law as a Means and as an End: Some Remarks on the Function of European and Non-European Law in the Process of European Expansion," and Franz von Benda-Beckmann, "Symbiosis of Indigenous and Western Law in Africa and Asia: An Essay in Legal Pluralism," give a long-term view of the conflict, but also of the interaction of law of European origin and indigenous law which comprises both the Americas and Africa.

The transfer of European law and European legal institutions to the non-European world must be considered an important process of acculturation, although it did by no means proceed in a linear manner. The introduction of European law and European legal norms was not a one-way street, as one would assume at first sight. Rather it was the result of a complex process of interaction to which the Europeans and the indigenous peoples, especially the small westernized intellectual elites in the colonial and semi-colonial territories, contributed in their own right, although often from a very unequal base. This is a particularly interesting aspect of the many-faceted nature of imperial rule. Today it is established beyond doubt that colonial rule was based, in most, if not in all cases, upon a delicate system of "unequal bargains" (Robinson) between representatives of the colonial powers at the periphery and the indigenous elites. An essential element of this system of "bargains" was the partial subjection to and, as time went on, the adaptation to legal norms and institutions of European origin. It goes without saying that this was much the same in semi-colonial countries where indigenous governments managed to retain a semblance of independence.

The Europeans who settled or traded in distant lands overseas took their own law with them, rather than let themselves be subjected to alien laws and legal institutions. Accordingly preference was given to the personal law principle; that is to say, in overseas countries subjected to European control, whether formal or informal, Europeans expected their legal disputes to be conducted according to the laws valid in their countries of origin. Above all they could not be prosecuted according to any other law than their own; indigenous or customary law did not apply to them. This was particularly important in Islamic countries, in as much as the Islamic religion in principle demanded the prosecution of all non-believers without mercy. This problem had been dealt with already in the thirteenth century in order to facilitate trade between the Ottoman Empire and the West: the capitulations granted to all Europeans exterritorial status in legal matters, and all litigation affecting them had to be conducted in special consular courts.

In the Americas these problems did not arise, because the Spanish and Portuguese invaders did not encounter here any effective

resistance; the indigenous states and empires usually succumbed without a fight. For the Conquista the spreading of the Christian religion
and of the legal practices common in their mother country were
much the same; they did not hesitate to use brutal repression to
impose not only their rule, but also the Christian faith and Christian
values, or what amounted to them, upon the indigenous population.
This ruthless process of colonization, associated with the enforced
imposition of Christianity and its codes of conduct, in total disregard
of all cultural achievements and traditions of these indigenous cultures which soon crumbled into nothingness, resulted, however, in a
massive depopulation. Due to the spreading of illnesses of all sorts of
European origins, the indigenous peoples passed away with
accelerating speed. After two generations of Spanish colonial rule it
could no longer be overlooked that the extreme maltreatment of the
indigenous peoples had most unwelcome effects on the economy.
Only now the Conquista considered it necessary to grant the Indian
population a minimum of autonomous existence, albeit only on the
basis of isolated village communities, and to provide them with a
semblance of legal protection; but this was done by laws especially
designed for the Indians, not European ones. The Ibero-American
case, however, cannot be called a process of acculturation in any
sense whatever; the introduction of laws of European origin was
merely undertaken in order to keep the indigenous population in
their subordinate place in colonial society.

Nowhere else did European colonial or imperial rule ever attain
this level of ruthless imposition of European values and law, associated with the wholesale destruction of all indigenous institutions,
save perhaps in a few extreme cases like the almost total annihilation
of the Hereros in German South West Africa in 1904/5. As a rule the
opposite trend was prevailing. From the eighteenth to the mid-
nineteenth century, a period in which informal techniques of colonial control were predominant, the colonial powers were usually
reluctant to impose laws and regulations of European origin upon
indigenous societies. Actual control by the colonial power was in
many cases still marginal, mostly limited to a few coastal areas. In
practice it would have been impossible anyway to implement such
laws and provide for the necessary sanctions. Accordingly indigenous legal institutions were mostly left alone, unless they directly
affected the status of the European traders, missionaries, settlers, or
officials. This was, however, a controversial strategy. Colonial expansion and imperialism were justified at home above all by the
argument that colonial rule brought civilization, justice, and Chris-

tian codes of conduct to still-undeveloped regions of the world. Charles Macauley was paramount among those who came to be acutely aware that the pursuit of these two alternative goals, namely the civilizatory mission of the colonial power on the one hand, and the advisability of non-interference with customary law, in order not to arouse the resistance of the local population against the benevolent rule of their colonial masters, could not easily be reconciled with one another.

There existed, however, great variations according to time, circumstances, and, in particular, geographical region. In those Islamic countries which came under the indirect rule of Western countries, such as Algeria, Tunisia, Morocco and Egypt, the personal law principle valid for the Europeans was gradually extended to so-called "protected persons" (*protégés*), who also usually were associated with the commercial activities of their European masters. Likewise consular jurisdiction was extended step by step to order personal affairs. Eventually all cases which concerned conflicts between Europeans and their *protégés* on the one hand and indigenous parties on the other were heard in so-called Mixed Courts, which conducted their business according to European law. Strictly speaking this practice affected only a rather small section of the indigenous population, but in substance it meant that in the Westernized sectors of the economy European law became absolutely predominant. It was no surprise that gradually customary law was influenced by Western legal practice also, though to a small and initially even negligible degree. Eventually there developed a dual system of law, one for the areas more affected by European informal control, and another for the masses of the people.

The Ottoman Empire itself was a special, though most interesting case. As Esin Örücü shows in her contribution, "The Impact of European Law on the Ottoman Empire and Turkey," the Ottoman Empire had always been governed in a decentralized manner, and although Islamic law was the basic law of the empire, the various peoples and religious groups were allowed to regulate their affairs according to their own legal traditions. In legal matters there had always existed a plurality of different customary laws side by side, depending upon the ethnic and cultural groups in question. This made it easier for the Ottoman rulers who wished to implement reforms according to the Western model to introduce elements of Western law considered necessary for the economic development of the empire, beginning with the Commercial Code in 1850. Certainly informal pressure for reforms, to which the Sultan was exposed by the Great Powers, hastened this process, but this coincided with the Ottoman rulers' willingness to modernize those sectors of the society relevant to economic modernization. The leaders of the new Turkish Republic, which came into being in 1923 after a final peace settlement had been reached with the Western powers, eventually embarked upon the wholesale introduction of Western law.

In China and Japan things took a different course, as is described in the contributions by Eric Seizelet, "European Law and Tradition in Japan during the Meiji Era (1868–1912)," and Paul H. Ch'en, "The Treaty System and European Law in China: A Study of the Exercise of British Jurisdiction in Late Imperial China." Both China and Japan had been forcibly opened up to Western trade and influence during the 1850's, but they reacted to this act of informal imperialism in very different ways. The Chinese empire was forced to accept much the same system of legal exterritoriality for the European colonists which had provided the basis for commercial exploitation of unequal terms previously imposed upon Japan, but it made no attempt to react against it. Japan, however, did the opposite as is well-known. In order to get rid of the treaty system which guaranteed a special legal status to all persons of Western origin, Japan embarked upon a deliberate policy of modernization. It began with the introduction of the Meiji constitution in 1868, which was an adaptation of the Central European constitutional monarchy to Japanese needs; likewise a Western legal system was created in order to lay the foundations for a speedy modernization of the country. Thereby the Japanese hoped eventually to become strong enough to be able to stand up against Western intrusions into their society.

In the colonial empires the development took a very different course. The British, the French, the Dutch, the Belgians, and the Germans harbored, in principle, substantially different ideas of how best to run their colonial empires. The British preferred flexible methods and, wherever possible, informal rather than formal rule; they rightly considered the strategy of indirect rule the most preferable and cost-effective method of colonial government. The French were inclined, although in theory rather than in practice, to impose upon their colonies their system of administration with the values and ideals attached to it; the assimilation of the indigenous population to the great French Republic was the guiding ideal. In practice these "privileges" were extended to very small indigenous minorities only, thereby creating, as it were, a special class of *protégés* who came to enjoy the advantages of French law, whereas the mass of the indigenous population was left to live under their customary laws. However, the inclination of French colonial rule to impose European rational standards upon indigenous societies wherever possible did not at all preclude the survival of a considerable variety of indigenous customary legal systems. As is shown by J.-L. Miège in his essay, "Legal Developments in the Maghrib 1830–1930," this was the case in the Maghrib, where French colonial authorities were confronted with an extremely diversified political situation, and with a great many different ethnic groups only loosely subjected to indigenous rulers, mostly of Islamic origin. The Belgians placed from the start all their cards upon the system of "indirect rule" through native chiefdoms, as this seemed to be the most cost-effective system of colonial administration, but in doing so they tended to give very little leeway to the local rulers. Rather they merely used them as instruments in order to civilize native society, as Filip Reyntjens demonstrates in his essay, "The Development of the Dual Legal System in former Belgian Central Africa (Zaire-Rwanda-Burundi)." The Germans sought to implement their system of *Landfrieden* in the colonial territories under their control in an equal fashion everywhere; they operated on the assumption that in all legal matters involving the maintenance of peace ultimate power should rest with the colonial authorities. This implied, at least in theory, that customary law was given in principle only a subsidiary status; it could always be overruled by colonial law. But here, as elsewhere, reality was different from principle; we find in the German colonies much the same wide variety of forms of indirect rule as elsewhere, and thus effective implementation of colonial law differed widely from region to region. The Dutch, in their turn, adhered to an older tradition of legal pluralism. In their colonies there existed one system of law applying to Dutchmen and other Europeans, and another for the various indigenous groups of the population. In principle both were given equal weight and practiced alongside one another; in reality Dutch law prevailed whenever conflicts arose, as is shown in C. Fasseur's essay, "Colonial Dilemma: Van Vollenhoven and the Struggle Between Adat Law and Western Law in Indonesia."

Although the various European colonial powers had different views about colonial rule, the differences of colonial government were in practice by far not as great as one would think. Actual colonial administration at the periphery by and large relied upon much the same strategies. Due to circumstances and scarce resources the European powers were forced to make use of the techniques of indirect rule, wherever possible, although in different degrees, depending on local circumstances and requirements. These techniques varied not only by colonial territory, but also within the individual territories a great deal. They also depended largely upon whether the respective chiefs could be effectively reduced to mere agents of the colonial power, or whether they retained considerable authority in their own right. This implies, in the present context, that European interference in the exercise of justice by the indigenous collaborating elites was often limited, and at times even negligible.

Reliance upon indirect rule implied, of course, that customary law had to be respected, at least to some degrees; otherwise the authority of the chiefs, upon which the system of indirect and subsidiary rule relied, would not have survived for long. Hence customary law not only survived the age of colonialism, but in some cases it was deliberately preserved and at times even strengthened by it. Indeed, in not a few cases artificial customary law came to be created anew by the colonial authorities, for instance in Indonesia. In principle therefore all colonial powers practiced in their colonial possessions a dual, or more correctly, a pluralist system of law. This was part of the informal "unequal bargains," upon which the stability of colonial rule rested at the periphery.

Even though the colonial powers had a vital interest in keeping customary law alive, as indirect and subsidiary rule with the assistance of indigenous authorities was largely dependent upon the continued acceptance of customary law by the indigenous groups, conflicts with the interests of the colonial power were inevitable. The legal and cultural views held by the public in the metropolis objected to the harsher elements of customary law practiced by the indigenous rulers in many parts of the colonial empires. One of the justifications of colonial expansion and rule always had been that the colonial power had a cultural mission; civilization and its values ought to be brought to the peoples in these distant, undeveloped regions, along with, if ever possible, the Christian religion, whereas superstition and inhumane practices had to be eliminated. Not all of this was mere cant; the great movement for the prohibition of slavery had been largely motivated by moral considerations only, and it has had lasting beneficial effects upon the peoples at the periphery. Especially in the British case moral considerations of this sort could not be neglected entirely, and this fact enticed colonial governments time and again to step in against particularly atrocious practices of customary law. But this policy had definite limits. After the so-called "Indian Mutiny" Queen Victoria explicitly forbade any further interference with Indian legal traditions. Besides, many of the principles by which Western humanitarian concern was to be met were in fact not really implemented; in these matters the colonial state was soft and hesitant rather than determined, let alone brutal. Even so the introduction of basic principles of European law into colonial society, like equality before the law or free access to the courts by anybody, had a considerable effect, at least in the long term. Though effective implementation may well have been minimal, these principles eventually provided arguments for the indigenous elites in their struggle for independence which could not easily be ignored.

However, the inroads into customary law by Western law were mostly instrumental. They were designed to provide the legal base for more effective colonial control in areas considered vital by the colonizing power, or to strengthen the predominance of the white ruling elite within indigenous societies. There were in particular two sectors in which the colonial authorities interfered with customary law: labor relations and landholding. In both sectors the colonial elites had vital economic interests. A successful economic "mise au valeur" of the colonies could not be achieved without forcing indigenous peoples to adapt to European labor regulations, and this could only be achieved by massive interference with their traditional work practices. As a rule, the weapon used in order to make the local population adjust to regular work in accordance with European standards was the introduction of individual taxation. Much the same was true with regard to landholding. In customary law individual landownership was almost entirely unknown, and so was the free marketing of landed property. This, however, collided directly with the interests of the white settler communities, notably with the running of plantations, but also with the economic exploitation of mineral resources, which according to Western rational rules required the full possession of the respective lands. According to Max Weber, an essential precondition for an effective capitalist economy is a unified rational legal system, which is created and, if need be, can be reconstructed, according to formal-rational principles. The colonial situation, with its complicated plurality of European, specially designed colonial, and customary law of diverse sorts, did in no way conform with this ideal-typical requirement. However, in the spheres of business and commerce, substantial interference by the colonial authorities with customary law was the rule.

As has been rightly emphasized, the colonial laws more or less forcibly imposed upon indigenous societies were strictly speaking not European at all, but rather laws especially designed for the colonial situation. To put it otherwise, there was no straight transfer of European law onto the periphery; rather, special colonial and state law were created whenever and wherever considered necessary. It was European only in as much as it embodied the principle of formal rationality of law.

Not surprisingly the prime objective of colonial law always was the preservation of peace, be it the *pax britannica* or the German *Landfrieden* or the French "rule of the law." The inroads of colonial law into customary law were thus deepest in the field of criminal law. Conflicts in this sector could all too quickly devolve into major crises affecting colonial authority as such. Accordingly the colonial authorities almost always reserved an ultimate say in the exercise of criminal justice for themselves; at any rate the local representatives of the colonial power had the right to interfere in matters of criminal punishment, if they so wished. In this sector the inclination to interfere with the usually harsh and brutal punishments of customary law was highest, not least because of public opinion at home, which disapproved of the brutal justice exercised by allegedly uncivilized indigenous peoples under the eyes of their European colonial masters.

On the whole, however, the colonial authorities were not interested in pushing hard for a modernization of the legal system as it evolved in the colonial situation. Any such policy would have run contrary to the strategy of "indirect rule" practiced almost everywhere. Besides, civilizing the native population was not considered by them their prime duty. On the contrary, there was much to be said for leaving the natives alone and letting them manage their own affairs in the ways in which they were accustomed, as long as this did not impair the rights and privileges of the white community, or the prerogatives of the colonial power. This policy was also supported on moral grounds; the Oxford School, for instance, pleaded for the preservation of the indigenous societies and their cultures, rather than for the imposition of European values and norms. In actual fact the colonial authorities usually were quite happy with the existing system of legal pluralism, which regulated the lives of the white ruling elites by state law in accordance with the principles of their own national legal traditions, while allowing the indigenous peoples to run their affairs according to local custom.

It goes without saying that the strategy of "indirect rule" depended upon the maintenance of traditional institutions, however alien those might be from a European viewpoint. Indeed, in order to stabilize the "intermediate rule" of various indigenous collaboratory elites, the colonial authorities often were driven to support traditional institutions, and even to prop up customary law, in order to further ensure its acceptance by the indigenous population. Likewise the colonial authorities at times stepped in to stop gross abuse of the existing customary law by individual rulers. Even if it was not the intention to enforce substantial changes in the exercise of customary law, in the long term the impact of such actions was felt nonetheless, whatever the initial intentions may have been. The colonial authorities were not aiming for any far-reaching policies of modernization; on the whole they wanted no more than to achieve a rationalization of customary law which would reduce conflict and make it easier to run the country smoothly. But even so the colonial authorities exercised considerable pressure upon the "intermediary elites" in order to make them abandon certain "uncivilized" elements of customarity. A good example is the informal influence exercised by the "residents" upon the chiefs in British West Africa.

The degree to which the colonial authorities instrumentalized the indigenous collaboratory elites for the pursuance of their objectives, including an adaptation of the system of customary law, varied greatly, according to time and circumstances, and also to the particular style of colonial government practiced by the European colonial powers. As Filip Reyntjens describes, interference with local authorities was particularly strong in former Belgian Central Africa (what is now the states of Zaire, Rwanda and Burundi), and it would appear that such interference is true also for French colonial rule. In West Africa the British made a particularly strong effort to practice "indirect rule," but, as Jarle Simensen shows in his essay "Jurisdiction as Politics: The Gold Coast During the Colonial Period," eventually they also ran into considerable trouble with the native tribunals. The British Raj was a special case; here colonial authority was shrouded in the traditional legitimacy of the former Mughal rulers. And as an inheritance from the British East India Company, here it practiced for the greater part of the continent direct rather than indirect rule, even though it sought the assistance of various intermediary collaborative elites, notably the Zamindars, a theme dealt with in H.-J. Leue's essay, "Legal Expansion in the Age of the Companies: Aspects of the Administration of Justice in the English and Dutch Settlements of Maritime Asia, c. 1600–1750." In the case of British India, the utilitarian philosophy, promulgated by Macauley, among others, had a stronger impact upon law making than anywhere else within the British empire, and interference with customary law was therefore at times considerable, though not always beneficial, as Dagmar Engels describes in her essay, "Wives, Widows and Workers: Women and the Law in Colonial India," in some detail. The Indian princes, on the other hand, discovered that the imperial legal system offered to them a splendid opportunity to carry on with their traditional chivalrous struggle for power and social status, though now in the form of endless lawsuits about property and inheritance. Colonial law and litigation in the Imperial Courts served as means for the Indian upper classes under the British Raj to fight traditional conflicts, as is vividly reconstructed in Pamela G. Price's contribution, "The 'Popularity' of the Imperial Courts of Law: Three Views of the Anglo-Indian Legal Encounter." The operation of the British and the Indian "law machines" alongside each other was full of frictions, but, as D.H.A. Kolff demonstrates in his essay, "The Indian and the British Law Machines: Some Remarks on Law and Society in British India," the old Indian legal system, though subjected to a great deal of change, nonetheless survived the British Raj.

Indonesia is a particularly interesting case. Here the Dutch authorities were initially intent to preserve *adat*, the indigenous customary law. But it proved difficult to adapt *adat* to modern requirements, and to run a colony with a variety of different legal systems seemed outrageously inefficient. Thus there ensued a long struggle to replace the existing dual legal system by a unified law of European origin, but eventually nothing resulted from this, as is shown by C. Fasseur in his essay, "Colonial Dilemma." Attempts to codify *adat* and thereby turn it into a modern rational legal system likewise failed.

Indigenous chiefs and judges were often quite willing to adjust to the new conditions in the colonial situation and to take up elements of colonial or European law whenever this seemed feasible. As F. von Benda-Beckmann shows in his essay, "Symbiosis of Indigenous and Western Law in Africa and Asia," customary law never had been merely the good, ancient law of former times, but had always been adjusted to time and circumstances. Obviously this process of silent adaptation did not come to a halt during the era of colonialism. Rather a process of symbiosis developed, in which the gap between customary law and colonial law became less and less marked. Indeed, it may well be said that by the time when colonial rule came to an end, customary law had long since ceased to be mere traditional law. In fact it had become a sort of neo-customary law no longer comparable to the customary legal usage of pre-colonial times.

Hence it is not surprising to see that the national liberation movements which assumed power from the former colonial powers in the 1950s and 1960s, however much they condemned colonial rule, were by no means enthusiastic about revitalizing indigenous customary law, let alone replacing the colonial legal system with it. On the contrary, they usually preferred state law with its centralized structure to the diversity of customary law, as it would help to create a new unified nation. But, as Martin Chanock points out in his essay, "The Law Market: The Legal Encounter in British East and Central Africa," colonial legal culture had long since established itself as separate from the metropolitan one. Hence the option for what used to be colonial law was not so surprising after all. Besides, efforts were being made to legitimize state law originating from colonial times by reference to customary law, as, for instance, land tenure in East African territories.[1] Consequently legal plurality is no longer the dominant pattern in the legal landscape of the postcolonial countries. The new rulers were intent upon modernization of their countries at any price, and in this respect state law was more useful than traditional law. Indeed, it may be argued that the careful preservation, and in same cases even resuscitation, of customary legal systems had been a skillful device of maintaining colonial control with a minimum of costs to the colonial power, and that this was no more justified than the imposition of law of foreign origin upon the periphery.

There is no doubt that during the period of European expansion the introduction of Western principles of law, although through the back door of special colonial law designed originally to maintain colonial control, had a lasting impact upon the societies in the non-Western world, and still continues to do so, which in hindsight may be judged at least in part as beneficial. The legal systems inherited from the colonial period, however much they have been amended in order to suit the interests of the new nations, are an essential element of the new social order which emerged at the periphery, almost always in a painful process, after the end of colonial rule. They are the product of a process of acculturation which may be judged beneficial, even though considerations of this nature had played but a very small, if any, role at all when these laws and legal institutions were introduced in the first place. Such processes of acculturation will be considered all the more important in an age in which the West has become acutely aware of its

1. Cf. the article by Chanock in this volume.

responsibility for the future well-being of the new nations of the Third World, which, after a long period of subjection to European imperialist rule, now are about to find their own way in history.

I

Law as a Means and as an End: Some Remarks on the Function of European and Non-European Law in the Process of European Expansion

JÖRG FISCH

Introduction

The motives behind European expansion have been and still are subject to debate. While political and economic factors usually are thought to have been particularly important, it seems obvious that law played a subordinate part, that it was a means and not an end in this process. It strengthened the European position overseas, the hold of the colonial powers over subject populations, and was molded according to this purpose.

There certainly can be no doubt that European expansion was not the result of the desire or decision to extend the area of validity of European law. From this fact, however, it cannot automatically be concluded that law always remained in the position of a mere means to quite different ends. It could and did in fact become to some extent an end in itself, especially in the nineteenth and twentieth centuries. It became an end in itself first on the ideological and propagandistic level, when European intervention was justified by the need to abolish or suppress so-called inhumane, barbarous, or at least progress-inhibiting customs and institutions. But the desire to spread one's own law or rather to change the extra-European law could become more than a mere pretext, and in fact influenced measures which otherwise did not promise to strengthen the colonial power's position or even threaten to endanger it. One example is the struggle against polygamy.

This is not to say that from a legal standpoint European expansion was a self-denying, idealistic and altruistic process. Law was indeed an important instrument of imperialism and of expansion in general, whether this was mainly of a political or of an economic nature. But on the other hand it also set some limits to European intervention and manipulation. Whether these limits were to the advantage or to the disadvantage of the indigenous population is open to debate – but limits they were. To name but two examples: once slavery was abolished the Europeans had to develop new methods to mobilize cheap labor, and once basic equality before the law was proclaimed it became at least more difficult to justify existing legal inequalities.

In order to illuminate the dichotomy between means and end with a contrasting example I shall first give a short survey of the same problem in the history of Christian missions. Christianization is a classic example of an end in itself, but in the process of expansion it became to a great extent a means for other ends.

After this preliminary example I shall sketch the role of both European and extra-European law in the process of European expansion. The second half of the eighteenth century is an important watershed. The development of legal thought, ideology and practice within Europe led to an increasing emphasis on equality before the law and on the civilizing mission of law (which until then had been mainly connected with Christianity). The result was a growing tension between the function of law as a means and as an end.

The role of European and extra-European law did also strongly vary according to the type of European domination and settlement. I shall distinguish between three types of colonies corresponding to the role of European settlers.

While only European law could become, in European eyes, an end in itself, the function of a means to an end was not limited to European law but could be assumed by non-European law as well. The instrument was law in general and not European law in particular. This is very important if one wants to understand the legal history of European expansion. If the end is European political or economic supremacy there is no way to decide *a priori* what legal means will best further this end. Indigenous law probably was used as often as European law as an instrument to keep the dominated populations under control. If, instead, only the function of European law is considered, the picture becomes distorted, because it appears that European law as such was an instrument of domination. It would be difficult to prove that by its very nature it was more of such an instrument than any other law. The only certain advantage it had was that the Europeans knew it better than other systems of laws.

But the corresponding disadvantage was hardly less serious: the indigenous population did not know and understand it.

The Vicissitudes of Religious Expansion

While it is obvious that the desire to extend the area of validity of European law never to any significant degree impelled Europeans to extend their activities into new areas, it is not less obvious that the spread of Christianity was one of the most powerful ends in itself that were connected with European expansion, and often preceded it. Individual missionaries may have had many motives, but it is difficult to doubt that the great majority of them would never have left Europe had they not believed it their duty or calling to extend Christianity. Of course they could not keep their work apart from the process of European expansion, and it is well known that in many cases they became the forerunners and pioneers of colonial rule. Objectively Christianization turned out to be a means to an end, although the same end – European rule – would probably have been the result even if the missionaries' attempt at conversion would have failed or if there had never been a missionary.[1]

While any end in itself can become, in a different context, a means for another end, it is more interesting to see whether for the missionaries themselves their own activities tended to become a means instead of an end. Such a process can be observed in the early phase of European expansion.

The Spanish crown never founded its claims to the Americas on the famous papal grants of 1493, because this would have meant a recognition of some kind of overlordship.[2] But the bulls were a very welcome instrument against competitors. They contained strong exhortations to Christianize the population of the areas discovered and to be discovered. Within the first few decades of the Spanish conquests in America there was a heated debate on these clauses. An influential group of missionaries was of the opinion that

1. For a general survey see Stephen Neill, *A History of Christian Missions* (London, 1964), and for two critical studies relating to Africa: Norman Etherington, *Preachers, Peasants and Politics in Southeast Africa, 1835–1880* (London, 1978) and Horst Gründer, *Christliche Mission und deutscher Imperialismus* (Paderborn, 1982).

2. For a full treatment of the arguments see Juan de Solorzano Pereira, *De Indiarum Iure Sive de Iusta Indiarum Occidentalium Inquisitione, Acquisitione, et Retentione*, vol. I (Leiden, 1672). The text of the bulls is in Frances G. Davenport, *European Treaties bearing on the History of the United States and its Dependencies*, vol. I (Washington, 1917), 49–83.

Christianization was a precondition for Spanish rule, that Spain
could lawfully annex the new territories only after at least the
majority of the population had been converted. It was a strange view
because it supposed that religious conversion would lead to voluntary political submission. The supporters of this theory, with Las
Casas himself as their champion, did not propagate Spanish conquest of Christianized territories, but they declared themselves convinced that Christianized Indians would of their own free will place
themselves under Christian, Spanish rule.[3]

This was a far-fetched interpretation of the papal bulls which was
incompatible with their wording, and had never been encompassed
either by the Spanish crown or the Popes. The bulls of 1493 and all
earlier, similar documents first granted the new lands and then
exhorted the grantee to Christianize the population, without making
the grant conditional upon the fulfillment of this requirement. The
attempt at reinterpretation is, however, interesting as an endeavour
to give the spread of Christianity absolute priority in European
expansion. The consequence was that, by a strange dialectics,
Christianization tended to be changed from an end in itself into a
means of expansion. Christianization became the foremost end, but
by this very fact it became a means to a different end, namely
Spanish rule, because the state did not accept it as an end in itself.
As the missionaries tried to monopolize expansion under their own
activities, they had to show that these activities had effects not just in
the religious and ecclesiastical field, but also with respect to the
extension of Spanish rule. Otherwise they ran the risk of being
declared bad Spaniards. The result was Las Casas's absurd contention that entire peoples of converted Indians would come of their
own free will under Spanish rule.[4]

Once the missionaries abandoned the position that the Christianization of the heathens was a duty regardless of other consequences, they became involved in discussions which allowed no final
decisions, because religion was no longer an end in itself. The
controversy was now whether Christianized or heathen Indians
would be better Spanish subjects. The missionaries affirmed that as
long as the Indians were heathens they were dangerous. They would

3. The most significant text is Bartolomé de Las Casas, *Tratado Comprobatorio del
Imperio Soberano y Principado Universal que los Reyes de Castilla y León Tienen sobre las Indias*
in Las Casas, *Obras Escogidas*, ed. Juan Pérez de Tudela Bueso, vol. 5 (Madrid, 1958),
350–423. For the general legal background cf. Jörg Fisch, *Die europäische Expansion und
das Völkerrecht* (Stuttgart, 1984), 205ff.
4. Las Casas, *Obras Escogidas* vol. 5, 342.

resent Spanish rule and remain rebellious. Once they were Christians there would be strong ties between them and the Spaniards. As long as they were a minority they would feel endangered by their heathen compatriots and thus become a kind of Fifth Column; once the majority were converted there would be a general Christian unity. Their opponents on the other hand could point at the danger of unrest, dissatisfaction, resistance, and rebellion if the Indians were not, religiously, left to themselves.

Behind this controversy there was a struggle for power, for the control of the Indians. The missionaries on the whole won the day not so much because they had the better arguments, but because they had the crown on their side. The settlers claimed the Indians as labor for themselves while the state wanted to control the Indians to some extent to prevent a full feudalization of the new societies. The church became an important power in this struggle and an instrument of control with strong interests of its own, but, ultimately, under the authority of the Spanish state.

There are two important points about these debates which can be connected indirectly with the problems of law and expansion.

1. Once Christianity had become a means instead of an end there was no way to decide finally whether one should try to convert the Indians or not. It was an empirical question, not an *a priori* one. The end was Spanish rule, not Christianization. In fact, there was no uniform answer to the question in the course of European expansion. The different states showed, from the sixteenth to the twentieth century, very different attitudes towards missionary activities. While the Spaniards and the Portuguese and later the French favored attempts at conversion, especially in America, the English and the Dutch were in most areas reluctant, and sometimes even prevented such work. All colonial powers, however, made their attitudes dependent on the specific circumstances of their position and of the surroundings. The Portuguese were more reluctant to support Christianization in Asia than in America; the Dutch favored it in some Asian areas when there was already a sufficient number of Christians, while in other areas they more or less prohibited it. Although in the eyes of many missionaries and of at least a good part of the Church Christianization continued to be an end in itself, it had become, in many respects, a means to further expansion.

2. While it was impossible to decide *a priori* whether Christians would be better subjects of European colonial powers than heathens, there was one undeniable danger in Christianization. Conversion held out the promise of Christian equality, that all Christians were

equal before God. This was, of course, in many respects an abstract
equality with little effect in practice. Nevertheless, it was there and
might have effects in the long run. At least it was no longer possible
to justify inequalities with differences between believers and unbelievers. Neither the churches nor the colonial states were fully prepared to accept the consequences. The result would be, in the long
run, the rise of independent churches: as the indigenous Christians
were not granted full equality with their European fellow Christians,
they refused to submit to their control. Therefore, in the end, at least
one of the fears of the settlers did materialize, that Christianization
would make indigenous Christians not better subjects but incite
them to resistance.

Missionary work thus can be seen from two perspectives, and
accordingly offers two aspects: the missionary aspect properly speaking and the pragmatic aspect. The first corresponds to the function
of religion as an end in itself while the second is connected with its
function as an end for other means. The same distinction between a
missionary and a pragmatic aspect will be made in the following
considerations with respect to law.

The Impact of Law Under the Ancien Régime, c. 1500–1750

Looking at the function of law in the first phase of European expansion, from c. 1500 to the middle of the eighteenth century, it seems
appropriate to distinguish between three types of colonies, according
to the importance of European settlers and indigenous people respectively. The role of European law was to a great extent a function
of the presence or absence of a European population overseas.

Before going into the details of expansion it is, however, important
to recall the fact that the European impact in many cases did not
begin with conquest and subordination, but with international relations either on the basis of equality or even of European subordination, especially in Asia, but also in Africa and even in America.[5]
European doctrine tried to suppress this fact later on, pretending
that real international relations were possible only between states in

5. Cf. Charles Henry Alexandrowicz, *An Introduction to the History of the Law of Nations in the East Indies (16th, 17th and 18th centuries)* (Oxford, 1967); id., *The European-African Confrontation. A Study in Treaty Making* (Leiden, 1973); Jörg Fisch, *Krieg und Frieden im Friedensvertrag* (Stuttgart, 1979), 548ff.

the European sense.[6] But this was wishful thinking projected onto the past. In those relations the Europeans usually tried to adopt procedures used by the extra-European side rather than to impose their own legal forms and figures. The reason was obvious. If they attempted to bind their counterparts with obligations that were meaningless to them, there was little chance of their being kept. Only when these international relations degenerated into one-sided impositions and more or less fictitious transactions did the Europeans no longer bother about the comprehensibility to the indigenous side and introduce their own notions. This was particularly the case in Africa and the United States in the nineteenth century.

The important fact about these international proceedings is that the Europeans did learn and were quite ready to use legal instruments and concepts of the other side, but that their propensity to do so declined with the strength of their position. It remains to be seen to what extent this holds also for internal affairs.

Colonies of Settlement

In several areas the Europeans met a sparse indigenous population hardly able to resist, and frequently decimated by the contact with the strangers by diseases, expulsion, and extermination. At the same time there was a fairly numerous European immigration. In time the indigenous population would become a minority; the settlement was then for all practical purposes organized as a European colony, with little contact with the surrounding population. This holds for large parts of the Americas. There were no doubts about the law to be introduced. For the settlers it was natural that they took their European law with them. Once the colony was established, its legal system tended to develop along its own lines. But this was just the consequence of the special conditions overseas, not of borrowing from indigenous law nor of a planned adaptation to a new, mixed society. European law was not a tool of imperialism but a concomitant of emigration. It was not imposed upon the settlers but claimed by them. To be allowed to live under European law was a privilege, usually not to be granted to the indigenous people. This attitude continued in the nineteenth and twentieth centuries, when in many colonies the possibility to become legally Europeanized was held out to natives. The conditions were, as a rule, so difficult to

6. Cf. Gerrit W. Gong, *The Standard of 'Civilization' in International Society* (Oxford, 1984).

fulfil that usually only a small minority qualified for the status of a
U.S. citizen (among the Indians) or of an *assimilé* and the like. The
great majority were largely left to themselves.

   In many areas there was not just a European settler society, but
also a society of forced immigrants, of slaves. They were as alien to
the country as the Europeans. The contrast to the latter is obvious.
There was no question of safeguarding the slaves' own law. They
were submitted to a harsh law designed by the Europeans, which
was not the law of the Europeans among themselves. This suggests
the extent of the colonial law machine. There was not just the
alternative of European and indigenous law, in the sense of the law
hitherto valid for the respective populations. Law making became a
much more elaborate process which could lead to entirely new law as
an instrument to rule over particular groups, or to the revival of an old
legal status like that of the slaves in Roman law.

   Nevertheless, the central fact of the colonies of settlement was the
transplantation of European law not to new populations, but to new
territories.

Commercial and Tributary Colonies

In Africa and Asia there was, up to the middle of the eighteenth
century, no question of vast European conquests. The contacts
usually started with trade, and later the Europeans tried to gain
superior positions by occupying networks of isolated strongholds.
Only gradually did there evolve larger areas under direct control,
first in Ceylon and on the Moluccas under Portuguese and then
Dutch rule, and later in Java under the Dutch. The British, up to
1757, had no important territories east of the Cape of Good Hope.
Moreover there was no significant European immigration. As a rule
there were but a small number of officials, military personnel and
merchants, most of whom intended to return to Europe after some
years of service, although many of whom never were able to do so.
Thus even in the places under direct European rule Europeans were
only a small minority of the population. Most of them were in the
service of a European state or a chartered company. To them it was
even more important and natural than to settlers to be under the
same laws as in Europe. This proved to be comparatively easy even
when they were living under foreign rule, due to an institution which
was much older than European expansion and which had nothing to
do with legal or territorial expansion. This institution was consular
jurisdiction, which had been developed for centuries in the coastal

towns of Europe, Africa, and Asia, especially in the Mediterranean, the Indian Ocean, and South East Asia. Legal systems differed considerably between various countries. Moreover the personal law principle was widely accepted especially in Asia. Thus foreign merchants were granted the privilege of living under and of settling their disputes according to their own laws. This was not seen as an infringement of the sovereignty of the local ruler, but rather as a means of attracting commerce without losing control over it. Typical is the medieval experience in the Mediterranean. The Islamic states were as a rule in the stronger position. But for various reasons Muslim traders usually preferred not to live in Christian countries, so that Christian merchant communities were built up in many Islamic Mediterranean towns. Although they were strictly subordinated to the local rulers, they enjoyed consular jurisdiction.

The basic institution of accommodation of foreigners thus already existed in Asia when European expansion began in the sixteenth century. But there was a point where expansion could change or even subvert the system. In the traditional system of consular jurisdiction mixed cases were either decided by the local authorities or by mixed courts, not by the foreign consul. There was a tendency in European consular jurisdiction, throughout the colonial period, to encroach upon mixed cases. The reason for this is clear. Europeans often considered it a privilege to be under European law and jurisdiction, while on the other hand the European authorities wanted to control their own people. However, the attempt at extension was certainly not made in order to extend European law and jurisdiction over non-European populations – the legal expansion did not go any further than the physical expansion of the Europeans themselves.

There was no basic change of attitude even where the Europeans did acquire full jurisdiction by conquest or cession, either in towns or in larger rural areas. On the whole there was a striking reluctance to accept jurisdiction over subject people.[7] Up to the late eighteenth century there was no serious European endeavor to develop jurisdiction over an indigenous population according to their own law. Nor were there attempts on a large scale to extend European law to the subject population. There was no real system at all. In the trading towns under European rule European courts were opened to some extent for the indigenous population who could, if they so wished,

7. Cf. for example John Ball, *Indonesian Legal History 1602–1848* (Sydney, 1982); T. Nadaraja, *The Legal System of Ceylon in its Historical Setting* (Leiden, 1972); Charles Fawcett, *The First Century of British Justice in India* (Oxford, 1934).

bring their disputes before these courts, but then had to submit to European law. This was most important in matters of trade. In the rural areas the colonial powers tried on the one hand to preserve the indigenous legal system and its agents, while on the other hand they attempted to control it. This was, of course, most important in the case of criminal law. But there was no attempt to create a new legal system or an entirely new administration of justice, and even less to introduce European law any further than Europeans were concerned. Indigenous subjects were left to themselves as far as this was compatible with European interests. The expansion of European law did not become an end in itself and not even a means to another end. European law remained mainly the privilege of the Europeans.

Feudal Colonies

In some areas, especially in Spanish America, there were both a numerous indigenous population and considerable immigration. In time a mixed society would develop and the legal system had to take account of both elements of the population. Thus neither of the two policies described above could be applied.

During the early phase of Spanish expansion in America there were strong feudal tendencies in that both leaders of expeditions and minor lords, who had either been granted vast territories or simply had conquered them, tried to build up jurisdictions of their own, especially over the population living on their estates. On the whole the Spanish state successfully managed to crush these tendencies and to build up a centralized state, although the big landlords remained very powerful. The Americas did not become feudalized in the sense of medieval Europe. On the other hand the colonial state the Spaniards built was still an ancien-régime state founded upon the legal distinction of groups with different rights, privileges, and duties. Thus in a looser sense it remained a feudal, early modern state. In such a system it was possible and normal to incorporate new groups, giving them a legal status of their own. The very thought of equality would have been misleading, because there was no equality among the Spaniards, either.

The Spanish crown claimed the Americas right from the beginning as part of its territory. There was no serious doubt that there had to be full incorporation, making the Indians Spanish subjects. But they were made a special category of subjects, a particular group with a legal status of their own. This status was defined by

Spanish law, which was thus vastly extended. There was no question of preserving indigenous law, of studying it so as to be able to administer it correctly to the subject population. That the Spaniards would use their law for the administration of the Indians was evident as far as they were concerned. Nevertheless it was a special law, differing in important aspects from the law valid in Spain: it was the law for the Indians.[8] On the whole theirs was a clearly subordinate status, although they were free. After long debates, the right to enslave Indians had been restricted to a few particularly resistant peoples and to cases of "just war". But the Indians were under heavy obligations for taxes and labor; they became a servile class more or less at the disposal of the conquerors. On the other hand it was not just a subordinate status, but one with its own rights. The Indians had some privileges, and there was legal protection. For example, one statute provided "that punishments for crimes against Indians be more severe than for crimes against Spaniards."[9] This was possible because equality was out of the question anyhow. The status of Indians was not defined simply by reference to the status of Spaniards, because in the feudal state various groups of Spaniards had a different legal status as well. Spanish law was introduced as Spanish law for the Indians and not as a general Spanish law for all Spanish subjects.

Nor was there a full Europeanization of the legal status of the Indians. They were allowed to retain many of their traditional institutions as far as this did not endanger the Spanish position. The Spaniards in particular built upon the Indian system of local government. This was a matter of expediency, as there were not enough Spanish staff, and the interference with matters of daily life would have increased the risk of resistance. From the legal side there was little missionary impetus. On the whole the approach was pragmatic; law was seen as a means to the end of entrenching Spanish rule. As far as the Spaniards wanted to control Indian society, they introduced their own law.

But legal policy was not influenced by the state only. The aims of the church and of the missionaries had legal consequences as well, especially with respect to customs considered as heathen, idolatrous

---

8. There was, in 1681, a compilation of all Spanish laws relating to the "Indies": *Recopilación de Leyes de los Reynos de las Indias*, 4 vols. (Madrid, 1973). The laws relevant to the Indians have been translated in *The Indian Cause in the Spanish Laws of the Indies*, ed. S. Lyman Tyler (Utah, 1980). Cf. José Maria Ots y Capdequi, *Historia del Derecho Español en América y del Derecho Indiano* (Madrid, 1969).

9 *Recopilación* 6, 10, 21, and Lyman Tyler, *Indian Cause*, 260.

or barbarous. The most famous cases were human sacrifices. More important became campaigns to enforce monogamy and to oppose so-called superstitious practices. Thus the missionary aspect entered legal policy, although it was not a product of legal but of religious policy – Christianization had proselytizing effects in the legal field. It is obvious that such measures were no direct consequence of the Spanish need to control the indigenous population and to mobilize their labor power. They thus were not means for a different end, but tended to become ends in themselves, connected with the primary end of Christianization.

From the Ancien Régime to the Modern Nation State: The Challenge of Egalitarianism

Legal and Material Equality

In the European tradition of natural law theory, including that of divine law, equal status of all persons before the law was a central tenet. But this referred to the original state of things only. In practice the legal position of an individual was defined by status and privilege, by birth, function and religion, with important inequalities between the various groups. In seventeenth- and eighteenth-century political theory original equality was stressed in the context of contractual theory, with its supposed state of nature. Yet the legal equality gained real practical importance only with the American and the French revolutions. They instituted legal orders built – at least ideally – upon full equality in all respects, expressly abolishing existing unequal rights. It is well known that this program was not fully realized. Important inequalities were not abolished, leaving some groups discriminated, the most important and the best known category being the slaves. Nevertheless it became increasingly difficult to justify and maintain such differentiation. In the Western countries there was in the nineteenth and twentieth centuries a gradual movement toward the realization of equality before the law. While this end was not fully achieved, it was virtually impossible to introduce new discriminations. Legal disabilities of slaves and women in particular were gradually abolished.

All this, however, refers to equality before the law. It is well known that legal equality does not necessarily lead to increased material equality. Legal equality in the first place meant the gradual disappearance of barriers between different groups, and thus led to increased opportunities which were seized mainly by those with greater means and abilities. Liberal competition favored those with the most extensive resources at their disposal. Those who hitherto had been discriminated lost their disabilities but also the (relative) privileges and protection they had enjoyed, and they became fully exposed to a competitive society. The only loss the upper classes gradually had to accept was that there were no longer full safeguards against loss of status in case of failure. Thus the egalitarian movement gave the same opportunities to all in theory, while in practice it favored the new bourgeois classes. Legal equality might even increase material inequality.

Yet these "advantages" had their limits. In theory the model of the competitive, materially unequal society built upon legal equality was ideally suited for European colonies. Especially where they were few in number the Europeans had such material advantages that there were hardly any doubts that they would monopolize wealth and power to a very great extent, and thus control those territories socially, economically, and politically. All the same, the system was nowhere applied. It was too risky. On the one hand there would be at least a minority of unsuccessful Europeans who, without a privileged position, could lose their status. On the other hand there was no safeguard against an indigenous group rising in the new dispensation. Considering the very small number of Europeans in most colonies, it was quite easy to outnumber them even at the top. If the aim was to maintain European rule and a superior position for the Europeans, the model of a liberal competitive society was too risky to be applied. Yet there was the secular movement toward legal equality, coming not from the colonies but from the mother countries themselves.

Colonial Inequality and the "Discovery" of Indigenous Law

Colonial policy was in a dilemma. It needed legal inequality which had become increasingly difficult to justify, to maintain or, even worse, to introduce. The dilemma did not, however, apply in the same manner to nor lead to the same difficulties in all of the three types of colonies distinguished above.

1. Colonies of settlement did not create any real problems. The number of immigrants increased enormously during the nineteenth century, so that for all practical purposes these colonies became European societies. Indigenous law had hardly any significance. But European law and law of European origin continued to be looked

upon not as a means of expansion but as a privilege. The indigenous populations were not so much legally discriminated against as left out of the legal system.

2. While up to the middle of the eighteenth century colonies of trade and tribute had played a minor role, not because of their economic weight but because of the area they had brought under direct European rule, they became by far the most important European possessions in the nineteenth and twentieth centuries. The first and most momentous acquisition was the British conquest of India. By the early twentieth century almost all of Africa and Oceania, vast tracts of Asia, and some minor parts of America had come under direct European control. Only in a few territories was there a significant European immigration, and even there the immigrants remained a small minority. As a rule European presence was limited to a tiny group of officials, soldiers and merchants.

3. The feudal colonies were built upon the very principles attacked and abolished by the revolutions in Europe, namely the distinction between different groups with graded rights and privileges according to their status in a hierarchically ordered society. In the long run it would have become increasingly difficult to justify and maintain such a system. But this problem was solved by the dissolution of the Spanish empire in America and the subsequent foundation of independent states. Typically none of them reproduced the feudal, colonial legal order; instead they all adopted more or less liberal systems. At the same time they became excellent illustrations for the dialectics of equality and inequality. While the Indians no longer had a special, discriminated status but had become citizens with equal rights, in practice their position very often deteriorated, because they had at the same time lost many of the safeguards they had enjoyed under Spanish rule. They had gained freedom and legal equality but not the means to achieve material equality.

For the colonies of trade and tribute the dilemma of securing European rule on the one hand and the general European drive towards legal equality on the other was particularly embarrassing. Under the *ancien régime* it might have been possible to develop feudal systems along Spanish lines, despite the lack of immigrants. But once the feudal state was abolished in Europe it was hardly practicable to reintroduce it overseas.

Two factors helped the Europeans to find a way out of their dilemma. The first was the insight that overseas the realization of the program of legal equality would have had more harmful consequences than in Europe. The indigenous systems of law, if it was at all possible to speak of systems, were built upon inequality and different status themselves. At least under European rule the realization of full equality before the law would mean the introduction of a basically European legal system. The consequences for the indigenous peoples would have been doubtful if not disastrous, especially in the case of a quick implementation. The new law would have been completely unfamiliar. In many cases it would have been at variance with the indigenous law or traditions. There was a good chance that it would have little effect, because it was not understood and could not be enforced, although it would have led to increased insecurity.

If the new law would have been enforced there would probably have been only a small Europeanized group who would have been able to take advantage of it, using it to the detriment of the vast majority. In short, the wholesale introduction of a modern European legal system seemed at least of doubtful value, especially from the perspective of the bulk of the indigenous population, while for the colonial power it seemed to contain the risk of unrest and resistance, thus jeopardizing European rule.

The second factor was at least in part a result of the first. European rule was seen as a kind of trusteeship. The indigenous, subject population had a right to be administered by their own law. Any other device would be tyrannical. This idea of a right to one's own law was, of course, connected with the doctrines of the historical law school. But it contained more pragmatic aspects as well. By declaring it a matter of justice to grant to everybody his traditional law, it allowed attempts at radical reform to be opposed not only in the legal but also in the social, economic, and political fields. In this view indigenous (and not European) law had a very important stabilizing function for European rule.

The doctrine of the duty of the conqueror to preserve indigenous law had another obvious advantage for the Europeans. It allowed legal inequalities to be retained and preserved even in an age which had proclaimed equality its foremost aim. Nobody expected the Europeans to submit to indigenous law, while indigenous law itself as a rule was not fully egalitarian either. Without recurring to the construction of a feudal system, the result was similar: European rule could rely on legal inequality, which, instead of appearing as a feudal feature, became a proof of good and enlightened government.

It certainly would be exaggerated to claim that the doctrine was "invented" in order to circumvent the effects of the spread of egalitarianism. Nevertheless it is interesting that important and successful movements to discover and codify indigenous law and traditions did not start before the late eighteenth century.

If taken too far the doctrine had, however, its pitfalls. If the preservation of indigenous law were to become one of the central aims of colonial rule, then the Europeans had best leave the natives to themselves and withdraw. If the existing law was to be retained, any interference from a nonindigenous agent was an evil, because those who interfered were less acquainted with the indigenous system than the natives themselves. Taken to its extreme this doctrine thus became anti-colonial.

In practice there were several other factors and arguments which led to the limitation of the doctrine of the preservation of indigenous law. First the doctrine referred mainly to the law itself, not necessarily to its administration. This usually was thought to be deficient because of lack of training of those who administered it, of insufficient control, and especially of arbitrariness, extortion, and corruption. Seen in this light, European interference became necessary in order to give the full benefit of indigenous law to the population concerned, by providing good order and government. The colonial power took over at least the control over the administration of justice and, in many cases, to some extent also the actual administration itself. The main reason behind this was certainly the desire to strengthen colonial rule. But it led more or less automatically to important legal changes too. While Europeans administered or controlled indigenous material law, they were bound to introduce, whether intentionally or unintentionally, parts of their own procedural law, all the more so as European interference was justified with the lack of good government in the pre-European system. But changes were not restricted to procedural law. European agents had to determine indigenous law, of which they knew little, especially when it consisted of unwritten customs. The colonial powers increasingly tried to determine and codify indigenous law by asking legal experts, collecting law-books and traditions, etc. But of course they were unable to achieve a complete codification, and, moreover, codification itself changed the character of the law. Whether it became less or more fluid is a matter of debate, but in any case it was stated increasingly by legal experts who relied on the codifications, and not by those who administered the collective knowledge of tradition.

Even if it had been possible to make a complete collection of all the relevant traditions and customs, it would have been impossible for a modern, centralized state with few agents to administer such a heterogeneous and ever-changing body of law, as the Dutch experience with *adat* law in Indonesia was to show.[10] If the traditional legal system (and not just legal traditions) was to be preserved, the traditional political and social systems would have to be fully preserved too, and this was incompatible with colonial rule.

Thus the realization of the principle that the subject populations were to be governed by their own laws led, as a consequence of European interference, to massive changes, especially in procedural, but also in material, law. Nor was this the only source of changes. The doctrine was basically relativistic, attributing its own intrinsic value to the legal system of any community. But this legal relativism was not absolute. The Europeans did not accept extra-European law as equal to their own law. There were absolute standards. If a law did not meet them, it had to be abolished or changed. Everywhere the colonial power reserved its right to judge on the merits of indigenous law. This fact found expression in formulas like "justice, equity and good conscience," but also in reference to "morality," "humanity," etc.[11] If anything was repugnant to one of these principles, it had to be abolished or changed. This gave a wide discretionary power to European agencies. It was, of course, not everywhere used to the same extent. Moreover it was only a residual category. It did allow important changes to be introduced, but it did not allow the introduction of a whole new legal system or code.

Those who advocated the preservation of indigenous law as far as it was compatible with European standards of morality, and especially with the interests of European rule, in many cases had great influence, for example in eighteenth century British India, among the Dutch in early twentieth century Indonesia, or in many British colonies in Africa in the twentieth century. But theirs never was the only voice. There were also advocates of wholesale legal reform and engineering, of vast codifications along European lines in a Benthamite style. Legal reform was not to be restricted to areas where it was unavoidable, but it had to be planned in order to promote social reform and social and economic development and progress. In many cases this attitude prevailed, and it led to very important codifications in various legal fields. The effects varied according to the sensitivity of a particular field of law to the European position. The more important European control was, the more important the changes in general were. Probably the area most affected was that of

10. See the article by C. Fasseur in this volume.
11. Cf. J.D.M. Derrett, "Justice, equity and good conscience," in *Changing Law in Developing Countries*, ed. J.N.D. Anderson (London, 1963), 144–153.

criminal law, as the maintenance of peace and order was the basic requirement for all other aspects of colonial rule. European agents had to control the administration of criminal law tightly, and in the long run it was difficult to do this without shifting to some kind of law of European inspiration. Once the political control of the country was secured, the introduction of law which facilitated economic penetration became of the utmost importance. Thus commercial and contract law, land law, and labor law usually were Europeanized to a great extent too, while there was much less change in family law, matters of inheritance, etc.

Thus the value of the doctrine of the preservation of indigenous law became highly doubtful, as in many fields that law was more or less displaced, sometimes gradually and sometimes by wholesale codification. But the doctrine became by no means useless, not only because it was still valid in important fields, but also because it enabled the colonial power to justify legal inequality in surroundings which gradually became more critical of it. The wholesale Europeanization of a legal system, the extension of the mother country's system to a colony, was out of the question. Indeed it would have been unjust and impracticable. Thus legal reform occurred only on the basis of the assumption that the colonies were legally different territories from the metropolis. Europeans were under European law, natives were under indigenous law, however Europeanized it might be. Sometimes the systems for Europeans and natives were very close to each other and partially merged, as in India. In other cases there were important differences, as in many parts of Africa or in Indonesia. This differentiation between Europeans and natives made it possible to maintain important inequalities or even to introduce new ones. There were special punishments for natives, special regimes for native land tenure (sometimes, however, with the aim of preventing the alienation of land to foreigners, including Europeans), and special systems of taxes or obligations to work which did not exist for Europeans. The discrepancies were even more obvious with political rights, which as a rule were reserved for Europeans.

Thus, in the colonies of commerce and tribute a kind of feudal legal system developed and was maintained, admittedly with important differences between the colonial powers and between their various possessions, but in all cases with different legal status, rights, duties, and privileges depending upon the membership of a particular group. The different cultural background and the different level of development sanctioned a clearly discriminatory legal system.

Legal pluralism is not a sufficient but a necessary precondition for such a system.

What has been sketched so far has been, on the whole, the function of law as an instrument of European rule, as a means to different ends. It is very important to see that this has to be said of law in general, and not only of European law. The question to what extent law will help to preserve or strengthen the political and economic position of a ruling power is empirical. Only pragmatic answers are possible, therefore. In many cases indigenous law was thought conducive to the end, in other cases the same applied to European or Europeanized law. These were the ruling powers' intentions. Whether the results would confirm the expectations was a different question which could be answered only *ex post*. One might suppose that, after all, legal policy was not of a decisive political importance: the end of European rule came in all areas within a short period regardless of the particular legal policy of the respective colonial power.

Nevertheless, in the process of European expansion, law certainly was not only a stabilizing factor for European rule but also an important agent for extending it, whether in the political or in the economic field. One of the most momentous achievements, from the point of view of European interests, was the maintenance of legal inequalities in surroundings which increasingly seemed to promote equality. Both indigenous and European law became instruments in this process. It must be emphasized that the European law used was law of European origin or inspired by such law, but not a complete European legal system. This allowed its use for purposes which would not have been compatible with its European context.

Law and Civilization: The Missionary Aspect

While it is obvious that law had an important function as a means to different ends in European expansion, especially in the intention of the colonial powers, it remains to be seen whether and to what extent it was also an end in itself. Did it have a pragmatic aspect only, or was there also a missionary aspect? As has been shown, this question can only refer to European law as a potential agent of change, not to indigenous law, which in European eyes embodied the existing state of things.

During the first phase of expansion, law was hardly seen as an end in itself, in that legal policy was not directed at social improvement and progress, at bringing the blessings of European civilization to unenlightened people. This aspect of expansion was connected with religion; progress was in Christianization. Nevertheless, the aims of the missionaries sometimes had consequences for legal policy as well, when they resulted in demands to introduce legislation which would further the propensity to become a Christian and abolish customs thought to be incompatible with Christianity.

From the middle of the eighteenth century there was a gradual shift in legitimation.[12] The aim which ultimately justified expansion and European rule was no longer the spread of Christianity but the spread of civilization, part of which was, of course, the European social and legal order. Law itself was increasingly seen as an agent of change, in the social but also in the economic and political field. Thus in propaganda and ideology the missionary aspect of law gained considerable importance. Legal changes were justified as serving social progress and contributing to the spread of civilization; a just legal order, fashioned according to European models, was part of a civilized order.

All this occurred on the ideological and rhetorical level. But it had a deep impact upon the indigenous elites inside and outside the colonies. The measures which were propagated and realized by the colonial powers, however, were mainly means to strengthen European rule. Yet there are indications that in many cases there was a real missionary aspect as well. The colonial powers legislated various social reforms which could hardly be seen as strengthening their own position, except perhaps in the very long run, while in the present and foreseeable future they sometimes even increased the risks of dissatisfaction and unrest. They aimed, for example, at the improvement of the position of women, at the abolition of practices thought to be cruel or barbarous, from polygamy and mutilating punishments to infanticide, from child marriage to ritual suicide, and also at the abolition of slavery and the slave trade. Seen from a perspective of the late twentieth century many if not most of these measures were the product of a rather narrow ethnocentrism, measuring all customs and values with one-dimensional European or Christian ("civilized") standards. This is, however, not the important point to be made here, but rather that, whether or not they were the result of ethnocentrism, these measures cannot sufficiently be explained as instruments to strengthen European rule. In the planning and realization of these measures, the desire for social reform and improvement of the living conditions of the indigenous

---

12 Cf. Fisch, *Die europäische Expansion*, 290ff.

people played a part not just in propaganda but also in reality. To a considerable extent they were the result of the specific colonial situation. The voices of missionaries and humanitarians were strongest in propaganda but not necessarily in actual legislation. Here the role of the administrators, especially of those of the lower ranks, of the real "men on the spot," should not be underestimated. They were not just scientific observers but had to act themselves. They had to administer laws and customs which were legal but sometimes repugnant to their own moral feelings. As it is easier to change legality than one's own morality, at least in the short run, there was considerable pressure from them to change or abolish customs and institutions they thought incompatible with European standards. In some cases this was even done despite fears that there might be widespread resistance, the most famous example being the abolition of widow-burning in India in 1829.

Thus the missionary aspect was a real and not just a propagandistic factor in legal policy. Nevertheless, it should not be overestimated either. The preservation and, if possible, the strengthening of the superior position of the colonial power was the highest criterion, and only fanatics advocated reforms at the price of the loss of colonial rule, which was, according to them, God's command. The missionary aspect was subordinated to the pragmatic aspect, but it was all the same real and not dictated by the latter. Its weight and influence are perhaps best shown by legal reform movements in countries not under European rule, like Japan and Turkey, where the wholesale introduction of European law was thought conducive to modernization. In such cases the situation was, in a sense, less complicated, because there was no colonial need to preserve legal inequalities. Yet the basic problems of changes in a legal system were the same.

There is a second and more complicated aspect of the function of law as an end in itself. It has been shown that in Europe and in the independent states of America there was, from the late eighteenth century, a gradual spread and increasing significance of the principle of legal (not material) equality. While the principle itself was more and more accepted, its specific realization, the abolition of legal discriminations of all kinds, took much more time and met with more resistance. Its spread to the colonies could become a real danger for the European powers. Fortunately for them they could point to the difficulty and injustice of introducing a unitary system of law of European origin, or at least of European inspiration, into societies with totally different traditions. The theory that peoples at

different stages of development and with different cultural backgrounds needed different laws was not altogether without foundation. But this was an evolutionary view which by its very nature
could not be maintained indefinitely. Understandably the first to
resent and reject it where those who thought themselves at the same
level of development with the Europeans, and who could best adopt
European law, the Westernized elites. To them the lack of equality
seemed nothing but discrimination. The reaction of the colonial
powers to this change was not altogether negative, and showed that
to be under European law was still considered a privilege for Westernized elites. Westernized natives had in many colonies the possibility to become subject to European law. Basically this was a means
to co-opt the indigenous elite, but it proved no real solution. Europeans, and especially European settlers, did not like the prospect of
a growing class of *assimilés*. The process became slow and cumbersome. Those who had been accepted were not treated as socially
equal, while at the same time they were estranged from their own
people. Full equality before the law could, in the end, only mean the
abolition of the privileged status of the Europeans and equality for
all indigenous peoples. Politically these demands have been extremely successful, if independence is taken as a yardstick. It was
difficult for the colonial powers to deny, in the long run, legal
equality to colonial peoples while this principle gained more and
more weight in their own states. Yet the difficulties the colonial
powers had used as a pretext for withholding equality, the extreme
differences between various groups, did not disappear after independence. A unitary legal system which frequently was established
either did not work at all, because it was too far away from reality, or
it became an instrument in the hands of the elite at the cost of the
masses. Full legal equality inside the new states is for most of them
still rather an aim than an achievement.

Thus equality did not become an element of European legal
policy, but it was an element of European origin which structured
the indigenous response to European policy. It showed that law
could have missionary aspects which developed a life of their own,
independently of European sponsors.

A Universal Legal Creed

Law has been presented here as a typical means for an end which, in
this case, was European rule, while on the whole its function as an
end in itself was clearly subordinated and could operate only within

the political framework. On the other hand Christian missions were typical examples of an end in itself (the spread of Christianity), which only in the second place became connected with pragmatic aspects of securing European rule. This classification is certainly persistent if one looks at the behavior, and especially at the intentions, of the European agents involved. It is different, however, if one looks at the successes. The aim of Christian missions was to Christianize the world. They had enormous success in all continents; Christianity became a truly universal religion. Yet they missed their ultimate aim: Christianity did not become the one religion of the world. Other important religions continued to flourish, and it is not to be expected that this state of religious pluralism will be changed in the foreseeable future. The ideal of a universal single creed remains utopian.

European legal policy in the course of European expansion at first certainly did not aim at anything like a universal legal doctrine. Yet there were elements, gradually developed in Europe from at least the eighteenth century, which could be seen in a worldwide perspective: equality before the law and civilization. The first was hardly propagated overseas, while the second was used mainly for ideological purposes. In the end, however, both have been spread and accepted all over the world and developed into a kind of universal legal creed. This creed or, as in the case of law it should rather be called, this doctrine, has been embodied mainly in the Universal Declaration of Human Rights of 1948 and in the two International Human Rights Covenants of 1966. All three documents contain rights and values which are declared to be valid all over the world, regardless of special circumstances like cultural development and religion. They thus form a universal legal creed, with civilization at its root, accepted by almost all states. It is obvious that they do not fully reflect reality. There is hardly any state which could subscribe to them if its practice would be taken as a standard. Yet on the other hand there are even fewer states which would dare openly contradict the principle of those international instruments. The same restriction applies, of course, to religious declarations: not all those who profess themselves Christians do live according to Christian precepts. Thus within the limited field of ideological influence European law has been more successful in the missionary sense than European religion, although there was much more missionary impetus behind religion than behind law. Obviously the missionary impetus was in law itself, or in certain of its tenets, rather than in those who administered it, so that, to some extent, it became a force independent of those who propagated it, and even turned itself against them. In this point there is a parallel with Christian missions. The denial of full equality (promised in the basic doctrines) led to the foundation of independent churches on the one hand and to the demand for political emancipation and independence on the other.

It seems possible and necessary, therefore, to distinguish between intentional and unintentional effects of European law and legal principles in the process of expansion. In the eyes of the Europeans, law, whether European or indigenous, was in the first place a means to an end: to secure European domination. This end had to be achieved within the framework of some limiting factors like the abolition of the feudal state after the French revolution. For a long time the end was fairly well achieved, while in the twentieth century the empires collapsed within a short time. This was partly the unintentional effect of forces spreading in and from Europe though they were not fully propagated overseas: legal equality, civilization, and human rights, which in the end were at least theoretically accepted all over the world. If they were fully applied they by necessity turned against the colonial order and thus against the Europeans.

The universal legal creed as defined by international instruments should not be mistaken, however, for the reality which continues to be much more diverse. Whether it will also develop toward more unity, or whether in the future cultural differences will increasingly find legal expression, remains to be seen.

2

The Impact of European Law on the Ottoman Empire and Turkey

ESIN ÖRÜCÜ

Introduction

Had it not been for the irreconcilability of Islamic law and Christian European law, and for the general Ottoman policy of leaving local indigenous laws intact, the title of this study might well have been "The Impact of Ottoman Law on Europe." By the fourteenth century the Ottomans were the rulers of the Balkans, and by the middle of the sixteenth century the Empire had expanded in the west as far as Vienna. It had become the largest in the world. In Asia it took in Asia Minor, Syria, Iraq, Palestine, and Arabia; in Africa, it included Egypt, Tripoli, Tunisia and Algeria; in the north it reached and included the Crimea; in Europe it stretched out to embrace the Balkans, the greater part of Hungary, and Austria. The Ottomans controlled the Black Sea and most of the Mediterranean. Under Süleyman the Magnificent the Empire was the strongest power in Europe.

However, the Ottomans did not colonize the territories they conquered. Unlike the Western European system of law, which was expanded partly by European settlers who carried the law of their homelands with them into their new settlements, Ottoman Islamic law was not transplanted.[1] The Ottoman Empire was organized for conquest and based on an expansionist policy, not on colonialism.

---

1. M. Rheinstein, looking over the total range of events which are referred to as "receptions," makes the observation that the consciousness and voluntariness of the process is essential in all cases. See "Types of Reception," in *Annales de la Faculté de Droit d'Istanbul* 6 (Istanbul, 1956), 31. This is to eliminate from the scope of the term *reception* those similar situations of independent parallel development, imposition, imposed reception, transplantation, penetration, infiltration, inoculation, and so on. See A. Watson, *Legal Transplants* (Edinburgh, 1974). Also see K. Lipstein, "Conclusions," in *International Social Science Bulletin* 9 (1957).

An administrative system and a system for collecting taxes were introduced into the conquered territories. The conquering army established fortresses and garrisons at strategic points and along the frontiers, and returned home. While Islamic law applied to the Turks left behind and to the few converted natives, the rest of the population in these conquered lands continued to live according to their existing laws in most respects.[2]

Although some European institutions left impressions on the Turks as early as the end of the fifteenth century, there was no interaction between Ottoman law and European law until the nineteenth. When this did happen it was not in the form of an interpenetration, but an impact of European law, largely that of the French, on Ottoman law. Europe did not expand into the Ottoman Empire, except for voluntary borrowings, imitations and adaptations, albeit sometimes under pressure, because no part of the Ottoman Empire was ever a colony. It is important to note this fact, since one of the most significant ways in which European expansion in its most essential aspect, European law, took place was via colonization. Even in the nineteenth century, when changes were introduced into the Ottoman legal system partly as a result of Western political demands and pressures, they were not impositions but rather imposed receptions, that is, not thrust from without, but received voluntarily by the appropriate organs of the legal system within. Law on the European model was deemed by the Ottomans to reflect Christian values and standards and therefore was repugnant to them. In the nineteenth century, when European law was at last used consciously by the Ottomans, this was done to modernize, Westernize, and secularize Ottoman law to a certain desired extent. It had no impact, for example, on personal statute and family law. This was to come later in 1926, again as part of a definite considered policy by the ruling elite of the Republic. In this study the encounters between European law and Ottoman law will be considered in three periods: the early, up to the nineteenth century; the later, nineteenth and twentieth centuries; and the last, from 1924 to 1929.

---

2. For conquests in Europe two regimes applied: all the new territories were under direct control of central administration except, in the eighteenth century, the republic of Dubrovnik, and the principalities of Moldavia and Wallachia, which were tribute-paying territories. See H.A.R. Gibb and H. Bowen, *Islamic Society and the West* (London, 1950), vol. I, 24–25.

The Early Encounters: The Period of Islamic Law (1299–1839)

The Turks accepted Islam over a period of 400 years, and by the tenth century nearly all were Muslims. Various Turkish tribes set up Islamic states in Asia Minor from the fifth century onwards, the most powerful one being the Ottomans. From the thirteenth to the nineteenth century Islamic law was the sole law of the Ottoman Turks.

Of the three periods, this early one, from the foundation of the Ottoman Empire in 1299 to the promulgation of *Tanzimat* (the Reorganization and Reformation) in 1839, is important for establishing the general picture and observing some of the peculiarities of the legal structure which were to have a bearing on future developments.

At this period the law of the land and the law taught in the *Medreses*, the universities of the day, was Islamic law (*Sheriat*), Islam being both a religion and a legal order. As already observed, the Ottomans did not impose their law *en bloc* upon the natives of the conquered territories. Where they settled, their own rights and liabilities were regulated by Islamic law as applied by the *kadis* and the *muftis* in the *Sheriat* courts, but they did not interfere with the laws and customs of those of other faiths. The question of native laws and customs, and how they were recognized by the Ottoman conquerors, has not been fully investigated, and there is no existing contemporary code of customary laws. These matters are important for the full understanding of the position in the fifteenth, sixteenth and the seventeenth centuries. In the absence of written codes it is difficult to state with certainty what matters were governed by what laws. It is well known, though, that the Ottomans did not extend the personal laws by which they governed themselves to the native population.

At this point it is important to distinguish the several categories of non-Muslims and their position in the Ottoman Empire. There were the *zimmis*, non-Muslims who lived in the Ottoman homelands, mostly in and around Istanbul. These were notably Armenian, Greek and Jewish communities, as well as Christian groups given asylum. In personal statute and private law their own religious laws and customs applied, and disputes were settled in their own Community Courts (*Cemaat mahkemeleri*). The Community Courts in Istanbul largely owed their existence to Mehmet the Conqueror's tolerance following the conquest of Istanbul in 1453 and to the imperial policy referred to earlier. The second category of non-Muslims were the people of the conquered lands in Europe whose own local indigenous customary law applied in the existing local courts. The third category were foreigners who mostly resided in Istanbul and later Izmir, and were concerned in trade. These people were granted special status, including residence privileges and the right to have their disputes settled by Consular Courts, which owed their existence to the Capitulations[3] and dealt with the problems of the increasing number of foreigners in the eighteenth and the nineteenth centuries.

Muslims and non-Muslims in the Empire were not of equal status. For example, non-Muslims were not allowed to go into the civil service. They also had to pay special additional taxes. Muslims constituted little more than half of the population,[4] and for them cultural, ethnic, and other differences were also important as far as equality before the law was concerned. Non-Muslims were free in their religious activities. They could become Muslims, and many did. However, since non-Muslims paid a special tax (*cizye*), which would be lost to the State on their conversion to Islam, this was not encouraged by the authorities. Another reason for the discouragement of conversion was the need for *devsirme* recruitment.[5] Generally it can be said then that, though the Ottoman Empire was an Islamic theocracy, in the implementation of Islamic law there was a pragmatic element.

During this period of early encounters, the general and basic common law of the Empire was Islamic. So, although different laws continued to live side by side with it with no apparent interaction and interrelationship, Islamic criminal law applied to all. In disputes between a Muslim and a non-Muslim it was Islamic law and

3. When Capitulations were first granted in 1537 to the French by Süleyman the Magnificent, allowing foreigners to be ruled by their own laws was by no means regarded as derogation of sovereignty. This was a concession granted to the French in conjunction with an offensive and defensive alliance. Under these Capitulations, later extended to other foreign nationals, foreigners were not subject to Ottoman Law, they paid no taxes, their houses and businesses were inviolable, their disputes were settled by the Consular Court of the defendant according to the law of their own land, and so on. Non-Muslem Ottoman subjects in foreign employment could also be given this privileged status. See G. Lewis, *Modern Turkey* (London, 1974), 37–38.

4. See generally C. Uçok and A. Mumcu, *Türk Hukuk Tarihi* (Ankara, 1985), 198–208, and for unresearched problems in this area, Gibb and Bowen, *Islamic Society*, 13–18.

5. The word means "collecting," and is used for the compulsory recruitment of Christian boys for training and eventual employment in the civil and the military service, a practice which started as early as 1360. On arrival in Istanbul the boys were formally admitted into Islam. See generally Lewis, *Modern Turkey*, 35–37.

the jurisdiction of the *kadi* that prevailed; and, whenever there were complaints against the decisions of Community Courts, these were investigated by the State authorities. In this sense only, Islamic law was the residual law. Since indigenous local customary law applied to non-Muslims living within the Empire, and since a multiplicity of personal laws existed, notably in Istanbul among the non-Muslim *zimmis*, it would be proper to call the Ottoman legal system at this period a plural legal system, but Ottoman law itself Islamic. The picture is a consequence of divergent linguistic, racial, cultural, communal, and religious traditions indigenous to the land. This pluralism led to legal pluralism, the decisive factor being the litigant's status rather than the subject matter of the dispute, except in criminal law matters, as mentioned earlier. Thus the primary connecting factor in choice of law was religion. No mixing of the laws took place and the laws of different sections of the population were allowed to co-exist independent of the basic law of the land. Unlike, for example, English or Roman-Dutch law in the respective colonies, in the enclaves in Istanbul and in the conquered territories, Ottoman Islamic law was not the general common law applicable to all inhabitants in all matters where their personal laws were silent, nor was it residual law filling in the gaps in those multiple personal laws. This was mainly due to its strictly religious character. Yet, Islamic law, the law of the State, was common to all persons, as distinct from the personal laws which governed special sections of the community.

How far did Islamic legal principles make inroads into the other laws in existence in the absence of a common religion and codified laws? This would be fascinating to investigate. The phenomenon could have occurred where these other laws were silent on a particular matter or where a dispute was between a Muslim and a non-Muslim. Was there or could there have been any interrelationship between Islamic culture and European civilization at this level? There is no known research into this.[6]

Private law in the Ottoman Empire remained purely Islamic[7] and more or less static until the collapse of the Empire in the twentieth century. Public law and administrative structure were primarily influenced by old Turkish political customs and by the organization of the Byzantine Empire and the Balkan states. The Roman concept of "imperium" was adopted by Mehmet the Conqueror in the fifteenth century and perfected later, with the sultans in the eighteenth

6. See Gibb and Bowen, *Islamic Society*, 13–18.
7. Yet see *ibid.*, 12–13 for various other authorities applying customary law and so on.

century combining the position of the caliph with that of the sultan. In spite of all this, in appearance the Ottoman Empire was always an Islamic state and the law of the Ottomans Islamic. It can be said that up to the nineteenth century, to our knowledge any encounters that did take place between Islamic Ottoman law and European law made no real impact on either.

Later Encounters: The Period of Islamic Law and Western Law (1839–1923)

Until the reign of Mahmut II (1808–1839) modernization movements had not touched the legal and administrative structures of the Empire. Mahmut came to power having had to sign an agreement of alliance with the feudal lords of Macedonia (*Sened-i Ittifak*) in 1807. Although similar to the 1215 Magna Carta in England, this one came to no fruition. He tried to modernize the central administrative structure as well as the army. Reforms were introduced in the civil service and in 1838 two criminal *kanunnames* applying to civil servants were promulgated. The Council of Judicial Ordinances (*Meclis-i Vala-yi Ahkam-i Adliye*) was set up in 1837. With the help of Mustafa Resit Pasa, the Grand Vezir, Mahmut II started a series of modernization and reform activities not attempted hitherto, and when he died in 1839, the *Tanzimat* movement (Reformation and Reorganization) was ready to take off. This movement started with the *Tanzimat Fermani* (The Charter), which may be seen as a move to introduce constitutional government that envisaged a whole series of reforms. It never assumed the form of a Constitution, nor did it create constitutional government, yet 1839 marks the beginning of a new era in Turkish history and heralds the transition from religious law to Western law. This period extends to 1923, the creation of the Turkish Republic. Forerunners of the receptions of 1926–1929 can be seen in it since one of the most striking features of the *Tanzimat* was the codification and Westernization of the legal system through adoption of foreign codes. Law reform activities in this period were the precursors of the later period of global receptions.

The *raison d'être* of the codifications was on the one hand new economic needs and ideological development in Ottoman society, and on the other, the pressure of the Western powers.[8] This double

8. For the importance of power relationships in legal borrowings see A. Kocourek, "Factors in the reception of law," in *Tulane Law Review* 10 (1936).

pressure to bring in foreign codes is apparent in the whole process of the Westernization of Turkish law prior to 1924. These precursors are "imposed receptions" since, although part of the development was an outcome of a voluntary desire to achieve a modern Western society, more pressing was the intervention of the Western powers, who were intent on ensuring that Western laws govern their own citizens, both in business transactions and personal statute. Foreign pressure was also exerted to create a law applicable to all living within the Empire, to give Muslims and non-Muslims complete equality before the law, in the civil service, and in other spheres. The Consular Courts already had a large say in dealings concerning foreigners. After 1856, any dispute between an Ottoman and a foreigner was resolved in the Consular Courts, and this was a clear intervention into the internal affairs and sovereignty of the declining Empire by the Western powers. The Ottomans saw that one law for all would ease this foreign pressure. Now, it had to be realized that if law were not secular it could have no unity. This becomes more poignant if that law is to be applied to members of a number of different religious groups. Therefore secularization of the law offered a solution.

The Empire had been declining since 1789. The adoption of Western institutions and techniques was regarded by the internal progressive groups as a means of Westernization, and Westernization in turn as a way of recovery from decline at a time when the Western powers, following the Renaissance, were surpassing the Ottoman Empire in all fields. The first move was to update the army and introduce military rules on the French and the Prussian patterns.[9]

Closer relations with the West necessitated Western institutions. Economic reasons dictated the introduction of such institutions, and the first came in the form of a Commercial Code in 1850 based on the French one. Commercial and maritime activities had increased and contact with the West was the paramount consideration. The existing institutions were deficient since they all relied either on customary law, which was changeable from area to area within the Empire, or on Islamic law, which was backward looking and proscribed such relations and the formation of certain types of companies. Capitalism was on the way in and had to be catered for.

9. As pointed out by J. Fisch, European law had gained an immense attraction for the western-educated élites in independent countries outside Europe in the nineteenth and twentieth centuries. See ch. 1 this volume.

In fact, the whole mechanism of administration had to be modernized and commercial activities made efficient. It was felt that the
solution was to introduce Western law.

The development of capitalism, the realization of the industrial
revolution, the progressive importance of commerce, the accentua-
tion of commercial and maritime laws, and the movement of
codification in the West could not be ignored any more. It became
increasingly cumbersome to attempt to regulate relations with
foreign powers through religious and local customary law. Problems
of foreign exchange, companies, and sales of goods that arose between the Ottomans and foreigners were difficult to resolve by
applying Islamic law. Commercial and maritime law, civil procedure, and even criminal law and procedure had to be secularized. As
a consequence, a new judicial organization became essential. To
prepare this reform, the already mentioned *Meclis-i Vala-yi Ahkam-i
Adliye* (Council of Judicial Ordinances) had been set up.

The need was felt for a secular law applicable to all citizens, a
Constitution, a Bill of Rights, and up to date rules on all aspects of
life. Through codifications of national law and imposed and voluntary receptions of foreign codes translated wholly or in part, the legal
system was touched for the first time. The old system was blamed for
not being unified and for being one of the many causes for the fall of
the Empire. In the words of Bernard Lewis:

> The promulgation in May 1840 of a new penal code did not at first appear
> to be a revolutionary step. The name given to it, *Ceza Kanunnamesi*,
> indicated a desire to remain within the existing tradition of Kanun-
> making, and the provisions of the Code, though influenced by French law,
> are mainly within the framework of the penal law of the *Sheriat* itself.
> There are, however, one or two significant changes, which prepared the
> way for the more radical legal reforms that were to follow. One of these is
> the affirmation of the equality of all Ottoman subjects before the law.
> Another is the preparation and promulgation of a legal code, consisting of
> a preamble and fourteen articles. This code marks the first tentative
> appearance in the Ottoman state, of the legislative principle and of a
> legislative body.[10]

This Code was original in character and was the first enactment
applicable to all in the Empire. Though primitive, it brought an end
to arbitrariness and combines *sheri* and customary sanctions. A new
and secular Code was introduced in 1851, the first to recognize a

10. B. Lewis, *The Emergence of Modern Turkey* (London, 1968), 109–10.

public suit against an offender. Later in 1858 yet another was introduced, mostly derived from the 1810 French Criminal Code, which remained in force till 1926. This Code can be regarded as the basis of Turkish criminal law. It was a translation with additional principles from Islamic law. Its later revisions were inspired by the Italian and German Codes.

A number of other Codes were enacted between 1839 and 1881. These include the aforementioned Commercial Code based on French models, largely the 1807 one, promulgated in 1850. This was a radical step, since it was to be administered in the newly (1840) established Commercial Courts. It can be seen as the first formal recognition in the Empire of a system of law and of judicature independent of the religious scholars (*ulema*) and dealing with matters outside the scope of the *Sheriat*. This Code did create special problems though, especially related to interest on investments, which was forbidden by Islamic law. In 1861 the Regulations on Commercial Court Procedures were introduced, based on the French model, and in 1863 a Maritime Code came into existence which was eclectic, being of French (1808), Belgian and Prussian origins.

Penal procedure was reformed in 1866 and a Code was promulgated in 1879 that reproduced the French *Code d'Instruction Criminelle* of 1807. Modern Criminal Courts and the concept of the public prosecutor entered the Ottoman Empire. This Code remained in existence until 1929. Civil Procedure was also taken from the French (1807) in 1881.[11] The first secular courts, the Commercial Courts, had already been set up in 1860. In 1868, the *Meclis-i Valayi Ahkam-i Adliye* was reorganized and divided into the *Divan-i Ahkam-i Adliye*, leading to the Court of Cassation on the French pattern, and the *Surayi Devlet*, leading to a Council of State, the basis of the administrative law system, modelled on the French again. In 1870 the *Divan-i Muhasebat* (*Cour des Comptes*) was established, once more on French lines. The legal aspects of the *Tanzimat* were supplemented in 1856 by the *Islahat Fermani* (Charter of Reformation), prepared under pressure from the West, establishing the equality of Muslims and non-Muslims under the law and the application of principles following the *Tanzimat* to all.

---

11. In 1861, a regulation was promulgated introducing French procedural law for commercial cases. In 1879, civil as well as commercial courts were established on a secular basis and given a secular Code of Procedure based upon the French model. See, E. Özsunay, "Legal science during the last century: Turkey," in *Inchieste di Diritto Comparato* 6 (Padova, 1976), 697.

In 1847 mixed courts had already been established for criminal
matters and in 1848 for commercial matters, and with the 1856
Islahat Charter, mixed courts were planned to resolve disputes between Muslims and non-Muslims in the areas of commerce and in
serious criminal matters (The *Meclis-i Tahkikat* in Istanbul). In 1864
a secular court system on four levels was designed, and in 1871 this
new structure was set up to function alongside the *Sheriat* Courts. By
1880 the system had been completed. For problems arising in the
area of personal statute, the old tradition of religious *Sheriat* Courts
and Community Courts continued to have jurisdiction for the respective groups in the population. The equality of Muslims and
non-Muslims had not been openly guaranteed in 1839, but in the
Islahat Charter of 1856, under Western pressure and contrary to
Islamic law. It is interesting to observe, however, that soon afterward a new privileged position was created both for non-Muslims
(*zimmis*) and for foreigners, which paradoxically infringed the newly
established principle of the unity of the law.

The first Ottoman Constitution of 1876 was inspired by the
Belgian Constitution of 1831 and the Prussian one of 1850, but
neither the Constitution nor the new Parliament lasted for long. In
1908 the same Constitution was put into effect for the second time.
The bulk of new legislation was "restricted to the technical aspects
of law and did not touch upon subjects such as family law and
succession . . . thus the most important part of private law, had not
yet been secularized."[12]

The first ever attempt at codification of Islamic common law was
the *Mecelle*[13] of 1870–1877, the earliest example of reducing Islamic
law to the form of a modern legislative enactment, a comprehensive
restatement of the law with the notable exception of family law and
the law of inheritance. Family law was only promulgated in 1917 in
the form of a decree, but remained in force for a mere two years. The
Mecelle was introduced after long deliberations only by leaving areas
of law that could be only applicable to Muslims outside its scope.[14]
It was to apply to all in the Empire. To supplement it there was the

12. H.V. Velidedeoglu, "The reception of the Swiss Civil Code in Turkey" in
Internation Social Sciences Bulletin 9, 61.
13. This enactment to a certain extent imitated Western drafting techniques. For
extensive information on Medjelle see S.S. Onar, "The Majalla," in *Law in the Middle
East*, ed. M. Khadduri and H.J. Liebesny (1955), 292–308.
14. It should be recalled here that Egypt chose to solve this problem by basing its
civil code on the French one, which was also strongly supported in the Ottoman
Empire by certain scholars as the solution.

Land Law (*Arazi Kanunnamesi*) of 1858, which reasserted Islamic rules in a national codification.

The *Mecelle* was of the utmost importance, since the discrepancies that existed between the Commercial Code of French origin and the body of scattered private law had to be resolved. The close relationship between commercial codes and civil codes is well known. Codification of the civil law was to be a first step to ease matters, although the problems arising out of the different origins of the two seemed almost irreconcilable.

By the end of this period the Ottoman legal system was firmly in transition from one legal orientation to another, and as an aspect of this transition, had developed a hybrid character.[15] The *Tanzimat* period was a period of reforms and its main characteristic was the increase of Western influence and the creation of a cultural and legal duality. Law in the Ottoman Empire was still pluralist, but through these later encounters with European law, Ottoman law itself ceased to be solely Islamic and the legal system became a mixed jurisdiction. Two bodies of law of different origin, reflecting the rules and principles of two of the major legal families in the world, the civilian and the Islamic, were in effect operative together, with the same force and independent of each other, applicable to the same body of people. Thus in the nineteenth century, the legal system in the Ottoman Empire was both plural, the communities still being subject to their own religious laws in private matters, and mixed. The two elements of this hybrid co-existed with two fully supporting judicial systems, separate rules, separate courts, separate judges, and inevitable overlaps. Whereas prior to *Tanzimat* there had been three types of Courts, now there were five: *Sheriat* Courts, Secular Courts (*Nizamiye*), Commercial Courts, Community Courts, and Consular Courts. All had different procedures and organizations, thus creating innumerable problems; conflicts as to jurisdiction and competence were abounding. This state of affairs gave rise to further problems such as legal education, measures to protect the judges from political interference, and guarantees for their independence. In 1879, the Judicial Organization Statute guaranteed judicial independence, introduced procuracy, and organized the execution of judgements. The institution of notary was set up. Advocacy had

15. White suggests that "a legal system can only be properly classified as hybrid if any existing duality or plurality in the legal culture is accepted as a permanent feature." See D. White, "Some problems of a hybrid legal system: a case study of St. Lucia," *The International and Comparative Law Quarterly* 30 (1981), 880. See also the discussion by Reyntjens on legal pluralism (ch. 6 in this volume).

been established in 1875 in Istanbul and the next year in the whole country. The first law school, set up in 1869, had been closed in 1876, to be reopened in 1878, becoming in 1900 the law Faculty in the newly established Istanbul University. In 1853 a special school was set up to prepare the *kadis* for their judicial office.

In sum, the positive aspects of this period are: the introduction of the concept of the rule of law; the realization of the first codifications; the systematization and codification of a section of Islamic law; the acceptance of Western law in areas where Islamic law did not provide an answer; the introduction of new court structures; and the promulgation of a citizenship law in 1869 to regulate the nationality problem. On the negative side: legal unity was totally broken down; foreign powers gained a degree of judicial power, which meant a diminution of Ottoman sovereignty; the *Seyhülislam* became a political power as Islamic law was reorganized; financial reforms failed; judicial organization did not have a strong basis, having been introduced by politicians rather than jurists; as a result there were no knowledgeable jurists to apply Western law, and the reform lost its meaning. In addition, the majority of the people in the Empire did not support these reforms.

Yet it was a step in the right direction, with possibilities for future development. As Hamson[16] points out, "One of the most important effects of this continuous modernisation was that in the law faculty of Istanbul a generation of jurists were trained to whom the principles of European law were familiar and whose minds were formed by those principles." This meant that to a certain extent the next stage of encounters could rely on this "accumulated experience."

Lewis emphasizes the important changes which took place in administration and law: "During the nineteenth century the Turkish reformers tried, by legislative enactment, to give Turkey the form and structure of a European state. European laws and judiciary, European ministries and administrative procedures were copied with more or less fidelity, usually from French originals, and promulgated by Imperial decree." The Sultan's government "offered to Europe the only evidence she would accept of progress and improvement that is, a movement towards a greater resemblance to herself." But "to European observers, their rate of progress seemed lament-

---

16. G.J. Hamson, "Preliminary Report," in *Annales de la Faculté de Droit d'Istanbul* 5 (Istanbul, 1956), 7–8. As E. Seizelet points out, a massive introduction of European law not only creates technical problems, but also problems of attitude and mentality. Yet, it also produces an *élite dirigeante*, as has been the case in Japan. See ch. 3 in this volume.

ably slow," and as the century rolled on the Sultan had to "give way to the pressure of events," and "a stream of new laws and institutions followed." Lewis concludes that "in European writings on the nineteenth century Turkish reforms, it has become a commonplace that the reforms were stillborn. . . . Yet a comparison of Turkey in 1800 with Turkey in 1871 will reveal many profound changes," though most of the "legal and administrative reforms were often ill-judged and incompetently applied."[17] However, the nineteenth century surely opened the way for the twentieth century reforms as well as creating that important element, an educated, enlightened élite.

The Last Encounters: The Period of Secular Western Law (1923–1929)

The outstanding period for our purposes started with the foundation of the Republic in 1923. The 1924 Constitution[18] of this new Republic, the product of a long evolution, but undoubtedly inspired by the 1875 Constitution of the Third French Republic and the 1921 Constitution of Poland, marks the beginning of this period. It was amended seven times and finally replaced by a new one in 1961, itself later replaced in 1982.[19]

Let us turn our attention to the eclectic, large-scale receptions that mark the Turkish legal system of today. The founder of the Turkish Republic, Atatürk, did not long tolerate the existence of Islamic law as the law of the land. The outward aspect of the people was dramatically changed through a number of social and cultural reforms related to dress, script, the calendar, etc., brought about by a series of law reforms.[20] A radical reorganization of the entire legal system transformed the Turkish "family life and way of living" to

17. Lewis, *Emergence*, 362, 115, 119, 121, 124, and 126 respectively.
18. The second one of the Republic, the first being in 1923.
19. In the preparation of these latter, although no single constitution was taken as a model, wide use was made of the Italian and West German Constitutions, with the provisions on economic development being inspired by the Indian Constitution of 1949 for the 1961 constitution and the 1958 French and the American Constitutions for the 1982 Constitution.
20. There are eight principal reform laws (*Inkilap Kanunlari*), whose unconstitutionality cannot be challenged even today (Art. 174 of the 1982 Constitution), establishing secular education and civil marriage, adopting the Latin alphabet and the international numerals, introducing the hat, closing the dervish convents, abolishing certain titles, and prohibiting the wearing of certain garments.

accord with the "common practice of civilized nations." The first move was to replace the *Mecelle*.

Through a variety of receptions, adoptions, and adaptations, the entire legal system was reorganized in an astonishingly short space of time. The outcome was: The Civil Code of 1926 (The Swiss Code and the Swiss Code of Obligations received *en bloc*); The Penal Code of 1926 (Adaptation of the Italian Code of 1889); The Commercial Code of 1926 (Based on the German Code of 1897 and the Italian Codes, therefore eclectic); The Code of Civil Procedure of 1927 (from the Swiss Canton of Neuchatel); The Code of Criminal Procedure of 1929 (The German Code of 1877); The Code of Supplementary Proceedings, Execution and Bankruptcy of 1929 (The Swiss Federal Code of 1889) and the Maritime Code of 1929 (The German Code of 1897). All Turkish citizens were henceforth subject to the same laws. The old legal system was abrogated *in toto*.

In 1928, the clause, "The religion of the Turkish State is Islam," was dropped from Article 2 of the Constitution. Bernard Lewis remarks that,

> the nineteenth century reforms had already removed large areas of law from the domination of the *Sheriat* and the jurisdiction of its exponents. On 8th April 1924 Mustafa Kemal had gone still further, and had abolished the separate *Sheriat* courts. But even after all these changes, the *Sheriat* still remained in force in most fields of family and personal law, and was still administered by judges who, though they sat in secular courts, were still to a large extent, by training and outlook, doctors of the Holy law. Throughout the period of reforms, the exclusive competence of the *Sheriat* lawyers in matters of family and personal status had been left intact. Kemal was determined to end it.[21]

When it was first decided to Westernize the legal system through fundamental reforms and codifications, there was an attempt to produce draft codes using modern foreign drafting techniques, while keeping the existing national content. This proved to be a fruitless exercise, since there was no agreement and the process of codification would have proved to be too lengthy. The Committee which had been set up for this purpose was dismissed.

A decision was then made to move outside the framework of the indigenous system of laws rather than to integrate the existing systems. Once the decision to receive foreign codes and use the tool of reception as the method of law reform had been made, a commis-

21. Lewis, *Emergence*, 272.

sion of twenty-six members was set up to translate the Swiss Civil Code and the Swiss Code of Obligations from the French version. Meanwhile the most important commentaries on civil law, criminal law, and so on were translated into Turkish by special committees sponsored by the Ministry of Justice. The radical nature of the reform when it came amazed most foreign observers. Within one year Turkish legal experts had produced four entirely new codes, with more to follow.

It is difficult to exaggerate the significance of the adaptation in 1926 of the Swiss Civil Code to Turkish needs in the development of Turkey. "This was the first time that a reformer had dared to invade the intimacies of family and religious life . . . and to do so, not by stealth, but by head-on-attack."[22] In receptions where two legal systems, the model and the recipient, are of two different legal families, the recipient usually becomes a mixed jurisdiction or a hybrid system, since as a rule, the recipient does not introduce change in the sensitive areas of family law and succession or even land law. This was the case in the Ottoman Empire between 1839 and 1923 and the legal system of that period became a mixed jurisdiction with hybrid character. However, the adoption of the Swiss Civil Code in 1926 was a unique example of the complete passage from one legal family to another. The technique of reception as a method of law reform was used to the extreme in this case. This instance is also an example of law being used not as a reactor to social change but as an initiator of social change. The purpose behind the reception of the Swiss Civil Code was to regulate and legislate the civil relationships of the people according to what was thought these relationships ought to be, and not according to existing custom, usage, and religious mores.[23] This reception was revolutionary and radically reformist, and can be summed up as a prime example of "social engineering through law." Of course Turkey did not suddenly change in the 1920s from a medieval Ottoman despotism to a modern democratic Western state. Western law had been in the process of being received into Turkey, albeit imperfectly and partially, for a period of at least one hundred years. Now,

---

22. *Ibid.*
23. In this way, the "normative repertoire" was not to be constituted by *adat*, Islamic, and government law together, as seen in legal pluralisms (see F. von Benda-Beckmann, ch. 14 in this volume). The centralized paradigm, the legal system emanating from the state, was strong (see M. Chanock, ch. 13 in this volume). Nevertheless, the gap between law and society remains in all legal systems, even when one takes a legalistic view of the law (see by D.H.A. Kolff, ch. 10 in this volume).

however, one thing was clear: the bases of the old legal system were totally destroyed. Although the purpose as stated by Atatürk was "to create completely new laws and thus tear up the very foundation of the old legal system," the reception of foreign laws in Turkey did not mean that the Turkish legal system would not have a peculiarity of its own. Turkey took over several foreign codes, both in the field of private and public law. They were of Swiss, German, Italian and French origin, which were brought into line with each other and with what was Turkish. As a consequence of the application and interpretation of the adopted and adapted codes by the Turkish courts, there came into being a Turkish civil law, a Turkish law of obligations, a Turkish law of civil procedure, and so on. In this connection, the importance of Article 1 of the Turkish Civil Code, which is an exact translation of Article 1 of the Swiss Civil Code, must be pointed out: "If no relevant provision can be found in a statute, the judge must decide in accordance with the customary law and, in its absence, in accordance with the rule which he would adopt, were he the legislator. In so doing he must pay attention to accepted doctrine and tradition."

Evaluation and Conclusions

From 1299 to the nineteenth century, there was no significant interaction between European law and Ottoman law, and no impact of one on the other, although they were in physical proximity from the fifteenth century onward.

In the nineteenth century, it was mainly French law which was received by the Ottomans, partly by imposed and partly by voluntary reception. The Ottoman legal system at this period had a dual character, as well as being pluralist. In some areas a blend occurred between the elements, making the legal system a hybrid in transition from an Islamic to a civilian system.

The twentieth century, especially the period 1924–29, saw the full impact of European law on the Turkish legal system. This remarkable period of voluntary receptions gave Turkey its civilian secular character, the blend this time being of the Swiss, Italian, German and French systems – systems themselves the product of inter-receptions over the centuries.

So it can be said in sum that both in the case of the Ottoman Empire and later of the Turkish Republic, the method through which the impact of European law took place was reception, the only possible route, considering that no part of the Ottoman Empire or the Turkish Republic was ever a colony of the West. Such voluntary global or large-scale receptions of foreign law are not frequent occurrences. Kocourek says that "such a reception has not occurred since the year 1495, when Roman law was received into Germany as common law, until the most recent times as in Japan, Turkey and China."[24] Zweigert and Kötz find the Turkish instance of receptions especially interesting and remarkable, since "nowhere else in the world can one so well study how in the reception of a foreign law there is a mutual interaction between the interpretation of the foreign text and the actual traditions and usages of the country which adopted it, with the consequent gradual development of a new law of an independent nature."[25] According to Lipstein "the problem of the reception of foreign law is one of the most fascinating presented by Western legal history" and "the reception of Western law in Turkey in 1926 provides a unique modern example, inasmuch as this reception was wholesale and deliberate."[26] Again of this reception, Hamson said at the 1955 Istanbul Conference of the International Committee of Comparative law that "this phenomenon of reception is one of the most striking juridical events during the last one hundred and fifty years."[27] Nowhere has reception been used to the extent it was in Turkey during the years 1926–1929. Not only is Turkey the classic example of a country where there has been one total reception of a code, in this case the Swiss Civil Code, but also it is the only country where within a span of five or six years the entire legal system was transformed almost exclusively by the use of the method of reception.

In such a case, there are always fears that the social system and the legal system will not accord. However, the results of recent surveys show that this transplanted formal legal system has indeed influenced even the rural areas of Turkey. The data

> suggest that planned legal change over time does indeed affect populations and institutions at the local level. . . . The fact that Turkey could adopt and ostensibly follow Western law codes in the face of popular support for the islamic religion may attest to Galanter's proposition that a

24. Kocourek, "Factors," 210.
25. K. Zweigert and H. Kötz, "An introduction to comparative law," in *An Introduction to Comparative Law* (Oxford, 1987), 184.
26. K. Lipstein, "Reception of Western law in Turkey," *Annales de la Faculté de Droit d'Istanbul* 6 (Istanbul, 1956), 11.
27. Hamson, "Preliminary report," 3.

legal system of the modern type may be sufficiently independent of other
social and cultural systems, that it may exist for long periods while
maintaining a high degree of dissonance with central cultural values.[28]

So it cannot be claimed that only trans-cultural and morally neutral
rules can be successfully received. The Turkish experience challenges this claim:

> Transplanted on a massive scale it (the law) can, of course, change
> completely the socio-economic identity of the recipient socio-political
> system. Law is system-conditioned but the system, too, is shaped by the
> law. In Turkey, for example, Swiss law was imported in the gigantic effort
> of the political leadership of that country to "secularise" Turkish society
> and "Westernise" its political system; the determination of Turkish lead-
> er, to succeed in their objective, finally caused the desired alteration of the
> existing socio-economic structure, by the imported legal system.[29]

Starr and Pool submit, "our data . . . suggest that the Turkish legal
revolution is a revolution in more than form . . . The use of the
courts by citizens extends to arenas formerly within the sphere of
religious law alone – to such an extent that these are now among the
most common kinds of cases."[30]

It is obvious that the reception of a code or codes based on
developed Western law by a developing country, or one with a
religious or traditional legal order, with the view of modernizing
society, is a method that must be used with delicacy, skill and
knowledge. This exceptional legislative method of inducing social,
cultural and legal change is a transitional one. Introducing a foreign
law into a different social *milieu* is a grave task. The results in Turkey
point to its success, while experience elsewhere suggests fundamental problems. What then makes the Turkish experience unique? A
number of factors are here submitted as hypotheses to explain the
success of this experience.

One group of explanations is of a general nature. Turkey itself was
never a colony. Even in the nineteenth century, Western powers and
their demands were external to the people, and changes, when they

28. J. Starr and J. Pool, "The impact of a legal revolution in rural Turkey," in *Law and Society Review* 8 (1974), 533–35.

29. E.K. Banakas, "Some thoughts on the method of comparative law: the concept of law revisited," in *Archiv für Recht und Soziale Philosophie* 67 (1981), 294.

30. Starr and Pool, "Impact," 554. People do apply and invoke most of the legal rules and do use the law in defense of their rights. This is seen by M. Channock (Chapter 13) as the criterion to determine whether legal rules are real.

came, were internally introduced. Most of the other contributions in this book trace legal impositions via colonization. There are fundamental socio-cultural consequential differences between the two routes, the external and the internal introduction of change.[31] It is also essential to stress that it was not just European law that was introduced, but a European way of life. The change was envisaged as a whole. The Turkish elite did not attempt to integrate the existing norms of diverse origin, they simply replaced them. Legal reforms were accompanied and strengthened by social and cultural reforms, the aim being to Westernize and modernize Turkey, an aspiration shared by the powerful elite, who had themselves been in close contact with Western cultures. Colonialists, with the probable exception of the French, who introduced "acculturisation," may have seen no benefit in modernizing the way of life of their colonized people. Colonial law may have been introduced mostly in those areas where it would make life more convenient for colonizers not interested in national integration.[32] The Turkish ruling elite definitely was interested in modernization and national integration. The benefits were obvious, and it seemed imperative that the country should be modernized. Already, for centuries, the army had been well educated, in contact with the West, and highly respected by the people. There was an affinity with the West, a dislike of the Russians, and deteriorated relations with the Arabs. The natural solution was to strengthen ties with Europe that were already begun about a century ago; to become European, legally, socially, and culturally.[33]

The second group of explanations is particular to the conditions of this historical accident. During the war of independence, internal debates had suggested becoming a mandate of the USA or a

31. This is one of the reasons why even the Chinese experience (see ch. 4 by P.H. Ch'en in this volume) is not parallel to the Turkish one, though one does encounter similar structures in both, such as the Consular Courts, which become in time a point of departure for legal expansion, as pointed out by J. Fisch (ch. 1 in this volume). However, it is imperative that all examples be evaluated within their own set of factors, rather than in a theoretical framework, since all historical accidents are diverse.

32. As F. Reyntjens shows in Zaire, Ruwanda and Burundi (ch. 6 in this volume).

33. The most important problem areas left are marriage and succession. The official legal system does not compromise or allow itself to be diluted by the social system on these points. It does however give concessions from time to time in the area of religious marriage and the children thereof, by promulgating "Amnesty Acts" in order that these relationships can be administratively corrected and thus legalized. Over sixty years, there have been seven such Acts. See for a discussion E. Örücü, "Extra-legal cohabitation in Turkey," in *Les Concubinages: Approache sociojuridique* (Paris, 1990), ed. J. Rubellin-Devichi.

protectorate of Britain. A firm decision was made for an independent, modern, viable Turkey. Feelings of nationalism and unification are very important at this point. National unity, an anathema to
colonial administrators, was the driving force of the ruling elite in
Turkey. This was succinctly encapsulated by Atatürk, "How happy
the one who says, I am a Turk!" The exceptional vision of this
charismatic leader surrounded by his admiring elite cannot be over-
stressed. Now that the country had been drastically reduced in size
within compact borders, the situation was more manageable. There
were only ten million people and eighty percent were illiterate. What
opposition there was, was initially fiercely suppressed. The clash
between the legal and the social systems diminished over the years,
as did the gap between them, through incentives, simplification, and
education. In the rooting of the system, the contribution of professors, mostly German and Austrian, such as Schwartz, König,
Neumark, and Hirsch, who were given sanctuary in Turkey before
the Second World War, and who held posts at the universities, must
be remembered.[34]

Now, we know that "however sophisticated and well-planned
technologically, development plans are ultimately hostage to a re-
fractory residual problem, usually referred to as 'the human
factor.'"[35] In Turkey, unofficial systems, such as old customs, in so
far as they are allowed to subsist, have to accord with the norms of
the legal system, the posited law.[36] If people use patterns of their
choice for organizing their affairs, when they fall foul of the norms of
the legal system, the legal system takes no cognizance of these
"social rules," whether orientated by customs or religion. The official program is geared to eliminate such personal choices. The
sources of law are predetermined only by the formal legal system. It
is worth remembering here that there is no legal pluralism in Turkey
and legal positivism is strongly upheld.[37] From time to time, fluctua-
tions from this position for vote-catching purposes can be seen, but
overall, there has been no significant change over the years. Ghosts
of the old way of life still looming in the background, haunting the
legal system, are not allowed to materialize.

34. For a very interesting history of this involvement see H. Widmann, *Exil und
Bildungshilfe. Die deutschsprachige akademische Emigration in die Turkei nach 1933*. (Bern-
Frankfurt/M, 1973). (Translated into Turkish in 1981).
35. I.M. Lewis, "Anthropologists for sale?," in *The L.S.E. Quarterly* 2 (1988), 52.
36. See ch. 6 in this volume by F. Reyntjens.
37. See F. von Benda Beckmann in ch. 14 in this volume.

3

European Law and Tradition in Japan during the Meiji Era, 1868–1912

ERIC SEIZELET

Introduction

On July 8, 1853, Commodore Matthew C. Perry entered Edo bay; he was empowered by President Fillmore to negotiate a commercial and economic agreement with the shogunate. It was not the first time that Western power had attempted to end the seclusion of the Japanese Empire, in order to oblige the shogunate to renounce the strict isolationist policy decided by the *shogun* Tokugawa Iemitsu in the early years of the seventeenth century. Perry's official request was somewhat comminatory, expecting a clear answer from the Japanese authorities within one year.

On January 30, 1902, Great Britain and Japan concluded a military alliance to contain the Russian advance in the Far East.

Superficially, there is no connection between these two events. As a result of tremendous changes which occurred during the period of the Meiji Restoration, however, the position of the Japanese Empire *vis-à-vis* the West was highly improved. The sudden appearance of the "black vessels" in front of the "capital of the Tycoon" obliged Japan to emerge from its lethargy, throwing the nation into a political crisis, which led progressively to the destruction of the *Bakufu* system, while threatening national independence. On the other hand, this alliance concluded with the most powerful maritime nation of the time was imbued with a great symbolic meaning, quite above and beyond the natural congruence of similar strategic and economic interests. It involved an evolution which was the consequence of years of strenuous diplomatic efforts aimed at the establishment of equal relations with the West, as well as the recognition of the central position of Japan in the Pacific area. In fifty years, Japan raised itself from a humiliated and dominated nation to the status of a great power. This shift was due to the success of the obsessive modernization process, involving all the components of Japanese life, including mainly the political institutions and the legal system.

These transformations must be singled out for two reasons. First, Japan was nearly the only Asian country to encounter the West while avoiding colonization. Second, the subsequent changes, though imposed from above by the enlightened elite, did not provoke any radical crisis which might have swept away those drastic changes. It does not mean that the modernization process did not meet fierce opposition. If internal and external tensions sometimes affected its course, its final objectives remained intact.

Was Japan psychologically or materially more prepared than Vietnam or Korea to resist Western pressures? Is it possible to identify a fundamental principle of stability that makes the reception and adaptation of Western institutions easier? Why was the introduction of Western law associated with the task of modernization, whereas local traditions – based on the primacy of ethics over law according to the Chinese model – seem to exclude any similarity or reference to the peculiar experience of the West?

Answering this question is difficult, since Japan developed its own dialectical perception of modernity and tradition, change and order, influenced by variations in international environment or internal balance of powers. As a result of precarious compromises, political decisions were greatly determined by historical development, mentalities, and shifts in the social and economical forces. The collapse of the *Bakufu* system in 1868 did not mean the complete disappearance of the feudal order; the massive introduction of European law in the Meiji period – though a decisive factor in the modernization process – did not necessarily involve the Westernization of Japanese society. Undoubtedly, the reform of the political system combined with the emergence of Western law notably affected the whole structure of the Japanese state, not in terms of a total and definitive eradication of the old order, but rather as a product of a cumulative process of acculturation and sedimentation. The result was a new synthesis, allowing Japan to cope with the national goal of opening the country while preserving her own identity.

The Acceptance of European Law: A Prerequisite to International Responsibility

It can be said that the introduction of Western law in Japan pro-ceeded from the sudden national awareness of the precariousness of the Empire's international situation in the middle of the nineteenth century. China's defeat in the Opium War (1840–1842) was a considerable shock to the Japanese elite. Consequently, the ability of the shogunate to face the "white peril" became a matter of great concern. Europeans and Americans could not tolerate the presence in the northern part of the Pacific of a "blockade" that obstructed their lines of communication with the Chinese mainland and flouted the most elementary rules of the *droit des gens*. They were determined to remove that obstacle through negotiation if possible, by force if necessary. Put in legal terms, the problem was to decide whether Japan could be enticed to enjoy the benefit of international law governing the relations between civilized nations. Had Japan any interest in obeying this "law"? What would the consequences be for the Japanese legal system itself?

The Applicability of European Law in Japan as a Universal Norm

Opening fire on foreign ships cruising near the Japanese islands, refusing diplomatic contacts except through the Dutch factory of Deshima in Nagasaki, putting innocent people shipwrecked on the Japanese coasts in jail, imprisoning foreigners who had transgressed the national edicts of seclusion, and attacking foreign legations and residents in Japan were considered reprehensible acts requiring stern punishments by the Western nations. In the first stages, their "gunboat diplomacy" appeared a rather tough means of making clear to the Japanese government that it had to follow the rules, habits, and customs commonly accepted by the nations of the world. Thus, Japan experienced a somewhat empirical and painful intro-duction to diplomacy, lacking as it did a comprehensive knowledge of the legal system inspiring these rules. On the other hand, obvi-ously, given the fact that Japan had decided by itself to be isolated from the rest of the world, Western powers were inclined to think that, as far as Japan was concerned, they were not obliged to respect international law. In fact, the decline of the *Bakufu* system, after two hundred years of dictatorship, gave them a strong incentive to attempt direct action regardless of legal niceties.

Certainly, after two hundred years of isolation, Japan was not well prepared for international law and modern international relations: the shogunate had no room for specialists in foreign affairs, and even the Japanese language was unable to express clearly the titles of diplomatic officials. Moreover, the dyarchic nature of the Japanese state, based on the separation between sovereign authority and political power, was progressively undermined by the fierce competition between the Kyoto Court and the Edo *Bakufu* during the later years of the shogunate. This domestic struggle complicated the determination of the supreme authority in foreign affairs, especially in treaty making. This situation required exceptional procedures: negotiations through the Dutch factory or naval officers, confusion of diplomatic and consular functions, and appointment of foreigners to act as provisional representatives of the Japanese government to the Western powers. In the middle of the nineteenth century, for administrative, psychological, and linguistic reasons, Japan was not successfully prepared to manage its encounter with the "Southern Barbarians."

However, the notion of "law of nations" was the first Western legal concept to be introduced in Japan, and through it, the Empire of the Rising Sun understood the necessity of adhering to a global system of law that provided guidelines for diplomatic contact. Enlightened intellectuals, all of them specialists in Western sciences (*Yôgakusha*), originally believed, with great optimism, that acceptance of this system was the best guarantee and protection for the survival of "small" powers such as Japan. In the long run, after the Meiji Restoration, they realized that this guarantee had to be strengthened by economical and military development. Nevertheless, for these elites, assimilation of this new kind of law was the *sine qua non* condition for attaining international respectability: the achievement of equal relations with outside countries depended partly on Japan's capacity to submit itself to the *droit des gens*.

Political and cultural Eurocentrism was the major difficulty in this process. Confusion, in the rudimentary legal terminology of the time, of various notions such as European law, universal public law, and Western national law created uncertainty. Did these European concepts refer to natural or positive law? Was it possible to neglect the specific socio-cultural context in which they were developed? How was one to reconcile in the legal field Oriental spirit and Western ability? Most of the xenophobic loyalists who were formerly addicted to the expulsion of the Barbarians – and later were to restore imperial rule in 1868 – finally understood that in order to catch up with the industrialized West, Japan needed a strong and centralized leadership, while admitting concomitantly that modernization should not jeopardize national identity. Separation of the modernization process from Europeanization was furthermore a vital priority: convulsions generated by the renovation programs were to be overcome in order to avoid a disastrous rejection of international law.

Eurocentrism was also in a way a handicap for Westerners. It is true that the nineteenth century was mainly characterized by the expansion of Western imperialism over the five continents. European countries developed a strong feeling of superiority, supported by their industrial and economic dynamism. They commonly shared the same vision of a Western cultural and political supremacy. International law was first the law of the Christian nations, and religious freedom was seen as an integral part of it. But Japan, throughout the seclusion period, had carried on a strict policy of persecution of Christianity. And one of the first acts of the new government was to confirm this prohibition, which was extended even to Buddhism, because of its former allegiance to the *Bakufu*. Though religious freedom was granted to foreign residents, it was very doubtful whether the powers would be satisfied by the continuation of religious discrimination between Westerners and natives. The question was therefore whether non-Christian nations were to be excluded from the scope of international law. Generally speaking, most European scholars assumed that diversity of thoughts and beliefs could not by itself hinder the building of a general community of law among the nations, since they were ready to conform to these "universal principles of civilization." In 1874, the Paris Institute of International Law proclaimed the theoretical equality between Eastern and Western nations, and thus admitted the legitimacy of the application of international law to non-Christian nations. Consequently, every state could join the community of nations, provided that its civilization showed compatibility with diplomatic and legal rules officially approved and recognized by this community. In other words, international law, as a fundamental basis for the organization of international society, was endowed with a universal dimension. So, as a result of this process of secularization, international law became the law of "civilized countries." It was even asserted that in Buddhist countries, this extension was easier than in Islamic nations. Particularly Japan, in contrast to China, appeared to be a more active and homogeneous community, able to adapt itself to change without plunging into anarchy. Nevertheless, it is worth noting that those "principles of

civilization" were mainly Eurocentric, since Western Powers, by
virtue of their "specific mission," monopolized the right to define
these criteria of "civilization."

The Implications of the Treaty System on Domestic Legal Order

In 1858, Holland, Great Britain, the United States, France, Russia,
and Japan signed five fundamental treaties which became a standard for similar agreements concluded at the dawn of the Meiji era
with other European states such as Sweden, Norway, and Austria.
These treaties contained stipulations for the exchange of ambassa-
dors and consuls, enjoying movement facilities in their respective
countries; opening of ports; freedom of trade; monetary convertibil-
ity; delimitation of restricted residential zones for foreigners in the
opened ports; privilege of extraterritoriality and consular jurisdiction; contractual tariffs; and most-favored nation clauses.

To the imperial loyalists, the conclusion of these treaties was
scandalous, not by their content – whose pernicious effects would
only be felt a decade later – but because they were imposed under
foreign pressure without imperial sanction. The shogun's nego-
tiators saw these agreements as merely concessions: the opening
policy was still in an embryonic state and their lack of international
experience did not allow them to weigh the repercussions of these
commitments. That foreigners would not be submitted to Japanese
law was of no importance, since barbarians did not deserve these
sacred laws. They did not wholly understand why the reciprocity of
several stipulations had been suggested – the right of settlement for
instance – whereas Japanese were still not permitted to go abroad.
Evidently, they were aware of the breach in the seclusion policy, but,
from their point of view, the treaties were completely external to the
domestic legal order. In fact, contrary to those treaties concluded in
1882 by the United States, Great Britain, and Korea, which specified that suppression of the consular jurisdiction would depend on
adjustments or modifications in Korean laws and procedures prior
to their application on foreigners, no similar conditions were prescribed in the treaties signed by the *Bakufu*. There was no explicit
link between the privileges granted to the Western Powers or any
criticism of the archaism in the Japanese legal system. Legally
speaking, nothing obliged Westerners to abandon their "dominant
position," even though the Japanese government was determined to
install modern institutions.

Reality was quite different. Westerners would not agree to the revision of the treaties in dispute until Japan had undertaken the building of a new *état de droit*. According to them, the Japanese legal system could not escape fundamental adjustments because it suffered so many deficiencies: confusion bred both by the lack of separation of powers and the absence of a dichotomy between criminal and civil laws; uncertainty deriving from a tradition of secrecy in administration and the division of the country in nearly 300 autonomous fiefs; the utmost cruelty of criminal laws, including wide use of torture; the inhumanity of death penalties, such as neck sawing; and the principle of criminal liability expanded to relatives or groups of which the defender was a member. The great variety of practices and customs scarcely brought the native law within the reach of Westerners. As for traditions stemming from the historical and cultural legacy of the Japanese Empire, they were useless: in the Antique period, Japan experimented with a centralized monarchy on the Chinese pattern, which declined rapidly. Prior to the introduction of the Chinese model, clan structures of administration were stamped with religiosity: norms were oracles, offenses were depicted as stains, and administration was devoted to the performance of rites. Feudalism was an obstacle to political unity and economic development. The Japanese were ruled by their personal status and not by law. Consequently, the idea of a body of pre-established laws formulated *in abstracto*, as well as the determination of mutual rights and duties, remained largely unknown.

From numerous diplomatic contacts after the Restoration, most famous of which was the Iwakura mission (1871–1873), from their observation of the European powers' attitude toward their Chinese and Korean neighbors, and from the reports written by the first grant-holders in Europe, the Japanese became more and more convinced that institutional modernization was a prerequisite to the solution of the treaty issue. As, in the long run, privileges conceded to foreigners turned out to be a danger to national independence, Japan strove to obtain a revision through negotiations, while continuing the task of internal renovation. Skillfully, perhaps because there was no alternative given the balance of powers, the Meiji government proclaimed its intention to observe the treaties concluded by the *Bakufu*. The possibility of unilateral denunciation was sometimes advocated as a tactical means to pressure Westerners, but the government knew perfectly well that a consensual revision of the treaties was far better than an unforeseeable showdown.

In the course of diplomatic talks which took place virtually without interruption from 1875 to 1898, the crucial issue was the nature

of the compensations that Japan was disposed to offer in order to
obtain the suppression of consular jurisdiction. In two reports produced in 1879 and 1885 at the International Law Institute, Sir
Travers Twiss, from Great Britain, emphasized the necessity of
guarantees concerning a fair application to foreigners of a modernized domestic law.

In this respect, was the formal commitment of the government to
codification reliable? Had these Codes to be submitted to the European powers' approbation? Was it necessary to appoint foreign
judges to Japanese courts – and at which level? On these various
points, Western scholars disagreed. According to Paternostro, the
Italian legal advisor to the Japanese Ministry of Justice, exceptions
to territorial sovereignty had to be strictly interpreted, and, given
the decisive progress achieved in modernization of the legal apparatus, the maintenance of jurisdictional privileges was henceforth
without basis. Finally, after hard negotiations with London (serving
as the leader of the Western powers in Japan), both parties agreed
upon the abolition of the consular jurisdiction in return for the
liberalization of settlement rights. On the other hand, Japan promised to delay applying the new treaties pending enforcement of the
Codes, and to produce detailed reports at different stages of the
codification process, as well as the translation into English, or any
Western language, of the Codes in draft. After the 1894–1895 Sino-
Japanese War, similar negotiations were conducted with all the other
powers and, consecutively, new egalitarian treaties came into force.

Needless to say, the treaty issue and the question of its impact on
domestic law considerably affected the political situation in Japan.
Liberal opponents to the Meiji oligarchy arising from the big resto-
rationist clans, Chôshû and Satsuma, asserted that the renegotiation
of the treaties could not be obtained without the popular mobilization of an elected assembly. To the government, anxious to reinforce
its grasp on the political institutions, such a claim was both un-
acceptable and immature. During the 1880s, the liberal and
nationalist opposition, appalled by the compensation proposed by
the government in Codes endorsed by the Powers and by the transformation of the Great Court of Cassation into a Mixed Court,
launched a broad movement of protest against the treaty revision. It
was marked by riots and assassination attempts on Cabinet members. The enforcement of the Meiji Constitution and the subsequent
opening of the Imperial Diet in 1890 rekindled the controversy:
"popular" parties constantly denounced the "shameful" attitude of
the Government, selling off and trampling underfoot national inde-

pendence. The Meiji oligarchy reacted by enacting numerous ordinances restricting freedom of expression and association, while bitterly criticizing the ambiguous behaviour of its adversaries, whose stiffened opposition to any compromise paradoxically was consolidating a humiliating *status quo*. Thus, the treaty issue was not only the main line of the Meiji diplomacy, but also one of the most important stakes in domestic politics.

The Modernization of Law in Japan

Though having scarcely emerged from its feudal age, Japan, thirty years after the Restoration of imperial rule, enjoyed a complete and comprehensive modern system of law, whereby her rank among "civilized" nations was at last fully recognized. The revival of imperial rule, along with the building of a "strong and rich state," *Fukoku Kyôhei*, as a national priority, involved the administrative and political centralization around the throne and thus, the creation of an unified legal order justifying "the suppression of the evil customs of the past." On the other hand, for the Western powers, the advent of an European-oriented *état de droit* based on procedures and laws compatible with Western norms of civilization was taken as a prime requirement for the revision of the treaty system. This double exigency governed both the ways of reception of European law and the task of legal institutionalization and codification.

The Ways of Reception of European Law

Translations were the primary sources of information and knowledge about European law. The *Bakufu*, with the Bureau of Investigation on Barbarian Books, *Bansho Torishirabesho*, had at its disposal groups of specialists devoted to the translation of foreign books and documents, who also served from time to time as interpreters to shogunal officials. This work was taken over by the Meiji Government and developed as soon as the task of codification was well underway. Nevertheless, in the first stages, these attempts met numerous obstacles. Most of these sources were translated from their Dutch and Chinese versions, so that the *Bakufu* decided to improve knowledge of foreign languages to make access to the original sources easier. The countless difficulties, mistakes, and misunderstandings created by these translations (made by administrators whose abilities in the legal and linguistic fields were rather superficial), can easily be imagined. By employing neologisms and paraphrases to express Western legal notions with no equivalent in Japanese, these men invented a new legal terminology. Most of them took active part in codification work; they were not mere subordinates. Some of them, like Mitsukuri Rinshô, were appointed to the Senate by the emperor, and later to the House of Peers prior to ennoblement.

Missions abroad were the second channel of information. Since the 1860s, the *Bakufu* had sent several diplomatic missions to Europe to deepen its understanding of the West: the Takeuchi Embassy (1862) and the Ikeda, Shibata and Akitake Tokugawa Missions (1864, 1865, 1867). In the travel notes or reports of these men can be found, in a colorful if not laudatory way, the first on-the-spot descriptions of the European legal systems. From 1862, the government gave grants for study abroad. Two holders, Nishi Amane and Tsuda Mamichi, became famous for the publication of the first Japanese textbooks on international law. The fiefs themselves followed the same path: as early as 1865, one of the most powerful clans, Satsuma, sent a delegation of warriors to Great Britain. Two years before, five more impatient *Samurai* had left Japan clandestinely to visit England. Among them was Itô Hirobumi, the father of the Meiji Constitution. This policy was continued by the new Government. Besides the Iwakura Mission, Itô Hirobumi's stay in Europe in 1882–1883 played an important role in the advent of constitutionalism in Japan. In addition, many higher civil servants and law professors were trained in the West.

The recruitment of foreign legal advisors was the cornerstone of the reception system. These advisors were attached to the Japanese Foreign Ministry to supervise legal modernization. From France, Bousquet participated in the first draft of the Civil Code based on a translation of the Napoleonic Codes; Boissonade spent most of his life in Japan, and his contributions in civil and criminal matters were highly appreciated. From Germany, Roesler took charge of the Commercial Code; in collaboration with Mosse, he rendered considerable assistance in constitutional matters; Rudolf was in charge of the judiciary. Sometimes their influence extended on political issues: Boissonade, for instance, was deeply involved in the settlement of the conflict which arose between Peking and Tokyo about the Ryûkyû archipelago (1874). In 1887, while Japanese public opinion was extremely divided on the diplomatic issue, he advised the Government to adopt a less conciliatory stand in the negotiations with the West on the treaty revision.

A fourth factor was the promotion of legal education. Initially established as a documentation center for shogunal officers, the Bureau of Investigation on Barbarian Books, founded in 1856, was raised to the status of a national school specialized in Western sciences, open to all samurai. In 1863, the first legal courses were inaugurated and the new Government confirmed this policy by inviting foreign professors to Japan. In 1877, the newly created Tokyo Imperial University was divided into four Faculties. Among them, there was a Law Faculty, which ten years later set up three chairs of French, German and Anglo-Saxon law. Apart from Imperial Universities, many private schools specializing in Western law also flourished: French law at the Meiji Law School and Anglo-Saxon law at the Tokyo Special School, which became later the well-known Meiji University and Waseda University respectively. The teaching staff included both native and foreign professors: at Tôdai (Tokyo Imperial University), Charles B. Storres and Edmund Ono taught English law together with their Japanese colleagues. Those Law Faculties, especially in the Imperial Universities, were fully integrated into the state administrative system, not only because they were at the apex of the national school organization, but also because they were mainly devoted to bureaucratic training. Given the close relations between State Universities and officialdom, the Law Faculties played a prominent role in the education of the political and administrative elite. Professors enjoyed considerable prestige. Hozumi Yatsuka, professor of constitutional law at Tôdai who studied in Germany, ended his career as member of the House of Peers and Palace Councillor. His brother, Nobushige, a distinguished specialist in comparative law, was trained in Europe, too. Ennobled by the emperor, he was promoted to the presidency of the Privy Council. All of them were greatly influenced by Western legal theories and methodologies: Max von Seydel and Paul Laband's thought made a deep imprint on Hozumi Yatsuka's doctrine of legal traditionalism, while Minobe Tatsukichi's liberal interpretation of constitutionalism was strongly colored by Jellinek's ideas.

The Task of Legal Institutionalization and Codification

Even prior to the introduction of constitutionalism, the first regulations pertaining to the fundamental structure of the state referred to Western legal concepts: separation of powers was explicitly advocated in the Instrument of Government, *Seitaisho*, promulgated in

June 1868. In April 1875, an Imperial Rescript promised the establishment of a constitutional government in gradual stages. Though
these formal proclamations were not fully consistent with governmental practice, they sounded very modern and liberal in theory.
Moreover, the Charter Oath, issued in April 1868 by the Emperor,
announced that deliberative assemblies would be widely established
and that all matters would be decided by public discussion. Simultaneously, although feudal territorial structures were not yet totally
dismantled, bicameral assemblies were created. The representative-
ness and competence of these deliberative organs were rather weak,
but strong enough to attest to the regime's will to open up to
"talented men regardless of rank." Even though these "democratic"
statements must not be misunderstood, it was undoubtedly a great
advance, compared with the situation prevailing under the shogunate, since access to administrative functions was no longer limited by
social status. Besides, in 1869, the old social hierarchy was abolished
and replaced by a new legal differentiation under the general label of
"imperial subjects" (Imperial Family, Peers, former Warriors and
Commoners). Consequently, the exorbitant privileges of the *Samurai*
class – such as the carrying of two swords – were also gradually
suppressed. In the same way, in order to fortify the new administration, the government itself did not overlook the problem of drawing
up a Constitution. After the first unofficial draughts produced by
two oligarchic leaders, Kido Takayoshi and Okubo Toshimichi in
1873, in 1876 Emperor Meiji ordered the Senate to submit a constitutional draft "based on the system established at the time of the
foundation of the nation and which will give due consideration to the
laws of the various nations." Foreign advisors were appointed to a
special bureau under the chairmanship of Prince-imperial Arisuga-
wa. In 1877, the publication by the Senate of a booklet entitled "The
Western States Constitutions," facilitated comparative research
and spurred on the constitutional debate within enlightened public
opinion. Afterward, as mentioned above, German scholars assisted
closely in the compiling of the final drafts. Even after the promulgation of the Constitution, one of the main drafters, Kaneko Kentarô,
who was graduated from Harvard, was sent to Europe and America,
in order to record the opinions of the most famous Western lawyers.
All of them praised the pragmatism, the wisdom, and the conservatism of the Japanese Government, so that the Meiji Constitution
came into force with the almost unanimous approbation of Western
specialists, while in Japan, liberals were somewhat disgruntled at

the prospect of a "Prussianisation" of the state.

In the private law field, initial studies were conducted in 1869, with the translation of the French Civil Code, under the responsibility of, successively, the Ministry of Justice, the Senate, and the Foreign Ministry (in 1886, when the diplomatic negotiations on the treaty revision were in a crucial phase), before returning to the Ministry of Justice. Foreigners undertook a large part in the researching and drafting, but decision-making was strictly reserved to a Japanese Committee composed of judges and senators. The first Civil Code, promulgated in 1890, was supposed to come into force three years after, but its postponement was decided by the Imperial Diet in 1892 after a long controversy. Redrafted along German lines, the new Civil Code was enacted in 1898. As regards commercial matters, the Meiji Government first adopted preliminary measures in order to remove hindrances to traffic and trade: monetary unification, banking system reform, improvement of communication networks and stocking, reorganization of commercial professions and transactions, and modernization of the insurance system. The drafting of the Commercial Code started in 1881, but the project written by Roesler in 1890 was carried along by the Civil Code turmoil. Once redrafted, the final Code was applied in 1899. The first attempts at the codification of civil procedures occurred in 1873, and the Code came into force in 1891. Until the 1890s, the major part of private law remained reliant on Tokugawa customary laws, which were compiled and recorded. Significantly, in the 1875 Regulations for the Conduct of Judicial Processes, it was stated that in civil cases judgements would be governed by custom in the absence of written law, and, in the absence of custom, based on reason, *Jôri*. It is commonly admitted that in these early days, Western law partly succeeded in penetrating the Japanese legal system through the judicial process as an expression of "reason."

Concerning criminal matters, by 1868 the Meiji Government had extended the Hundred Laws, *Osadamegaki Hyakkajô*, applied in the Tokugawa lands, to all feudal domains. From 1868 to 1871, criminal reforms were merely a mixture of Chinese and shogunal laws, without any influence from the West. These regulations were, however, publicized for the first time, whereas, according to feudal practices, the deterrent effect of criminal laws depended on secrecy. The Amended Criminal Regulations (1873) specified a general attenuation of penalty scale, including some gradual concessions to Western ideas. But Boissonade's contribution was decisive, by introducing in the Japanese criminal institutions the principle *nulla poena, nulla crimen sine lege*. The so-called Old Criminal Code came into force in 1882, completed by the procedural Code of Criminal Instruction, which provided for a full set of hierarchical criminal courts. These two Codes were revised in 1908 and 1890, respectively, along German lines.

Of course, legal codification likewise affected the Japanese judicial system. Modernization of the judiciary implied a step-by-step separation of the courts from the administration, which was consecrated by the Courts Organization Law (1890); statutory independence of judges became legally and constitutionally guaranteed; and cases were secured against interference from the executive.

To sum up, three conclusions can be drawn: 1) Among the main consequences of the legal institutionalization and codification process was the marginalization of common law systems for two reasons: first, to the proponents of a Prussian style governing monarchy, the British form of constitutionalism was not reliable; second, Anglo-Saxon law was less suitable for the purposes of systematization than other European legal systems; 2) competition between various systems of law provoked important discrepancies, especially between French-style civil drafts and German-style commercial drafts; 3) the promulgation of the first Codes before 1890 was likely prompted by political overtones – the treaty issue – but also by the prospect of the Meiji Constitution enforcement and the impending opening of the Imperial Diet. Given the hostility of the political parties, the ruling oligarchy probably tried to present the new Parliament with a *fait accompli*.

Tradition as a Permanent Symbol of Identity

The massive introduction of European law in such a peculiar political, historical and cultural environment did not only entail technical difficulties: attitudes and mentalities ossified by centuries of seclusion and feudalism could not be easily changed. But within thirty years, Japan appeared as a modern state, ready to join the community of nations. The national fabric, however, was far from impregnated with this amazing transformation. One should rather say that under the strong leadership of the Meiji Government, legal modernization preceded social change in Japan. The risk was real of dysfunction between superstructural renovation and the survival of traditions and values which were not at once affected by the 1868 *coup d'état.* Transplantation of European law was essentially congruent with national restructuring, while having to be consistent with the national spirit and polity. The following illustrates something of the reception process as well as its pitfalls.

European Law and the Legitimacy of Power

It may be assumed that the Meiji Restoration was basically a "revolution" in the literal sense of the word, not only because the *coup* was stirred up by a few "imperial" fiefs which subverted the shogunate, but also because the new Government pretended to return to the antique monarchy, *Osei Fukkô*, which had flourished during the eighth century along with the reception of Chinese institutions, but had then been overshadowed by seven hundred years of military rule. It was even doubtful whether this quest for direct imperial rule was relevant to the historical facts, since most of the Japanese sovereigns were incapable of containing the irresistible thrust of the warrior class to whom they willy-nilly "delegated" their political prerogatives. But this claim was highly paradoxical: restoring the heroic day of Jimmu *tennô* – the first human emperor of the Japanese dynasty – on the basis of institutions imported from T'ang China was not very pertinent. In addition, the so-called return to the antique monarchy was not compatible with the actual situation created by the abandonment of the isolationist policy in the middle of the nineteenth century. Above all, this "revolution" on behalf of the emperor was carried out while keeping imperial authority impotent: the future Meiji Emperor was still minor, and his father, *Kômei tennô*, who constantly advocated the expulsion of the Barbarians, did not personally favor the destruction of the *Bakufu*. Even within the imperial camp many loyalists believed that the emperor, once restored in his supreme authority, must remain aloof from politics.

Thus, the restoration of imperial rule was far from removing all ambiguities. By attacking the *Bakufu*, imperial loyalists were breaking the feudal framework in the name of a superior and transcendent loyalty which legitimized their subversive goals. By advocating the return to the ancient monarchy, they evidently did not rely upon any reasoned analysis of the real function of the imperial throne in the preshogunal times, but rather upon the actualization of a new type of "tradition" which was "reconstituted" in order to secure its own power and to focus national energy around a charismatic authority, serving as a symbol of progress and order.

As a result, in the institutional field, the Supreme Affairs Ministry,

Dajôkan, which had been the central organ of government in the eighth century, was reactivated, and high-ranking Court Nobles, *Kuge*, from the Kyoto aristocracy, held the prestigious posts of imperial advisors. That structure was reshuffled in 1885, when the creation of a modern Cabinet system established the oligarchic supremacy over the state machinery. The period 1868–1873 unquestionably marked the peak of this policy of return to antiquity, together with its political and ideological implications: union of Court and rites, wherein formal imperial rites and ceremonies were revitalized and officialized. However, from 1875, the *Dajôkan* system moved toward constitutionality and eventually lost its "fundamentalist" connotations.

At this time, the Meiji Government had to deal with the problem of the constitutional formulation of the monarchical status. It was a matter of great significance, since the cabinet had to make a decisive choice among various European models: a British type of parliamentary monarchy, a democratic monarchy inspired by the French Revolution, or a Prussian oriented authoritarian monarchy. It is well known that, in 1881, following serious internal dissensions and the rise of liberal agitation, the government, concerned with the protection of imperial prerogatives, chose the Prussian form of constitutionalism in order to preserve monarchical preeminence as a shield against further political deviations. But at the same time, the oligarchs came down strongly in favor of a legal formulation of the imperial will, implicitly rejecting the Confucianist views as a contrary to the rule of law.

Since Japan's specific experiences did not provide any valuable cases of institutionalization and rationalization of monarchical power through law, the full impact of European law might have been anything but decisive. All the provisions of the Meiji Constitution could be found in the old German States Constitutions, except for the expression of the cardinal principles of the national polity, *Kokutai*: "the Empire of Great Japan is governed by an emperor belonging to an unbroken line of sovereigns since the divine foundation of the nation, and for ages eternal, combining in himself the rights of sovereignty." Furthermore, the justification of monarchical pre-eminence was not the Constitution itself, but the instructions bequeathed by the Sun Goddess, Amaterasu-Omi-Kami, and the imperial ancestors through successive generations of emperors. So, there was no innovation in introducing constitutionalism, but only a legal clarification of these heavenly instructions, as they were originally depicted in the first Japanese historical sources, the *Kojiki* and the *Nihon Shoki*. The Constitution thus embodied the imperial myths described in the Japanese theogony as the basis of sovereignty. The emperor was bound by the Constitution, but only in so far as it was taken as a part of this divine heritage, and he was only accountable for his acts to his ancestors.

Their German advisors strove vainly to warn the Japanese against such an irrational description of the national polity: if the power organization deriving from the monarchical preeminence was to be discussed, the Japanese drafters never admitted any foreign interference in the definition of the imperial institution. As such, the Japanese monarchy was extolled as basically different from its European counterparts, founded on an irrelevant compromise, in the Japanese context, between the conflicting rights of the king and the people. The Prussian model was essentially viewed as a state philosophy inspiring both the political machinery and the power relationships, but without any implications for the source of sovereignty or legitimacy. Therefore, the Japanese *Kokutai* appeared to be the most perfect expression of a pure and genuine monarchy, serving as a powerful weapon for nationalist mobilization. This conception of legitimacy relying on myths and legends was mostly fictitious. But the framers of the Meiji Constitution could not fail to marvel at the exceptional dynastic continuity, its incomparable antiquity and the remarkable durability of its *auctoritas*, which obviously contrasted with a fluctuating political leadership. They discovered in the immemorial intimacy between the imperial Household and the nation the mystery of Japanese uniqueness. In a way, the Government paid all the more attention to the constitutional transcription of the Japanese "*Kokutai* splendour" – formulated in the first article of all constitutional drafts – since the description of the organic structure and administrative competence of the state was largely shaped by Western influence. But, by erecting imperial legitimacy as the sole symbol of national identity, the oligarchs initiated a harmful alteration of constitutionalism, since the compulsive force of the Meiji Charter was invested in a pre-existent institution which was not only the main impetus source within the state, but its creative impulse as well.

The legitimacy issue, too, was a tremendous problem for the political opposition to the Meiji Government. Rising against the clan oligarchy was somehow interpreted as an attack against the throne itself. When, in the early years of the Meiji era, liberals demanded the convocation of an elected assembly, these formal "democratic" convictions reflected in fact heterogeneous aspirations and frustrations emanating from numerous social categories excluded by the new regime: proletarianized *samurai*, overburdened peasants, former *Bakufu* officials, loyalists disappointed by the inferior situation left to their fiefs in the new imperial state, and genuine liberals. Later on, in the late 1870s, when the Senate produced a constitutional draft focussing on "the sharing of political rights between the sovereign and the people," on a British pattern, it was mainly because members of the Upper House were rejecting both Rousseauist extremism and unrestrained Westernization. They found in the most liberal parliamentary systems sophisticated instruments for control over an Executive suspected of yielding to the reform mood. A decade later, the newly inaugurated Diet became the scene of repeated clashes between the Cabinet and political parties, which revealed a hidden rivalry for the control of the bureaucratic machinery and monopolization of the imperial will. In short, confronted with a government promoting both modernization and tradition, the political opposition felt rather off-balance, whether it was discredited as an obstacle to national development because of its impulsiveness or ultraconservatism, or whether its fighting spirit was blunted by the dream of an indolent consensualism. At any rate, the "attractive" force of imperial preeminence was so strong that even to the political opposition itself, there were no current source of legitimacy. Protection of the throne and national polity was always explicitly mentioned as the first principle of all political parties, even though this claim covered different meanings or contents. As for the debate on European institutions, discussions implied strategic stakes – the most suitable type of regime for Japan – as well as tactical ones, embracing competition among the ruling elite and between government and opposition.

European Law and Moral Values Hierarchy

This question can be examined from two sides. On the one hand, did the recognition of individual rights bring about significant changes to tradition? On the other hand, how far did it affect the Confucian conception of the family-state? As to the first question, following the enforcement of the constitution and the enactment of the new codes, the relationship between the government and the governed and the subjects' rights and duties were henceforth legally organized and well defined. Nevertheless, this task had to overcome many difficulties and remained partly incomplete.

If modernization implied the overhaul of the whole shogunal system, the spirit governing the feudal institutions endured the formal abrogation of the *Bakufu* legal framework and deeply impressed the new laws or judicial practices. Throughout the debates about the first Civil Code draft, some Japanese compilers objected to the translation of the French *droit civil*, by Minken, because granting rights, *Ken*, to commoners, *Min*, was unthinkable. During the preliminary deliberations about the Meiji Constitution, the question of the subjects' rights was never included in the governmental top priorities. At the Privy Council, the advisory organ undertaking the constitutional drafting, a few councillors stated that only the monarch possessed rights, whereas subjects had to be ruled by a "status." Itô Hirobumi himself had to fight in order to impose a legal conception of rights. Rights – as well as the Constitution itself – are bestowed by the monarch. The idea of fundamental rights invested on every human being as expressions of individual dignity was entirely discounted. Furthermore, these rights could not be considered *vis-à-vis* the imperial prerogatives and were only exerted "under the limits of the law." In other words, the finality of legislative intervention was not protection but restriction. The content of rights was fixed by law through due legal process: according to the German concept of *Rechtstaat*, the "law state" proceeded from a central and absolute authority as the source of general guidance for administrative actions and subjects, but did not impose any limitations on lawmakers.

Similarly, in the field of criminal law, until the enforcement of the first Code in 1882, the old principle of discriminatory penalties according to social conditions was still applied. Appellate jurisdiction was unknown to shogunal courts. Under the *Bakufu* system, suits against superiors or petitions over the head of one's lord were condemned as contrary to moral obligations and as a cause of disturbance in the immutable order of the relationship between superiors and inferiors. Violations of this prohibition were sternly punished, even if the claim was justified. It will also be noticed that since the first Criminal Code, crimes against the Imperial House and state security were also repressed. In the Meiji period, Criminal Law developed as a bulwark against liberal movements: the promulgation of the first Criminal Code coincided with the enforcement of numerous special laws on Public Meetings (1880, 1890), Press (1875, 1887, 1897), Libel (1875), Publications (1883, 1887, 1893) and Peace Preservation (1887, 1898), which were very useful to control political agitation. So, there is no exaggeration in stating that criminal law served as an auxiliary to administrative centralization around oligarchic power.

Under these circumstances, the birth of a legally defined individual rights consciousness was all the more problematic, since, because of the cultural inhibitions peculiar to a highly hierarchical society, claims for individual rights were shaking the holistic values and moral obligations with which every member of the group had to comply. As these behavioral norms provided security and assistance for the community itself, the pretension to individual autonomy through personal rights appeared to be eminently disruptive, indeed even subversive, since it meant the exclusion from all internal mechanisms of protection induced by these compulsive relationships, as well as the rejection of effective means of dispute settlement within the group, through resort to external procedural rationality deprived of the lubricating function devoluted to moral categories. Until the Pacific War, and perhaps even today, mentalities and social attitudes remained largely dominated by the *Giri Ninjô* pattern, and not by legal standards.

From many points of view, the outcome of the codification process was not the complete upheaval of the society, but rather, through European legal concepts and procedures, the perpetuation of the old moral order adapted to a new type of governance. Besides, like most of the Confucian nations, the Japanese inherited a deeply rooted feeling of suspicion toward Western jurisdiction, still preferring the discretion of conciliatory procedures to obtrusive suits. These psychological factors explained both the weakness of the Japanese bar, which was not provided for criminal actions until 1882, and the peculiar conception of lawsuits, *Uttae*, viewed, even in civil litigations, as disciplinary complaints or petitions to a superior rather than as a legal arbitration between equal and opposite claims.

As to the second question – on European law and the Family-State ideology – the imperial rule of the Restoration established a direct and immediate link between the emperor and his subjects. Primarily, the monarch substituted himself for the *shôgun* in the suzerainty relationship, and, as mentioned earlier, after 1869, all Japanese became imperial subjects. At the same time, the restored monarchy turned out to be an imperial mysticism – a so-called theocratic-patriarchal constitutionalism – linking both the emperor and the people in an emotional symbiotic relation: on the one hand, the state was identified as a big family, on the other hand, loyalty to the throne was closely likened to filial piety.

The family institution was erected in the microcosm of the state. Hierarchical ties among family members and kinship were considered as national standards for the relationship between the emperor and his subjects. Family was firstly a patrilinear filiation group devoted to its own perpetuation. This typical feature, though genealogically delimited, did not exclusively rely on biological consanguinity, but rather on the interaction of natural and adoptive filiation, in order to maintain the continuity of the household entity. The ritualized expression of this requirement was ancestor worship, wherein the living community, bound together under the leadership of the family head, is connected to the unbroken lineage of the clan ancestors and founders.

During the Meiji era, the main contribution made by the theorists of imperial absolutism, who systematized historiographical and philological tendencies which had grown up under the *Bakufu* system, was to make imperial dynastic continuity directly relevant to the basic family unit, both as the patriarchal symbol of national unity and the apex of a transcendent ethical order. Whereas, traditionally, the imperial institution was not subjected to popular worship, absence of differentiation between loyalty and filial piety resulted in the combination of the domestic entities' preservation, as sanctified by appropriate rites with reverence for the throne. In other words, obedience to the emperor as descendant of the ancestors of the Japanese race was nothing more than submission to the family head embodying the clan ancestors' authorities through parental rights over the household. As a sacred obligation of reverence, such an obedience was nothing but the transfiguration of parental loyalty chains connecting each individual clansman to his eponymous ancestors, the family to the state. The only difference between imperial ancestor worship and clan or family ancestor worship lay in their respective scope, not in their nature. This intrinsic solidarity was seen as the foundation of the genuine cohesion of the Japanese race. The Family-State ideology was thus closely associated with the institutionalization of the monarchy's cultural role as paragon of traditional values.

To that end, education, through the famous Imperial Rescript on Education – the blueprint of the school curriculum – and State Shinto became instruments of mass indoctrination. Loyalty and filial piety appeared as the pivot of national identity, the most significant expression of indigenous virtues handed down by the ancestors. National beliefs were sublimated by State Shinto – a typical creation of the Meiji period – devoted to the penetration of imperial worship as civic duty transcending all kinds of religious faiths.

Could these conceptions be inserted in a legal scheme? Throughout the national debate about the postponement of Boissonade's

Civil Code draft, at the dawn of the 1890s, traditionalist scholars stated that legalization of intrafamilial relations – in terms of mutual rights and duties – involved harmful mechanization of loyalty and filial piety contrary to national ethics. This suggested that the controversial point did not concern only the contents of the Code, but the opportunity of codification itself, although Boissonade ensured that the bulk of family law was created by Japanese jurists. Besides, the drafting of a new Civil Code under German influence met with the same traditionalist objections. The result was a dual conception of the family institution: legal codification consolidated the position of the household head – parental rights, birthright, primogeniture – in a modern formulation of feudal values extended to the whole society. Of course, it must be understood that such a legal definition of the family institution did not exhaust obligations deriving from the filial piety precept. Similarly, it is conceivable to affirm that even though the Meiji Constitution clothed the emperor in the guise of a limited constitutional monarch, loyalty to the throne was not constrained by the legal organization of relationships between the sovereign and the people.

Conclusion

The Meiji oligarchy's ambition was to conciliate Western legal formalism attached to normative values with Eastern ethics based on moral edification. Nevertheless, the implementation of this policy proved to be uneasy: the Meiji Government could not set aside the past without creating a vacuum undermining the modernization process. The destruction of the *Bakufu* did not mean so much the destitution of the old scale of values as its absorption by the imperial system. Reference to tradition, therefore, remained unavoidable, first, as means of legitimatization of a tottering regime, second, as a need for social stabilization and rallying point urged by the modernization process, and third, as both a protection against encroachment from the West and as a moral palliative for Japan's inferiority in industrial and economic achievements. It must be also noted that traditions proved to be a dynamic impulse, since they were mostly remolded by the ruling elite for the fulfillment of new national goals.

In relation to European law, tradition cannot be seen from an exclusively antithetical point of view, but rather in both a dialectical and a diachronic perspective. Certainly, the implementation of such a heterogenous legal system sometimes gave rise to scepticism. It is also true that the introduction of European law did not open the way to political liberalism, since *de facto* evolution toward parliamentary government at the end of the Meiji period coincided with the penetration of imperial worship and the reinforcement of ideological orthodoxy in order to counter the rise of socialism. As a matter of fact, the interaction between European law and tradition provided the ruling oligarchy with powerful legal and moral instruments of social restructuring and domination, whereby the Japanese monarchy developed as a global political, ideological and religious system which, in the end, inhibited the growth of constitutionalism in Japan.

BIBLIOGRAPHY

In French

Bruno Gollnisch-Flourens, *Ouverture du Japon et droit de l'Occident* (Paris, 1978), 2 vols.
Eric Seizelet, *L'institution impériale endroit public japonais depuis la restauration de Meiji* (Paris, 1984) 3 vols.
Noda Yoshiyuki, *Introduction au droit japonais* (Paris, 1966).

In English

Carol Gluck, *Japan's Modern Myths. Ideology in the Late Meiji Period* (Princeton, 1988).
Richard H. Minear, *Japanese Tradition and Western Law. Emperor, State and Law in the Thought of Hozumi Yatsuka* (Cambridge, 1970).
Arthur T. von Mehren, *Law in Japan. The legal order in a changing society* (Cambridge, 1962).
Robert E. Ward (ed.), *Political Development in Modern Japan* (Princeton, 1968).

In Japanese

Inada Masatsugu, *Meiji Kempô Seiritsu-shi* (History of the Making of the Meiji Constitution) (Tokyo, 1978), 2 vols.
Ishii Ryôsuke, *Meiji Bunka-shi Hôsei-hen* (History of Meiji Culture: Legislation) (Tokyo, 1964).

Nakamura Kichisaburô, *Meiji Kenryoku no Hôteki Kôzô* (Power and Legal Structure in the Meiji Period) (Tokyo, 1977).

Kawashima Takeyoshi, *Ideologii to shite no Kazoku Seido* (The Family Institution as Ideology) (Tokyo, 1980).

4

The Treaty System and European Law in China: A Study of the Exercise of British Jurisdiction in Late Imperial China

PAUL H. CH'EN

Introduction

The Sino-British Treaty of 1842, signed at Nanking to conclude the conflict arisen from the "Opium War," marked a new period of British involvement in China. Among several other stipulations in this treaty, China agreed to open five ports to accommodate various British commercial activities, and these five treaty ports consequently provided the British government with a strong foundation to exert its influence in China. As the volume and speed of Sino-British intercourse increased, more treaties were later ratified to consolidate and expand British interests; and until these so-called "unequal treaties" were finally terminated in 1943, the British government enjoyed a wide scope of privileges, including extraterritorial jurisdiction in China.

The exercise of British jurisdiction, along with the introduction of modern Western ideas and values, also confronted Chinese society with novel questions. The problem of how to react to the new situation shaped by Western influence was an urgent concern for the Chinese leaders, who were also desperate to secure China's independence from foreign intervention. Through the treaty system China was forced to enter into the family of nations, making various adjustments to reduce the tensions between the Chinese traditional order and modern Western forces. Such adjustments occurred, consciously or subconsciously, bridging the gap between the Chinese and Western concepts of law and justice. The adjustments were also reflected in the establishment of legal institutions to facilitate the exercise of British jurisdiction on the one hand, and to implement many programs to reform the Chinese legal system on the other.

In discussing modern Chinese civilization, however, many historians tend to neglect the impact of the Western legal institutions in China, partly due to the moral and political implications of the exercise of extraterritorial jurisdiction. Many Chinese scholars have, understandably, stressed their strong nationalistic concern by criticizing the imposition of British jurisdiction. Their resentment has also been intensified by the fact that nations including the United States, France, Germany, and Japan followed the British example and took advantage of the weak Chinese position to conclude various "unequal treaties" with China. By contrast, owing to the existence of moral issues in "Imperialism" and the "Opium Wars," many Western scholars have been apologetic in their interpretations with regard to the impact of European institutions.

In order to obtain a more realistic view of the impact of European law in China, this paper will examine the exercise of British jurisdiction in China under the treaty system during three stages of its involvement in late Imperial China. The first stage started with the Treaty of Nanking in 1842 and continued up to 1857, illustrating the experiments in adopting a workable formula for the exercise of British jurisdiction. The Sino-British Treaty of Tientsin (1858) brought the experiences of British jurisdiction into the second stage, in which various institutions were established to facilitate an efficient administration of justice. The intervening years between 1876, when the Chefoo Convention was ratified, and 1912, when the Republic of China was founded, witnessed the third stage of the exercise of British jurisdiction in Imperial China.

In response to the rising Chinese nationalism and the various law reforms initiated during the Republican era, however, the exercise of British jurisdiction finally came to an end in 1943. Undoubtedly, to the Chinese and British authorities who worked out the first treaties, the formula of extraterritorial jurisdiction seemed to provide a practical solution to some pressing judicial problems between the two nations. But, during the course of subsequent developments, the treaty system succeeded in introducing the Western ideas of law and justice to China. The impact of European legal principles and institutions continued to affect the Chinese legal order, even after the termination of the treaty system. Thus, the significance of the exercise of British jurisdiction in China has, in its many dimensions, gone beyond a mere political expediency in the scale of history.

The First Stage (1842–1857)

Historically, the legal status of foreigners has been a matter of concern to the Chinese. In the T'ang dynasty (618–907), if a *hua-wai-jen* ("a person beyond transformation," i.e., "a foreigner") had a legal dispute with a foreigner of the same ethnic group, his case was to be decided in accordance with the laws of his own group. If two parties were of different ethnic backgrounds, the case was to be determined by the Chinese authorities according to Chinese law. Thus, pursuant to this principle, disputes between Chinese and foreigners were decided by Chinese law. As the prototype of extraterritorial jurisdiction, the T'ang practice concerning foreigners in China was adopted by later dynasties, but with some modifications.

The traditional practice became much more elaborate in the Yüan dynasty (1279–1368), as the issues of jurisdiction became complicated, owing to the existence of several ethnic groups (such as Mongols, Central Asians, and Chinese) in China proper. Since these groups were all under the domination of the Mongolian rulers in China, theoretically they were not foreigners in the strict sense. They were, however, so different from one another that a sophisticated system of jurisdiction was established to govern their legal disputes.[1] With a large influx of foreigners to China in the Ming (1368–1644) and the Ch'ing (1644–1912) periods, the problem of jurisdiction became much more important and delicate. This problem was especially pressing during the latter half of the Ch'ing dynasty, when Western powers began to demand a higher trade volume as well as extraterritorial protection for their subjects residing in China.[2]

Extraterritorial jurisdiction in its modern form in China began with the Treaty of Nanking (1842), which followed the first Anglo-Chinese War, more commonly known as the "Opium War." Although the Treaty did not mention specifically the provision of extraterritoriality as such, the opening of the five treaty ports (Canton, Amoy, Foochow, Ningpo, and Shanghai) and the appointment of Superintendents or Consular Officers to serve as medium of

1. For a discussion of the exercise of jurisdiction during the Yüan dynasty see Paul H. Ch'en, *Chinese Legal Tradition under the Mongols* (Princeton, 1979), 80–88.

2. For a discussion of the early European contact with China and the issue of extraterritoriality, see Hosea Ballou Morse, *The International Relations of the Chinese Empire*, vol. 1, *The Period of Conflict, 1834–1860* (Shanghai, 1910), 41–62. Also see G.W. Keeton, *The Development of Extraterritoriality in China* (London, 1928), vol. 1, 1–95.

communication, as stipulated in Article II, provided a base for the development of extraterritorial jurisdiction. With the anticipation of having more British subjects reside at these ports to expand commercial activities, the Foreign Office in London was eager to obtain a guideline with regard to extraterritorial jurisdiction concerning any possible future conflict between British subjects themselves and between British and Chinese parties. In response to the letter written by Lord Aberdeen, dated January 4, 1843, Sir Henry Pottinger, who was then the British plenipotentiary, followed the advice of the Foreign Office and conducted further negotiations with his Chinese counterpart, Kiying. Their meetings succeeded in incorporating some regulations dealing with British jurisdiction into the General Regulations of Trade, published on July 22, 1843.[3]

Pursuant to Articles XII and XIII of the Regulations, it was agreed that disputes between British and Chinese parties should be first settled amicably by the British Consul. When the case could not be resolved in this way, then and only then would the Consul request the assistance of a Chinese official to consider jointly the true merits of the case and decide equitably. It was also established that British subjects involved in criminal cases were to be tried by British officials according to British law, and that the Chinese criminals were to be tried by the Chinese authorities according to Chinese law. These provisions thus served as the first official framework for the exercise of British jurisdiction in China.

In order to settle several important pending issues subsequent to the termination of the "Opium War," Pottinger and Kiying signed the Supplementary Treaty at Hoomun Chai (the Bogue) on October 8, 1843. Article II stipulated that the General Regulations of Trade should be in force from that time onward at the five ports, and consequently the formula of British jurisdiction meted out in the Regulations was officially incorporated into the Supplementary Treaty. In addition, the principle and procedure of extradition were outlined in Article XI, thus making the Supplementary Treaty more effective in expanding British extraterritorial jurisdiction.[4]

With the removal of various difficulties mentioned in the letter of Lord Aberdeen, an "Act for the better government of Her Majesty's subjects resorting to China" was passed by Parliament and prom-

3. For the complete text of the General Regulations of Trade: *The Maritime Customs, Treaties, Conventions, etc., between China and Foreign States* (Shanghai, 1917), vol. 1, 383–89.

4. For the complete text of the Supplementary Treaty of Hoomun Chai see *The Maritime Customs*, vol. 1, 390–99.

ulgated in 1843.[5] This act, in its Sections I and III, empowered the Superintendent of Trade to enact laws and ordinances, subjected to the conditions and limitations so prescribed by Her Majesty, for governing British subjects in China. This special arrangement thus placed British subjects in China under the authority of the Crown instead of Parliament. Section IV, however, provided that all such commissions, instructions, Orders in Council, and all laws and ordinances so to be made to facilitate the administration of British subjects in China should be laid before both Houses of Parliament, as soon as conveniently possible after they were made and enacted. Since British subjects in China were too far away from London to be ruled directly and effectively by the central government in England, this Act was to confer the legislative power upon the Crown and the Superintendent of Trade, so that English laws and ordinances suitable to the local Chinese conditions might be established. For fear of possible abuse of the legislative power, measures to check and review such enactments were adopted in Section IV, thus maintaining a fine balance of power between the Crown and Parliament.

On January 24, 1844, Ordinance No. 1 (1844) of Hong Kong was enacted to implement the above-mentioned Act, by rendering all British subjects in China within the jurisdiction of the Courts of Justice at Hong Kong and subjecting them in all matters to the laws of England. On April 17, an Order in Council was issued to clarify and specify points of jurisdiction. In order to reduce any injurious effect resulting from exercising British jurisdiction in China to the territorial sovereign, a circular was released on November 22, stressing:

> It is essential that Her Majesty's Consular Officers in China should bear in mind that, in conferring upon them powers of jurisdiction of such a comprehensive and unusual character, it is the desire of Her Majesty's Government that those powers should not be needlessly or lightly employed; but that, on the contrary, whenever differences can be adjusted in a conciliatory manner, such a termination should be promoted and recommended, and whenever crimes are to be punished, certain and speedy, rather that severe, punishment is to be preferred.[6]

This circular further prescribed three courses of proceeding, namely a summary decision, a decision with assistance of assessors chosen from the British community, and a recourse to the criminal tribunal of Hong Kong. To ensure a smooth administration of justice in a

5. For the complete text of this Act of 1843: E.W.A. Tuson, *The British Consul's Manual* (London, 1856), 204–05.
6. Ibid., 230.

new setting in China, however, the circular realistically instructed
that it was not necessary to deal with crimes according to the strict
definition of English law, so as to pay attention to the local circumstances and necessities.

   During the preparation for the exercises of British jurisdiction in
China, Hong Kong soon became the center of British activity in
China. On March 4, 1844, the Criminal Court for British subjects in
China opened for the first time in Hong Kong to decide two cases,
one involving the murder of a seaman and the other involving the
manslaughter of a Chinese boatman. Pursuant to the Ordinance No.
15 of 1844, the Supreme Court of Judicature at Hong Kong was
formally opened on October 1 of that year. To reduce the difficulty
of uncertainty concerning the jurisdiction of various courts in
China, an Order in Council was further issued on June 13, 1853 to
strengthen the legal structure in Hong Kong and to define the
respective jurisdictions of the Supreme Court of Hong Kong and of
the Superintendent of Trade and the Consular Officers.[7] With its
good intention of simplifying and unifying legal matters, however,
this Order in Council could not avoid the pitfalls caused by the limit
of consular jurisdiction and the inconvenience in sending a legal case
to Hong Kong from China for trial (especially the difficulty in
collecting sufficient evidence to obtain a conviction from a Hong
Kong jury).

   These pitfalls were not entirely avoidable because of the strict
limitation of the treaty terms, for the right of British Consular
Officers to exercise any jurisdiction in China depended on the extent
to which the right had been conceded by China under the treaty
agreements. The situation was complicated by the lack of legal
knowledge or administrative resources among the Consular Officers.
The burden became heavier because of the increase of the trade
volume and the influx of a heterogeneous mass of people hurrying to
China in search of fortune. As a result, in order to bypass the
shortcomings of the Consular Officers, many merchants and others
of the British community in China took their cases either directly or
by appeal to the Supreme Court of Hong Kong. In the meantime,
the legal structure, as formulated by the Order in Council of 1853,
continued to operate within the boundary of the treaty terms
through the first stage of development.

   7. Keeton, *Development*, 193–95.

The Second Stage (1858–1875)

The Treaty of Nanking set a precedent for Western powers to conduct new relations with China. Following the general lines of this Treaty, the Sino-American Treaty of Wanghsia and the Sino-French Treaty of Whampoa were signed on July 3, 1844 and October 24, 1844 respectively. Similar trade privileges were extended to Belgium in 1845, and to Sweden and Norway in 1847. But the expectations and demands were frustrated by anti-foreign sentiment in Canton, where the local Chinese authorities even refused to receive on an equal footing any Western diplomatic representative. The tension led to the British request of direct communication with the central government in Peking, yet such request was nevertheless repeatedly denied by the Chinese.

To resolve the impasse, finally, two events of 1856 – the Arrow incident and the murder of the French missionary Auguste Chapdelaine – were used as convenient casus belli by the British and French governments to employ force against China, resulting in a quick military victory and the occupation of Tientsin in 1858. Negotiations for peace followed and were joined by Russia and the United States. New treaties were signed by the Chinese authorities with Russia on June 13, with the United States on June 18, with England on June 26, and with France on June 27.[8]

Along with trade privileges, certain extensions of British consular jurisdiction were granted in the Treaty of Tientsin. Article IX allowed British subjects to travel, for their pleasure or purpose of trade, to all parts of the Chinese interior under passports. If a British subject so travelling committed a crime, he was to be handed over to the nearest Consul for punishment, but could not be subjected to excessive restraints in the meanwhile. Article XV stipulated: "All questions in regard to right, whether of property or person, arising between British subjects, shall be subject to the jurisdiction of the British authorities." In addition to such exclusion of Chinese jurisdiction from cases involving only British subjects, Article XVI further created an important framework for the exercise of British jurisdiction in China. It continued as follows:

Chinese subjects who may be guilty of any criminal act towards British

---

8. For the complete text of the treaties with Russia, the United States, England and France: *The Maritime Customs*, vol. 1, 85–100, 404–21, 713–28, and 814–39 respectively.

subjects shall be arrested and punished by the Chinese authorities
according to the laws of China.

British subjects who may commit any crime in China shall be tried and
punished by the Consul or other Public Functionary authorized thereto
according to the laws of Great Britain.

Justice shall be equitably and impartially administered on both sides.[9]

Article XXI also provided procedures for the extradition of Chinese
criminals escaping to Hong Kong or on board British ships, so as to
bring them to justice. In addition, the Treaty stipulated items of
other judicial nature such as Sino-British joint efforts to suppress
piracy, and the protection of British persons and property. With
these new terms of extraterritorial jurisdiction granted by the Treaty
of Tientsin, the British authorities began to reexamine the role and
function of the Supreme Court of Hong Kong and the Consular
Courts. As a result, an Order in Council of March 9, 1865 abolished
the traditional exercise of jurisdiction by the Supreme Court of
Hong Kong over British subjects in China, and, in replacement,
established a new court, "Her Britannic Majesty's Supreme Court
for China and Japan," to be situated at Shanghai.[10]

Pursuant to this Order in Council, the Supreme Court for China
and Japan was to have one judge (entitled the Chief Judge) and one
assistant (entitled the Assistant Judge), who had to have been
members of the Bar in England. Within every Consular district,
with the exception of that of Her Majesty's Consul at Shanghai, a
Provincial Court with both civil and criminal jurisdiction was to be
established. Under this arrangement, the Supreme Court for China
and Japan thus had its original jurisdiction in the Consular district
of Shanghai and concurrent jurisdiction with the several Provincial
Courts. In practice, with regard to civil matters, every Provincial
Court and the Supreme Court for China and Japan should have
been a Court of Law and of Equity, a Court of Bankruptcy, and
should have had all the powers, rights, and duties appertaining to
the office of Coroner in England, although certain other functions
were exclusively reserved for the Supreme Court for China and
Japan. Be it a Provincial Court or the Supreme Court, however, the
Order in Council emphasized that every Court was to promote

9. Ibid., 409.

10. For the complete text of this Order in Council: Sir Edward Hertslett, *Treaties,
Etc., between Great Britain and China and between China and Foreign Powers; and Orders in
Council, Rules, Regulations, Acts of Parliament, Decrees, and Notifications affecting British
Interests in China* (London, 1896), vol. 2, 424–60.

reconciliation and to encourage and facilitate the settlement in an amicable way of any suit or proceeding pending before it.

With regard to criminal matters, for a case other than assault endangering life, cutting, maiming, arson, or house-breaking, the offender was normally to be tried by a Provincial Court in a summary way and without assessors. If the penalty prescribed for an offense was heavier than the maximal measure which a Provincial Court had power to impose, the Court was to reserve the case to be heard and determined by, or under the special authority of, the Supreme Court for China and Japan. Because of the insufficient legal training among most Consular Officers, the Order in Council provided the procedure for appeal in criminal cases so as to reduce the extent of any injustice possibly caused by a Provincial Court. On appeal, concerning any question of law arising during such a trial, the Supreme Court for China and Japan was to consider the matter and thereupon reserve, affirm, or amend the judgement, conviction, or sentence made by a Provincial Court. The Judge of the Supreme Court for China and Japan was empowered to cause any convicted person to be imprisoned in China or Japan at any place approved by one of Her Majesty's Principal Secretaries of State as a place of imprisonment for these offenders or, alternatively, to cause any offender to be taken to Hong Kong for the execution of punishment, if such a measure was deemed expedient.

The Order in Council moreover provided steps for settling legal disputes arising between British subjects and foreigners by stipulating: "Where a foreigner desires to institute or take any suit or proceeding of a civil nature against a British subject, the Supreme or other Court, according to its jurisdiction, may entertain the same."[11] The term "foreigner" in this Article 117 of the Order in Council was, however, ambiguous, for there was a possible clash, if the category of foreigners included the Chinese, with the terms prescribed in the Treaty of Tientsin. The difficulty also resulted from the wording of Article 4 of the Order in Council. This article stipulated: "All Her Majesty's jurisdiction exercisable in China or in Japan for the judicial hearing or determination of matters in difference between British subjects, or between foreigners and British subjects . . . shall be exercised under and according to the provisions of this Order, and not otherwise."[12] Although Article 117 confined its jurisdiction to matters of a mere civil nature, the language of

11. Ibid., 450.
12. Ibid., 430.

Article 4 specified such matters be adjudicated, in principle, according to the provisions of the Order in Council. By comparison, however, Article XVII of the Treaty of Tientsin governed that disputes between British and Chinese subjects be first settled by the British Consul in a friendly manner, and that only when the Consul failed to arrange them amicably should he then request the assistance of the Chinese authorities to consider together the true merits of disputes and decide equitably.[13]

Owing to the ambiguous wording, if the term "foreigner" included the Chinese, there would be an overlap of jurisdiction between the Order in Council of 1865 and the Treaty of Tientsin; such an overlap could be interpreted as an extension of British jurisdiction beyond the terms originally confined in the Treaty of Tientsin. Although no specific measures were taken to clarify the ambiguity, the Supreme Court for China and Japan in practice seemed to regard its jurisdiction over Chinese plaintiffs in such disputes between British and Chinese subjects as simply an elective matter, thus ignoring the issue of a possible conflict with the treaty terms.[14]

The interpretation concerning the term "foreigner" was further complicated by two issues related to the status of British subjects, one being the treatment of the British subjects of Chinese origin and the other being the privilege of British subjects in the service of the Chinese government. Having all the appearance of Chinese and speaking like natives, British subjects of Chinese descent often established themselves in Chinese villages, buying land and engaging in business and even local politics. When they were charged with some offense or had a legal dispute with native Chinese, then and only then would they claim their British nationality to benefit from the protection of extraterritorial jurisdiction. Disturbed constantly by the confusion caused by those British subjects of Chinese origin, the British authorities finally published a notification in 1866, instructing: "Anyone so offending is liable to be taken by the Chinese

---

13. *The Maritime Customs*, vol. 1, 409.

14. In a case reported in the *North China Herald*, dated February 11, 1875, an English defendant claimed before the Supreme Court that the original decision given by a court at Foochow in favor of the Chinese plaintiff was invalid because of the participation of the British Consul with a Chinese official during the trial. The Supreme Court denied the motion and ruled that any rights given the Chinese plaintiffs under the Order in Council of 1865 were permissive only. For a discussion of this issue: Roger Dubrock, "A study of the treatment accorded the Chinese plaintiffs in the Civil Summary Division of Her Majesty's Supreme Court for China and Japan from 1875 to 1885, as evidenced in the Law Reports contained in the North China Herald" (Seminar Paper, The Harvard Law School, 1967), 9–10.

authorities to the nearest Consular port to be handed over to the British Consul for punishment, in the same way as any other class of British subjects would be punished for a similar violation of the Treaty."[15] In 1868, a circular was further issued to stress that those British subjects of Chinese descent who established residence in China and concealed their nationality could no longer claim the same protection accorded to British subjects in China. To retain original privileges for themselves, the circular instructed such persons to adopt some dress or custom clearly distinguishing them from natives. The measure meted out in the circular was justified by the consideration that "it was never contemplated that extraterritorial rights should extend to any but those whose birth, dress, language, and habits plainly distinguished them from Chinese subjects."[16]

Likewise, the British authorities encountered difficulty in defining the status of British subjects employed in various capacities by the Chinese government. The Chinese Customs Service, for instance, entrusted its British personnel with highly responsible tasks. The Service, established in 1854 through a joint Chinese and foreign action, was renowned for its impartial administration of the Chinese treaty tariff. In addition to the performance of ordinary customs routine, the Service, under the leadership of Inspector General Robert Hart, began to provide the Chinese government with such important functions and services as the promotion of higher education and the negotiation of diplomatic matters with foreign powers.[17] The question of status was specifically raised in 1862 when a British subject attempted to sue a fellow countryman for acts done by the latter in his capacity of a Chinese Customs official.

In response to this delicate question, however, the law officers of the Crown held: (1) that such persons in the service of the Chinese government did not by virtue of such service cease to be "British subjects" under the terms of the Order in Council of 1853, and (2) that they were not civilly liable for acts done by them officially in the service of the Chinese government.[18] While many British merchants resented this explanation and continued to insist that the British officials of the Chinese Custom Service be liable in a Consular Court for acts done by them in excess of their legitimate powers, the British

15. Keeton, *Development*, 246.
16. Ibid.
17. For a detailed discussion of the Chinese Customs Service: Stanley Wright, *Hart and the Chinese Customs* (Belfast, 1950).
18. Keeton, *Development*, 236. For some diplomatic dispatches discussing the status of British subjects in the service of the Chinese government: ibid., 298–304.

authorities ignored the complaint of the merchants by sustaining the special status of British officials in the service of the Chinese government. On other other hand, there was no doubt whatsoever that the Consuls themselves were subject to the jurisdiction of Consular Courts in China. Indeed, George Whittingham Caine, then British Consul at Hankow, was charged in 1873 with embezzling public funds and was sentenced to two years' imprisonment.

Under the treaty system, the Provincial Courts and the Supreme Court for China and Japan were active in exercising British jurisdiction in China. At Shanghai, on May 1, 1864, a different court styled "Mixed Court of the International Settlement" was also opened. The establishment of the Mixed Court was prompted by the need to grant the Shanghai municipal council the special jurisdiction over those foreigners who were not represented by any local consul. Cases of the Court were to be heard by a Chinese official with the participation of a foreign assessor.[19] Due to the efforts made by the first British assessor, Chaloner Alabaster, the Mixed Court enjoyed a considerable amount of authority. The Assessors, as the lawfully appointed representatives of their Consuls, thus participated in the Mixed Court not merely to watch the cases, but also more importantly, "to examine into the merits of the case and decide it equitably," pursuant to Article XVII of the British Treaty of Tientsin.

As the United States, England, and France each had a separate Settlement at Shanghai, the first two countries joined in organizing the International Mixed Court, while France operated a different court at Shanghai. Initially, the Mixed Court exercised jurisdiction over the whole amalgamated British-American Settlement, and only over criminal cases within its boundaries. For an offense involving heavier penalty than the maximal power of the Court, the case had to be transferred from the Settlement to the City Magistrate for trial. In October of 1864, the jurisdiction of the Mixed Court was extended to civil cases in which British subjects were plaintiffs and those against natives in foreign employ, thus relieving the burden of the British Consul at Shanghai with regard to the administration of justice in civil matters.

The British Consul at Shanghai started in 1867 new negotiations with the Chinese officials, in order to consolidate the authority of the Mixed Court, resulting in the draft of Rules for the Mixed Court (styled in Chinese "Regulations relating to the Establishment of an

Official North of Yang-king-pan"). The draft was submitted to the Chinese authorities in Peking and the diplomatic body for approval. On April 20, 1869, the text of the Provisional Rules for the Mixed Court was promulgated, giving a wide authority to the Court to exercise jurisdiction over the Shanghai International Settlement. But the Mixed Court continued to be a Chinese Court (i.e., Office of the Official North of Yang-king-pan) in nature and as such was entitled to claim the rights which belonged to every Chinese Court. Because of the unusual nature of the Mixed Court, the improvement of the Court's practice was urged by the Consular Body in 1875. When the Chefoo Convention was signed between China and England in 1876, many suggestions for improvement were incorporated into the Convention, thus opening a new stage of the exercise of British jurisdiction in China.

The Third Stage (1876–1912)

In 1875, a young British consular officer, Augustus Raymond Margary, was killed along with five Chinese members of his party during an expedition to China's Southwest by a Chinese armed band in Yünnan. The British government decided to make full use of this incident to press for more tariff and commercial privileges in China. The Chinese authorities, under the pressure of an ultimatum, reluctantly concluded with the British representative on September 13, 1876 the Sino-British Agreement for the Settlement of the Yünnan Case, more commonly known as the Chefoo Convention.[20] The Convention included three sections: the first section related to the settlement of the Yünnan incident, the second section concerned both the Sino-British official communication and the judicial proceedings in mixed cases, and the third section involved trade, transit duty, and other commercial matters.

The principles of British jurisdiction as secured in the Treaty of Tientsin was reaffirmed by the Convention. It also provided new recourse for the settlement of legal disputes between British and Chinese subjects. With regard to crimes affecting British subjects, the Convention authorized the dispatch of the British officers to the scene of investigation. It further prescribed that the Chinese authorities in Peking would later invite foreign representatives to consider

20. For the complete text of the Chefoo Convention: *The Maritime Customs*, vol. I, 491–99.

measures for the better administration of justice at treaty ports. The subsequent negotiations in Peking, however, did not lead to a fruitful result, and the Provisional Rules of the Mixed Court promulgated in 1869 (to be valid for only one year) thus had to remain in force by ways of extension of validity. The situation prompted the British government to concentrate its effort on reconstructing the Supreme Court for China and Japan. On August 14, 1878, an Order in Council was issued and, in relation to the reorganization of the Supreme Court for China and Japan, Articles 9 to 22 of the former Order in Council of 1865 were thereby revoked.[21]

The Order in Council of 1878 instituted a Chief Justice and an Assistant Judge of the Supreme Court for China and Japan. The Assistant Judge was to hear and determine such civil and criminal cases as the Chief Justice from time to time directed, and such cases were also entitled to a rehearing before the Chief Justice. The Chief Justice was to sit with the Assistant Judge for rehearing, unless the absence of the latter was unavoidable; and if there were any difference of opinion, the opinion of the Chief Justice was to prevail. To relieve the heavy burden of the case load, a separate court, "Her Britannic Majesty's Court for Japan" was created; it had a Judge and an Assistant Judge, and was to hold its ordinary sittings in Japan at Kanagawa. Either the Chief Justice of the Supreme Court or the Judge of the Court for Japan had to be a British subject and had, at the time of his appointment, to have been a member of the Bar of England, Scotland, or Ireland, of not less than seven years' standing.

In November of 1878, the British government established the "Rules of Her Britannic Majesty's Supreme and other Courts in China" to regulate matters related to the prosecution of criminal cases.[22] Rules governing the conduct of practitioners in Provincial Courts were further promulgated on March 22, 1881.[23] Along with the new measures governing the legal practice, various steps were taken to clarify the earlier confusion concerning the ambiguous meaning of the term "foreigner," as provided in the order in Council of 1865. As a result, on October 25, 1881, a new Order in Council was issued, defining the term "foreigner" as "a subject of the Emperor of China or of the Mikado of Japan, or a subject or citizen of any other State in amity with Her Majesty." This definition thus

---

21. For the complete text of the Order in Council of 1878: Hertslett, *Treaties*, 610–15.
22. For the complete text of the Rules of 1878: ibid., 617.
23. Ibid., 618.

prevented further speculation on the scope of the term "foreigner" with regard to the exercise of British jurisdiction.[24]

The earlier practice of the Supreme Court to regard its jurisdiction over Chinese plaintiffs in mixed cases as an elective matter was also under review. In repealing Article 117 of the Order in Council of 1865, a more detailed version of the provision was given by the new Order in Council of 1881, which said in its Section 47 (Subsection 1):

> Where a foreigner desires to institute or take a suit or proceeding of a civil nature against a British subject, or a British subject desires to institute or take a suit or proceeding of a civil nature against a foreigner, the Supreme Court for China and Japan, and the Court for Japan and a Provincial Court, according to the respective jurisdiction of the Court, may entertain the suit or proceeding, and hear and determine it; and, if all parties desire, or the Court directs, a trial with jury or assessors, at a place where such a trial might be had if all parties were British subjects, but in all other respects according to the ordinary course of the Court.[25]

Pursuant to the above provision the Supreme Court was able to deal with civil suits between British and foreign (including Chinese) subjects, thus formulating a solid foundation for the further exercise of British jurisdiction. Also, in view of the urgent need to maintain peace and public order in a concession or settlement, this Order in Council authorized Her Majesty's Minister in China to join with other Ministers of any foreign powers in amity with England in establishing Regulations for the municipal government of foreign concession or settlement in China. In addition, various stipulations of diverse nature such as prison regulations, mortgages, bills of sale, and suits by or against partners were included in the Order in Council.[26] To administer more effectively the jurisdiction over suits or against foreigners, another Order in Council was issued on August 3, 1886, amending a portion of the previous Order in Council.[27] A new rule authorizing a table of fees to be levied by Her Majesty's Courts in China, Japan, and Korea was issued on October 1, 1888, reducing many possible irregularities of the functionaries in the Courts and thereby maintaining a standard form of various legal expenses.

In 1890, after having accumulated almost fifty years' experience

24. Ibid., 619.
25. Ibid., 628.
26. Ibid., 622–28.
27. Ibid., 633.

of exercising British jurisdiction in China, the time seemed ripe for
the British to provide a formal machinery for the effective administration of justice. A major act, entitled the "Act of Parliament to
Consolidate the Foreign Jurisdiction Acts," commonly cited as the
Foreign Jurisdiction Act of 1890, was finally established on August
4, 1890.[28] Section 1 of this act conferred the power of exercising
jurisdiction upon Her Majesty the Queen, and section 5 further
authorized Her Majesty the Queen in Council to direct by Order the
implementation and extension of enactments in relation to the exercise of British jurisdiction in a foreign country. Section 6 directed
any official having authority derived from Her Majesty to send
persons charged with offenses cognizable by a British court in a
foreign country for trial to a British possession. Section 7 stipulated
that the punishment of convicted persons should be carried into
effect in such a place as might be determined by Order in Council.
Section 9 conferred upon Her Majesty the Queen in Council the
power to assign jurisdiction to British courts within the Foreign
Jurisdiction Act. In order to prevent any abuse of power, however,
every Order in Council made by virtue of this act was to be laid
before both Houses of Parliament for review.

In pursuance of this Act, an Order in Council was issued in 1904
to create a substantial system for the exercise of British jurisdiction
in China and Korea, and was laid before both Houses of Parliament
on February 14, 1905. This Order in Council had 171 articles which
were arranged into nine separate parts, namely, "Preliminary and
General" (Articles 1–6); "Constitution and Powers of Courts" (Articles 7–34); "Criminal Matters" (Articles 35–88); "Civil Matters"
(Articles 89–117); "Procedure, Criminal and Civil" (Articles 118–
128); "Mortgages and Bills of Sale" (Articles 129–150); "Foreign
Subjects and Tribunals" (Articles 151–154); "Regulations" (Articles 155–159) and finally "Miscellaneous" (Articles 160–171). A
Schedule of Repealed Orders was also attached to the end of Part
IX.[29]

Within the framework provided by the Order in Council, a court
styled "His Britannic Majesty's Supreme Court for China and

---

28. For a discussion of the significance of the Foreign Jurisdiction Act of 1890:
Skinner Turner, "Extraterritoriality in China" in *The British Year Book of International
Law* 10 (1929), 57–58.

29. For the complete text of this Order in Council: Godfrey E.P. Hertslett, *Treaties
Etc., between Great Britain and China; and between China and Foreign Powers; and Orders in
Council, Rules, Regulations, Acts of Parliament, Decrees, Etc., affecting British Interests in
China* (London, 1908), vol. 2, 834–89.

Korea" was established at Shanghai. This Court was to have one Judge and as many Assistant Judges as might from time to time be required; and every Judge was to be, at the time of his appointment, a member of the Bar of England, Scotland, or Ireland, of not less than seven years' standing. When the Judges, or any two of them, sat together to hear and determine cases, such court was regarded as "the Full Court," and the opinion of the Judge was to prevail if there was a difference of opinion among members of that Court. By comparison, every commissioned Consular Officer, with the exception of those at Shanghai or other exceptions made by the Secretary of State, was to hold in his Consular district a Court (i.e., a Provincial Court). Like its predecessors, this Order in Council thus authorized the Supreme Court to have its original jurisdiction in the Consular district of Shanghai and concurrent jurisdiction with the several Provincial Courts.

This Order in Council further dealt with the criminal matters in Part III, covering subjects such as local jurisdiction over criminal cases, apprehension and custody of accused persons, trial with jury or assessors, summary trial, preliminary examination, charges, punishments, inquest, statutory or other offenses, authority within 100 miles from the coast of China, deportation, appeal and reserved cases, and fugitive offenders. In addition to various provisions concerning civil matters, the Order in Council stipulated from Part V through Part IX other measures related to criminal and civil procedures, mortgages, and miscellaneous matters.

Soon after the promulgation of this Order in Council, steps were taken to draft comprehensive Rules of Court, resulting in the compilation of a text entitled "The China and Korea Rules of Court, 1905," to become effective on January 1, 1906.[30] The Rules consisted of 320 articles in five parts, thus covering almost every important aspect of legal jurisdiction in this substantial text. Also, in order to regulate the sittings and procedures of the Full Court in China, "The China (Full Court) Rules of Court, 1910" came into force. When an appeal from a Provincial Court reached the Supreme Court, the Judge could order that it be heard by the Full Court.[31] The British government further established "The Summary Jurisdiction Shanghai Police Rules, 1910" to authorize the exercise of

30. For the complete text of the China and Korea Rules of Court, 1905: W.B. Kennett, *Rules of Court, 1905–1916* (Shanghai, 1918), 1–138. Also see Hertslett, vol. 2, 890–1033.

31. For the complete text of the China Full Court Rules of Court, 1910: Kennett, *Orders in Council, 1904–1915* (Shanghai, 1916), 141–42.

summary jurisdiction by the Captain-Superintendent.[32] Indeed,
through the operation of these various Orders, Regulations, and
Rules, many important English legal institutions were introduced
into China, and by 1912 a comprehensive English legal order had
been established there to facilitate the exercise of British jurisdiction
under the treaty system.

Owing to the Treaty dated August 22, 1910 between Japan and
Korea, the exercise of British jurisdiction over the British subjects in
Korea officially came to an end when Korea became part of the
Japanese empire. The termination of British jurisdiction in Korea
led to the promulgation of "The Korea Order in Council, 1911."[33]
Pursuant to this Order in Council, all the references to Korea both
in the Order in Council, 1904 to 1910, and in all Rules of Court were
omitted from the provisions, thus making the exercise of British
jurisdiction in China more unified and consistent.

By a gradual process of evolution the British machinery for exercise of jurisdiction in China had become complete by the beginning
of the Republican era in 1912. The operation of the British legal
system not only endured the political upheaval immediately after
the Revolution of 1911, but also performed its function effectively
through the first decade of the new Republican regime. Under the
Order in Council of 1925, the British government continued to
administer various judicial matters through the activities of the
Supreme Court, the Full Court, and the Provincial Courts. With the
emergence of Chinese nationalism after 1925, local political movements began to advocate forcefully the total termination of extraterritoriality in China. In conjunction with the development of
international politics, especially the Japanese invasion of China and
the outbreak of the Second World War, the Allied Powers finally
agreed to abolish the system of extraterritoriality and related rights
in China. On January 11, 1943, the "Sino-British Treaty for the
Abolition of Extraterritoriality and Related Rights in China" was
signed, and the ratification was exchanged on May 20, 1943. With
the implementation of this Treaty, a century of the exercise of
British jurisdiction in China under the treaty system finally came to
an end.[34]

32. For the complete text of the Summary Jurisdiction Shanghai Police Rules,
1910: Kennett, *Orders*, 154–59.
33. For the complete text of the Korea Order in Council, 1911: Kennett, *Orders*, 97.
34. For general discussion of the implication of the treaty system in China: John K.
Fairbank, "The early treaty system in the Chinese world order" in *The Chinese World
Order* ed. John K. Fairbank (Cambridge, MA, 1968), 257–75. Also see Jerome Ch'en,
China and the West (London, 1979), 285–331.

5

Legal Developments in the Maghrib, 1830–1930

J.-L. MIÈGE

Introduction

The Maghrib is one of the most interesting areas for studying the spread and overseas implementation of French Law. The diversity of its peoples, the different dates of French rule in the three countries (from 1830 in Algeria, 1881 in Tunisia, and 1912 in Morocco), and the regional peculiarities, both in terms of peoples and of colonial policy, have produced an extremely varied range of developments. At the beginning of the nineteenth century, prior to French rule, the whole of pre-colonial North Africa was characterized by the coexistence of four legal systems: Islamic law, Berber customary law, laws peculiar to the Jewish minorities, and the capitulations applied to Europeans.

The Pre-colonial Situation

The Islamic law of orthodox Sunni Islam, based on the *shari'a* and applied to virtually all inhabitants, derives throughout North Africa from the same sources (*usul al-fiqh*): the Quran (the revealed book); the *sunnah* (traditions based on the *Hadith*); the *ijma'* (the infallibility of the consensus) and the *qiyas* (legal reasoning by analogy). Nonetheless, there are differences of nuance from country to country, and sometimes even quite marked differences. Although, it is essentially the *Maliki* school which prevails, particularly in Morocco and Algeria, there are significant groups of Hanafites in Tunisia and Khariji-Ibadis in M'zab (south Algeria) and in Jerba (Tunisia).

One should also remember the varying degrees of influence of surviving local customs (*'adah*), which are given consideration by legal authorities. The special case of Sharifian Morocco is

particularly worthy of note, where the force of local customs had just
begun to be felt in the nineteenth century. In fact this country was
scarcely touched by European influence, except for some modifications (in particular in the area of criminal law), which were limited
to the port towns, and which had precious little effect on the functioning of the centralizing *makhzan*. Ottoman Algeria was only
slightly affected by the legal influence of Turkish customs, unlike
Tunisia, which, although quasi-independent, was to be heavily
affected by the Tanzimat local variant of the Ottoman reformist
movement, under the rule of the reformist beys. It was also here,
more than anywhere else, that the weight of European-based ideas
was felt, exemplified by the abolition of slavery as early as 1847.
Berber customary law maintained its full force in certain regions of
Algeria (Kabylia and Aurès) and over a very large area of, if not
most of, Morocco. With its basis in tradition, it was the *Kanun* in
Algeria and the *Orf* or *Izref* in Morocco which defined the practice of
each community, particularly in criminal matters. Passed on orally,
this contrasts with Islamic law, which is essentially a revealed body
of law. Both under Ottoman rule and under the authority of the
Sharifs, Jews everywhere had maintained their peculiar, Judaeo-
Moorish status and the courts of law which protected and enforced
the rules of this personal status. They were also subject to discriminatory legislation of varying harshness, which was enforced with
varying degrees of stringency according to the region.

Lastly, Europeans were bound by capitulations. Based on the
body of rules regulating the relations of the Christian powers with
the Ottoman Porte and the Barbary states, it had two aspects: one
was connected to the letter of treaties, the other derived from a
whole local and international legal tradition. This body of legislation
unilaterally conferred certain privileges and specific exemptions not
only on the nationals of European states, but also for local people
who traded under the flag and under the protection of consuls (the
so-called "protected"). The granting and strengthening of these capitulations had been commonplace since the beginning of the century.

Developments under European Influence

This was the existing mixed legal basis which French intervention
maintained as a whole, but with different developments that varied
according to the different countries' statutes and the reactions of
their populations.

The annexation of Algeria to France, by decree of July 22, 1834, applied to all inhabitants, be they Berbers, Jews, or Arabs, and made them French subjects, but definitely not French citizens. After annexation they remained subject to their own laws and customs. Thus the concept of personal status remained intact in private law, and for more than a century it was to be the keystone of the legal structure built by the sovereign power. Nonetheless, in Algeria the tendency to keep Islamic law within these limits, in order to ensure that it was more rigidly confined, became apparent very early on. Indeed, assimilationist ideas were quick to develop. *Habous* (property in portmain) was abolished at the time of the July Monarchy. Local justice was declared subordinate to French justice by a decree of September 1842. The *Beytal Mal* was gallicized after the Second Republic and a law on personal status was enacted in 1882. The whole century was marked by major land legislation. This series of decisions culminated in the decree of April 17, 1889 regarding the organization of Islamic justice, whereby the European justice of the peace became the court of general jurisdiction for Muslims. The *qadi* retained jurisdiction only over personal status matters, thus effectively remaining the law for those who were not French citizens, i.e. virtually all Muslims. French citizenship could only be obtained by an individual's choosing and conferred equality of legal status with those born French. The general legal definition and the effect of an individual's choosing to adopt French nationality were clearly expressed by the Senadisconsul on 1865 July 14, 1865:

> The muslim native is a Frenchman. However, he will continue to be subject to Islamic law. He may be admitted to serve in the army and navy, and he may be employed in the civil service in Algeria. At his request, he may be granted the rights of a French citizen. In such a case, he is then subject to the civil and political laws of France.

This illusory idea of Muslims individually applying for citizenship waned over the course of the year, as did the commitment of the administration, which ended up being frankly hostile to the "naturalization" of Muslims. Between 1865 and 1900 there were only 1,151 new citizens, which is little more than thirty per year:

The intense legislative activity of the inter-war period was to reaffirm this ambivalent tendency, with in particular, the abolition of Arab taxes in 1918, the land law of 1926, and the laws of 1930 on the personal status of Muslims. The fact remained that the legal situation was far removed from the reality of everyday life. Algerian

Number of Naturalizations of Muslim Algerians

Period	Total	Average per year
1865–1900	1,151	32
1901–1908	1,440	180
1929–1937	2,760	345
TOTAL	5,351	105

legal practice, which has been well studied by Charnay, was indicative of these discrepancies. There continued to be very little enforcement of any laws that even remotely related to personal law (personal status) until after the Second World War.

In the protectorate of Morocco policies remained more conservative. The *dahir* of August 4, 1912 invested judicial powers in the Sultan, who continued to exercise them through the *qadis* on the one hand and the *pashas* and *qaids* on the other. This was the codification of a traditional Moroccan Islamic right. Here again it is necessary to distinguish between the two areas: personal status on the one hand and civil and commercial law on the other. The first area merely involved some administrative reforms with the creation of a genuine Minister of Justice in 1913, whose task it was to supervize all the *qadis* in the Empire, and with the *dahir* of July 10, 1914, which covered the regulation of native civil justice. The legal profession itself was reorganized in respect of the posts of *qadi*, *oukil* and *adoul*, and an appeal court was set up in 1921. This traditional justice of the *qadis* remained strictly under the control of the French authorities, who could examine their records, report any irregularities, and hear the grievances of any persons to be tried. In the second area, that of civil and commercial law, there was an increasing alignment with French-based law (cf. below).

The Jewish world was to develop quite differently in Algeria and in the two protectorates. From the outset their position already varied significantly from country to country: treated as a mere fact in Tunisia, more harshly in Algeria, and variously from region to region and according to their activities in Morocco, the Jews traded for the Sultan and enjoyed a privileged position. Their legal status was not immediately affected by French intervention. The Jewish community in Algeria retained its courts (decree of October 22, 1830), presided over by a head with a Hebraic board (decree of June 22, 1831). However, the isolated and highly urbanized Jews were soon to come under Western influence. As early as 1833, the head of the Jewish community said that his fellow Jews "would easily adapt to the civil and commercial laws of France providing that they did not contravene the law of Moses."

While retaining the law of Moses, the Jews became increasingly subsumed under the laws applied to Europeans, with the reduction in the powers of the rabbinical courts (August 1834), the abolition of these courts in 1841 and 1842, the duty to register on the civil registry, and, in the case of a Jewish marriage, the duty to also register it with a French civil registry official (1834). The setting up of an Algerian consistory court in Algiers in November 1845 and of provincial consistory courts in Oran and Constantine marked "the end of the old Jewish world, which was subsequently on its way to becoming fully assimilated to French Judaism, whose institutions it adopted." The large-scale naturalization of Algerian Jews was commonplace as early as 1848. Gradual assimilation (the tendering of property owned by Jews with French nationality in June 1851) prepared the way. The collective naturalization was passed by decree on October 24, 1870. Having become French citizens, the native Jews of Algeria saw their actual and personal status governed by French law. The 34,000 Algerian Jews were integrated into the French population. The definition of an Algerian Jew of October 7, 1871 aimed to exclude Tunisian and Moroccan Jews from the collective naturalization, by specifying that it applied to "those Jews born in Algeria before the occupation, or those born after the occupation of parents settled in Algeria at the time of the occupation." The implementation of these decrees caused problems in the case of the Jews of M'zab (annexed in 1882) and more generally for all those in the Saharan territories that became French after October 24, 1870. The Administration refused to accept them as French citizens. The lack of a Civil Registry and the relative slowness in setting one up allowed a significant number of Jews from the two neighboring countries to make use of this right, acquiring French passports while travelling or staying in Algeria. This meant that in the subsequent decades one could find nuclei of native Jews in Morocco and Tunisia claiming French citizenship and thus enjoying the privileges of the capitulations.

As regards the Berber world, it is interesting to note the two contrasting policies followed in Algeria and Morocco. Both of these countries attempted to bring together, codify, and fix these traditions, but whereas in one of them they were widely enforced, in the other they were rather limited. Algeria tended to pursue a policy of assimilation. Attempts were made to encourage Berbers to become naturalized, although with very little success, or even to convert them. By the end of the century, the White Fathers of Lavigerie, who had translated the Bible into the Kabylian language, had seven institutions in Kabylia. The results were disappointing, but the very effort well illustrates the thinking behind the policy of "Kabylia privilege," which was based on the belief that Berbers were more assimilable than Arabs. Schooling was more systematically promoted here, and in the legal sphere the emphasis was on restricting traditions as much as possible. A law of May 2, 1930 marked an important step, in that it touched on personal status. It affected the position of Kabylian women by setting the age for marriage and specifying the cases when marriage was not valid. This was backed up by the law of May 19, 1931 which dealt with inheritance. In practice, these complicated decrees met with local indifference and were hardly ever enforced.

By way of contrast, in Morocco French legal and administrative activity was aimed at maintaining the status quo. Virtually any type of proselytism was forbidden. General Lyautey, the resident general, had Sultan Moulay Youssef seal the *dahir* of September 11, 1914, which provided for "respect of the traditional status of the Berber tribes, who have laws and customs of their own dating back to ancient times." This constituted an unambiguous defense of the principle of autonomy and of the special nature of the legal status of the Berber tribes. This policy was supported by the *dahir* which codified the working of the traditional legal *jemaas*, and was followed by ten vizierial decrees between 1915 and 1928 and two binding residential circulars (1924). This whole arrangement was protected by the famous Berber *dahir*, the date of which (May 16, 1930) was, ironically enough, exactly the same as that of the opposite laws passed on Berbers in Algeria. This *dahir* exempted the Berber tribes from the law of the Quran, once again officially recognized their traditions, and provided that appeals against judgements of the *jemaa* courts could be heard in a French court in criminal cases, and before traditional appeal courts in personal status cases.

The system of capitulations itself developed in different ways. It had been particularly widespread in Morocco with the practice of the native "protected," which I do not discuss here. It is sufficient to note that up until 1913 numerous natives, among them some of the wealthiest, were still managing to acquire this highly advantageous status. The problem was solved immediately in Algeria by all authorities relinquishing their privileges. In Tunisia this relinquishment took a little longer, but was nonetheless fairly easily achieved, with the exception of the Italian government. In the peculiar case of Morocco things were somewhat different. Article 9 of the Franco-German agreement of November 4, 1911 provided that, following an interim system, the consular courts would close the day a European-type legal system was set up. The *dahir* of August 12, 1913 was to specify how this was to be enforced. "Although as of 1 January 1913 protection cards will cease to be issued," it stated that "those natives who were under French political or consular protection on 31 December 1912" continued to be subject to the jurisdiction of French courts for their lifespan.

The "protected" remained under the consular protection of the European powers until the system of capitulations was discontinued. Most of the European powers were quick to relinquish this privilege: Portugal, Russia, Spain, Norway, and Sweden in 1914; Denmark in 1915; Belgium, Italy, and the Netherlands in 1916. The French authorities, on the other hand, abruptly discontinued these privileges just after the declaration of war against the belligerent enemies Germany and Austria. The United Kingdom and the United States continued to retain the system of capitulations. The United Kingdom was not to give it up until July 1937, in exchange for France doing likewise in Zanzibar. The Americans did not follow suit until the eve of independence.

French Justice

All over North Africa alongside these traditional laws, which had been retained, modified, or updated, a French-based legal system was introduced in a dual guise, either deriving from the competence of the French courts, or the competence of what could be called secular justice, in that it applied to all French subjects whatever their religion. The case of Morocco is the clearest example of this. The *dahir* of August 12, 1913 set up in the territory of the protectorate tribunals of instance and courts of first instance, as well as an appeal court presided over by French magistrates. These French courts were competent to deal with civil and commercial cases *ratione personae*. They not only had the power to deal with crimes committed by French citizens or French nationals and Europeans whose protecting power had relinquished capitulations, but also with certain crimes committed by Moroccans. Their powers were particularly wide-ranging in administrative matters, totally replacing sharifian jurisdiction: the right to pass judgement in such cases was the exclusive prerogative of the French courts. The system developed in favor of the *makhzan* courts, their powers in civil and commercial matters being recognized by a residential circular of August 15, 1914. All criminal cases involving Moroccans were referred to the courts of the *pashas* and the *qaids* – not the *qadis* – although the maximum sentence they could pass was limited to two years imprisonment. More serious cases were referred to the Grand Vizier. The *dahir* of November 11, 1913 established a criminal *medjhess* with the power to examine the most serious cases. These various reforms were acknowledged by the dahir of April 1926. The French courts in Morocco and Tunisia had the same powers. Intense legislative activity rounded off these administrative reforms throughout North Africa, introducing French principles into a number of areas. One of the best examples of this was in the area of water. All stretches of water were declared property of the state regardless of previous traditions and customs. Regarding enforcement, regional peculiarities were always taken into account (the Tunisian decree of September 24, 1885 and the Moroccan *dahirs* of July 1, 1914 and November 8, 1919).

Conclusion

It therefore seems that on the basis of a situation that was initially very complex, but nonetheless reasonably similar throughout North Africa, the development of the legal system there was characterized by two mains trends: one tending towards assimilation, in particular in Algeria, the other tending towards conservation, while updating the relevant traditional institutions with different nuances, in Morocco and Tunisia. All in all the coexistence of different laws, the complex interplay of the two great French and Islamic legal systems, the different applications according to the status and nature of the countries, and the richness of legal invention and adaptation make the Maghrib an outstanding area for the study of European impact on colonial legal systems.

BIBLIOGRAPHY

Annuaire de l'Afrique du Nord (Paris, 1963)

Blanc, François-Paul, "La justice au Maroc sous le règne de Moulay Youssef" in *Histoire des grands services publics au Maroc de 1900 à 1970* (Toulouse, s.a.).

Caponera, D.A., *Le droit des eaux dans les pays musulmans* (Rome, 1976).

Castro, Francisco, "La codificazione del diretto privato negli stati arabi contemporanei" in *Rivista di Diritto Civile*, XXXI (1985), 387–447.

Charnay, Jean-Paul, *La vie musulmane en Algérie d'après la jurisprudence de la première moitié du XIXe siècle* (Paris, 1965).

Chouraqui, R., *Les juifs d'Afrique du Nord* (Paris, 1952).

Gellner, E. and Micaud, C. (eds.), *Arabs and Berbers. From tribe to nation in North Africa* (London, 1973).

Girault, A. and Milliot, L., *Principes de colonisation et de législation coloniale* (Paris, 1936).

Lacoste, C., *Bibliographie ethnologique de la Grande Kabylie* (Paris, 1962).

Lambert, J., *Cours de législation algérienne, tunisienne et marocaine*, (Algiers, 1952).

Lourde, A., *Les origines capitulaires du protectorat de la France sur le Maroc* (Perpignan, 1984).

Miège, Jean-Louis, *Le Maroc et l'Europe* (Paris, 1961/1964), 4 vols.

Montagne, Robert, *Les Berbères et le Makhzen dans le Sud du Maroc* (Paris, 1930).

Pascon, P. and Bouderba, A., "Le droit et le fait dans la société composite: Essai d'introduction au système juridique marocain" in *Bulletin Economique et Social du Maroc*, XXXII (1972).

Rivière, P.L., *Traité de Droits marocain* (Caen, 1950).

Rondot, Pierre, *L'islam et les musulmans d'aujourd'hui* (Paris, 1958), 2 vols.

Surdon, G., *Institutions et coutumes des Berbères du Maghreb* (Tanger, 1938).

6

The Development of the Dual Legal System in Former Belgian Central Africa (Zaire-Rwanda-Burundi)

FILIP REYNTJENS

Introduction

The phenomenon of legal pluralism has given rise to a great deal of scholarly writing. I shall, therefore, refrain from analyzing the concept in general terms, and rather address myself to its operation in former Belgian Central Africa. In order to identify the subject dealt with in this paper, suffice it to say that I understand legal pluralism as "the existence, in a given society, of different legal mechanisms applied to identical situations."[1] While this phenomenon is in fact universal, due to the high degree of social pluralism characteristic of these societies, it is a particularly striking feature of Third World legal systems. This is obvious as soon as one accepts that legal pluralism is the corollary of social pluralism: François Gény, and Aristotle and Montesquieu before him, had already insisted upon the link between social data ("donné social") and juridical construction ("construit juridique").[2] Thus in John Griffiths' terms "a situation of legal pluralism . . . is one in which law and legal institutions are not all subsumable within one 'system' but have their sources in the self-regulatory activities of all the multifarious social fields present, activities which may support, complement, ignore of frustrate one another."[3]

While this description is, rightly in my view, very broad, we are concerned here with a more concrete situation: it is generally an

1. J. Vanderlinden, "Essai de synthèse" in *Le pluralisme juridique*, ed. J. Gilissen (Brussels, 1971), 19.
2. F. Geny, *Science et Technique en Droit Privé Positif* (Paris, 1911–1924); in particular see vol. 4, 60.
3. J. Griffiths, "What is legal pluralism?," *Journal of Legal Pluralism* 24 (1986), 39.

aspect of the global process of modernization introduced by colonial
rule, whereby a state law of European inspiration was superimposed
upon a multitude of folk laws (be they customary or religious). The
assumption was that the first set of norms would eventually displace
the second, but for the time being two or more normative systems
were left to coexist in the same geographic area. In an attempt to
clarify the mechanisms of this meeting of legal orders, Hooker has
proposed the distinction between two classes of law: the "dominant"
and the "servient."[4] The first, generally referred to as "positive law"
in European legal theory, encompasses the sources of state law, formulated and applied by the institutions of the modern (colonial or
post-colonial) state. In a situation of legal pluralism, the determination
of the normative weight of the servient or unofficial system, insofar as it
is allowed to subsist, is theoretically made according to the norms of the
dominant system. This article will illustrate this relationship with
regard to the introduction of Belgian-inspired law in Zaire, Rwanda
and Burundi. I shall avoid the technical detail, and examine the larger
policy-issues involved in the meeting of two laws.

The Political Context

From the earliest days on, when Zaire was still the Congo Free State
under the personal rule of King Leopold II of the Belgians, the
colonial policy officially adhered to was that of indirect rule. In
contrast with the French, at no time have the Belgians considered
attempting the social, cultural or legal assimilation of the populations in their African territories. An early report on the administration of the Congo Free State, submitted to the King, draws the
logical inference from that option. It states that "we do not believe
that it is necessary to have the law intervene to settle disputes
concerning private interests between indigenous parties; these continue in principle to be judged by local chiefs in conformity with
local custom."[5] However, at the same time the report clearly implies that this situation is to be temporary.

Recognizing a *de facto* situation, the Royal Decree of October 6,
1891[6] stipulated that "the indigenous chiefdoms shall be recognised

---

4. M.B. Hooker, *Legal Pluralism. An Introduction to Colonial and NeoColonial Laws*
(Oxford, 1975), 4.
5. *Rapport au Roi-Souverain*, published in *Bulletin Officiel (B.O.)*, 1891, special issue
(7bis), 175–76.
6. *B.O.*, 1891, 259.

as such, provided the chiefs have been confirmed by the Governor General . . . in the authority given to them by custom." Article 5 goes on to state that "the indigenous chiefs shall exercise their authority in conformity with usage and custom, provided these are not contrary to public order and the laws of the state." However, "the chiefs shall be placed under the direction and control of the district commissioners or their representatives." An administrative instruction quite clearly spells out the general idea behind this text: "it is appropriate to ensure the domination of the state through the medium of the indigenous chiefs, who must be made into our most active auxiliaries. . . . The native chiefs have a real influence on their peoples, and if they feel supported by us they will be able to have our ideas prevailed and eventually imposed, thanks to our support."[7] Clearly, while the Belgians proclaimed to rely on the existing political and judicial structure, the organization of the Congo was based on the principles of indirect rule in name only. As is made obvious in the administrative instruction quoted above, the chiefly structure was essentially considered a convenient vehicle for European penetration.

A similar situation is found in Ruanda–Urundi. When the Belgians conquered the territory from the Germans in 1916, they found Rwanda and Burundi to be two highly organized kingdoms, where a policy of indirect rule appeared to be the obvious choice. This option was adhered to in one of the first legal texts applied in the territory: article 4 of the Law–Ordinance nr. 2/5 of April 6, 1917[8] states that "the sultans (name originally used for the designation of the kings of Rwanda and Burundi) exercise, under the direction of the Resident, their political and judicial authority within the limits and in the manner determined by indigenous custom and by the guidelines of the Royal Commissioner." As had happened in the Congo, very soon the kings and the chiefs in Ruanda-Urundi were reduced to a role of mere agents of transmission and implementation of commands emanating from the colonial authorities.[9]

This evolution appears to be the inevitable consequence of the fundamental contradiction of a policy of indirect rule, which on the one hand purports to respect traditional institutions, while on the

7. "Etat Indépendant du Congo, Département de l'Intérieur," *Recueil Administratif* (Brussels, 1900), 355. This instruction accompanies an Order taken in execution of the Decree of October 6, 1891 on the indigenous chiefdoms.

8. *Bulletin Officiel du Ruanda-Urundi (B.O.R.U.)*, 1924, no. 4, supplement, 4–5.

9. See particularly on Rwanda: F. Reyntjens, *Pouvoir et droit au Rwanda. Droit public et évolution politique, 1916–1973* (Tervuren, 1985), 71–177.

other attempts to "civilize" native society. Therefore, White has rightly argued that "the classical concept of indirect rule might be said to contain the seeds of its own destruction."[10] In fact, Belgium was not the only colonial power to fall into the trap of that contradiction. Lord Hailey, with the authority that is his, wrote:

> If originally there was some difference between (direct and indirect rule) in principle, there is today far less distinction in practice. . . . Those governments . . . which have relied in principle on the use of traditional institutions are seen to have so transformed them in the process that Africans of a past generation might find it difficult to recognise them.[11]

Imperfect Legal and Judicial Pluralism During the Colonial Period

General Framework

The option of both legal and judicial pluralism was unequivocally adhered to in early organic legislation. The principle of legal pluralism was confirmed in the basic text ruling the Congo upon becoming a Belgian colony in 1908. Article 4 of the Act of October 18, 1908 on the government of the Belgian Congo (*Charte Coloniale*)[12] stated that "the natives of the Belgian Congo who are not matriculated[13] enjoy the civil rights recognized to them by the legislation of the colony and by their customs, inasfar as these are not contrary to the legislation or to public order." Similarly, judicial pluralism was recognized from the outset, although there existed no organic legislation on indigenous justice until 1926, when the decree of April 15, 1926[14] organized the activities of the existing courts and created new "native" courts unknown in customary law.

However, while two systems of substantive law and two judicial hierarchies were left existing together, the relationship between a dominant and a servient system is explicitly confirmed in the Congolese system. The pluralism is therefore called "imperfect."

Before enquiring into this relationship, it must be noted that the

---

10. C.M.N. White, "Indirect Rule," in *From Tribal Rule to Modern Government*, ed. R. Apthorpe (Lusaka, 1959), 195.

11. Lord Hailey, *Native Administration in the British African Territories* (London, 1950–53), vol. 4, 36.

12. *B.O.*, 1909, 65.

13. The concept of matriculation (*immatriculation*) will be discussed later.

14. *B.O.*, 1926, 437.

analysis will be limited to matters of private law. Indeed, like in the other African territories, the principle of legal pluralism was rejected very early on in criminal matters. Article 84 of the Decree of April 27, 1889[15] established the rule of written law for the treatment of offenses. However the text went on to state that "if the offense has been committed by a native against another native, the *Officier du Ministère Public* may leave the accused to the effective jurisdiction of the local chief and to the application of indigenous custom." As this possibility was very rarely used,[16] for practical purposes there was no question of legal pluralism in this area. The early exclusion of criminal law from the ambit of custom and chiefly competence was of course consistent with the colonial ideology of the "civilising mission" which the European powers purported to undertake in their African possessions. In reality, however, leaving the power of the sword to native rulers was considered contrary to public order and an obstacle to the maintaining of *Pax Belgica* in Central Africa.

Imperfect Legal Pluralism

A number of rules and principles of the dominant system defined the boundaries of the validity of the norms of the servient system. I shall briefly discuss three of these limiting concepts.

Legislation   Article 18 of the Decree of March 17, 1938,[17] in line with article 4 of the *Charte Coloniale* mentioned above, stipulates that "when legislative or executive provisions aim at the substitution of native custom by other rules, the native courts shall apply these provisions." Therefore, if a rule of customary law is contrary to a rule of written law issued specifically for application to the native population, it cannot be applied by the courts. Thus the Decree of July 9, 1936[18] forbade the offering for marriage of girls below the age of nubility; the monogamous marriage was imposed by Decrees of July 5, 1948[19] and April 4, 1950[20]; the Decree of February 10, 1953[21] established successoral rights in immovable property in favor of all

15. *B.O.*, 1889, 87.
16. O. Louwers, *Elements de droit de l'Etat Indépendant du Congo* (Brussels, 1907), 338–56.
17. *B.O.*, 1938, 219.
18. *B.O.*, 1936, 941.
19. *B.O.*, 1948, 969.
20. *B.O.*, 1950, 497.
21. *B.O.*, 1953, 430.

descendents and the surviving spouse; and a Royal Order of July 19, 1954[22] consolidated the legislation on the labor contract for natives.

Cases also arose where a native was in a position to claim rights under a particular legislation without being removed from the effect of customary law. The Congolese were then in a position to combine the application of both sets of normative systems, if there was no opposition between written and customary law. The Decree of February 10, 1953[23] on individual immovable property is an example of such legislation. However, interventions of this sort by the colonial legislator have been rather scarce, occurring mainly toward the end of colonial rule.

Public Order   The notion of "public order" as a limitation placed upon the application of customary law was the equivalent, in francophone Africa, of the "repugnancy clauses" found in African countries with a common law tradition.[24]

"Public order" in article 3 of the *Charte Coloniale* or "universal public order" in article 18 of the Decree of March 17, 1938 in fact means colonial public order. Colonial scholarship has stressed the need for a flexible concept of public order in a situation where two social and legal orders cohabit. Thus Sohier stressed that "it is a public order which is more tolerant and takes into account the special fabric of native society."[25] But here again, as is consistent with a "dominant-servient" scheme, this flexible notion of public order was considered temporary and contingent, as the colonial public order was expected to gradually align itself on the metropolitan model.[26] As its main theorist has pointed out, the public order doctrine was essentially seen as an element in the colonization effort: "(By public order) we understand that the native personal law, even if its respect is accepted by the coloniser, shall not prevail when it is contrary to a rule considered essential for the success of the task of colonisation."[27]

A few examples may serve to illustrate the operation of the notion

22. *B.O.*, 1954, 1430.
23. *B.O.*, 1953, 430.
24. A. Durieux, *La Notion d'Ordre Public en Droit Privé Colonial Belge* (Brussels, 1953). Allott confirms the similarity of the concept in Commonwealth Africa. See A.N. Allott, *Essays in African Law* (London, 1960), 197.
25. A. Sohier, "A propos de la notion d'ordre public en droit privé colonial belge," I.R.C.B., *Bulletin des séances*, 1953, 546.
26. Thus e.g. M. Verstraete, *Droit Civil du Congo Belge*, vol. I: *Les Personnes et la Famille* (Brussels, 1956), 56.
27. H. Solus, *Traité de la Condition des Indigènes en Droit Privé* (Paris, 1927), 303.

of public order. Thus the fact that the termination of a marriage by divorce in a complex of bride-exchange arrangements would result in the dissolution of all related marriages was held to be contrary to public order.[28] The prohibition of usury was deducted from the same principle,[29] which also served to gradually abolish all forms of domestic bondage.[30]

"Natives" It was of course consistent with the basic economy of the system that customary law should apply to natives only. The concept of "native" seemed so obvious to the legislator that the Decree of 1926 on the native judicial organization did not deem it necessary to define the term.[31] However, we have seen that article 4 of the *Charte Coloniale* restricts the application of customary law to the natives who are not registered. Not before 1952[32] was the registration (*immatriculation*) of natives organized by law: two Decrees of May 17, 1952, completed by a Decree of December 8, 1953, on the one hand allowed the natives to obtain their matriculation and thus abandon their "customary status," and on the other removed the registered natives from the competence of the native courts. One of the conditions for obtaining matriculation was "to show by one's training and way of life a state of civilisation implying the ability to enjoy the rights and to fulfill the duties provided for by the written laws."

Only a very limited number of Congolese obtained matriculation (only 217 families were registered in 1958), while in Ruanda-Urundi less than a dozen applied for the status. In practice, therefore, this limitation of the field of customary law has had little impact.

Imperfect Judicial Pluralism

Although there were, in both the Belgian Congo and Ruanda-Urundi, two separate judicial hierarchies, one called "principal" (i.e. colonial and of European inspiration), the other "customary,"

28. E.g. Tribunal du Parquet du Kibali-Ituri, April 3, 1951, *Journal des Tribunaux d'Outre-Mer (J.T.O.)*, 1952, 166.
29. See e.g. Tribunal du Parquet du Ruanda, July 17, 1953, *J.T.O.*, 1955, 26; Tribunal du Parquet du Lualaba, July 27, 1954, *J.T.O.*, 1955, 76.
30. For further examples, see J. Sohier, *Répertoire Général de la Jurisprudence et de la Doctrine Coutumières du Congo et du Ruanda-Urundi* (Brussels, 1957), 512–27.
31. J. Vanderlinden, *Essai sur les Juridictions de Droit Coutumier dans les Territoires d'Afrique Centrale* (Brussels, 1959), 138.
32. In fact, a first attempt at matriculation had been tried in 1895, but it had been a failure.

here again the relation between a "dominant" and a "servient" system
was clear. While the dominant "principal" judicial organization had
been set up in the early days of colonial rule, only in 1926 was the
first text organizing the "native" courts promulgated. In principle,
the division of competence between these two judicial orders was
very simple: in civil and commercial matters the "customary" courts
heard all cases arising between non-registered natives, provided the
issue was not determined by a rule of written law (except in the cases
mentioned above where rules of written law purported to replace
those of customary law), while the "principal" courts decided the
other cases (i.e. those involving Europeans and registered natives,
where *ipso facto* only written law was to be applied). However, the
operation of the customary courts was controlled by the principal
judicial system, and more particularly by the *Tribunal de Parquet*
(staffed, by the way, by a member of the Public Prosecutor's office
[*Ministère public*]). The *Tribunal de Parquet* had the power to transfer
(*évocation*) a case pending before a customary court, or revise or
annul a decision of such a court.[33] When it is noted further that the
judges of the customary courts were appointed by the colonial
administration and that the District Commissioner was allowed to
preside over all the native courts of his district, it becomes clear that
the judicial pluralism was very imperfect indeed, and that the "customary" courts in fact functioned under the guardianship of the
colonial judicial and administrative hierarchy.

This judicial pluralism was not only imperfect or "hierarchical,"
it was also, as Lamy has rightly pointed out,[34] mixed. The "European" courts indeed had a mixed competence *ratione materiae*: as
courts of general jurisdiction, they were to apply customary law if
natives chose to file their case with them. The customary courts were
mixed in both their composition and the law they applied: on the
one hand Europeans sat on the bench (in some cases their participation was mandatory, in other cases it was optional); on the other
hand these courts applied written legislation (in cases where a law
modifying custom required the customary courts to apply the replacing legislation) as well as customary law.

33. For further information of these means of control, see Vanderlinden, *Essai sur
les Juridictions*, 149–151; J. Herbots, "Les techniques du recours en droit coutumier
congolais," *Revue Juridique et Politique*, 1966, 215–20.
34. E. Lamy, "Les juridictions mixtes de droit écrit et de droit coutumier dans les
pays en voie de développement: évolution et situation au Zaïre, Rwanda et Burundi,"
Rapports Belges au XIIe Congrès de l'Académie Internationale de Droit Comparé (Antwerp-
Brussels, 1986), vol. I, 12–14.

Interaction Between the Two Laws

The meeting, in both substantive law and procedure, between two legal systems has inevitably led to a great deal of interaction. This is two-way, but I shall not dwell here on the influence of traditional law on official law.[35] The most conspicuous influence is of course that of written law on customary law.

Let me first make it clear that it is not possible in this paper to discuss a number of general (and admittedly important) influences on the evolution of the customary law. These are of a social and economic nature, and include the introduction of a monetary economy, urbanization, education, Christian religion, and the penetration of "modern" ways generally. The following comments are limited to interactions of a legal nature.

A general point, which has been stressed elsewhere in Africa, must be briefly recalled: the replacement of an oral legal culture by a written one. To the precolonial oral customary law succeeded a written customary law: minutes of court proceedings were held, registrars kept books and statistics, case-law was reduced to writing. A good deal of the flexibility which characterized the traditional legal process was thus lost, which in turn led to the transformation of the substantive customary law.

Related to this tendency toward the bureaucratization of the judicial system is the position of "traditional" judges. Not only were they appointed by the colonial authorities, they were also placed in an insecure position, torn between the norms of the Belgian administration and the demands and expectations of the indigenous population. Grévisse, writing about the crisis of the customary courts in the 1930s and 1940s, notes: "Used to remembering and not to reasoning, the natives see the sources of their memory dry up and the habits of their life fall apart . . . there are no rules left which are not jeopardised, no obligations that are not dependent on one or more conditions, or even, worse, contingencies."[36] In the eyes of the native population, these "traditional" judges did not represent much: they had very little legitimacy, as their right to judge and punish had been given to them by the whites. Hulstaert therefore

35. Although the subject is important, it would lead us too far. Suffice it to say that, up to the present day, norms and values of folk laws penetrate the official legal system, thus "corrupting" it in a way similar to the impact of (e.g. affective) "traditional" norms penetrating the bureaucratic state administration. See for instance F. Reyntjens, "Chiefs and burgomasters in Rwanda: the unfinished quest for a bureaucracy," *Journal of Legal Pluralism*, 25–26 (1987), 71–97.

36. F. Grévisse, *La Grande Pitié des Juridictions Indigènes* (Brussels, 1949), 33.

noted that "the bankruptcy (of the native courts) resulted from the
fact that they were too often instruments in the hands of the white
man, who tends to favorise, tolerate or disturb custom in favour of
his own interests."[37] A Flemish colonial novelist vividly expressed
the same feeling: "Our wise judges and elder clan chiefs were not
allowed to settle disputes anymore, replaced as they were by dec-
orated judges who decided cases in brick buildings according to
incomprehensible laws."[38]

This leads us to the next point. Francescakis[39] has rightly stressed
the importance of the "jurisdictionalisation" of disputes. The
tendency of the customary courts, because they were no organic
emanations of a customary system, to create new customs (notably
by their habit of "territorialising" personal customary laws) will be
illustrated later, when I shall briefly discuss the emergence of urban
custom. But it must be noted already now that the courts of written
law, which (as was indicated above) enjoyed full jurisdiction even in
purely customary matters, weighed heavily upon the evolution of the
customary courts' case law. Again, this was identified as a problem
long before these issues became fashionable in legal anthropologists'
circles. Thus Sohier wrote in the early 1950s: "The imbalance
between European and native courts and the increasingly frequent
intrusion – often unconsciously and difficult to ascertain – of the case
law of the European courts in the customary domain shatter the
traditional law."[40] This assessment is strikingly illustrated by the
fact that the native courts themselves increasingly invoked the exception of public order – a patently European concept – to justify
their refusal to apply certain rules of folk law. A court went as far as
considering the payment of interest on a loan to be contrary to
public order.[41] In an attempt to do well, the white men's custom was
obviously misunderstood. This penetration of European norms in
the case law of native courts, based on the fear of revision by the
Tribunal de Parquet, has also been noticed elsewhere. Saltman, for
instance, has shown that the local conflict-solving agency of the

37. G. Hulstaert, "Feu la coutume indigène?," I.R.C.B., *Bulletin des séances*, 1950,
156–157.
38. J. Geeraerts, *Ik ben maar een neger* (Amsterdam, 1962), 237.
39. Ph. Francescakis, "Problèmes de droit international privé de l'Afrique noire
indépendante," Académie de Droit International, *Recueil des Cours* (Leiden, 1964),
vol. 2, 304.
40. Sohier, "Les juridictions européennes du Congo et le droit coutumier," *J.T.O.*,
1953, 67.
41. Tribunal de secteur Lubelike, Judgment nr. 573, *Bulletin des Juridictions Indigènes*, 1942, 151.

Kipsigis of Kenya, the *kokwet*, became increasingly influenced by the way decisions are made in the (official) magistrate's court, and that it relied on case-to-case precedent cited from the official courts.[42]

Finally, a number of specific and purposeful interventions by the colonial authorities furthered the evolution from original customary law to colonial customary law. Both the promulgation of legislation designed to abrogate or modify custom and the use of the concept of public order to achieve this have already been referred to. This "streamlining" of customary law inevitably entailed profound change. The idea of the "invention of tradition"[43] to qualify processes of this sort was not invented in the 1980s. Already in 1944, Rubbens had published a paper called "The late native custom";[44] and in 1956 Sohier wrote a booklet on the subject of the transformation of custom.[45] In fact, from the outset the colonial authorities recognized that the so-called indigenous courts were to be an important instrument of change. Only a few years after the reorganization of native justice by the decree of 1926, the *Procureur Général* of the Elisabethville Court of Appeal published a revealing instruction on the subject.[46] Sohier insisted on the fact that the principal mission of the native courts was "the consolidation of the family and social order of our subjects." Noting that most litigation in these courts consisted of "*palabres de femmes*," i.e. actions in divorce and repression of adultery, he advised when solving these cases to "always see the need to strengthen the indigenous family and to regularise morals."[47] "*Coutume évoluée*," developed custom, was the euphemism used to describe the neo-traditional law thus emerging.

Transformation in Action: The Emergence of Urban Custom

The doctoral thesis of Professor J.M. Pauwels, entitled "Choice of Law and Genesis of a Uniform Urban Custom,"[48] offers a

42. M. Saltman, "Indigenous law among the Kipsigis of Southwestern Kenya" in *Access to Justice*, ed. M. Cappelletti (Alphen-Milan, 1979), vol. 3, 327.

43. E. Hobsbawm and T. Ranger, eds., *The Invention of Tradition* (Cambridge, 1983).

44. A. Rubbens, "Feu la coutume indigène," *Lovania*, 1944, no. 4, 60–64.

45. J. Sohier, *Essai sur la Transformation des Coutumes* (Brussels, 1956).

46. A. Sohier, *Pratique des Juridictions Indigènes (Notes sur l'Application du Décret du 15 Avril 1926)* (Brussels, 1932).

47. Ibid., 6.

48. J.M. Pauwels, *Rechtskeuze en Wording van een Eenvormige Stadsgewoonte in de Inlandse*

remarkable analysis of the process of interaction and transformation mentioned above. The phenomenon of the birth of urban custom is not only interesting as a privileged and accessible laboratory for the study of the relations between different legal orders, it is also highly relevant in a country like Zaire, where about 40 percent of the population is urbanized.

Pauwels's research shows that, during the crucial first fifteen years of the implementation of the 1926 legislation on the customary jurisdictions, a law of European inspiration in fact replaced customary law. A typical example can be found in the rule that the wife must live with her husband: not only was this norm contrary to the uxorilocal customs, but it also went against the majority of customs allowing a wife to visit her parents at regular intervals and to leave the household from time to time.[49] Other examples can be found in the rules on polygamy and concubinage.

Pauwels notes that these examples, as well as the pressure exercised in favor of the patrilineal system, show that the basic policy behind the action of the colonial authorities was the introduction and protection of the monogamous nuclear family. Such a policy required the acknowledgment of the power of the father over his children, the sanctioning of irregular cohabitation, the strengthening of the authority of the husband over his wife, and the taking of measures against polygamy. This influence of Western law on the indigenous case-law was found in most fields. In a conclusion on "Eurafrican legal acculturation," Pauwels cites the law of marriage (rights and duties of spouses), the law of adultery (the attempts by the colonial authorities to abolish damages in favor of criminal sanctions), the law of concubinage (the refusal to give any effect to obligations arising from the relationship, on the basis of the rule of *Nemo auditur propriam turpitudinem allegans*), the law of succession (the granting of rights to the surviving spouse and the children), land law (the application of municipal bye-laws), and the law of contract (especially the introduction of the civil law principle of consensuality in the contract of sale).[50] It is striking that the written law has not penetrated the customary legal system through the regulation of

---

Rechtbanken te Leopoldstad (Kinshasa), 1926–1940 (Tervuren, 1967). Although the text is in Dutch, an excellent summary in French (605–31) makes the thesis accessible to a wider readership. Likewise, the annexes (administrative texts and judicial decisions) are in French (541–604). The study has also been summarized in J.M. Pauwels, "Les origines du droit urbain de Kinshasa," *Revue Juridique du Congo*, 1968, 341 ff.

49. Pauwels, *Rechtskeuze*, 116–17.

50. Ibid., 519.

conflicts of laws, but rather through a quasi-legislative way, where the desire to impose a uniform "custom," based not on the principle of personality but on that of territoriality, prevailed. As soon as the fundamental option for a uniform law was taken, the relations of power between the indigenous judges and the representatives of the European administration inevitably led to an imbalance in favor of the ideas of Western-inspired law.[51]

Developments after Independence: Unification and Codification

While colonial rule has profoundly modified customary law, no formal attempts at unification of the laws had been undertaken by the Belgian administration. Legal and judicial pluralism were of course not contrary to the ideology of colonial rule.

Independence has, in all African countries, brought a fundamental change in this respect. Legal pluralism was felt to be an obstacle against attempts at national integration and nation-building: "Like the Kings of France, the African leaders have understood that legislative unity in every field can help towards realising national unity."[52]

The first constitution of the Congo (Zaire) upon independence (June 30, 1960) was in fact an Act of the Belgian Parliament, the "Fundamental Law" of May 19, 1960,[53] which contained no specific provisions on the relations between folk law and state law. However, article 2 stated that the existing legislation was saved insofar as it was not explicitly abrogated: the 1926 legislation on the native judicial organization thus remained in force, and with it the existing situation of legal and judicial pluralism. The relationship was re-established explicitly in the constitution of August 1, 1964.[54] Article 123, para. 1 stated that "the courts apply the law, and custom only inasfar as it is in conformity with the laws, with public order and with good morals." Although the existence of custom was further recognized, this provision affirmed the primacy of written law over custom and confirmed the existing limitations on the application of

51. Ibid., 520.
52. G. Kalambay, "La situation actuelle des droits civils congolais: droit écrit et droit coutumier et perspectives d'avenir," *Problèmes sociaux congolais (CEPSI)*, September 1967, no. 78, 96.
53. *Moniteur Belge*, 1960, 3988; *Moniteur Congolais*, 1960, 1535.
54. *Moniteur Congolais*, special issue of August 1, 1964.

customary law. The subsequent constitutions have all carried similar provisions (however, no further reference is made to "good
morals," which in the mind of the draftsmen seem to be included in
the concept of "public order"). While some authors have claimed
that the positive requirement of "conformity" of custom with written law instead of the previously used negative "not contrary"
further diminished the ambit of folk law,[55] I believe with Pauwels
that the relationship between the two legal systems remained essentially the same,[56] although it must be admitted that the new vocabulary undoubtedly reflected a commitment to further the integration of both systems. This idea is further strengthened by the fact
that the subsequent constitutions provide guidance in particular
fields of law, e.g. regarding certain principles on the freedom of
persons to choose their spouse. Verhelst has noted that the constitutional draftsmen intended to propagate institutions like the nuclear
family, and that it must be assumed that the courts were instructed
to modify rules of folk law in such a fashion as to make them conform
to the constitutional and statutory model.[57]

The implementation of this option of unification took quite some
time in Zaire, but was pursued in a systematic manner. The first
area tackled was that of the judicial organization. The Code of
Judicial Organization and Competence of 1968[58] unified the judicial
system in one single hierarchy of courts, which were to apply written
or customary law, whichever was appropriate. According to the
exposé des motifs, the aim of this reorganization was "to wipe out the
last traces of racial discrimination and to consecrate the integration
of custom in the national law by ending the dichotomy of judicial
organs."[59] From the *tribunaux de paix* at the bottom to the *Cour
suprême* at the apex, the courts were thus expected to take a unifying
attitude in applying both sets of law. As in other countries, the
reform was underpinned by the hope that "through the case law, it
will engender a merger of modern and traditional laws, in effect a

55. See e.g. A. Durieux, *Droit Ecrit et Droit Coutumier en Afrique Centrale* (Brussels,
1970), 21–22; L. Lobitsh, "Le passé, le présent et l'avenir de la coutume congolaise
dans l'intégration des droits," *Revue Congolaise de Droit*, 1971, no. 1, 108; E. Lamy,
"Bilan actuel de l'intégration du droit zairois et ses perspectives d'avenir," *Revue
Juridique du Zaire*, special issue 1974, 123–24.
56. Pauwels, "La constitution du Congo et le droit coutumier," *Etudes Congolaises*,
1964, no. 9, 13.
57. T. Verhelst, *Safeguarding African Customary Law: Judicial and Legislative Processes
for its Adaptation and Integration* (Los Angeles, 1968), 10. Occasional Paper No. 7.
58. Ordinance-Law of July 10, 1968, *Moniteur Congolais*, 1968, 1343.
59. *Moniteur Congolais*, 1968, 1340.

kind of common law."[60] However, the effective operation of this reform has incurred considerable delay, so much so that Lamy estimated that by the mid-1980s only about one quarter of the Zairean population effectively lived under the regime of unification, the majority remaining subject to the customary courts which continued in operation pending the installation of a *tribunal de paix* in the area.[61]

While under the new system all courts are "mixed" regarding the applicable law (written law and custom), only the *tribunaux de paix* will remain partially mixed in their composition (two assessors are added to the professional judge if the court is to apply customary law).

The second stage in the pursuit of unification addressed the issue of substantive law. While the interventions of the colonial legislature (the promulgation of laws purporting to modify custom in particular fields) and judiciary (the application of the "public order" clause) had led to a "streamlining" of customary law – which was fundamentally transformed in the process – the situation is very different when legislation attempts to completely replace entire areas of customary law. It is typical that such attempts at wholesale unification of areas of the substantive law were undertaken only after independence: indeed, after the unification of the judicial system, Zairean written law has aimed at invading the two core areas of legal pluralism, i.e. land law and family law. On the one hand, the Land Code of 1973[62] organized the legal status of all immovable property as well as sureties; on the other hand, the Family Code of 1987[63] imposes a uniform set of rules concerning persons and the family. In theory, therefore, hardly any matter is left to customary law in 1988. However, given the absence of *tribunaux de paix* in large parts of the country, one is faced here with the paradoxical situation that customary courts are supposed to apply statutory law exclusively.

Rwanda and Burundi tend toward the same aim. Both countries, being very small, have found it easy to unify their judicial systems. Judicial dualism was abolished just before independence in 1962: like in Zaire after the 1968 reform, the unified hierarchy of courts applies written or customary law, whichever is appropriate. The unification of substantive law is a slow process in both countries,

60. P.F. Gonidec, *Les droits africains* (Paris, 2nd Ed., 1976), 280.
61. Lamy, Les juridictions mixtes, 21.
62. Act no. 73–021 of July 20, 1973, amended by Act no. 80–008 of July 18, 1980.
63. Act no. 87–010 of August 1, 1987. This code has entered into force on August 1, 1988.

although they have the enormous advantage that apart from some
minor regional variations, folk laws are similar everywhere. At the
end of the 1960s, Rwanda drafted Codes in the areas of land law and
law of persons and the family. Opposition to both drafts forced the
government to shelve them; however, an extensive research and
consultation process is currently underway for a Code of Persons
and the Family, and signs are that this may result in legislation in
the years ahead. For its part, Burundi promulgated a Code of
Persons and the Family in 1980.[64]

Conclusion

There is a basic difference of attitude toward legal pluralism and
unification between the colonial rulers on the one hand, and the
leaders of independent Zaire, Rwanda, and Burundi on the other. It
was consistent with colonial policy to recognize legal pluralism: this
recognition was not only induced by a feeling of cultural superiority,
it was also – like the choice of a policy of indirect rule – imposed by
reasons of expediency and administrative convenience. Furthermore, the colonial authorities were not interested in national integration, quite the contrary. The leaders of the newly independent
nations, for their part, wished to do away with legal (and for that
matter, social) pluralism and strived toward national (e.g. legal)
unification, but were faced with a situation of legal pluralism imposed upon them by the facts of life.

   Although these starting-points were so different, in fact there
exists a great deal of continuity between both policies. On the one
hand, while the colonial administration pretended to respect custom, they transformed it beyond recognition; on the other hand,
while the leaders of independent countries attempted to legislate
unity into existence, they faced an effective resistance to their endeavour. In both cases a considerable degree of pluralism remains,
with large portions of the population living under the aegis of
neo-traditional law. Gonidec has rightly noted that "there appears
to be a divorce between law wanted by the African leaders, for
instance statute law, and the law lived by a large fraction of the

---

64. Law-Decree no. 1/1 of January 15, 1980 (*Bulletin Officiel du Burundi*, 1980, no. 3,
83). See on this subject: J.M. Pauwels, "Le Code de la Famille burundais de 1980,"
Jahrbuch für afrikanisches Recht, 1981, 73–98.

population."[65] There exists another source of continuity between both regimes. Written law, or state law or official law as one may prefer to call the dominant system, has remained the same in its relation to customary law, or folk law or unofficial law, as one may prefer to call the servient system. The "maker" of the dominant system may have changed, but not the system itself, which is still as alien as it used to be: its ideology, concepts, categories and techniques remain those that emerged in the 19th century European nation-states. Therefore, the "legal fetishism" of the leaders of independent Africa seems somewhat unrealistic: experience shows how difficult the imposition of official law is, and the persistence of situations of legal pluralism is a likely perspective for many years to come.

65. P.F. Gonidec, "Réflexion sur l'état et le droit en Afrique," *Penant*, 1984, no. 783, 22.

7

Legal Expansion in the Age of the Companies: Aspects of the Administration of Justice in the English and Dutch Settlements of Maritime Asia, c. 1600–1750

H.-J. LEUE

> ... the Inhabitants and Commerce of this place are much
> increased, and many complaints have lately been for want of a
> due course for the administration of Justice, ...
>
> (Madras Public Consultations, 1678)[1]

Principles

When the English and the Dutch East India companies began their
careers at the opening of the seventeenth century, neither parent
state took the trouble or thought it advisable to lay down in any
detail the principles which were to govern the management of the
administrative and judicial affairs of the newly formed corporations.
As A.B. Keith has explained, the charter granted by Elizabeth I to
the EIC on New Year's Eve, 1600, merely provided in summary
fashion for the Company's right to "... make, ordain, and constitute such and so many reasonable laws, constitutions, orders, and
ordinances, as to them ... shall seem necessary and convenient for
the good government of the said Company ... or for the better
advancement and continuance of the said trade and traffick." Keith
concludes that "they were further authorized to impose such pains,
punishments, and penalties by imprisonment of body or by fines and
amerciaments as might seem necessary or convenient for the observation of such laws and ordinances. Both laws and punishments

1. H.D. Love, *Vestiges of Old Madras, 1640–1800*, vol. I, (London, 1913), 405.

must be reasonable and not contrary or repugnant to the laws, statutes or customs of the realm of England."[2]

In a similar vein, article 35 of the *octrooi* granted in 1602 by the States-General of the United Netherlands, empowered the VOC "east of the Cape of Good Hope, to enter into treaties and alliances with princes and potentates in the name of the States-General; to make peace and war; to build stations and fortresses; to inflict punishment – including capital punishment; to administer its trading stations; to appoint and dismiss governors, military commanders and judicial officers; and to establish other services necessary for the maintenance of good order and justice and the advancement of trade."[3] In addition, this important article laid down that all servants of the VOC had to take their oath first on the States-General and only afterwards on the Company, thus giving expression to the determination of the parent state to safeguard his suzerainty.

Thus, instead of attempting to regulate practical details in noncommercial fields, the English crown and the Dutch republic contented themselves with a position of overlord and invested their companies with full powers of self-management – legislative, executive, and judicial. Their main proviso – unambiguous in the English charter, less explicit in the Dutch *octrooi* – was that the rules and regulations made by the companies must not be repugnant to the laws of the parent states.[4]

The newly founded companies, going through a time of trial and error which did not end before the middle of the century, made use of their powers when, and to the extent to which, occasion arose. The earliest jurisdiction of VOC and EIC was in practice confined to the planks of their ships. However, after a few years, fortresses on land were added to the floating fortresses, and administration and jurisdiction spread from the sea to the shore. This meant that the ships' councils, hitherto in charge of that measure of administration and jurisdiction which was deemed indispensable, had to detach embryonic local governments, and it meant further that these landbased authorities had to deal not only with their "own" people, but with a growing number of "natives," too. Given their basic aims, power and profit, the companies had no difficulty in realizing and in

2. A.B. Keith, *A Constitutional History of India, 1600-1935* (London, 1936), 4–5. See also C. Ilbert, *The Government of India* (Oxford, 1898), 475–476, and M.P. Jain, *Outlines of Indian Legal History* (Bombay, 1972), 6–7.

3. J. Ball, *Indonesian Legal History, 1602-1848* (Sydney, 1981), 2. The preceding article (article 34) established the monopoly of the VOC.

4. Cf. Ball, *Indonesian Legal History*, 28 ff., on the "concordancy" principle.

accepting that local conditions had to be taken into account in one way or another wherever their Asian subjects were involved, and that to that extent the rule of European law, proclaimed or simply implied in the charters as a matter of course, had to be qualified.

It was in accordance with the "first things first" temper of the pioneering years that this principle was more or less acted upon, before it was put on paper. In the VOC, the directors thought it necessary first to reaffirm and clarify the validity of Dutch law. In 1621, two years after the Company, by conquering Jacatra (the future Batavia), had acquired its long sought-after Asian rendez-vous and capital, and when the essential parts of its organization were taking shape, they advised their lieutenants to adopt in the VOC territories certain laws of Holland and West Friesland. In cases not covered by these laws the administration of justice was to be according to the "common civil laws as practised in the United Netherlands."[5] Eleven years later, in 1632, governor-general Hendrick Brouwer (1632–1636) was reminded in his instructions "that the administration of rightful justice was the foundation of good and well-ordered government. . . . [Article 1 of the instructions] required the Governor-General and Council to ensure that at Batavia and all other places under the dominion of the VOC justice was administered in accordance with the instructions and customs usually observed in the United Netherlands Provinces in both civil and criminal cases."[6]

Meanwhile, in 1625, governor-general Pieter de Carpentier (1623–1627), confirming the applicability of Dutch law as enounced in 1631, had laid it down that in using that law regard should be had as far as possible for local conditions.[7] This policy had already been followed in two ways. First, shortly after his conquest of Batavia, governor-general Jan Pieterszoon Coen (1618–1623 and 1627–1629) had appointed a "captain" of the important Chinese community in the person of his friend Su Ming-kang, alias "Bencon" (1580–1644). This functionary represented his people toward the VOC authorities and dealt with minor matters which occurred among his flock.[8] In

5. Ball, *Indonesian Legal History*, 29. See also G.C. Klerk de Reus, *Geschichtlicher Ueberblick der administrativen. rechtlichen und finanziellen Entwicklung der niederländisch-ostindischen Compagnie* (Batavia, 1894), 134.

6. Ball, *Indonesian Legal History*, 10 and 29; Klerk de Reus, *Geschichtlicher Ueberblick der Compagnie*, 81 n. 1, 87–88, 134.

7. Ball, *Indonesian Legal History*, 29; Klerk de Reus, *Geschichtlicher Ueberblick der Compagnie*, 134.

8. L. Blussé, *Strange Company, Chinese Settlers, Mestizo Women and the Dutch in VOC Batavia* (Dordrecht/Riverton, 1986), 51, 81.

addition, when setting up a College of Aldermen (*College der Schepenen*) for his newly-won capital, Coen had added the captain of the Chinese to the three citizens and two Company servants, who were to constitute the College. This body, called *Bank der Schepenen* (Court of Aldermen) in its judicial capacity, underwent many changes in later years, and it even appears that the representatives of the Chinese community were excluded altogether from its ranks in the later seventeenth century. The principle of grouping the population along "national" lines was, however, extended with the growth of Batavia and was applied in other settlements, too, with each of the different communities being concentrated in a particular quarter and each as a rule receiving its own chief or chiefs who looked after minor affairs.[9]

Toward the middle of the seventeenth century, when the age of adventure and experiment drew to its close, attitudes had not changed, but they were now laid down in the first collection of Dutch colonial laws, the "Statutes of Batavia."[10] This work had been undertaken by the "High Government," as the governor-general and his council had come to be styled, because the directors at home had, for years on end, promised to send comprehensive instructions for the administration of justice, but had never in fact acted up to their words. The "Statutes," collected and arranged by Johan Maetsuycker, a future governor-general (1653–1678), were promulgated under governor-general Anthony van Diemen (1636–1645) in 1642 and were made applicable in Batavia itself as well as in the "outstations."[11] Their concluding passage, summarizing the past and foreshadowing the future principles of judicial administration, stipulated in essence that "where no special provision was made in the Statutes of Batavia the law to be applied was

9. There was, it is true, nothing new about these arrangements, since a limited jurisdiction used to be conceded to resident groups of foreigners all over the Eastern Seas, and when the Portuguese arrived, they had readily conformed to this pattern, but it is remarkable how swiftly the VOC followed such precedents. Cf. Ball, *Indonesian Legal History*, 61; K.S. Sandhu, "Indian settlement in Melaka," in *Melaka, The Transformation of a Malay Capital, c. 1400–1980*, vol. 2, (Kuala Lumpur, 1983), 174–211; L. Dermigny, "Escales, échelles et ports francs au Moyen Age et aux temps modernes," in *Les Grandes Escales* vol. 3 (1974), 212 ff.; J.S. Furnivall, *Netherlands India. A Study of Plural Economy* (Cambridge, 1939, reprinted 1967), 36, 45; L.F.F.R. Thomaz, "Malaka et ses communautés marchandes au tournant du 16e siècle," in *Marchands et Hommes d'Affaires Asiatiques dans l'Ocean Indien et la Mer de Chine, 13e–20e Siècles*, ed. D. Lombard and J. Aubin (Paris, 1988), 31–48.

10. Cf. Ball, *Indonesian Legal History*, 31–33. The "Statutes of Batavia" became the "Old Statutes" when "New Statutes" were completed in 1766. See Ball, 33–35.

11. Cf. Ball, *Indonesian Legal History*, 32–33.

the 'laws, statutes and customs of the United Netherlands'. If these did not cover the case the 'written Imperial laws' were to be used in so far as they were in accordance with and practical in view of conditions in the Indies."[12]

In the English East India Company, the legal position was not nearly as clear, but it is comparable to the Dutch case all the same. The orthodox view, established by judicial opinion in the last century, has been that English law was introduced into the Company's settlements by the charter of 1726.[13] Why such a late date should once have been postulated is now merely of technical interest. Suffice it here to say that M.P. Jain, one of the foremost legal historians of India, who is himself a lawyer, while quoting the established judicial opinion approvingly, states in unequivocal terms: "The first Charter having a bearing on the question of introduction of the English law in . . . [the Presidency Towns] is the Charter of 1661. It is the first, and indeed the only Charter, which in express terms introduced English law into the East Indies. It authorized the Governor and Council of a settlement to judge all persons belonging to the Company, or that should live under them, in all causes, whether civil or criminal, according to the laws of the Kingdom of England."[14]

From an historical point of view, even 1661 is much too late a date. Already in the earlier decades of the seventeenth century, so it seems, there was little doubt among those responsible that English law was to be the ultimate basis of all the Company's activities, legislative, executive, and judicial, at home as well as overseas. On the other hand, the very vagueness of the "constitutional" documents may perhaps be said to have amounted to an official recognition of the policy pursued all along, a policy which, just like that of the rival Dutch company, never lost its pragmatism and had regard for local conditions wherever this seemed advisable. At Madras, the adjudication of petty cases was originally left in the hands of the "adigar," the native hereditary village headman and "choultry"

---

12. Ibid., 32. Cf. Klerk de Reus, *Geschichtlicher Ueberblick der Compagnie*, 136; M.H.J. van den Horst, *The Roman Dutch Law in Sri Lanka* (Amsterdam, 1985), 50–51. In another place "the Statutes of Batavia called on all Vice-Governors, Presidents, Justices and Judges in 'far-off countries, towns and places' under Dutch sovereignty in the East Indies, to regulate themselves according to its provisions as far as the constitution of such countries, towns and places should admit and allow." Ball, *Indonesian Legal History*, 32.

13. G.C. Rankin, *Background to Indian Law* (Cambridge, 1946), 1; Jain, *Outlines*, 440; C.M. Setalvad, *The Common Law in India* (London, 1960), 12–13; idem, *The Role of English Law in India* (Jerusalem, 1966), 8–9.

14. Jain, *Outlines*, 472.

justice[15] who, insofar as he was not acting from motives alien to his task,[16] could be expected to administer traditional indigenous norms. Even after 1654, when the "choultry" judges were servants of the Company, indigenous customs were apparently respected. A different kind of indigenous forum was the traditional caste tribunal, which probably functioned at least in each of the larger castes represented at Madras. However, so little is known about them that we cannot even say in what respects they provided an additional, and to what extent they were an alternative, mechanism of conflict resolution.[17]

In the infancy of the settlement, the reason for keeping the "adigar" as well as the caste panels was probably a lack of interest in the affairs of Madraspatnam, the future Black Town, and a more or less genuine respect for the superior power of the local Indian overlord. Later on, when Fort St. George became less vulnerable and when Black Town, too, had received a modest fortification, this respect dwindled away and the original lack of interest in the life of the non-European communities turned into a deliberate legal dualism. The most striking instance of this policy was the creation of a mixed European and Asian "Mayor's Court" at Madras in 1688.[18] Half a century after the acquisition of the site, Madras had grown into a populous place, and the then leading man of the EIC, Sir

15. On the "choultry" court cf. C. Fawcett, *The First Century of British Justice in India* (Oxford, 1934), 208; Ilbert, *The Government*, 18–19; Jain, *Outlines*, 14–16; Keith, *A Constitutional History of India*, 47–48; Love, *Vestiges*, 451–452 and passim; A.F.T. Reyes, *English and French Approaches to Personal Laws in South India, 1700–1850*. Thesis submitted for the degree of Doctor of Philosophy in Law, St. John's College, Cambridge, 1986 (University Library, Cambridge, PhD 14737), 22.

"Choultry" is a South Indian word "meaning a hall, or shed, or loggia, used either as a resting-place or for purposes of business." Ilbert, *The Government*, 19, n. 1. See also Hobson-Jobson, Henry Yule and A.C. Burnell, *A Glossary of Colloquial Anglo-Indian Words and Phrases* (London, 1903), 211–212. In Pondicherry French the word was spelt "chauderie" or "chaudrie," and the judge holding court there was the *juge de la chauderie*: See M. Thomas, *Le Conseil Supérieur de Pondichéry, 1702–1820* (Paris, 1953), 104 ff.; Reyes, *Approaches*, 184.

16. "Adigar Kanappa who had inherited the office from his father, abused his power at the Choultry in various ways, the most serious of which was his connivance at the stealing of children for being sold as slaves." Jain, *Outlines*, 15. See also Love, *Vestiges*, 126 ff.

17. Cf. Keith, *A Constitutional History of India*, 47; Fawcett, *The First Century*, 164, 169, 173–74, 183.

18. The charter which established a municipal corporation and a Mayor's Court at Madras, was granted by the EIC in 1687. It was implemented in 1688. Cf. Fawcett, *The First Century*, 203–06; Jain, *Outlines*, 19–26; Keith, *A Constitutional History of India*, 46–47; Love, *Vestiges*, 497–503; Reyes, *Approaches*, 21–22. On the Mayors' Courts established under the charters of 1726 and 1753, cf. below.

Josiah Child, accordingly felt that the time had come to associate the heads of the indigenous population with the governance of their town. Typically, the occasion for this resolve was a need for money, with the Company desiring to improve the fortifications of Madras and deeming it advisable to levy the necessary taxes with the consent of the people. In order to exchange acquiescence in taxation for a measure of representation, Child obtained the permission of James II to constitute Fort St. George, and the populous Black Town under its protection, a municipal corporation on the English model, with the mayor and aldermen sitting as the Mayor's Court "with power to 'adjudge all causes whatsoever . . . between Party and Party whoever . . . in a summary way according to Equity and Good Conscience.'"[19]

The decision to include among the aldermen representatives of all communities may have been made easier by the awareness that similar solutions had been tried out long ago by "other European Nations in India," as the charter modestly veiled its reference to the Dutch East India Company,[20] which was still setting the standard in many matters concerning Europe's intercourse with Asia. In spite of the wording of the charter – the Mayor's Court "was to consist of a 'Mixture of the most discreet, best, and honestest of all sorts of people,' and the aldermen 'especially should be made up of the Heads and Chiefs of all the respective Casts'"[21] – the promotion of Madras to a municipal corporation should perhaps not be regarded as an early manifestation of the spirit which, much later, was to lead to the introduction of representative institutions in the British Empire. Indeed, it is questionable whether Corporation and Court were more of a success than Batavia's civic bodies, which have been qualified as so many Potemkin villages. Fawcett writes that "when in 1692 the Company expostulated with the Madras Government for having too many English Aldermen and desired that most of them should be supplied by 'the heads of the severall foreigne Casts,' the

19. J. Shaw, *The Charters of the High Court of Judicature at Madras and the Courts which Preceded it* (Madras, 1888), quoted after Reyes, *Approaches*, 21.

20. Love, *Vestiges*, 497. See also Fawcett, *The First Century*, 204.

21. Shaw, *The Charters of the High Court of Judicature at Madras and the Courts which Preceded it* (Madras 1888), quoted after Reyes, *Approaches*, 21. Jain explains: "The Corporation . . . was to consist of a Mayor, twelve Aldermen and from 60 to 120 Burgesses." (*Outlines*, 21.). He adds that "at least three Aldermen were required to be covenanted British servants of the Company while the remaining nine could belong to any nationality. The break-up of the first twelve Aldermen appointed by the Charter itself was as follows: Englishmen, 3; Hindus, 3; Frenchmen, 1; Portuguese, 2; Jews and Armenians, 3" (Ibid., 22.). Muslims are conspicuous by their absence.

reply was given that it was found difficult to reduce the number of English Aldermen, as the Armenians refused to accept the office, the Jews qualified for it had left Madras, the Portuguese were unwilling to officiate for fear of their countrymen settled at St. Thomé, and it was not safe to confide in the Musselmen."²² However, the principle of indigenous association with the Company's administration and jurisdiction had been established, and was maintained even when, nearly forty years later, municipal corporations and mayors' courts of a less straightforward kind were set up in all three English presidency towns in India – Madras, Bombay, and Calcutta.

In so far as there were, during the first two or three generations, significant differences between EIC and VOC in the field of administrative and judicial practice – in the sphere of the EIC there was e.g. neither a capital settlement like Batavia nor a centralized overseas administration, nor a collection of colonial laws comparable to the Statutes of Batavia – these were probably due partly to national tradition, the English being less systematic and preferring to "stumble into wisdom,"²³ and partly to the unequal experiences which their countries were going through. While the Seven Provinces settled down to a quieter life after the 1630s, when the tide had turned in their long struggle for independence, the British Isles ran into the heavy weather of their civil wars and revolution. Thus, it was not before 1657 that Cromwell's charter, taken over with few material changes by Charles II in 1661, brought about the EIC's transformation into a company with a permanent stock of capital, a step which had been taken by the VOC a whole generation earlier. Even then the Company, vulnerable after 1688 because of its close relations with the former Stuart régime, did not really come to rest, having to defend its monopoly again and again. However, the long-term development of England's Asia trade did probably not suffer in all these vicissitudes, and the evolution of the Company's administration and jurisdiction were also apparently little affected.

Admittedly, these are matters which will become clearer only after a good deal of systematic comparative research has been undertaken. What can be said today is that both great East India

22. Fawcett, *The First Century*, 204. See also Love, *Vestiges*, 503. Whether Reyes, *Approaches*, 21–22, is right in saying, "The Mayor's Court came to represent an exclusively English outlook", will have to be borne out by detailed research. Jain, *Outlines*, 22 n. 2, points out: "From the 'Minutes of Proceedings' in the Mayor's Court, 1716–1719 (Madras Govt. Press), it appears that the various castes continued to be represented amongst the Aldermen and Burgesses even as late as 1719."
23. G. Radbruch, *Der Geist des englischen Rechts* (Göttingen, 1956), 64.

companies adhered during the whole length of their existence to the same principle, as far as the law to be administered in their overseas settlements was concerned. European law, that is to say, the law of the state from which a company derived its authority, reigned supreme – either directly as the law which was in force in the metropolis, or indirectly in the shape of company-made rules and regulations – but local customs and circumstances were taken into consideration. The question of the judiciary was settled in like manner, and also at an early date, never to be reopened during the age of the companies. Both VOC and EIC entrusted the administration of justice together with the general administration and all other functions to their allround servants, who in this way were made merchant-judges,[24] merchant-administrators, -soldiers, -diplomats, and so on. As has been mentioned, "non-official" Europeans or Asians – freeburghers of the Dutch settlements, free-merchants of the English settlements, or representatives of non-European communities, like the Chinese "captains" – were sometimes vested with quasi-judicial powers, sometimes only consulted. But even where the merchant-judges acted on their own, they were to pay attention to the local circumstances of a case, a requirement which was probably facilitated by the fact that only very few of those vested with judicial powers had any previous knowledge of European law.[25]

Interests

The Europeans carried their law with them wherever they went. Nothing else would have been possible, for purely legal reasons, where they remained subjects of their sovereign or citizens of their republic. Even in places where they were strangers and guests, it was natural for them to cling to what they knew. This disposition can be found in many cultures and is e.g. at the root of the consular institution. The fact, therefore, that European law was made the law ruling the overseas settlements poses no problem, at least

24. I borrow this term from Fawcett, *The First Century*, vol. 6.
25. An exception from the rule that no professional lawyers should be appointed as judges was made when, in order to check the illegal and increasingly harmful competition of the interlopers, the EIC obtained a charter from Charles II that empowered it to establish admiralty courts (1683) (cf. Fawcett, *The First Century*, 121–56, 202 ff; Jain, *Outlines*, 19–21). Under this charter civil lawyers were sent out to Bombay and Madras. However, the admiralty courts soon fell into decay.

not at first sight. On closer scrutiny, however, the question arises why the companies should have claimed to make European law applicable, on principle, to all their subjects, Europeans and Asians alike.

It was a matter of course that Europeans, company servants and others, preferred to be judged according to the law of their mother country if there was a dispute among themselves. It is also obvious that they preferred their own law in suits against Asians, but why European law should have been regarded as applicable – even if only on principle – in cases concerning only Asians is not at all evident. It may actually seem puzzling in view of the fact that the merchant-judges whom the companies charged with the administration of justice, who were rarely familiar with the law of the parent state, tended to interpret quite extensively the provision that local customs and conditions should be considered. So, whence the insistence on the supremacy of European law?

The answer is, in a nutshell, that the Europeans were seeking, right from the beginning, not only profit, but also power, not only trade, but also dominion. Trade alone may have been possible, at least in the beginning, when only one European nation, the Portuguese, penetrated into the Eastern Seas. Pure trade might even have been profitable. However, trade was never the sole aim. For various reasons – ingrained fear and hatred of that hereditary enemy, the Muslim; lust for plunder; European rivalries spilling over across the seas, etc. – the Europeans wanted, if not dominion of the high seas, illusory in the age of sail, then certainly control of strategic sealanes and areas, and they also wanted the indispensable corollary, the secure base on land. On the whole, there was up to the end of our period a balance of threats between the Europeans and the Asian powers, with the Europeans being stronger at sea and the "country powers" stronger on land.[26] Normally the Europeans respected this truth. If they forgot or ignored it, as in Josiah Child's disastrous war against the Great Mogul (1685/86), a bloody reminder followed promptly. The European beachheads, however, did not really belong to the continental sphere, but were rather elements of maritime power.

At any rate, this is what the Portuguese and after them the companies strove to achieve, in many instances with success. They felt extremely uncomfortable in factories of the Surat or Canton type

---

26. Those South-East Asian states who were themselves maritime powers were of course vulnerable.

where they were guests, and guests among other guests, of Asian potentates whom they usually regarded as dangerously unreliable, and whom they imagined as constantly bent upon a thousand vexations. Their common desire was, therefore, to make the factories European territories in the full sense of the term, that is to say, far ends of European lines of power. Batavia's early history is an example among many: At first an unfortified, smallish trading place dependent upon the good-will of the local prince, it was walled in without permission and victoriously defended in 1619, the year of its "foundation." Where such a procedure was impossible, as in Surat, the Great Mogul's main port-city, the second-best solution might have been to weigh anchor and shift to a more suitable place. The general tendency was to escape, wherever possible, from the overall balance of threats by making the more important settlements immune from the pressures of the surrounding country powers.

The claim to make European law, at least in theory, the "lex terrae" of the settlements and of the tiny extra-muros territories belonging to them was thus only a reflex of the urge to be master, the sole master, in one's house. This "house," however, was as much a "factory," that is to say a market and a store, as it was a stronghold, and as a factory it was expected to work smoothly and profitably. This meant for instance that the companies were seeking not "good," but functional government, a government geared to the necessities of a foreign merchant-sovereign, and this kind of government could very well be provided by the merchant-judge-cum-administrator. Contrary to the professional lawyer, against whom there seems to have been, right in the middle of his spectacular rise, a widespread and intense aversion, the company servant made guardian of the law could be expected to avoid costly, formalistic, long drawn-out litigation, and thus to save the time and money of all concerned. At the same time, the merchant-judge may have seemed to be a much more pliable instrument in the hand of his employers than the professional lawyer who pretended to a certain independence. This, however, was wishful thinking, if not cynical make-believe.

The East India companies differed from later business corporations in two important respects. They were, as has already been discussed, designed to act the part not only of commercial enterprises, but of something very different as well, namely quasi-sovereign powers. At the same time, their economic functions were as yet insufficiently developed, even in terms of contemporary expectations. Experienced directors and servants were painfully aware

that the companies lacked the instruments necessary for a proper
financial management, a management which would have enabled
them to attempt something approaching "maximisation of
profits."[27] It was also common knowledge that the companies were,
more often than not, badly served by their own representatives and
employees, and unable to effect a lasting change in this vital respect.
With great effort, they could sometimes rouse themselves to destroy,
but they could not yet control.[28]

Just like many of the servants of the "estado da India" before
them, most company servants had strong private interests which
often ran counter to the corporate interests of their masters. As one
historian of this still rather neglected side of the age of the companies
put it, the typical company servant had come out in order "to make
a fortune; the quicker the better."[29] This appetite could only have
been whetted by the awareness that – given medical ignorance as
well as European clothing and unrestrained eating and drinking
habits stubbornly clung to in the tropics – less than half of those who
came out as temporary emigrants would live to see their distant
homes again.[30] A clearsighted contemporary drew the obvious conclusion from this state of things when he remarked that "he who
makes haste to get rich, cannot be innocent."

In a world such as this, any function which did not hold out
prospects of making money in excess of the – admittedly rather
meagre – official pay, was bound to be unpopular,[31] and was therefore either shunned or made profitable, by hook or by crook.[32]

27. Cf. F.S. Gaastra, "The shifting balance of trade of the Dutch East India
Company," in *Companies and Trade*, ed. L. Blussé and F.S. Gaastra (Leiden, 1981),
54–55, 65 ff. See also K. Glaman, *Dutch Asiatic Trade, 1620–1740* (Copenhagen, 1958),
1 ff.; 244 ff.; H.-J. Leue, "Die europäischen Asien-Kompanien, 1600–1800," *Geschich-
te, Politik und ihre Didaktik* 15 (1987), 12–28.
28. Cf. J. Hicks, *A Theory of Economic History* (Oxford, 1969), 100.
29. I.B. Watson, "Indian merchants and English private interests: 1659–1760," in
India and the Indian Ocean, 1500–1800, ed. Ashin Das Gupta and M.N. Pearson
(Calcutta, 1987), 302. Cf. P. Spear, *The Nabobs. A Study of the Social Life of the English in
Eighteenth Century India* (Oxford, 1963), 14.
30. Cf. P.J. Marshall, *East Indian Fortunes. The British in Bengal in the Eighteenth
Century* (Oxford, 1976), 214 ff.: Blussé, *Strange Company*, 173; C.R. Boxer, *The Dutch
Seaborne Empire. 1600–1800* (London, 1977), 208–09; *Hobson-Jobson*, 24; Spear, *The
Nabobs*, 67–68, 87–88.
31. Cf. the difficulties to find candidates for the (adulterated) Admiralty Court at
Madras: Love, *Vestiges*, 559; ibid vol. 2, 30; Jain, *Outlines*, 20, n. 2. These difficulties
are characteristically passed over by Fawcett, *The First Century*, 206–07.
32. François Valentijn calls the post of secretary to the Batavian "Weeskamer"
(Orphan Board) "one of the most profitable little offices": Klerk de Reus, *Geschichtlicher Ueberblick der Compagnie*, 155, n. 1. It is very unlikely that his remark refers to the
official salary of the secretary.

Nevertheless, it is undeniable that there was a certain demand for company justice not only on the part of Europeans, but among the Asian population of the companies' settlements, too. The Europeans, birds of passage as nearly all of them were,[33] and eager to return home rich, were obviously interested in the security of their property and in its safe transfer home, either for their own benefit or for that of their heirs. Thus, when the directors of the EIC solicited for a new charter in the 1720's, their purpose seems to have been to obtain courts, the decisions of which could not easily be challenged at home, particularly in matters of inheritance. Indeed, this is what the Company secured through the charter granted by George I in 1726, a document which, apart from establishing Mayors' Courts not only in Madras, but also in the other two presidency towns, Calcutta and Bombay, conferred the status of King's Courts upon the regular courts of the settlements. Such King's Courts, even if far from the ultimate seat of power, could be expected to command greater respect in England and to find more acceptance on the spot.[34]

A measure of acceptance – indispensable, as Tocqueville noted, for any judicial system – was also forthcoming from the Asian subjects of the companies. Most of them had come to the European settlements in order to stay, and as the true citizens of their adopted homes, they expected probably not less security than the fleeting population of "White Town." As has already been mentioned, such security could be demanded, as far as the "personal law" of the different communities was concerned, either from the traditional caste tribunals and similar institutions, or from the agents of the "state." If a plaintiff or, according to the circumstances of the case, a defendant, found that his interests would be better served by the Company authorities, it was only natural for him to apply to them, which seems to have happened more often than either the Europeans or the indigenous umpires liked.

A push-effect must have been produced by the comparatively unsettled state of the indigenous society. In the "newly-sprouted plural societies of the European settlements, with their overly materialist ethics and their heavily mixed castes, ethnic groups and religious communities," it could not have been an easy task to find

33. In the English settlements there was no comparable counterpart to the sedentary Dutch "freeburghers." The English freemerchants were all eager to return home as soon as possible, as were practically all company servants.

34. Cf. Fawcett, *The First Century*, 214 ff.; Keith, *A Constitutional History of India*, 18; Jain, *Outlines*, 43 ff.

umpires of generally recognized impartiality and rectitude. Those "who were recognized by the . . . [European] establishment as the leaders of society were not necessarily so accepted by the various segments of . . . [the indigenous] society."[35] As for the pull, this would have made itself felt even if the indigenous society would have been intact, because the relative ruthlessness which was a major characteristic of the European judicial process could not but be attractive to many. Nevertheless, one must beware of concluding all too hastily that the European courts were popular.

The notion that European courts of law were popular among the Asian subjects of the companies or that, alternately, Asians were litigious, goes back perhaps to the eighteenth or even the seventeenth century, when it was found that some courts were, at least temporarily, unable to cope with their work. For instance, a few years after the new Mayors' Courts had been set up under the charter of 1726, the directors of the EIC complained: "Little did we imagine that the number of suits at Fort St. George should rival those of one of the principal courts at Westminster Hall. This can be owing only to a vexatious temper, or to a wanton desire to try the experiment of law suits upon the coming of this new charter."[36] This need not be wrong simply because the London directors, or the French at Pondicherry, couched their observations in such arrogant terms.[37] However, what we can glean from such evidence with any certainty is simply that some courts had, at any rate from time to time, more work to do than they could dispose of without undue delay, but this is insufficient to prove their "popularity." The correct answer may be that the number of cases brought before particular courts – in other words, the demand for European judicial services – was high compared with "supply." This demand may very well have been low in relation to the volume of litigation disposed of by non-European tribunals or in comparison to the overall needs for conflict resolution, needs which, for a variety of reasons, may largely have remained inarticulate.

35. S. Arasaratnam, *Merchants, Companies and Commerce on the Coromandel Coast, 1650–1740* (Delhi, 1986), 286.
36. Love, *Vestiges*, 245.
37. Cf. Thomas, *Le Conseil Supérieur*, 112; see also M.N. Pearson, *The Portuguese in India* (Cambridge, 1987), 94.

Arrangements

With respect to the administration of justice, Arasaratnam describes a case brought by Rawson Hart against the Madras shroff[38] Gopaldas Nundalal in 1734:

> Hart had charged compound interest for money that was due to him from the shroff on a bill of exchange from Surat to Madras. Nundalal argued in court that compound interest was never known or practised among merchants in Madras. The Mayor's Court found in favour of Nundalal and added that compound interest could not be admitted in any English court of record[39] and was contrary to the express laws of England. Hart thereupon appealed to the Governor-and-Council, which set aside the Mayor's Court judgement and found in his favour. It held that compound interest was a just charge, confirmed by custom in Madras, Bengal, Surat and most other parts of India, the disallowance of which would prejudice the credit of Madras. So here we have two conflicting opinions and there is no further evidence of cases of this type to pursue the matter further.[40]

In this case, like in so many others, we learn only which law the judges claimed to have applied – English law in the Mayor's Court, and local customary law in the court of appeal formed by the Governor-and-Council. What they really did – whether they followed any norms at all, whether they decided freely from case to case,[41] or whether they indulged, from whatever motives, in arbitrariness, taking the law as a mere pretext – is a question which can be answered only after a close scrutiny of the particular case. That is to say, on close examination of the applicable law, European and/or indigenous; of the exact circumstances of the case in question; and perhaps, of contemporary accounts and comments, such as those of the Company's Standing Counsel and Attorney, who was of course a professional lawyer, and who after 1732 periodically examined the records sent in by the Company's major courts.[42] In general terms, we still know much too little about the actual administration of justice of the different "East India" companies, great and small. So

---

38. A money-changer, a banker, from Arabic *sarraf*: cf. Hobson-Jobson, 831–832.

39. Court of record: "a court whose proceedings are formally enrolled and valid as evidence of fact, being also a court of the sovereign, and having authority to fine or imprison." The *Oxford English Dictionary*, 2nd ed., 1989.

40. Arasaratnam, *Merchants*, 281–82.

41. Cf. M. Weber, *Wirtschaft und Gesellschaft. Grundriß der verstehenden Soziologie* (Tübingen, 1972), 394; M. Weber, *Economy and Society, An Outline of Interpretive Sociology*, vol. 2 (Berkeley, 1978), 654.

42. Cf. Fawcett, *The First Century*, 223–24; Jain, *Outlines*, 50.

much, however, we can say even today that the different fields of law
were tilled with different intensity.

Personal Law: The Theory and Practice of Non-interference

A field of which the companies normally fought shy was what later
came to be known as "personal law," that is, "in general the family
law, with especial reference to marriage and succession . . . determined by reference to the religion which . . . [an individual] pro-
fesses or purports to profess or is presumed to profess."[43] Whether in
Batavia, in some "out-station" like Melaka, Formosa or Ceylon, or
in an English settlement like Bombay, Madras or Calcutta, everywhere there was an unmistakable tendency to keep clear of the
natives' disputes and to leave them, as far as might be, to their own
devices. Like the indirect rule of a later age, this policy was no mark
of respect for the alien culture, but rather an expression of the desire
to save money and trouble in a field of administration and jurisdiction which was not regarded as particularly important. To meddle
in matters of "personal law" risked to stir up unrest and to occasion
expenses in an area which was at once sensitive and, under normal
circumstances, of little concern to the companies.

Fortunately a legal dissertation submitted a few years ago, one of
the rare exceptions from the rule that there is as yet a great lack of
recent detailed studies on legal expansion before 1750, enables us to
get a clearer insight into the actual working of a dualistic administration of personal laws – its motives, its mechanisms, and the
largely unforeseen problems springing from the very dualism of the
system.[44] Although this study ranges from the seventeenth century
far beyond the "1750" demarcation, and although it is mainly concerned with the question of to what extent and in what sense Hindu
personal law, as it came to be applied by mid-nineteenth century at
Madras and at Pondicherry, had been conditioned by the legal
traditions of England and France, it is most useful for us because of
its account of the eighteenth-century legal system of Madras.[45]

As has already been pointed out above, the Corporation and the

---

43. J.D.M. Derrett, *Religion, Law and the State in India* (London, 1968), 39.
44. Cf. Reyes, *Approaches*.
45. Cf. Reyes, *Approaches*, 389. Reyes, it is true, deals only briefly with the institutions outside the Mayor's Court, but what he has to say on this particular forum is
remarkable. The established legal histories, on the other hand, present a complete
picture of the judicial set-up, but do not care to show in detail how it worked. An
attempt will therefore be made here to glean the essential points from both.

Mayor's Court, which had been functioning at Madras from 1688 onwards, were replaced under the charter of 1726 by remodelled institutions of the same name, institutions which were also established at Bombay and Calcutta. This time the purpose was not to win the goodwill of the native population, but to establish a forum which enjoyed the authority of a King's Court; thus the sizeable indigenous representation of the charter of 1687 was reduced to two aldermen, who could be subjects of any prince or state in amity with Great Britain. "In practice," says Jain, "no non-English alderman was ever appointed."[46] In addition, the jurisdiction of the Mayor's Court was confined to civil matters, criminal cases being handed over to the Governor and Council.[47] The offense of high treason did not fall into the purview of the court constituted by the Governor and Council, but otherwise they were competent, and no appeal to higher authority was apparently possible. With regard to the Mayor's Court, "the first appeal . . . lay, within fourteen days, to the Governor and Council, from where a further appeal could be lodged, within fourteen days, with the King-in-Council in all matters involving 1,000 pagodas or more. Thus, for the first time, a right of appeal to the King-in-Council from the decisions of the courts in India was granted."[48]

This did, however, not complete a presidency town's judicial system as instituted in 1726. From our point of view it is particularly important to note that in matters of civil law there functioned, below the Mayor's Court, not only the councils of the various castes, but also the indestructible Choultry Court. At Madras, governor Macrae and his council soon after the proclamation of the new charter had resolved that those members of council who were "Justices of the Peace should be also Justices of the Choultry to decide small causes up to Pags. 20. Realizing, however, that this plan would render decisions by Justices, who were incidentally members of a superior Court [the court of the Governor and Council], liable to an appeal to the inferior Mayor's Court, the [Madras] Government determined . . . [after a few weeks] to erect a Sheriff's Court in

---

46. Jain, *Outlines*, 49.
47. Ibid., 45, 47. Fawcett, eager as always to put in a good word for his compatriots, stresses to institution of trial by jury (*The First Century*, 217–218). Jain, on the other hand, points to the fact that criminal justice was vested in the executive, "certainly . . . a retrograde step" (*Outlines*, 47, 49). For a systematic comparison between the systems of 1687 and 1726, see Jain, idem, 49–50.
48. Jain, *Outlines*, 45–46. The pagoda was a South Indian gold coin equivalent to 8 shillings: cf. L. Dermigny, *La Chine et l'Occident. La Commerce à Canton au XVIIIe siècle, 1719–1833* Vol. III (Paris, 1964), 1565.

which such petty causes should be decided."[49] This solution, however, found no favor with the directors in London, and from mid-
1729 the Justices of the Peace again sat at the Choultry.[50]

Whereas the Choultry Court had always been, and was to remain,
a court where a rough and ready "palmtree justice" was dispensed
in petty causes, liable to rehearing in a superior forum, the arbitration of the heads of caste was meant to be a self-sufficient branch of
jurisdiction and to extend to small as well as big matters of personal
law. This is, at any rate, how Reyes reads the charter of 1726 and the
texts relating thereto. One of these documents was forwarded to
Madras, Bombay, and Calcutta together with the "judicial charter"
itself and bears quoting again:

> We think it necessary here to acquaint you that this new Charter . . . is
> principally designed for the Government of Europeans and what relates
> to them directly, or wherein the Natives may be concerned with them. We
> add, and do you acquaint the Mayor's Court for your and their constant
> observance, that the Gent(ues) and other Natives having particular cus-
> toms of their own in the disposal of their deceaseds' Estates, you must by
> no reasons intermeddle therein, but leave the management intirely to
> themselves, for fear of the unforeseen mischiefs that may arise if their old
> customs are broke into: and further, that they be allowed to live in the full
> enjoyment of the priviledges of their respective Casts, provided they do
> nothing to the prejudice of the English Government.[51]

Reyes comments: "Questions of succession and inheritance are
specially marked as areas best left to be decided according to indigenous law. But 'privileges of their respective Casts' might be
understood as embracing any variety of customs and usages. Thus,
the Company suggests that Indians be left, in fact encouraged, to
decide their disputes themselves."[52] If, however, Indians insisted on
having their suits decided by the Mayor's Court, then English law
must be applied, and English law only. The latter point was elaborated by the London directors a few years after the inauguration of
the new courts:

> Such differences that happen between the Natives, in which the King's
> subjects are not involved, these may and should be decided among
> themselves, according to their own Customs or by Justices or Referees to

---

49. Love, *Vestiges*, 243.
50. Ibid.
51. Quoted after Love, *Vestiges*, 241.
52. Reyes, *Approaches*, 25.

be appointed by themselves or otherwise as they think fit; but if they request and choose them to be decided by English laws, these and those only must be pursued, and pursued too according to the directions in the Charter: and this likewise must be the case when differences happen between Natives and subjects of England, where either party is obstinate and determined to go to Law.[53]

After the French occupation of Madras (1746–1749), when it had been felt that a new charter had become desirable, the English East India Company went even a step further and "expressly excepted from the jurisdiction of the Mayor's Court all suits and actions between the natives only, and directed that these suits and actions should be determined among themselves, unless both parties submitted them to the determination of the Mayor's Court."[54] This provision, together with the charter of which it was an important part (charter of George II granted in 1753), remained in force until the end of the century when George III issued new letters patent establishing so-called "Recorders' Courts" in Bombay and Madras. It gave rise to a lot of difficulties and abuses, but before examining these consequences of the EIC's judicial policy, an attempt should be made to understand its underlying motives.

Until 1726, legal dualism in Madras had meant respect for the decisions of the caste councils, but also an active taking into account of indigenous customs by the English or English-dominated judicial institutions, particularly the Mayor's Court, which, when it was created by the charter of 1687, had received a sizeable indigenous representation. After 1726, the new Mayor's Courts, having practically lost all non-European members, were first discouraged and then even debarred from "entertaining a suit and action between . . . natives until both parties involved in a matter submitted it for the court's determination."[55] What had changed, what endured? As has already been pointed out, the charter of 1726 was solicited in order to obtain for the English courts of the settlements the status of King's Courts because these, as such, would command respect not only on the spot but at home as well. For this purpose, it was perhaps deemed necessary to make the new Mayor's Courts as "English" as possible – not, it is true, by saying as much in the charter itself, but by giving instructions to the governments of the

---

53. Dispatch of EIC to Madras, dated 12 February 1731, para. 112, Letter Book vol. 21, 174 (quoted after Fawcett, *The First Century*, 224–25).
54. Fawcett, *The First Century*, 225.
55. Jain, *Outlines*, 55.

presidency towns to "pursue" English law only. However, having
departed from the established practice in such an important respect
for the sake of the Company, its servants, and the European community at large, it was necessary to consider the interests of the
non-Europeans, too, and here the course followed hitherto was on
principle continued. That is to say, the Company adhered to its
policy of minimum interference with matters of personal law; therefore it was, under the changed circumstances, only consequent to
make non-Europeans look for conflict resolution outside the Mayor's
Court. If, however, an Asian subject insisted on submitting its cause
to that court, it was free to do so on the clear understanding that the
court would have to base itself on English law only, substantive and
adjective. In other words, the Company did not really want to
change its judicial policy, but it was eager to introduce a new
element – the higher status of the Mayors' Courts – and it adjusted
the judicial set-up accordingly.

So much for the probable intentions. The consequences turned
out to be quite different. The "natives," far from being deterred by a
purely English court, flocked to it in large numbers, larger than it
was sometimes able to cope with.[56] This was not only troublesome
for a bench which was required to stick to English law – in actual
fact, the Company's injunctions were interpreted quite liberally[57] –
but it also provoked difficulties of a different kind. After all, every
case of personal law brought at some stage before the Mayor's Court
was a case withdrawn from the jurisdiction of the caste leaders, who,
having cause to fear for their authority, repeatedly asked for remedy,
until the charter of 1753 prohibited the Mayor's Court from taking
cognizance of any case involving two Indian parties unless they
submitted it unanimously. Even then, however, there were ways and
means of dragging a reluctant party before the Mayor's Court so
that the caste leaders' grievance persisted.[58]

It is one of the merits of Reyes' thesis to have shown that the
British policy-makers had to consider at least two kinds of Indian
interests, those of the caste leaders and their loyal followers, and
those of a considerable number of individuals who preferred the
services of a European court to the traditional means of conflict
resolution. But what exactly prompted an Indian citizen of Madras
to stray from his flock? Was there really, as the London directors,

56. Cf. Reyes, *Approaches*, 37, 37 n. 26, 52–53.
57. Cf. below n. 62.
58. Cf. Reyes, *Approaches*, 38, 38 n. 27, 54; Jain, *Outlines*, 55; Fawcett, *The First Century*, 225.

taken aback by the volume of litigation in the reformed Mayor's Court, tended to think, "a vexatious temper, or . . . a wanton desire to try the experiment of law suits"?[59] Or are we to assume that the impartiality of many caste elders was in doubt? Basically, there seem to have been two reasons for an Indian subject of the Company to prefer the Mayor's Court to a caste council. One was the superior power of the European bench, i.e. the certainty that its decision would be enforced. The other was the probability that in the case of a success more would be gained by the decision of a European court. In the words of Derrett: "The secret of the flood of Indian cases to the early British courts, such as the Mayor's Courts, lay in the immediacy and violence of the remedies offered. . . . The chances of losing a good case were high, but if one won, the prizes were larger than would be available under the native system. . . . [the Indian] could not only get his decrees executed, without relative delay or appeal, to the great discomfiture of the opposite party, but he would be able to gain legal advantages of which the native legal system knew nothing."[60]

That the prizes were apt to be larger in a system which was designed to arrive at "decisions" rather than at a consensus is obvious. But why should a caste decree, as a rule, not have been executed as speedily as a court decree? An answer to this question can, given the present state of research, only be tentative, but it should be attempted. In Hindu society, the caste tribunal had from time immemorial been a powerful institution. In "pre-British times,", says Derrett, "its jurisdiction was as wide, as important and as effective as that of the civil and criminal court."[61] Its main source of authority was religion, and its sharpest weapon was excommunication. However, even under "normal" circumstances "litigation over property and debt would not constitute 'religious' issues,"[62] and Madras society was not at all normal from the orthodox point of view. It must have been a jumbled-up "plural" society with "overly materialist ethics"[63] where the typical elements of Indian society had first to fall into place. However, before that could

59. Cf. n. 38.
60. Derrett, *Religion, Law and the State*, 279.
61. Derrett, *Religion, Law and the State*, 81 and 274–79.
62. Reyes, *Approaches*, 40 n. 29. Reyes goes on to say: "to invoke excommunication as a penalty in these instances, would run the risk of the sanction against an individual being ignored by the other members, thereby undermining the authority of the heads of caste even when acting in religious matters."
63. Cf. n. 35.

be accomplished, traditional values and institutions were apt to be perverted.

There is indeed an endless flow of complaints about corrupt practices among Madras caste elders, and some of these allegations would have been well-founded. But many were trumped up or exaggerated in order to be used as weapons. What Colebrooke later remarked about Bengal is probably also true of the decline of caste arbitration at Madras: "Every dissatisfied party unable to impeach the award of an arbitrator without proving partiality or corruption, set about calumniating the arbitrator, and imputed corruption to him simply, that he might obtain a revision of the award."[64] Such a course of action could be tempting, if there was much to gain or little to lose, and it was feasible because the Mayor's Court was in effect a court of appeal: the British allowed revisions of caste awards even if both parties had pledged themselves to abide by the eventual award.

In other words, neither did the British share their authority with the native leaders in a clearly circumscribed field of jurisdiction, nor did they delegate the powers necessary to uphold the authority of the caste tribunals. The consequences which such a state of things could produce have been made very plain by Reyes. Analyzing in detail a number of cases recorded in the papers of the Mayor's Court and in other sources of the time, Reyes illustrates the inner contradictions of a system which looked to the traditional authorities of the indigenous society for administering personal law and for preserving, more generally, a good order among the Company's Asian subjects, but which, at the same time, withheld the power required: "So long as force or coercion remained the prerogative of the state alone, the effort to keep indigenous litigation apart from English courts was doomed to failure."[65]

As has been stressed above, we have only the – incomplete – records of the Company courts to rely upon. There are no known records of caste panels or similar indigenous tribunals, so that we do not know how many or how few disputes were decided in the traditional manner without ever coming to the notice of the Europeans. In many cases, however, the authority of the traditional umpires was challenged by one or the other party, and if that happened the matter would end up with a Company court, whether the Europeans liked it or not.

---

64. Henry Thomas Colebrooke's note on the reasons for the decline of caste arbitration in Bengal, quoted after Reyes, *Approaches*, 54 n. 45.
65. Reyes, Ibid., 53.

Thus, an important end of the 1726 arrangement was defeated. Another injunction of the London directors was also honored in the breach because, if the Mayor's Court took cognizance of a case involving two Indian subjects, it was not always found possible or desirable to stick to English law exclusively.[66] In other words, as things turned out, the Mayor's Court which functioned between 1726 and 1753, was not as different from its predecessor as the charter and the Company's instructions had meant it to be. After 1753, however, when the Court could no longer take up a suit between two natives unless it was submitted by both parties, it would indeed be justified to speak, as Jain did, of a denial of justice to the Indian citizens.[67] It is true, there were loopholes.[68] The charter's exclusion from the Mayor's Court of the "Indian natives of Madraspatnam" could be construed to mean that every Indian citizen of Madras born outside the jurisdiction of the Company was allowed to appeal to the Mayor's Court.[69] Another expedient which came to be widely used was the nominal transfer of claims to Europeans, and there was even a chance to drag a reluctant adversary before the Court.[70] In many instances, however, the Mayor's Court was out of reach from an Indian citizen, while the authority of the caste panels had not at all gained in the process. This does not mean that the panels were idle, but if a party was obstinate and willing to run the risk of caste opprobrium, it need not even have bothered about appearing before arbitrators, because contrary to the years 1726–1753 the Mayor's Court would not now take up the matter in the end.[71]

In a way, legal dualism is an attempt to have the cake and eat it too. In the long run the companies could not escape the lesson that there is an inherent contradiction between the claim to be master, the sole master, in one's house, and the desire to keep clear – for whatever reasons – of a good deal of what is going on in that house. Therefore, after some vain "stopgap measures," as Reyes calls

---

66. *Ibidem*, 42, 46–47, 53
67. Cf. Jain, *Outlines*, 58.
68. Cf. Reyes, *Approaches*, 53–57.
69. Bombay was a notable exception. Here the Mayor's Court "took the view that the 'natives' of Bombay were all British subjects because of the fact that Bombay had been ceded to the British Crown in full sovereignty by the Portuguese and, therefore, the restrictive words in the Charter did not cover them. The native inhabitants of Bombay were never actually exempted from the jurisdiction of the Mayor's Court." Jain, *Outlines*, 62.
70. Cf. Arasaratnam, *Merchants*, 288; Reyes, *Approaches*, 55–57.
71. Cf. Reyes, *Approaches*, 54.

them,[72] the EIC returned to the pre-1726 solution. In 1798 a new charter superseded the charter of 1753, establishing so-called "Recorders' Courts" in the place of the Mayor's Courts of Madras and Bombay; Calcutta, having replaced Madras as the most important English settlement in India, had received its "Supreme Court" already in 1744.[73] The Recorders' Courts, which in due course became the Supreme Courts of Madras and Bombay,[74] again applied, as the original Mayor's Court once had done, English law and indigenous customs as well, without thereby forfeiting their status as King's Courts. This time, however, the "Heads and Chiefs of all the respective Casts"[75] were not represented at the Bench.[76] While the idea of equality was finally beginning to assert itself in Europe, in Asia the partnership which may have existed here and there between Europeans and "orientals" was rapidly melting away before the growing European sense of superiority. But even if there had been indigenous brother judges. European law would progressively and inevitably have overgrown Asian customary law.[77] After all, one cannot monopolize power and share it at the same time.[78]

Objects of Closer Interest: Commerce and Public Order

The policy of non-interference in matters of personal law being inspired by considerations of expediency, company servants did not

72. Ibid., 57.
73. *Ibidem*, 62–65, and Jain, *Outlines*, 88, 138–39.
74. Cf. Jain, *Outlines*, 141.
75. Cf. n. 21.
76. Cf. Jain, *Outlines*, 139–40.
77. Cf. Reyes, *Approaches*, 63–64. The delegation of the necessary powers to the leaders of the indigenous communities would, in the long run, not have removed the dilemma either, because delegates act, by definition, in the name and with the consent of the higher authority on which they depend, and are liable to correction by that authority, which, wherever it interferes, abandons its aloofness at least temporarily. There are examples from the VOC's legal history which show that this was bound to happen. One is the case of a Chinese lady of Fort Zeelandia on Formosa, the widow of a rich merchant, who after the death of her husband would have got nothing under Chinese law, but eventually received "the cash in hand and 40 percent of the real property whereas the grandfather and the sons shared 60 percent. . . . The Dutch authorities [had] ordered the . . . [Chinese chiefs] to make an arrangement according to Chinese customs and law, but by which the widow was not wronged according to Dutch law." J.L. Oosterhoff, "Zeelandia, a Dutch colonial city of Formosa (1624–1662)," *Colonial Cities, Essays on Urbanism in a Colonial Context*, ed. R.J. Ross and G.J. Telkamp (Dordrecht, 1985), 58; see also B.H.M. Vlekke, *Nusantara, A History of the East Indian Archipelago* (Cambridge Ma., 1944), 173.
78. This was soon to be demonstrated by the fate of the indigenous "law officers," particularly the Islamic law officers who were associated with the administration of

hesitate to intervene more systematically if this seemed advisable in the – true or alleged – interests of their masters. Such a necessity arose, for instance, in Batavia in 1639 when the big Chinese entrepreneur Jan Con "who had been . . . instrumental in [the fortification of Batavia and in many other] important contractual engagements with the Company since the foundation of Batavia in 1619," died insolvent.[79] The authorities had been feeling all along that it was necessary "to put an end to the 'manifold frauds and malversations committed in the Chinese house of morning',"[80] and they now took the opportunity of the Chinese tycoon's bankruptcy in order to establish an "onchristelijke Boedelkamer" or "non-Christian Estate Chamber." This body, first set up in 1640 and comprising among its *boedelmeesters* company servants as well as Chinese citizens, was to mediate in the execution of solvent or insolvent estates of Chinese and other non-Christian citizens of Batavia, and did so with such success that the accumulation of capital and the emergence of a Chinese property-owning middle class were encouraged.[81]

With this example the borderline between family and commercial or contractual law, indistinct anyhow, has already been crossed. Another instance in which Asian "personal law" and other fields of law overlapped, was the problem of the joint responsibility of a Hindu family for obligations resulting from commercial ventures of one of its members. Here the tendency was to bring the joint-family obligation to an end if families had divided *de facto* and had operated separately for years.[82] However, as Arasaratnam points out, "it is

---

criminal law in Bengal. At first very powerful (at least in theory) because they represented the (Islamic) criminal law of the land, they were, parallel to the gradual supersession of the Islamic law by Company-made rules and regulations, reduced to the role of advisers. See J. Fisch, *Cheap Lives and Dear Limbs. The British Transformation of the Bengal Criminal Law 1769–1817* (Wiesbaden, 1983), 108ff. An alternative course which would have consisted in making them a partner in the administration of the emergent Anglo-Indian criminal law was sometimes recommended by the home authorities, but was stubbornly resisted on the spot. See Jain, *Outlines* 246–247.

79. Blussé, *Strange Company*, 50.
80. Ibid., 69. Already in 1624 a *Weeskamer* (Orphan Board) had been established for orphaned children of Christian parents or, at least, fathers. See also Klerk de Reus, *Geschichtlicher Ueberblick der Compagnie*, 154–156; Ball, *Indonesian Legal History*, 24.
81. Cf. Blussé, *Strange Company*, 70, 82–83; Klerk de Reus, *Geschichtlicher Ueberblick der Compagnie*, 156–58; Ball, *Indonesian Legal History*, 24.
82. Cf. Arasaratnam, *Merchants*, 282–86, 292 f. The "joint-family, the core of the Hindu personal law and its most difficult – to newcomers its least comprehensible – part" (Derrett, *Religion*, 400) has been defined by Sontheimer as "a property-acquiring, -managing and -enjoying unit centering around the relationship between father and son according to traditional law." See G.–D. Sontheimer, *The Joint Hindu Family. Its Evolution as a Legal Institution* (New Delhi, 1977), XX. It may sometimes,

difficult to assert whether there was a change or not [under European influence] without knowing the extent to which joint family estate was held in traditional practice to be inviolable, even in areas of high mobility, such as the coastal ports" of Coromandel.[83]

It is obvious that, the smooth functioning of their factories being uppermost in their minds, the companies and their servants took a much closer interest in commercial matters than in personal law. However, in the absence of a commercial "Reyes" – and one which, ideally, would focus its attention on the pre-1750 period – we cannot do more than point again to the basic field of forces. Not only was there in each company the inbuilt contradiction between corporate and private interests, but different private interests, too, would often rival each other: possibly the example quoted in the beginning of this section is a case in point. The least one can say in that instance is that it would be rash to equate the Mayor's Court with "private" and the Governor and Council with "corporate" interests. The governor of an English presidency town was at once head of the executive, legislator, chief justice, and a big trader in his own right,[84] and the same holds true of high company functionaries everywhere. For them the path of duty must have been hemmed with temptations.[85]

In criminal matters which, as such, directly affected not only the proper functioning, but the security of the settlements as well, the Europeans apparently never had any doubt that they themselves must take charge, and that the law to be applied was to be European law, i.e. the law of the parent state and/or company law, adjective as well as substantive.[86] Only if it came to inflicting capital punishment on a Muslim was there marked caution, and even then only if the neighboring potentates were Muslims, and if the Europeans had to be careful not to offend these neighbors.[87] After 1765, when the

---

but need not take the form of "a conglomeration of relatives of one household, i.e., a residential unit . . . [with] joint living, commensality, property held in common, and participation in common family worship" (ibid., XVIII).

83. Arasaratnam, *Merchants*, 293.

84. A well-known example is Thomas Pitt, the grandfather of William Pitt the elder. Having begun his career as a successful interloper, he was made governor of Madras (1698–1709) and acquired the famous Pitt diamond, which was later sold to the regent of France for 135,000 Pounds Sterling. Cf. Love, *Vestiges*, vol. 1, 461–462; vol. 2, 1–102; P.J. Marshall, "Private British trade in the Indian Ocean before 1800," in *India and the Indian Ocean 1500–1800*, ed. Ashin Das Gupta and M.N. Pearson (Calcutta, 1987), 286–87; Watson, "Indian merchants," 311–12.

85. Cf. Arasaratnam, *Merchants*, 258–65.

86. Cf. Fisch, *Cheap Lives and Dear Limbs*, 2.

87. In the instructions accompanying the charter of 1726 (see above), the governor

EIC, by now a formidable "country power" in its own right, had become the virtual ruler of Bengal, Bihar, and Orissa by acquiring the "diwani," i.e. the responsibility for finance and some aspects of justice, Warren Hastings' policy of leaving the Nawab in nominal charge of the "nizamat" – defense and law and order – did not prevent the governor or his successors from introducing changes which altered the Bengal administration and jurisdiction beyond recognition.[88] However sincerely individual EIC servants and the directors at home might have wished the Company to remain a mere prop and paymaster of the indigenous régime, "as strangers, the British could not rely on the traditional structure of power."[89] In order to maintain themselves, the merchants turned conquerors had to gain a firm grip on law and order, and for this purpose criminal jurisdiction was even more important than it had been formerly.[90]

Evaluations

There was no justice that a little money wisely distributed could not buy: this is how Alexander Hamilton, a Scottish country captain, judged the courts of Madras when he wrote down his experiences in the 1720s, having roamed the Eastern Seas from one end to the other for thirty-five years, and having visited nearly all important trading places from Mokka in the West to Japan in the East.[91] Admittedly, the captain had not much sympathy with the English East India

---

and council at Madras were still exhorted by the London directors to be mindful of Muslim power and susceptibility: "You must also be very careful to avoid as much as possible putting any of the Moors to death, unless the crime is of a very high nature, such as Murther and Pyracy, and the proofs thereof be very positive and plain, lest the Mogul's Governours make it a handle for raising disturbances, of which it may not be easy to foresee or prevent the ill consequences." Love, *Vestiges*, 241–242. In the 1680s, François Martin at Pondicherry had even more reason to be wary, since his infant settlement was still at the mercy of the surrounding country powers. Cf. F. Martin, *India in the Seventeenth Century*, ed. L. Varadarajan (Delhi, 1981–85), 1075f.

88. This transformation is the subject of Fisch, *Cheap Lives and Dear Limbs*.

89. Fisch, Ibid., 134.

90. The counterpart to the administrative and judicial penetration of Bengal by the British was their increasing participation, diplomatic and military, in the game of Indian power politics, particularly in times of intensified European rivalry. See P.J. Marshall, *Bengal: The British Bridgehead. Eastern India 1740–1828* (Cambridge, 1987), and S. Förster, "Imperialismus aus Versehen? Die britische Eroberung Indiens, 1798–1819," in *Britische Übersee-Expansion und britisches Empire vor 1840*, (ed. J. Osterhammel, Bochum, 1987).

91. Hamilton's verdict has often been quoted. See e.g. Arasaratnam, *Merchants*, 293; Jain, *Outlines*, 23.

Company and its servants, but there are other indictments of a
similar kind and only recently Arasaratnam has painted a very
somber picture of the conditions prevailing under company rule,
concluding that "there seems no contrast in essence between the
exercise of power in . . . [the European] enclaves and in the neigh-
bouring hinterland administrations."[92]

On the other hand, an Indian contemporary of Captain Hamilton, and one who is not suspected of having been partial to the
English or to foreigners in general, has left a Sanskrit poem in which
the following verse is to be found:

> Never do they seize the flow of others' wealth unlawfully. They tell no
> untruths. They create a marvelous object. They themselves inflict punish-
> ment upon their offenders in accordance with the law. Now you must
> accept that there are virtues even in the "Hunas" who are sinks of
> iniquity.[93]

Derrett has established that the place mentioned elsewhere in the
text as the haunt of the "Hunas" is none other than Madras and
that these "Hunas" are therefore neither, as a later Indian trans-
lator of the poem suggested, the White Huns who devastated northern India in ancient times, nor, as one English sanskritist thought,
the Portuguese, but rather the British.[94] The value of the compli-
ment paid to them is enhanced by the fact that the author of the
poem, the Telugu-speaking Brahmin Venkatadhvarin, an extremely
popular satirical poet of the later seventeenth century, had even less
sympathy with strangers and unbelievers than Captain Hamilton
had with the EIC.[95] The "image" of the Madras administration can
therefore, at least temporarily, not have been too bad.

92. Arasaratnam, *Merchants*, 264–65. Cf. Blussé's verdict on the administration of
justice in seventeenth-century Batavia: Blussé, *Strange Company*, 257. Very critical
eighteenth-century remarks on the servants of the *Compagnie des Indes* are quoted in
Thomas, *Le Conseil Supérieur*, 72 ff.

93. Derrett, *Religion, Law and the State*, 227. The "marvelous object" referred to in
the verse was apparently a clock. Derrett explains: "The ability of the British to
import manufactured goods, and indeed the skill of Europeans generally in clock-
making and the like would go far to endear them to a nation like the Indian. . . . What
really interested the Hindu observer was the incredible ability to inflict penalties, to
administer justice, to one's own immediate associates, irrespective of their influence
and without fear of their resentment. Justice without fear or favour was evidently a
foreign characteristic, a British quality recognised by even so hostile a critic as the
learned author. What really hurt was that such ingenious and law-observing people
should not patronise Brahmins and indigenous scholarship and should not observe
the lavatory and other taboos of their high-caste neighbours." Ibid., 227–28.

94. Ibid., 226 and 222 n.1.

95. Ibid., 226–227.

There are also those historians who, mostly apologists of British imperial rule writing around the turn of the century or between the wars, liked to contend that the European settlements would not have grown as much as they did in wealth and in population, if conditions there had not compared favorably with those prevailing under the indigenous potentates. This reasoning seems plausible, but did the European enclaves really have to offer more to the average "immigrant" than security of life and property in order to attract him from the hinterland, or did they remain attractive even if the crying abuses depicted by Arasaratnam were known to occur from time to time? An answer to this question, let alone an overall evaluation of European jurisdiction in Asia, must await the results of a good deal of fresh comparative research, not only in the legal, but also in the social history of European expansion in the Eastern hemisphere. The same applies to a comparison between the standards of justice in the overseas settlements and at home.[96]

G.M. Trevelyan has this to say about the masters of rural England, the Justices of the Peace:

> In the middle years of the [eighteenth] century, Fielding, Smollett, and other observers of the injustices of life, bitterly satirised the irresponsible power of the J.P.s and its frequent misuse in acts of tyranny and favouritism. There was a corrupt type of J.P. known as 'trading justices', men of a lower order of society who got themselves made magistrates in order to turn their position to financial profit. But generally speaking, the Justices who did most of the work in rural districts were substantial squires, too rich to be corrupt or mean, proud to do hard public work for no pay, anxious to stand well with their neighbours, but often ignorant and prejudiced without meaning to be unjust, and far too much a law unto themselves.[97]

Was the average merchant-judge-cum-administrator closer to the "trading justice," or could he, like his landowning elder brother, cousin, or social "better" at home, afford to be above temptation? All that we can presumably say at this stage is that the administration and jurisdiction of the companies, and that of the "Estado da India" before them, was in essence an extension overseas of the

96. Cf. Thomas, *Le Conseil Supérieur*, 103, where, with regard to the French East India Company's judicial organization, the author asserts: "Notre organisation judiciaire était . . . supérieure à celle de la métropole et à celle de l'Inde musulmane ou brahmanique." The quality of the justice dispensed is of course a different matter.

97. G.M. Trevelyan, Illustrated English Social History, vol. 3: *The eighteenth century* (Harmondsworth, 1964), 108.

European Old Régime. And this meant not only the export of oddities, abuses, and injustices, but also, on principle, a rule of law. However much the merchant-judges may have been either unwilling or unable truly to administer the law, the principle that their duty was to apply permanent, uniform norms to individual cases, without fear or favor, had been established at the very outset and was as such never overturned.

Seen from this angle of vision, the sixteenth century and the age of the companies, c. 1600–1750, together form that epoch in the history of Europe's legal expansion into Asia during which the "subsumption" principle had been introduced, but was only haltingly implemented, because the necessary determination and the proper instrument, a professional and independent judiciary, were lacking. The next epoch did not begin before, in the second half of the eighteenth century, the "new conquistadores" appeared on the Indian scene, and before Europe's development itself took a decisive turn, ushering in a time of comparatively rapid and fundamental change. Then at last, with the professional lawyer gradually supplanting the lay judge-administrator in the more important courts, the theory and the practice of European jurisdiction in Asia came closer to each other. However, after the middle of the nineteenth century the momentum of the reform movement was spent, and progress toward the – still loudly proclaimed – ideals slowed down perceptibly. Significantly, a full-scale introduction of European law and legal institutions was only attempted in Meiji-Japan and, later on, in Kemal Atatürk's Turkey, that is to say in countries where an indigenous power élite had staked their all on a cultural revolution, convinced that nothing less held out hopes of survival in the modern world.[98]

98. Cf. Örücü's and Seizelet's contributions to this volume.

8

Wives, Widows and Workers: Women and the Law in Colonial India

DAGMAR ENGELS

Introduction

The history of women and colonial law in nineteenth- and early twentieth-century India is marked by a number of well-known issues, such as the legal abolition of female infanticide and *sati* (widow burning), the Hindu Widows Remarriage Act, the Age of Consent and the Child Marriage Restraint Act.[1] These acts suggest that the position of women within the family was of particular concern to the colonial legislators and deserves separate analysis. The editors of this volume suggest we highlight the encounter of two types of law, in the fields of property rights in land and of labor law, that is, a more or less class-based investigation of the impact of colonial law in Asia and Africa. This essay offers a different approach. Instead of class as the leading category for the analysis of law in colonial societies I have chosen gender. A gender-oriented analysis of law in the colonial setting assumes that the female experience of the law differs from male experience. Moreover, legislation – by men – on issues involving women and the predominantly male application of law in these cases reflects gender relations and gender stereotypes of the colonizing and colonized societies.

Most legal initiatives which concerned women dealt with problems which were linked to Hindu high-caste customs. In addition, they were justified with reference to Hindu scriptures. The colonial legislators claimed to be reinstating the true meaning of the *shastras*, that is authentic Hindu tradition, which had been misinterpreted

---

1. On the last two Acts, see Geraldine Forbes, "Women and modernity: the issue of child marriage in India," *Women's Studies International Quarterly* 2 (1979), 407–19; Dagmar Engels, "The Age of Consent Act of 1891: colonial ideology in Bengal," *South Asia Research* 3 (1983), 107–29.

during the past centuries allegedly for the sake of material and lascivious gains of Indian men.

Social legislation dealt with personal, as opposed to public, law. While the latter "sought to subordinate the rule of 'Indian status' to that of 'British contract'"[2] and thus to reshape and rationalize Indian legal affairs, colonial personal law – at least by definition – followed Hindu and Muslim traditions. According to J.D.M. Derrett, the outstanding scholar of Indian law, the early British lawgivers in India were predisposed to accept this division, because at home a similar division existed. Most matters of personal concern such as marriage and divorce, testaments, and religious worship were covered by ecclesiastical law. Moreover, Hastings and his colleagues believed their advisers who forecast serious opposition if the British interfered with personal and social issues.[3]

Taking the legal abolition of *sati* in 1828 as an example, the meaning of tradition in the colonial legal discourse will be examined. Implicitly, we will explore the duality laid out by Derrett. Does the division between Western rational public law and Indian traditional personal law stand? In addition, why did the British authorities in India spend as much energy as they did on trying to improve the situation of a tiny minority of Indian women, namely orthodox high-caste Hindu women, while ignoring the situation of the majority of women – of lower caste, outcast, *adivasi* and Muslim background? This essay will thus mainly focus on Hindu women and colonial law.

The acts, though reflecting conditions of a minority, were binding for all Indians, or at least all Hindus. They thus strengthened tendencies, often mentioned as Sanskritization or Brahminization, which propagated the validity of orthodox norms for the whole of Hindu society. The impact such policies had on other than high-caste women will be examined by looking at the implementation of the Hindu Widows' Remarriage Act of 1856, which legalized the remarriage of Hindu widows – against orthodox Hindu customs.

A gender-oriented analysis of colonial law does not imply that the class background of women was insignificant for their encounter with colonial law. In the last section of the essay we shall analyze factory law which regulated women's work to find out how far class,

2. D.A. Washbrook, "Law, state and agrarian society in colonial India," in *Modern Asian Studies* 15 (1981), 654; for the quoted terms, see B.S. Cohn, "From Indian status to British contract," *Journal of Economic History* 21 (1961), 613–628.

3. J.D.M. Derrett, *Religion, Law and the State in India* (London, 1968), 233; for a critical comment, see Washbrook, "Law," 651.

in addition to gender, determined the legal position of women. During the closing decades of the nineteenth-century women, mostly from a tribal, low-caste Hindu or low-class Muslim background, took up work in the organized sector, that is in mills, mines, and plantations. Underground and night labor as well as maternity were problems which required legal regulation. How far did the law protect women workers' interests? Did factory law reflect traditional or capitalist gender norms, and is Derrett's alleged division between personal and public law valid in the case of women factory workers' "public" rights?

The Abolition of *Sati*

In 1829 Lord Bentinck, the Governor-General, legally abolished *sati*, the practice of Hindu widow-burning. *Satis* were women who, allegedly voluntarily, agreed to be burnt on their husbands' funeral pyres as a demonstration of their close marital unity with the deceased and as an outward sign of their impeccable purity. By doing so they gained spiritual merit for themselves and their fathers' and husbands' families. It is hard to estimate how many women became *satis*. However, the extraordinary spiritual gains attached to the practice and the publicity which each *sati* received suggest that the custom was not particularly common in eighteenth-century India. But its publicity made it difficult for anybody to ignore it. Thus in the 1820s, as Michael Anderson has recently argued, the debate on *sati* "marshalled sufficient moral indignation among the British, both in India and at home, to break away from their policy of putative non-interference in indigenous legal relations."[4]

Administrators in the 1820s, however, did not understand their interference as a violation of Hindu social customs. Hindu society, particularly in Bengal, the British stronghold in early nineteenth-century India, was regarded as "a civil society paralysed by a barbaric, shastrified tradition," which was to be improved by "a rational, efficient state legal system bearing the enlightened policies of civilization and true Hindu principles."[5] During the colonial period this view of India and British colonialism was hardly challenged. As late as 1928, *sati* was still portrayed as a symbol of India's

4. Michael Roy Anderson, "Sati: the social history of a crime," School of Oriental and African Studies LLM Essay, July 1, 1988, 5–6.
5. Ibid., 6.

degeneration and Britain's civilizing duty, although the custom of *sati* had all but disappeared.[6]

During the 1980s, the dichotomy of Indian barbarism and British civilization which was implied by the colonial discourse on *sati* was challenged by Indian sociologists and historians. Value judgements were replaced with a historical contextualization of the practice and its legal abolition. First, Ashis Nandy's analysis of *sati* in early nineteenth-century Bengal emphasized the socially and culturally destabilizing impact of British rule. *Sati* had a long tradition in Bengal, but it reached epidemic proportions due to historical developments around the turn of the nineteenth century. Gender relations, in this case an extreme form of sexual control, were modified in the wake of colonial conquest.[7]

The historical contextualization has been taken further to include the legal debate.[8] Lata Mani analyzed the discourse on women as part of a specific "colonial knowledge" which was produced in support of British colonial dominance. The discourse on *sati* was placed in the context of the historiographical debate on the Bengal Renaissance and the Indian social reform movement. Rammohan Roy, the father of the Bengal Renaissance and the social reform movement, initiated the legal abolition of *sati*. But the modernity of these developments was questioned because of the colonial state's contradictory impact on development in India. The politically and economically restrictive conditions of colonial rule provided but a narrow space for genuinely modern ideas and implied the limitations of Rammohan and the following movement he initiated.[9] Social reform was hampered by colonial politics which propagated reform without allowing the emergence of self-conscious social classes in India to back such changes.

6. E.J. Thompson, *Suttee: A Historical and Philosophical Enquiry into the Hindu Rite of Widow-Burning* (London, 1928), 140–41, quoted in Anderson, "Sati," 49.

7. A. Nandy, "Sati: a nineteenth century tale of women, violence and protest," in *At the Edge of the Psychology. Essays in Politics and Culture*, ed. A. Nandy (New Delhi, 1980), 131.

8. Lata Mani, "The production of an official discourse on sati in early nineteenth century Bengal," in *Europe and its Others*, vol. I, ed. F. Barker et al (Colchester, 1985), 107–27; also published in *Economic and Political Weekly*, "Review of Women's Studies" 21, no. 17, April 26, 1986, 32–40; "Contentious traditions: the debate on *sati* in colonial India" in *Cultural Critique*, Special Issue, ed. A.R. Jan Mohammad and D. Lloyd: "The Nature and Context of Minority Discourse II," 7 (1987), 119–56; also published in *Women and Ideology in modern India*, ed. Kumkum Sangari and Sudesh Vaid (New Delhi, 1988).

9. S. Sarkar, "Rammohan Roy and the break with the past" in *Rammohan Roy and the Process of Modernization in India*, ed. V.C. Joshi (New Delhi, 1975), 46–68.

The legal debate on *sati* was less concerned with women and social reform than with Indian, in particular Hindu, tradition, which the British claimed to protect, Rammohan contested, and orthodoxy defended. However, based on a specifically colonial interpretation of Brahminic texts which ignored contradictory interpretations and folk culture, tradition was reconstituted under colonial rule. While Brahminical texts provided the means, women's rights and status became the area of the re-articulation of tradition. Tradition became interchangeable with culture and religion, and was referred to as a timeless and structuring principle of Indian society which colonial officials claim to have reinstated in India after the "Islamic interlude." The modernity of reformers and officials was expressed in their concern for social issues and in their reliance on the written as opposed to the spoken word. The preservation of tradition was called upon both to justify and to oppose social legislation, but also to legitimize the British presence in India.

Women were at the intersection of all these lines of thought. They provided the area of the discourse between colonial officials and the indigenous male elite on *sati* – and later in the century on widow or child marriage. However, while the focus changed, the main concern of the legal discourse remained the same: not women's welfare, but social reform to support conflicting claims to moral superiority, political power, and representation.

The debate preceding the abolition of *sati* as well as the few court cases against relatives of *satis* portrayed women as victims, and invested men with control, power, and activity.[10] Men, it was alleged, forced women on to the funeral pyre, but they could also act as reformers to forward the cause of female emancipation. Although *satis* could have been seen as the epitome of female power and courage, they were turned into speechless victims of male greed and an obsolete interpretation of Hindu scriptures. By propagating the dichotomy between male activity and female passivity, British officials introduced Victorian gender stereotypes into orthodox Hinduism, which had venerated or feared female power. For half a century, until Hindu Revivalism rediscovered the ideological potential of female power, the colonial definition of female emancipation excluded respective indigenous moralities from political consideration.[11]

10. Anderson, "Sati," 46.
11. Ibid., 51; for a discussion of Hindu revivalism and feminity, see T. Sarkar, "Nationalist iconography: image of women in nineteenth-Century Bengali Literature," *Economic and Political Weekly* 22, no. 47, November 21, 1987, 2011–2015;

Widow Remarriage

In 1856, Iswar Chandra Vidyasagar, Bengali intellectual, college
teacher and social reformer, succeeded in his long campaign for an
improvement of the conditions of child widows.[12] To sponsor social
reform the Indian government passed the Hindu Widows' Remarriage Act, which legalized the marriage of Hindu widows. Until then
high-caste widows, in accordance with orthodox Hindu ideology,
had not been allowed to enter wedlock, although they were often
below the age of puberty when their husbands died. As a consequence, offspring from extramarital relationships were illegitimate
children. In contrast, remarriage without sanctions was widely practiced among the non-twice-born Hindu and the tribal population.

Concern for female purity and fear of female sexual power were
cultural reasons for child marriage and the restriction of widows.
Economic reasons were important as well. Marriage and dowry
were a heavy burden for the parents of daughters. Fathers and
mothers tried to marry daughters as soon as acceptable bridegrooms
appeared. Often a dowry for a young girl was lower because her
family could not be pressed for more money by hinting at her
approaching puberty. After puberty a girl was less pure and, if she
belonged to an orthodox high-caste family, it was difficult to find a
spouse for her. Once a widow, in ritual terms, a woman survived as
the useless half of her husband. But she could be useful as an unpaid
maidservant in her husband's family, who no longer created expenses for nice saris, jewelry, or tasty food. According to the *Day-
abhaga* school of law in Bengal and the *Mitakshara* school in the rest of
India she had but the right of maintenance out of her husband's
estate. Even if her husband had installed her as sole heiress, she was
not allowed to sell it off unless it was in the interest of the next male
heirs. Relatives kept a close eye on her, and her low ritual status
could well help to make her give in to her relatives' bullying. A
widow, like any other woman, had unlimited rights only to her
stridhan which she had received from her parents or husband as a gift
or had inherited from her mother.

The actual position of the propertied widow in a joint family
depended very much on her ability to defend her rights. The misuse
of such women through their abduction into brothels by male kin

Dagmar Engels, "The limits of gender ideology: Bengali women, the colonial state,
and the private sphere, 1890–1930," *Women's Studies International Forum* 12 (1989), 4.

12. Asok, Sen, *Iswar Chandra Vidyasagar and His Elusive Milestones* (Calcutta, 1977).

while they were young and helpless was, for example, a common theme in contemporary Bengali fiction.[13] Mature widows were not so easy to get rid of. Widows did not resort to the colonial state in order to get married, but to defend their livelihood. Male relatives tried to cheat widows of their share, particularly if the income stemmed from urban business, which was more difficult to control than rural assets.[14] Others threatened to take widows to court when they insisted on their rights as documented in their late husbands' wills.[15]

Some families treated young widows so badly that they were forced to leave their matrimonial homes. The late husbands' families took this as a step which implied the forfeiture of any rights to property and maintenance. Under such circumstances widows had to go to court to secure their maintenance, once they realized that they could no longer depend on their own families. In 1931, the Calcutta High Court overturned a 1928 court order which had denied Sajani Sundari Debi, a widow, her rights of maintenance. She became a widow in 1906. The family property was divided in 1910 and since then she had been treated badly. Finally in 1925 she was unable to cope any longer. She left her in-laws' house, but found it impossible to rely on her father and brother, who were both in debt. As she had married into a rich family, her gains through the court's ruling were considerable. Her in-laws were ordered to pay Rs 1,326 for the jewelry she had left behind, and Rs 80 a month for her regular maintenance, backdated to the time she had left their house.[16]

If a child widow was the sole heiress, her guardianship became a contentious point. In 1915, for instance, Atanu Nandan Tagore died leaving "considerable property . . . and an infant widow, Akhoy Kumar Debi."[17] Akhoy Kumar's mother soon claimed the guardianship, which was contested in court by Sarala Sundari Debi, a cousin of the deceased.

As the evidence from these court cases suggests, the contentious point about widowhood was very often an economic issue. It is thus not astonishing that those clauses of Act XV of 1856, which

13. P. Mitra, *Premendra Granthabali* (Calcutta, n.d.), 1–48.
14. *Mathura Sundari Dasi v. Haran Chandra Saha*, Indian Law Report (ILR) 1916, 43, Calcutta 857.
15. *Poorendranath Sen v. Hemangini Dasi*, ILR 1909, 36, Calcutta 75.
16. *Sajanisundari Dasi v. Jogendrachandra Sen*, ILR 1931, 58, Calcutta 745.
17. *Sarala Sundari Debi v. Hazari Dasi Debi* and *Gossain Dasi Debi v. Hazari Dasi Debi*, ILR 1915, 42, Calcutta, 953.

regulated the economic implications of remarriage, proved to be the most problematic. Section 2 of the Hindu Widows' Remarriage Act rule that a widow on remarriage lost her rights of inheritance and of maintenance. This was logical in so far as in orthodox Hindu law a widow had the right of maintenance as the surviving half of her husband's body. Accordingly an unchaste widow did not succeed to her husband's estate, but after succession living an unchaste life did not alter her rights. While a widow could have an extra-marital relationship provided she started it after succession to her husband's estate, wedlock was punished with the forfeiture of property.[18] Thus, it could be argued that orthodox high-caste families were tempted into the acceptance of the Act by the economic gains a widow's marriage implied for her former family. However, reality was very different.

Until well into the twentieth century few high-caste widows made use of the legalization of widow remarriage, and remarriages often led to social ostracization of the family. The female age of marriage rose with the spread of education, and there were less child widows for whom Vidyasagar as well as Gandhi found remarriage opportune.[19] What was the significance of Act XV of 1856, including its economic regulations?

Lucy Carroll, in an analysis of Indian High Court rulings, has analyzed the judicial intricacies which followed the passing of the Hindu Widows' Remarriage Act. While Hindu law prohibited the remarriage of twice-born widows, its statutory reform permitted the marriages of all Hindu widows, irrespective of their caste background. Simultaneously it could be interpreted as subsuming all Hindu widows under its economic "punishment" clause. In 1896, Justice Ranade of the Bombay High Court, for instance, accepted that the Act was meant to bring relief to a part of the population. But he insisted that the individual sections were statutory Hindu law and thus valid for the whole Hindu population. In a case in point, on remarriage a Sudra widow lost her inheritance which she would happily have kept forty years earlier, because her caste traditionally accepted widow remarriage without economic sanctions.[20]

The jurisdiction of the Calcutta High Court was equally restric-

18. Lucy Carroll, "Law, custom, and statutory social reform: the Hindu Widows' Remarriage Act of 1856," *Indian Economic and Social History Review* 20 (1983), 365.

19. Dagmar Engels, "The Changing Role of Women in Bengal, c. 1890–c. 1930, with Special Reference to British and Bengali Discourse on Gender," unpub. PhD. thesis (London, 1987), 45–83.

20. Carroll, "Law," 372–75.

tive with regard to a widow's property, albeit based on a different interpretation of the Act XV. Here High Court judges took over the role of Brahminical *pandits* and interpreted the Act within the logic of Hindu law. A Hindu widow who converted to the *Brahmo Samaj* and got married under the provisions of the Special Marriage Act (secular wedding for non-Hindus) was nevertheless stripped of her inheritance. The judges ruled that her inheritance was due to her being the surviving half of her late husband's body. On remarriage she became half of another man's body and was forced to give up her late husband's worldly goods. Lucy Carroll rightly questions the logic of such reasoning. Why, in an Act opposed to Hindu law, was Hindu law referred to when economic aspects were at stake?[21]

Only the Allahabad High Court judges avoided passing sentences reflecting high-caste interpretations of the Hindu Widows' Remarriage Act, when the contestants came from a low-caste or tribal background. In 1889, the Court ruled that Nandi, a sweeper's widow, was entitled to retain the land she had inherited from her late husband – despite her remarriage. Her husband's brothers had filed a suit against her and had won in two lower courts. The High Court Judge, however, held that if remarriage had been accepted before 1856 without the forfeiture of property, Act XV was not meant to apply. This case became the precedent for all future court rulings by the court. In Allahabad customary law was accepted, albeit in a frozen form: evidence was only accepted when it proved the custom in question as existing before 1856.[22]

As in the case of legislation on *sati*, the jurisdiction on widow remarriage showed a striking concern for Brahminical tradition. In both cases there was a pragmatic reason for the nature of the decisions. Written evidence supported high-caste tradition and was thus more readily available than oral evidence in support of low-caste or tribal practices. However, as with legislation on *sati*, where the dichotomy between noble tradition and corrupt society served a political purpose, jurisdiction on widow remarriage made more than pragmatic ends meet. Due to their social background British and Indian judges on High Court benches in India identified more easily with Brahminical values which stressed the male prerogative over women, rather than with more egalitarian concepts which could be found among lower castes and tribals. Consequently female ownership of property, in particular immovable property, aroused male

21. *Ibid.*, 369–71.
22. *Ibid.*, 367–69.

suspicion. Significantly, a Hindu woman's *stridhan* was rarely anything but jewelry, money, clothes, and household utensils. Thus
under the conditions of British rule in India even an initiative meant
to ease social reform for women ended with the curtailment of
women's control over their lives. Law, as agent of social reform
under colonial conditions, almost inevitably favored religious orthodoxy and male conservatism.[23]

Labor Law

Labor law which regulated women's work in contrast to men's
concentrated on women in the organized sector which was regulated
by the Indian Factories Act of 1881. Law played a more important
role for women workers in mills, mines, and plantations than social
reformist law did in the lives of the majority of Indian women. The
latter was put into practice when it enforced existing trends, as in
the case of the Child Marriage Restraint Act.[24] In contrast, the
Hindu Widows' Remarriage Act never succeeded in overcoming the
aversion of Hindu society against widow marriage. However, violation of social legislation rarely ended in court. As such crimes mostly
happened within the family, representatives of the state found it
hard to investigate unless a member of the family came forward with
evidence. In addition, appearance in court was almost inevitably
regarded as a blur on female honor.[25] Thus it was circumvented at
all costs – unless a considerable amount of money was at stake.

In contrast, the law prohibiting women's night and underground
work or regulating maternity leave referred to women in the public
world of large economic concerns, and was enforced more easily.
Lobbies, as we shall see, were not content with scoring ideological
points. But ideological concerns, such as political legitimation via
social reform, received much more publicity – at the time of the
respective legislation, and later from historians. A wide literature on
social reform exists in contrast to barely an article on women and
colonial labor law.[26] The "underdogs of empire" have so far been
the "underdogs of history."

23. Compare, *Ibid.*, 382–84.
24. By the late 1920s, due to female education and the agitation of the nationalist
movement, middle-class girls were later given into marriage irrespective of the law.
25. For an examination of these arguments, see Engels, "The age of consent act",
and D. Engels, "The politics of marriage reform in the 1920s," in D. Conrad, W.
Menski, eds.
26. Radha Kumar, "Family and factory: women in the Bombay cotton textile

Here we shall look at women and the law in Bengal's organized economic sector during the four decades before the Depression drastically reduced the number of female employees. Bengal was the most industrialized province in India at the turn of the century, but industries were still scattered islands in the sea of agriculture. The organized sector, comprising mainly the jute mills in and near Calcutta, coal mines near the Bihar border, and tea plantations in Darjeeling, employed only a tiny number of people compared to agriculture and the labyrinthine, unorganized bazaar economy of the cities. On average one out of every three workers was a woman.[27] The ratio was highest in tea plantations, where women tea pluckers were the backbone of the production process, and lowest in jute mills, where relatively high wages attracted migrant male labor from north India.[28]

Legal interference in the organized sector was minimal. Mills, mines and plantations in Bengal were owned by British agency houses.[29] Factories and mines were regularly inspected, but more detailed reports in the 1920s showed that working conditions were extremely poor.[30] Legal initiatives reforming women's working days reacted to pressure from companies and international organizations, which the Indian government could not ignore as easily as high mortality rates of women and children due to long working hours, bad sanitary conditions, and poor pay.

In the Raniganj coalfields in western Bengal, most mining families were labor tenants living on land owned by the mining companies.

industry, 1919–1939," *The Indian Economic and Social History Review* 20 (1983). The most comprehensive examination of labor in colonial India more or less ignores women: M.D. Morris, *The Emergence of an Industrial Labour Force in India* (Berkeley, 1965).

27. India Office Library and Records (IOLR), Royal Commission on Labour in India, (hereafter RCLI), Vol. V, Part 1 (London, 1931); RCLI "Reports of the Royal Commission on Labour in India," IOLR, *Reports from Commissioners, Inspectors, and Others*, Vol. XI, 1930–31, (hereafter RCLI, "Report"), 8–9; *Census of India*, (hereafter COI) 1931, V, 2 (Calcutta, 1933); RCLI, *Memorandum on Labour Conditions in Bengal. Prepared for the use of the Royal Commission on Indian Labour, 1931* (hereafter RCLI, *Memorandum*) (London, 1931), Section V, Welfare.

28. R. Das Gupta, "Factory labour in Eastern India: sources of supply, 1855–1946. 'Some preliminary findings,'" in *The Indian Economic and Social History Review* 23 (1976), 277–329.

29. See A.K. Bagchi, *Private Investment in India* (Cambridge, 1972); R.K. Ray, *Industrialisation in India: Growth and Conflict in the Private Corporate Sector, 1914–47* (Delhi, 1979).

30. West Bengal State Archives (WBSA), Commerce Department/Commerce Branch (Comm./Comm.), April 1923, B77, "Report of Dr. D.F. Curjel on the Conditions of Employment of Women before and after childbirth." (Curjel Report).

They worked part-time as miners and part-time as cultivators in their fields. Women went down into the mines together with their husbands or male companions and relatives. After the men had cut the coal, women gathered it into baskets and carried it up to the surface by climbing either a series of ladders or, more commonly, some inclines to the hoist. Women working underground were usually paid jointly with their male companions and were entitled to a share of 40 percent of the wage. Surface workers, often groups of single women from nearby villages, earned lower wages. They lived in poverty and depended on meager company allowances in the case of maternity, sickness, or the death of a family member.[31]

Until the late 1920s mine owners tried to oppose any attempt to restrict female employment in mines, because women provided cheap labor. Moreover, while women worked, mining companies saved the extra expenses of paying family wages to male workers. In 1923, however, mine owners had to concede the first of reformist demands when children, who had been employed in picking coal, were banned from going underground. This implied a restriction on female underground labor; women who had taken their babies underground now had to look for surface employment unless there were relatives or elder children to look after their children. Above ground the tasks for women were limited. They either carried coal to the coking yard or moved sand for use in stabilizing the pit walls.[32]

After 1925 the mining industry suffered the worst slump in its history and had to lay off workers.[33] It was in this context that the reformist pressure of women's organizations and the International Labour Organisation was at last rewarded. This pressure was part of a worldwide campaign in the wake of the First World War to fight poverty and exploitation as causes for physical degeneration. The war had shown the need for a more healthy and sturdy physical human stock, and the Russian Revolution intimidated governments of industrialized countries sufficiently to give in to reformist social

31. C.P. Simmons, "Recruiting and organising an industrial labour force in colonial India: the case of the coal mining industry, c. 1880–1939," *The Indian Economic and Social History Review* 23 (1976), 466–67; Kamini Roy, "Women labour in mines," *Modern Review*, April 1923, 511–513; "Curjel Report," App. E, 2–7, 12; *Annual Report of the Chief Inspector of Mines in India* (Calcutta, 1905), 2, quoted in Simmons, "Recruiting," 461; RCLI, Vol. IV., Part 2, 108, 119–20; R. Raychaudhury, "Living conditions of the female workers in the eastern collieries (Bihar and Bengal) from 1901 to 1921," *Quarterly Review of Historical Studies*, 24, 4, 1381 (1984–85), MS., 5.
32. WBSA, Comm./Comm., Feb. 1924, A37 and Sept. 1927, A14–15; "Curjel Report," App. E, 3; RCLI, Vol. IV, Part 2, 119–20.
33. WBSA, Comm./Comm., Sept. 1927, A 16 and K.W.

demands. Infant and maternal health were the most important of all these concerns. In postwar Britain the activities culminated in the 1918 Maternity and Child Welfare Act, "which envisaged the provision of a network of infant welfare centres."[34] In India the recommendations and conventions of postwar international organizations, such as the League of Nations and the International Labour Organisation, were influential in condemning labor conditions of women workers. But such lobbying only proved successful once it coincided with the interests of mining capital in India.

In 1929 legislation was introduced which required the female underground labor force in Bengal and Bihar to be reduced by ten percent each year. Coal managers who for years had argued the need for cheap female labor now adopted the strategy of limiting overproduction through the reduction of female underground labor, without risking the social unrest which male redundancies could have caused. Whereas in the mid-1920s roughly a third of the total and underground labor force respectively were women, in 1938 they constituted but 11 percent.[35]

The gradual decline of female underground labor was a questionable achievement, in respect to the poverty of the women and their lack of alternative income. Women reformers from outside the mainstream middle-class organizations, who had actually inspected the mines, did not believe that underground work was unsuitable for women. They argued that the air was manageable and that the baskets were lighter than the loads women in the construction industry were used to carrying in the open air. Moreover, because the wages were better than elsewhere, women working underground were described as looking healthier and stronger than other women working outside the home.[36]

In addition, mining women came from an *adivasi* background where the sexual division of labor was less rigid than among Hindus or Muslims. Women were used to agricultural work with the men of the family. Underground labor as a family unit had matched the same pattern, and had guaranteed that women received part of the wages for household expenditure.[37]

These circumstances were ignored by women reformers lobbying

---

34. Anna Davin, "Imperialism and motherhood," *History Workshop Journal* 5 (1978), 43.

35. Simmons, "Recruiting," 462–63.

36. Roy, "Women Labour," 511–13, "Curjel Report," App. E, 4.

37. IOLR, *Report of the Labour Enquiry Commission*, (hereafter *Labour 1896*) (Calcutta, 1896), 21; Simmons, "Recruiting," 459.

against underground labor. The Women's Indian Association urged
the Government of India to prohibit underground labor and to

> restore women to their normal functions and health and lessen the evil of
> intemperance among the men-miners, ensure a higher standard of dom-
> estic life, save the life of the infants and improve the physique of the new
> generation.[38]

As a reason for the men's excessive drinking they argued that
husbands had to wait for their meals too long. Thus they asked for
the domestication of women:

> If the comforts of the house are guaranteed by the presence of wives there
> to perform the domestic duties under reasonable conditions, the whole
> standard of living will be raised, even if there be a temporary decrease in
> wages.[39]

The professionalization of housewifery, as propagated in Europe
and the USA after the First World War to put working-class women
from factory lines back into the home, found support in India as
well. However, its supporters were women from middle-class families who could use such trends to enhance their position within the
family. But their arguments were taken up by mine owners and
colonial administrators when they suited the interests of coal magnates. For tribal women miners, the ideology was highly inappropri-
ate, because their position in the family traditionally depended on
their labor outside the house. The very fact had turned tribal families into ideal mine workers. Their sexual division of labor, based on
complementary male and female contributions to the process of
agricultural and coal production, had neatly matched the conditions
of mining in Bengal coal fields. Early reformist initiatives had been
rejected by mining companies with arguments referring to this sexual division of labor.[40] However, as the delay in the legal prohibition
of female underground labor showed, the law was not concerned
with ideologies, but with profit margins. Indian and Western gender
stereotypes were used to justify the legal situation which suited the
mining capital.

In contrast to badly paid work on plantations and dangerous

38. Anonymous, "Against underground labour for women," *Modern Review*, Nov.
1922, 659–60.
39. Ibid.
40. Simmons, "Recruiting," 459; *Labour 1896*, 21; RCLI, Vol. V, Part I, 177.

mining labor, in jute mills Hindus and Muslims – rather than tribals from the bottom of the ritual hierarchy – made up the bulk of the workforce. Before 1890 the vast majority of the jute labor force was recruited from nearby Bengali villages or the surrounding districts. After 1900 the growing flow of migrant laborers from Bihar, Orissa and UP diminished the significance of the Bengali element in the workforce. As wages for manual labor in the jute industry were higher than elsewhere, there was no labor shortage, and men mono-polized the better paid skilled jobs.[41]

Women in jute mills were employed on unskilled jobs, particular-ly in the preparation and finishing departments, where the degree of mechanization was limited. Between 1890 and 1925 the number of women workers increased from 12,000 to 55,000, but the overall tendency in the industry was for fewer women to be employed compared to the number of men. In the finishing or hand-sewing department women were paid by the piece, which relieved the managers from the task of supervision. Managers showed them-selves as liberal-minded when they allowed women to work any time. Yet the freedom of women to take time off for cooking, eating and nursing was circumscribed by the very low piece-rates. Still, women liked the sewing department because it was safe for children to play there.[42]

Women worked long hours because they needed to earn as much as possible – they did not have to work continuous or regular shifts. Others could take their places. During the 1880s men, women, and children worked eight to nine hours per day in the mills. Once the mills were equipped with electric light in the 1880s women often worked fifteen to sixteen hours a day, and a system of night shifts was introduced. In 1891, the Factory Act was amended in "recogni-tion of night work by women in factories in which work is arranged on the shift system." Workers were not allowed to work more than 11 hours at a stretch in 24 hours and were required to have one and

---

41. National Library Calcutta, (hereafter NLC), B. Foley, *Report on Labour in Bengal* (Calcutta, 1906), 14, App. I, ix; IOLR, Government of India, (hereafter GOI), Home Department, Judicial Branch (Hereafter Home/Judl.), Febr. 1896, A423, 440; RCLI, Vol. V, Part 1, 4–5, 8–11; *Report on the Working of the Indian Factory Act* (FA) 1911, 3; IOLR, *Report of the Indian Factory Commission 1890* (hereafter *Factory Commission* 1890), Parl. Papers 1890–91, Vol. 59, male witnesses, 90. Das Gupta, "Factory Labour," 299.
42. IOLR, *Indian Factory Labour Commission*, Vol. II, Evidence, Parl. Papers 1909. Vol. 63, witness 165, 242–43; *FA* 1912, 3; "Curjel Report," App. A, ix; *FA* 1912 onward report regularly on wages and on the difference between the pay of men and women.

a half hours of rest. In addition, the working week of women was
limited to a maximum of 60 hours.[43]

The number of working hours excluded the extra hours women
worked outside the factories. Women bore the double burden of
house and mill work. In the villages where the Bengali operatives
lived the first warning whistle sounded at 3 a.m. Whereas men could
sleep until they were about to leave for work, women got up to fetch
water, light a fire, prepare some breakfast, and look after the children. At 4 a.m. women and children left for the factory to work a
minimum of 10 to 11 hours. Afterwards they waited for one to three
hours to be accompanied home by their male relatives. They spent
15 to 16 hours in the mills before they could return home to their
shopping, cooking, and washing. Their working day lasted from
three o'clock in the morning until ten or eleven o'clock at night.[44]

Despite the heavy workload of women inside and outside the
mills, the regulations for the amended Factories Act were widely
ignored. By 1896 the length of working shifts in Bengal jute mills
was a growing cause for concern. A special commission initiated by
the Dundee jute lobby found that in some mills, particularly in the
Hasting Jute Mill, women and children under 14 years of age were
employed for twenty-two and fifteen hours at a stretch respectively.
The owners of the Hasting Jute Mill, Messr. Birkmyre Brothers,
even provided an extra sleeping room for the children of working
mothers. The special commissioner suggested that these women had
most probably worked in another mill during the day, and argued
that female night work had a bad impact on family life and on
children who were dragged into mills. As ten hour shifts were the
legal maximum in Scotland, the Dundee jute entrepreneurs complained about unfair competition. While women and children undoubtedly worked abnormally long shifts, Dundee and Calcutta
were major competitors in the world market, and the Government of
India declined to take any new legislative initiative. The Government took the view that women went to and from work with male
escorts and should thus work the same hours. The Bengal National
Chamber of Commerce argued against any interference, because
workers found "their tasks both remunerative and delightful."[45]

After the turn of the century colonial authorities became more

43. R.K. Das, *The Labour Movement in India* (Berlin, 1923), 56; RCLI, "Report,"
37–38; IOLR, GOI, Home/Judl., Feb. 1896, A467.
44. IOLR, *Report of the Indian Factory Labour Commission 1908* (Simla, 1908), 46–47.
45. IOLR, GOI, Home/Judl., Febr. 1896, A405–68.

concerned about the long hours worked by women. It became public knowledge that women worked extra hours on Sundays in the winding and reeling departments, while other women worked regularly through the nights and the following day at domestic labor. Then the slump of 1908–1910 forced jute companies to curtail production. Mills were closed on Saturdays and the average working week was reduced to four days or forty-eight hours. In the aftermath of the slump, as in the 1920s in the mining industry, reformist legislation on women's labor followed. In 1911 women's work in the mills was restricted to the hours between 5:30 a.m. and 7 p.m. The Factories Act of 1912 prohibited the employment of children under nine years of age and limited the working-hours to seven for so-called part-timers between the age of nine and fourteen years. In 1922, part-timers were redefined as children between twelve and fifteen years of age, who were entitled to six hours work per day. But under the conditions in the hand-sewing department it was easy to ignore any restrictions relating to the working hours of children or women.[46]

The long hours of millwork, unhealthy and disruptive of family life, were subject to external pressures for labor reform. In October 1919, the International Labour Conference in Washington adopted a convention, which the Government of India later ratified, fixing eleven hours as the minimum night's rest for working women. In 1926, when the same conference decided to set up a committee to examine the fulfillment of the convention, British politicians in Whitehall showed concern about the state of affairs in India. It appeared that only 13,000 out of 53,000 female jute workers in Bengal had the required night's rest, and the Secretary of State for India asked the Government of India to investigate whether the climate in Bengal or the special circumstances of shift work justified the exemption of jute workers from the convention.[47]

During the 1920s, with a growing demand for jute in the world market, the Indian Jute Mill Association (IJMA), which included all but a couple of mills worked millhands harder than before. In 1921, its members agreed on a fifty-four hour week, six hours below the legal limit. But this and other agreements were accompanied by efforts to increase the extraction of absolute surplus labor, that is, to pay less for more work. The cuts were achieved in two ways:

46. Das, *Labour Movement*, 64; IOLR, *Report of the Textile Factories Labour Committee. Factory Labours in India* (Bombay, 1907), 11, 25; RCLI, *Memorandum*, V. Welfare; "Curjel Report," App. A, vii.
47. WBSA, Comm./Comm., Jan. 1929, B265–67.

management either reintroduced a sixty hour week, as happened for nine months in 1920–1921 and for twelve months in 1929–1930, without paying higher time-wages; or the multiple shift was replaced by the single shift system, which increased the individual workload and led to the loss of jobs. By 1926 work was done in single shifts in nearly half the Bengal jute mills. The crucial issue at stake in these changes was the abolition of the *khoraki* payment, an allowance for one day enforced idleness. Under the multiple shift system laborers worked an alternating four and five day week, but received an allowance for the missing fifth day in every second week. Workers' dissatisfaction was also aroused by the alteration of the piece workers' fixed task in proportion to the increased working hours and the generally low wage level at a time when the cost of living was going up rapidly.[48]

Despite legal change little happened to ameliorate working conditions. Mill managers were left by factory inspectors and the Department of Commerce of the Bengal Government to alter the structure of the working day according to their needs. In contrast in 1920–1922 and again towards the end of the decade, when workers went on strike to protest against low wages and rising prices, police stepped in on behalf of mill owners to restore "law and order."[49]

Women in jute mills were trapped between two worlds and got the worst of both. According to the traditional patriarchal values of Muslim and Hindu society they had lost their status by migrating to the Calcutta mills. Male workers thus showed little concern for the labor conditions of their female colleagues and for the reluctance of mill owners to implement reformist laws.[50] In fact, women laborers were gradually marginalized because of the sufficient supply of male labor and the mechanization of the production process. In 1927, the chairman of the IJMA referred to the benign effect of single shifts on the workers' family life, but he "forgot" to mention that the restructuring of the labor process would, as a secular trend, exclude women.[51]

During the 1920s increasing attention was paid to family ideology. As we have seen in the case of women miners, in jute mills, too,

48. Bagchi, *Investment*, 279; RCLI, Vol. V, Part 1, 410; RCLI, "Report," 37–38.
49. WBSA, Comm./Comm. July 1921, 40–42, F 2-R-67; Dipesh Chakraborty, "Conditions of knowledge of working-class conditions: employers, government and jute workers of Calcutta, 1890–1940," in *Subaltern Studies II*, ed. Ranajit Guha (Delhi, 1983), 259–310.
50. "Curjel Report."
51. *FA* 1927, 30–31; 1928, 12; 1930, 18; 1931, 7; WBSA, Comm./Comm. Jan. 1929, B261–66.

concern for mothering and housewifery accompanied the marginalization of women in the production process. In this context reformers suggested a change of law for the protection of mothers and children. The debate on maternity benefit and maternity leave was initiated by a Convention of the International Labour Conference, which had also regulated women's night rest. The Draft Convention suggested a six week leave before and after child birth, accompanied by sufficient benefits for women in commercial and industrial undertakings. Resuming work, women should be entitled to two extra breaks of thirty minutes each during their working hours while they were breastfeeding their babies.[52] Throughout the 1920s the Convention remained unhonored in Bengal. Instead a *laissez faire* policy on maternity benefit and leave was adopted, which suited the company interests in the respective branches of the organized industry. Women in tea plantations who were essential for the production process received benefits from the planters on a voluntary basis; mining women, being part-time workers and backed by agricultural families, were not regarded as being in need and jute workers received nothing:[53]

> The type of labour, moreover, must be kept in mind, particularly with respect of female labour in jute mills. Normal family life is notoriously absent among the labourers in jute mills . . . The peculiar type of the female labour in the jute mills does not conduce to the creation of schemes which presuppose normal family relations.[54]

Women were regarded as victims of the unfavorable conditions and themselves immediately responsible. To avoid or delay legal obligations of companies toward employed mothers, women were said to be needing education, not money. Women were accused of having "abused" voluntary benefit schemes, such as those set up in the early 1920s by the Baranagore and Kelvin Jute Mills, by taking the money and going to work elsewhere. Moreover, money alone would have implied that even child-mothers of twelve or thirteen years of age would have been supported.[55]

Legislative initiatives which succeeded in Bombay were rejected in Calcutta, with the argument that they were modelled on conditions in

---

52. WBSA, Comm./Comm., April 1921, A1–13; July 1921, A38–39; Dec. 1924, A40–54; July 1925, A32–68.
53. "Curjel Report."
54. WBSA, Comm./Comm., Dec. 1924, A54.
55. WBSA, Comm./Comm., Dec. 1924, A48 and July 1925, A47, 68.

the Bombay cotton mills, where the female labor force was said to be numerically more important and more permanent. Moreover, workers in Bombay were said to live in regular families, thus making their reproduction worth the support. Finally, however, even in Bombay, family ideology was used to justify female redundancy. During and after the Depression the working day and the labor force were restructured to extract more surplus labor. After 1934, while the male labor force increased, the number of women in Bombay cotton mills did not.[56]

Conclusion

The legal discourse on *sati* defined women as passive victims, while the colonial definition of tradition undermined chances for indigenous social change that could have ameliorated the condition of women. Colonial social reformist law was at best ignored, but more often it hampered improvements or had deteriorating effects on women's lives. High-caste Indian and Victorian gender stereotypes, such as the propertyless woman, worked together to the disadvantage of Indian women in the jurisdiction following the Hindu Widows' Remarriage Act. British interference or non-interference with social custom was secondary, because colonial law was less a matter of principles and more a matter of changing political interests. "Public law" on women workers did not rationalize Indian custom, but supported or justified employment policies of mine and mill owners. In all these cases, colonial, patriarchal, and capitalist concerns came first, women's social and material interests second.

56. WBSA, Comm./Comm., Dec. 1924, A40–54; July 1925, A32–68; Radha Kumar, "Family and factory."

9

The "Popularity" of the Imperial Courts of Law: Three Views of the Anglo-Indian Legal Encounter

PAMELA G. PRICE

Introduction

The Indian case of the encounter of European and non-European systems of law has, it appears, special characteristics. As the sociologist of law, Marc Galanter, has noted, there has been an "eager and unfaltering embrace of Western law" which did not take place in Southeast Asia, Japan, or Africa.[1] In the 1960s, India had the second largest legal profession in the world in absolute numbers, and in proportion to its population India had many more lawyers than other new states (see Appendix).[2] In this article I will take two established approaches and one emergent approach to the encounter in India, and outline how each implicitly or explicitly addresses the question of the nature of the encounter in general, and the significance of litigation in particular. The three approaches are: 1) legal history, 2) the sociology of law, and 3) cultural history. For the first two approaches I examine the synthetic attempts of three scholars. No major synthetic attempt has yet appeared in the field of cultural history, so this part of the article is more suggestive of future directions for discussion.

---

1. M. Galanter, "Indian law as an indigenous conceptual system," in *Social Science Research Council, Items* 32 (1978) 3/4, 43.
2. M. Galanter, "The displacement of traditional law in modern India," in *Journal of Social Issues* 24 (1968) 4, 77.

Legal History

The acknowledged master of Indian legal history has been J.D.M. Derrett, formerly of the School of Oriental and African Studies, University of London. Author of a great many pieces of legal scholarship, Derrett's general interpretation of the introduction of Western law into India is found in two articles, "The British as patrons of the shastra" and "The administration of Hindu law by the British."[3] Here Derrett focuses on the development of Anglo-Hindu law and its relationship to those sacred texts which representatives of the East India Company in the late eighteenth century designated as authoritative sources of the law of Hindus.

As the Europeans began to acquire territory in India in the seventeenth century, they were obliged by the "constitutional" law of the kingdoms or empires within which these territories lay to manage disputes in their jurisdiction in a manner agreeable to Indians.[4] Muslims claimed to be governed by rules derived from the Quran and textbooks written by specialists of the *Shari'a*, while Hindus recognized, in a manner unclear to Europeans, authority in the sacred Sanskritic texts, the *shastras*. However, no centralized legal system had prevailed in India, and these sources were consulted with widely varying regularity and results.

The British East India Company established courts in the seventeenth century to deal with cases involving Europeans and Company servants in their jurisdiction; however, Britons were reluctant to take responsibility for Indian disputes until 1765, when the Company accepted the *divani* or rule of the Eastern Provinces of northeast India. After 1765, Company courts became subject to the appellate jurisdiction of the Privy Council in London, and royal courts were established by Royal Charter. Appointees of the Crown staffed the latter, and members of the English Bar served in them. Both sets of courts were established as more territory came under British rule in the eighteenth century. These two systems of courts were merged in 1861, when the imperial judicial system took form as a group of mutually independent superior appellate courts (the High Courts of Bombay, Madras, and Calcutta), each subject to the Privy Council and each at the top of a pyramid of inferior courts in the districts. The High Courts heard appeals from courts of first instance situated in major district towns, and had limited original jurisdiction. For

3. J.D.M. Derrett, *Religion, Law and the State in India* (London, 1968).
4. Ibid., 275.

most of the nineteenth century the District Courts and High Courts were staffed mostly by Britons, while lower level courts were staffed by Indians. Outside the High Court the practitioners were Indians educated at law colleges in India. Few were professionally qualified in either Islamic or Hindu classical systems of law, because the demands of a career in the imperial courts precluded the possibilities of such specialization.

The Anglo-Indian judicial system differed radically from pre-imperial dispute management. Derrett lists the variety of Indian courts as: 1) tribal government, with slight influence from outside pressure; 2) "a hierarchy of political governors" in rural areas who took administrative action to solve problems which family, caste, village, or district leaders could not solve – "unanimity being more important that abstract justice"; 3) *panchayats* or *ad hoc* committees of castes, which might consult the *shastra* when the parties were of high caste status; and 4) Brahmin sub-castes, which would more frequently consult the *shastras*.[5] All of these types might be found over a small geographical area and none "were suitable for sudden transference into other spheres"; hardly any were "conformable to British presuppositions about judicial administration."[6] Derrett states that the state dealt with robbery, murder, and major disturbances. Royal authority, loosely defined in the Indian context, supported the decisions of caste *panchayats*.

The Anglo-Indian judicial system was alien to India in its organization, procedures, and principles of adjudication. However, its substantive law developed into a hybrid of Indian and British traditions. Derrett's main goal in these articles is to explain how the hybrid developed and what its nature was. He continuously points out that, even if imperial law had some roots in Indian law, it was still far from popular usage.

After the assumption of rule in the Eastern Provinces, the courts of the British East India Company became popular with Indian inhabitants of the area. Derrett finds this popularity in the Company's "readiness and sureness of execution and attachment" combined with the consultation of Indian expert opinion. The public found in the new system possibilities to harass their "enemies."[7] The flow of cases became a flood and the system quickly reached the point of breakdown as accusations of corruption and inefficiency

5. Ibid., 278.
6. Ibid., 278.
7. Ibid., 232.

were raised against the courts' Indian assistants. Warren Hasting's Plan of 1772 and the Administration of Justice Regulation of April 11, 1780 gave responsibility for the law and sentences to *pandits* (Brahmins proficient in the *shastras*), consulted by European judges, on listed subjects only, though they might be consulted for other subjects. The listed subjects were inheritance, marriage, caste, and other religious usages and institutions. Indian jurists had convinced Company representatives that the laws of the Hindus on these matters had to be ascertained from the *shastras*. The representatives, not being knowledgeable in either Sanskrit or styles of Indian legal reasoning, were predisposed to accept the *pandits'* arguments regarding the significance of the *shastras*, because of their familiarity with the division in Britain between "courts temporal" and "courts christian" (bishops' courts). The notion of an ecclesiastical law with its own specialists was congenial to British models of judicial organization at the end of the eighteenth century. The Company made no effort to collect evidence of local or caste custom, which, in fact, diverged considerably from the sacred texts. In 1781, the jurisdiction of the King's courts was extended to include the litigation of Hindus, in accordance with their laws and usages for listed topics. As the Supreme Court began, therefore, to utilize the services of *pandits*, pressure developed throughout both court systems to use precedent in making decisions and the principle of *stare decisis* was adopted throughout.

British ignorance of shastric learning was increasingly felt to be unsatisfactory. In the 1770s, the Company had begun the patronage of shastric learning and, with the expansion of the responsibility of the Supreme Court, the work accelerated. Over the next 60 years old texts were translated into English, new compendiums of laws were drawn up and translated, and new shastric texts made their appearance. Thus began a long, complicated process through which a subtle and abstract indigenous legal tradition became restated and reworked in the more concrete British legal terminology, and given alien meaning in the context of a completely different system of judicial procedure. Even though, however, the adjective and substantive law of the empire were alien to indigenous dispute management, the Anglo-Indian legal system came to replace local tribunals widely in the course of the nineteenth century (caste and village tribunals continued to function in some contexts). The courts ceased for the most part to consult *pandits* after 1864, and judicial knowledge of Hindu law was assumed at that time. In part because the distance between shastric injunction and actual practice became increasingly to be recognized, Anglo-Indian justices claimed that they were interested in actual practice; however, the requirements for proof of custom were so stringent that it could not come to play an important role in decision making:

> The British method of deducing the law from the European textwriter's idea of what the Pandits meant, coupled with whatever might be deduced from the translations of a few prominent Sanskrit legal texts, and put cheek-by-jowl with decided cases (which might not correctly reproduce the traditions in the locality) enabled the law to be deduced in a most artificial and remote manner, the despair of scholars able to read the Sanskrit original authorities.[8]

As Anglo-Hindu law developed, the supplementation of shastric rules and the blending with British rules occurred:

> New legal institutions, such as English-type negotiable instruments were expected to supplant the traditional customary law, or like insolvency, were expected to be grafted upon Hindu institutions . . . Where the texts provided no explicit indication of the way in which a right was to be worked out, or how a particular disposition should be construed, English rules filled the gap. This happened frequently even without conscious reference to Justice, Equity and Good Conscience, the residual source of law, since . . . the judges were not aware that in applying English Common Law or Equity they were doing anything else but expounding the Hindu law on the point. So many rules of English law seemed to be merely rules of universal law.[9]

Derrett also argues, however, that judges often discovered the Hindu law through importation, or that Hindu institutions could not have been applied effectively without importation. He also comments that there was evidence that judges attempted to avoid allowing analogies from the English system to affect their judgement, and that it was common to refuse to apply an English rule. Anglo-Indian law developed in a "piecemeal" fashion:

> Sometimes the *smrti* [ancient texts] was taken as a standard, and the commentators ignored, while at others the commentators were supposed the only valid authorities, whatever the *smrti* might appear to say literally. At times the commentators themselves were followed if local usage supported them; at others the local usage could be presumed. In all cases,

8. Ibid., 298.
9. Ibid., 311.

once the line of decisions had been established, the court was reluctant to depart from it even when it was shown that the *dharmashastra*, treated historically, went the other way . . . It is evident that learning in Anglo-Hindu law did not keep pace with historical research into the *dharmashastra*, perhaps because certainty of titles was more important that the satisfaction of the somewhat erratic academics of the period.[10]

In 1930, a process of the reform of Anglo-Hindu law began which reached its culmination in the Hindu Code of 1955–1956, after Independence. Even though nationalists charged that shastric law had become "fossilized" under British rule, the reformers who made the Hindu Code exhibited little interest in turning to shastric scholarship as sources for the code. The Hindu Code has some of its roots in Anglo-Hindu case-law. It also looks to the values of the influential and cosmopolitan sector of the urban population and the academic theory on law (in reference to the Code's relation to actual Hindu practice at the time, Derrett comments that it "has little to do with Hinduism by any possible definition of the term").[11] In defense of Anglo-Hindu law, Derrett notes that the writers of the Hindu Code were cautious in approaching Anglo-Hindu law and avoided undoing previous legislation:

> Nothing done in 1955–1956 suggested that in so far as the British amended, modified, abrogated or supplemented the law their administration had been mischievous or misdirected.[12]

Derrett often notes, as have many scholars, that Anglo-Hindu law differed widely from local usage. However, in his description of the development of this law as "piecemeal," he points to a flexibility in the tradition, on which Marc Galanter elaborates (below). However, insofar as Derrett addresses himself directly to the issue of the popularity of the courts, he points to their initial novelty and continued usefulness for Indians as arenas within which to harass their enemies. This is also a theme upon which sociologists of law elaborate.

The Sociology of Law

Attempts at a synthetic view of the Anglo-Indian encounter come from two American sociologists of law, Marc Galanter and Robert

10. Ibid., 300–01.
11. Ibid., 322.
12. Ibid., 320.

Kidder. These two scholars have related views, with some differences in emphasis and interpretation. They both differ from Derrett in discussing general categories, institutions, and processes, and de-emphasizing unique events.

Marc Galanter's work can be seen in two phases. In his early, modernization phase he focussed on the novel characteristics of what he termed the "modern" legal system in India. His later work examines the ways in which this legal system shows its adaptation to Indian structures and values.

In an article published in 1968, Galanter describes the British imperial legal system as a "unified nationwide modern legal system" with features common to legal systems in an industrial society, including "uniform territorial rules based on universalistic norms, which apportion rights and obligations as incidents of specific transactions, rather than fixed statuses."[13] This system he juxtaposed to that obtaining in pre-British India, with the latter having "innumerable overlapping local jurisdictions and many groups . . . [enjoying] one or another degree of autonomy in administering law to themselves."[14] Galanter found innovational elements in the imperial legal system in the "new avenues for mobility and advancement," in the possibilities for new allies outside local arenas, and in the freeing of property and persons from "hereditary prescriptions making possible a wider range of 'market' transactions."[15] The courts further offered "new channels for dissemination of norms and values from governmental centres to towns and out to villages" and they presented "new methods of group activity and new images of social formation."[16]

Lawyers, in particular, disseminated a new national legal culture as they translated local interests into the terms of official norms and assisted in the organization of India into a modern nation-state. This activity of translation Galanter elaborates upon as a way of describing in general terms the relationship between traditional society and the institutions of the modern legal system. Instead of being passively acted upon by the new system, traditional society used the modern legal system to reach its own goals and to enforce its own restrictions. Litigation activities could express traditional interests and groupings.[17]

13. Galanter, "Displacement," 66.
14. Ibid., 66.
15. Ibid., 76.
16. Ibid., 76.
17. Ibid., 83.

After Independence in 1947, the imperial legal system was further consolidated and rationalized, and the system of courts received further unification. The Constitution established a secular federal republic with a parliamentary system and a strong central government. A section of the Constitution, "Directive Principles of State Policy," called for the development of Indian society as a modern welfare state, and to this end, central and state legislatures released legislation to encourage economic development and facilitate social reform, "extending governmental regulation to many areas of life previously immune from official control."[18] Two examples of the extension and consolidation of the modern legal system are the Hindu Code, which for the first time applied a set of rules to all Hindus, and the legislation and constitutional provisions regarding caste.[19] Here the attempt has been to eradicate barriers among Hindus with the visualization of a non-communal society, a single national community.[20]

This reform legislation represents more of the values and vision of the Western-educated, "advanced" sectors of Indian society, a relatively small, if growing, minority. Galanter argues that in this way a dual legal system, a legacy of the colonial period, has been perpetuated. He finds, however, such a situation obtaining in "most modern societies," where one finds common trends in "barrowing, consolidating and modernising national legal systems."[21]

Galanter refers to the common observation in the nineteenth and twentieth century that a flood of litigation moved to the Western-style courts. He interprets this utilization of the courts in several ways. This movement probably represented "the mere transfer of old disputes to new tribunals."[22] He points out that isolating a dispute in Anglo-Indian courts, away from local and confining contexts, enabled "larger prizes" for the winners, since both the compromising and negotiating nature of local tribunals were avoided. Galanter agrees with Derrett that the new courts offered new opportunities for harassment and adds:

> They also gave rise to a sense of individual right not dependent on opinion or usage and capable of being actively enforced by government, even in opposition to community opinion.[23]

18. Ibid., 79.
19. Ibid., 80.
20. Ibid., 81.
21. Ibid., 85.
22. Ibid., 69.
23. Ibid., 70.

In his later work on the Indian legal system Galanter has been less interested in what was novel in the system, and more interested in understanding the "eager and unfaltering embrace of Western law" – those ways in which the system can be said to have become "indigenous" to India. In 1972, he published an article on the failure of government attempts to establish village-based tribunals, as an alternative to the costly and slow courts. Galanter concluded that, rather than serving as a radical alternative, these *nyaya panchayats* ended up serving to extend the procedures and values of the national legal system. They were "not an abandonment of the modern legal system, but its extension in the guise of tradition."[24]

In asking why there was such a relative scarcity of well-organized and powerful actors and well-developed alternatives to the national legal system, Galanter decides that, even though the system is severely criticized, it has become "so thoroughly domesticated": "That is, indigenisation on the ideological/programmatic level failed because the law had become 'indigenous' on the operational/ adaptive level."[25] Here Galanter emphasizes the adaptiveness of the imperial system rather than its novel features. He points out that British institutions and rules were combined with structural features of the pre-British system and with pre-British rules; the borrowed elements themselves were exposed to more than 150 years of "pruning in which British localisms and anomalies were discarded and rules elaborated to deal with new kinds of persons, property and transactions."[26] Here he reiterates his earlier points about the significance of the legal culture of the lawyers and the ways traditional interests use the legal system, becoming, in so doing, transformed by that system.

Even if Galanter argues that the imperially-based legal system has become indigenized, he remains (in 1972) preoccupied with that condition frequently referred to: its "lack of congruence with underlying social norms."[27] ("The Indian situation is perceived as deficient or even pathological . . ."[28]). Galanter concludes that the Indian system is measured against "expectations which are in part projections of the working myths of modern legal systems."[29] He

24. M. Galanter, "The abortive restoration of indigenous law in India," *Comparative Studies in Society and History* 14 (1972) 1, 60.
25. Ibid., 63.
26. Ibid., 63.
27. Ibid., 66.
28. Ibid., 66.
29. Ibid., 66.

suggests that we question our expectations of the "normal" in legal systems. The Indian experience, on the contrary, shows that law does not have to be "historically rooted in a society," nor need it be "congruent with its social and cultural setting," nor that it have "an integrated purposive character."[30]

In a more recent general statement Galanter sees more congruence between Indian society and its modern legal system than he found earlier. In the course of work on a major study of the judicial doctrine of protective discrimination, he found that, in certain structural ways, the modern system bears marks of pre-British organization. Galanter had expected to find a "fixed hierarchically-established doctrine," because, as a modern legal system, the Indian system had "doctrines of authority and precedent and the hierarchical organisation of courts."[31] A range of factors, including the pressures of case load, turnover of judges, and limitations of legal research, had acted to transform the law into something different. The doctrine was equivocal and the equivocation was fully institutionalized:

> What purported to be pyramidal hierarchy establishing fixed doctrine turned out to be a loose collegium presiding over an open-textured body of learning within which conflicting tendencies could be accommodated and elaborated.[32]

Galanter links the development of this patterning of judicial doctrine to two alternatives, neither exclusive of the other. He notes that the history of law in modern India has shown the interplay between the "nationalisation of legal activity" and the "continuing drive for self-regulation in many sectors of social life."[33] This tension between authoritative high law and local law-ways had been, also in Galanter's view, a characteristic of the pre-British system. It is possible, therefore, that what one finds in judicial doctrine today is an Indian way of accommodating this tension in a modern system. Or, a second alternative, it is that the experience shows "universal features of the accommodation of diverse normative orderings in the legal systems of complex heterogeneous societies".[34] Rather than looking at the activities of individuals in litigation, Galanter has

30. Ibid., 66.
31. Galanter, "India law," 45.
32. Ibid., 45.
33. Ibid., 46.
34. Ibid., 46.

taken a general cultural and structural view of the relationship between India and its national legal system.

Robert Kidder's article from 1978 goes in somewhat different directions. Kidder argues that Western law has certain characteristics which put it in the same relationship to all societies "regardless of culture." These characteristics are: 1) centralization or the existence of "externally determined agendas" – external to local societies; 2) agendas which are determined not only by local interests and local conflicts, but also by "economic and political policy needs defined by remote but influential actors," and 3) criteria for employment in courts which are based on "generalised, external standards."[35] Kidder says that all of these characteristics produce alienation between internal society and the external legal system, whether the latter exists in the United States or India.

Kidder, however, still shows preoccupation with the issue of the popularity of Western (or external) courts in India and the rate of litigiousness in Indian society. He is careful to note that popularity of these courts refers to the frequency of their use, but not to a wide appreciation of the quality of their justice:

> Almost every account of Indian responses to this "Western" institution carries the same message: courts were the object of rampant abuse and manipulation. Every trick in the book is described in detail: perjury, falsification of evidence, procedural manipulation in order to stalemate opponents with delay, and bribery of court personnel. Touts stirred up conflict in the villages and then brought the opponents to lawyers who paid for this service. People's cynicism about the quality of English justice was only matched by their ambivalent, gambler-like hopes for personal success. Litigants were pictured either as innocent dupes of an alien system or as convincing aggressors grabbing for fortunes from their inexperienced opponents.[36]

Kidder argues that the Western courts in India were in fact diametrically opposed in the principles and procedures of their practice to the principles and procedures of dispute practice in local, caste-based communities: "The result was that court decrees, rather than settling disputes, often added to the many already existing devices used by disputants to pursue their opponents."[37] The courts

---

35. R. Kidder, "Western law in India: external law and local response," in *Social System and Legal Process*, ed. Harry M. Johnson (San Francisco, 1978), 168.
36. Ibid., 160.
37. Ibid., 161.

were so alien to traditional "authority channels" – caste, familial, and territorial tribunals – and to traditional methods of mediation, that the Western system supported falsehood. Customary practice was so "distorted beyond recognition by simplistic judicial routines of interpretation," that "the only way to support truth was by lying."[38] Picking up on a point made by Galanter in 1966, Kidder argues that, in the face of the break with community norms which court involvement entailed, it was local "malcontents" who dragged everybody else into courts where alien judges had little capacity to sort out the fabrications of "troublemakers" from village authorities.[39] He adds that, in a period of accelerated economic change, the courts were also scenes of confrontation between the defenders of the status quo and those seeking marks of status consistent with their success at self-improvement. Here Kidder cites the example of caste groups attempting to escape from the incidences of low-caste status. He concludes his discussion here by noting:

> The terms of conflict were altered by the new judicial presence. An element of change became a real alternative for those with reason to resist local authority, as well as for those seeking to solidify unstable but advantageous definitions of local authority. Judicial decrees supporting the status quo could not support it, because the strategies and alliances needed to win produced important changes in local relationships.[40]

This continuous testing of authoritative limits produced and produces expansion in litigation, while "the net effect of much Indian litigation is to engage courts as additional agents in prolonged episodes of conflict that are periodically suspended by temporary compromises."[41]

Kidder began by saying that he was concerned with structure, though he continues, in making his over-all point, with a discussion of the culture of local communities. In the next section I will discuss how a cultural history approach can respond to several issues raised in the two main approaches discussed above.

38. Ibid., 163–64.
39. Ibid., 164.
40. Ibid., 165.
41. Ibid., 167–68.

Cultural History

The cultural history approach to the encounter between British and Indian legal systems is part of a wider trend in the study of the social and political consequences of British imperialism in India. This trend involves establishing the main principles and values of social and political action in the period preceding the establishment of imperial government, and then discussing transformations in indigenous society under imperialism. Or, the practitioners of this approach find in the records of the period of imperial rule evidence of indigenous values and institutions which are undergoing transformation. One outstanding characteristic of this approach is the willingness to consider that the cultural logic of indigenous institutions followed principles of organization and practice which were different from contemporary Western institutions in important ways. This approach finds that at the same time that the makers of British policy in India proceeded with misconstructions of the aims and values of "native" society, imperial institutions evolved in a dialectic relationship with local society: the institutions of the rulers and ruled transformed each other throughout the period of imperial rule. As this trend has developed, new assessments of indigenous, pre-colonial society and culture and new assessments of the imperial experience have appeared.

From the nineteenth century, as Indian studies developed among Westerners, the major focus and fascination for scholars was caste, conceived of as a rigid, conservative institution which ordered all significant aspects of a person's life. Caste, quite simply, was thought to explain most of what was distinctive in Indian history, as giving social stability to a people otherwise at the mercy of oppressive, violent, and chaotic dynastic rulers.

In this general vision of Indian society, Brahmin priests are at the apex of a stratified system in which the principles of status are organized primarily around notions of purity and pollution. Conceptions of status in relationship to structures of Indian polities and ideologies of royal power played a relatively minor role in these scholarly formulations. This preoccupation with caste led to a tradition of inquiry in which the "isolated" village, organized into caste communities living in harmony with each other, provided the basic unit of analysis. Discussion of the pre-British legal systems similarly tended to focus on local, village-based, community dispute management. From this vision has come the suggestion that disputing was fairly well contained in local tribunals. This tradition of analysis focusses on disputing in family, caste and village "channels of authority."

A recent article by the historian Ronald Inden heralds a shift in scholarly models to a focus on the fluid boundaries of kingly status and domains in India. Inden points out that this focus was fore-shadowed in the work of A.M. Hocart (1883–1939):

> He argued that caste should be seen as a hierarchy of ritual offices centered on a king [or local lord] and having as their purpose the performance of the royal ritual for the benefit of the entire community. . . . Castes, according to Hocart, were not a peculiar irrational social institution confined to India; nor had they at their very point of origin swallowed up kingship; on the contrary, they were themselves offices of the state.[42]

With this perspective castes – and villages – are systematically put into a social and political framework which transcends the internal political concerns of villages. Recent formulations of the general principles of authority and status in the framework are markedly different from the bounded and rigid characteristics of "caste society." These formulations have important implications for recent conceptions of the significance and meaning of much litigation activity in India.

Recent discussions of the nature of status and authority in the old regime conceptualize polities organized according to principles of authoritative incorporation. Here special status accrues to powerful figures and/or heads of kin groups or other communities which share in the rule of authoritative domains. The holders of these shares are ranked, not necessarily by an absolute scale of values, but in relation to each other. These shareholders are integrated into both their immediate domain and into superior domains through rituals of incorporation.

For example, Mughal emperors distributed *khelats*, which included sets of clothes, to warriors and local rulers in the ritual of imperial assemblies. This clothing represented the body of the emperor, to which the recipient was ritually joined.[43] The ritual presentation indicated that the emperor shared his authority over his imperial domain with the recipient, who offered his own gift(s),

42. R. Inden, "Orientalist constructions of India," *Modern Asian Studies* 20 (1986) 3, 436.
43. B.S. Cohn, "Representing authority in Victorian India" in *The Invention of Tradition*, ed. E. Hobsbawm and T. Ranger (London, 1983), 168.

called *nazar*, in a returning vow of obedience to imperial will. In this manner the recipient joined his inferior domain to that of the emperor and recognized the superiority of the emperor, at the same time as his own local authority received imperial recognition and protection. The local authority of the recipient was theoretically enhanced because, in receiving the *khelat*, he shared in the superior royal substance/status of the emperor. At the same time as the local ranking of the recipient was enhanced, and presumably he was recognized as first among the other leaders in his locality, he was ranked in the emperor's assembly *vis-à-vis* the other bearers of *nazar*. The Mughal Empire brought an innovation to political ranking in India, in that, through the *mansabdar* system, some ranks were given an absolute value. However, for the most part, in some localities this conception of absolute value did not take hold, and relative ranking was prevalent.

Conceptions of political incorporation among relatively ranked sharers of authority in a domain appear to have been spread over a wide range of levels of political engagement in the old regime. Scholarly attention has recently focussed on south India, and Tamil country in particular,[44] but evidence of fluid boundaries in segmented polities throughout the subcontinent exists.[45] From village domains to chieftaincies, and from little kingdoms to regional monarchies, leading figures took part in rituals of incorporation and shared in the control and rule of polities large and small. The implication of these findings for our survey here is that political status, far from being clearly and absolutely defined, was continuously subjected to challenge by competitors for rank. In such a fluid system, without fixed values of rank, the boundaries and substance of control were not set and were subject to continual dispute by

44. See A. Appadurai, *Worship and Conflict under Colonial Rule: a South Indian Case* (Cambridge, 1981); N.B. Dirks, *The Hollow Crown. Ethnohistory of an Indian Kingdom* (Cambridge, 1987); D. Ludden, *Peasant History in South India* (Princeton, 1985); B. Stein, *Peasant State and Society in Medieval South India* (Delhi, 1980); P.G. Price, "Competition and conflict in Hindu polity, ca. 1550–1750: the integration and fragmentation of Tamil and Andhra kingdoms," Presented at the eighteenth European conference on Modern South Asian Studies, Tällberg, Sweden; D.D. Shulman, *The King and the Clown in South Indian Myth and Poetry* (Princeton, 1985).

45. See D.H.A. Kolff, "The end of an ancien régime: colonial war in India, 1798–1818," in *Imperialism and War. Essays on Colonial Wars in Asia and Africa*, ed. J.A. de Moor and H.L. Wesseling (Leiden, 1989) Comparative Studies in Overseas History, no. 8; N.P. Ziegler, "Some notes on Rajput loyalties during the Mughal period," in *Kingship and Authority in South Asia*, ed. J.F. Richards (Madison, 1981) 215–251; R. Inden, "The Hindu chiefdom in Middle Bengali literature," in *Bengali Literature and History*, ed. E.C. Dimock jr. (East Lansing, 1967), 21–46.

competitors for enhanced authoritative status. Much of the work of dispute management, then, involved sorting out the claims of shareholders to land and labor, irrigation rights, and temple and assembly honors in village, chieftaincy and royal domain. Among chiefs, little kings, and regional kings, challenges to status were similarly common – thus, the reputation of dynastic rule for anarchy and chaos. Competitors in the old regime fought over "land," yes, but land was not owned, but held and ruled, even in small plots; thus, rural dispute management involved sorting out claims very much tied up with issues of status and authoritative dominance. Characterizing Tamil kingship recently, David Shulman wrote, concerning "the diffusion of power and basic weakness of the centre":

> The king is less a source of compelling power and creative direction of affairs than the focus of a delicate balance, the embodiment of the community's consensus, which finds expression in his powers of arbitration. This consensus is, moreover, primarily achieved through conflict. The king's role is inherently agonistic, in that it pits him against an endless series of potential rivals and replacements, each with his own claim to legitimacy and equal power.[46]

Village men were consistently, through demands for military labor, called into participation in the competitions organized by chiefs and kings, petty and large, as they confronted and threatened each other and their rivals over issues of status and domination in and among authoritative domains. Understanding that land was not "privately owned" in pre-British India expands our appreciation that political domains were not necessarily territorially bound. Chiefs and kings and their warriors did not defend "homelands" so much as they were involved in contests over status involving continuously shifting relationships. As André Wink has written:

> In India . . . sovereignty was primarily a matter of allegiances; the state organized itself around conflict and remained essentially open-ended instead of becoming territorially circumscribed.[47]

Ironically, then, even though political ritual at all levels emphasized incorporation/integration, the sharing of ruling authority gave rise to considerable disharmony and confusion over boundaries of rela-

46. D.D. Shulman, "On South Indian bandits and kings," *The Indian Economic and Social History Review* 17 (1980) 3, 306.
47. A. Wink, *Land and Sovereignty in India: Agrarian Society and Politics under the Eighteenth-Century Maratha Svarajya* (Cambridge, 1986), 27–28.

tionships. Speaking of the level of engagement above the village domain, the historian Dirk Kolff asserts that what contemporary (eighteenth century) Britons termed "notorious treachery" characterized political relations in the old regime. Having a limited conception of belonging to territorially fixed domains, which had to be defended, warriors found it in their interest to fight for whomever, at a point in time, offered them the best terms.[48] Force, therefore, was not so important a political tool as "conciliation, gift-giving, sowing dissension among and 'winning over' an enemy's local supporters."[49] A man of ruling status did not hope to extinguish the claims of his rivals so much as to detract from their status, or, as Kolff describes, have "an impact on the performance of the other participants in the public drama as far as staged within one's political horizon."[50] In Indian political conception, one did not aspire to expand one's administration so much as to manipulate political forces in localities, weakening one's antagonist such that he would become incorporated into one's (open-ended) domain, with a demonstration that he accepted one's authority.

The system of status competition and dispute management outlined briefly above was not completely destroyed with the imposition of imperial peace. Research on the landed elites of the nineteenth century suggests that their seemingly endless inheritance and succession litigation in imperial courts represented a transformation of this traditional style of disputing through the conceptual forms and procedures of the Anglo-Indian legal system. Rural magnates, chiefs and petty kings, reincarnated as revenue paying *zamindars* in the Permanent Settlements, far from being the enfeebled dissolutes of imperial prose, showed remarkable persistence and strength of purpose in their political objectives, pursuing old and new royal relationships. Litigation played an important role in landed politics, as rajas and ranis and their rivalrous kin struggled in related processes of status competition and the maintenance of ritual forms of rule.[51] Here I briefly examine several aspects of *zamindari* litigation in the Presidency of Madras in the nineteenth century. I do not mean to confine royal values and relationships to *zamindaris*, as I discuss

48. Kolff, "Colonial war," 26.
49. Wink, *Land and Sovereignty*, 27.
50. Kolff, "Colonial war," 45.
51. See P.G. Price, *Resources and rule in Zamindari South India, 1802–1903: Sivagangai and Ramnad as kingdoms under the Raj*. Ph.D. dissertation, University of Wisconsin-Madison, 1979; Price, "Raja-dharma in nineteenth century South India: land, litigation and largess in Ramnad Zamindari," *Contributions to Indian Sociology* 13 (1979) 2, 207–39.

later. However, the role which litigation played in the adjustment of
indigenous royal political culture to imperial ruling is seen most
clearly here. I also do not mean to imply that local structures of
ruling and disputing were not importantly altered in the political
culture of the new empire. However, in important ways elements of
a political culture in which the boundaries of authoritative domain
were fluid and continuously subject to challenge and negotiation
survived, both in spite of and through the new forms of dispute
processing.

Company officers made Permanent Settlements, creating landed
estates in the first years of the nineteenth century in Madras. It has
commonly been observed that, in giving titles in land and marking
boundaries, the imperial government froze relations which had been
fluid. The new regulations are thought to have prevented the shifting of boundaries of domains and of the personal statuses of not-
ables. However, giving lineal boundaries to units of land which had
previously been vague in geographical definition was not the same
thing as freezing warrior groups into stagnating and rigid relationships. The point of the famous, drawn-out, expensive litigation
of landed families was not that legal judgments fixed relationships,
but that relationships retained elements of flux and, particularly in a
new context, continuously sought boundaries of status and meaning.

The selection of a new king, great or small, had often been a
violent procedure in pre-British times. In the nineteenth century
royal kin with a ruling house attempted to establish their status and
domination through litigation, challenging the title-holders' right to
rule. The meaning of belonging to a royal house was debated, in a
sense, as women as well as men frequently sought to claim the
zamindari title. Among *zamindari* families, struggles over rank and
status were carried on in legal manipulation. Under the cover of
challenging adoptions, for example, the *zamindari* families of Pitta-
pore and Venkatagiri on the Andhra coast competed for prestige
and control in the last half of the nineteenth century. All of the
"tricks" which Robert Kidder details in the selection quoted earlier
– and more – were used in these combats. However, as Kolff reminds
us, tricks and treachery were an important part of political relations
in the eighteenth century, and their appearance in nineteenth-
century court rooms need not be seen as a particular perversion of
the imposition of an "external" legal system. *Zamindars* and their
rivals, kin and non-kin, showed their local strength and their power
by buying great numbers of witnesses, hiring the most brilliant and
costly Madras lawyers, and maintaining small brigades of hangers-

on, who claimed fees for dubious services in the cause of extensive litigation. Through the rhetoric and terminology came the demands for honors and rights to ritual performances. A major preoccupation of the litigation show was competition over ruling status in a domain.

A focus on the fluid organization of authority in domains has more explanatory possibilities than assisting in an interpretation of *zamindari* litigation. Conceptions of fluid boundaries of rule, an inheritance of a pre-bureaucratic political culture, pervade, it appears, all aspects of political life, from competition for dominance among village bosses to the formation of factions in political parties. Scholarly focus on caste membership as the central defining element in a person's life has drawn attention away from the ways in which Indians conceptualize personal rank and domination in spheres of authority. Marvin Davis's work on Bengal discusses the nature of authority in domains in his area:

> Torkotala villagers . . . regard the king – whatever his actual *varna* [caste category] – as . . . [warrior-like] and look upon him as the exemplary political figure. . . . Each head [of a physical-cum-social division] replicates the function of a king, as it were, within a more limited realm. . . . Individuals and groupings of individuals at every level of social organisation are thus seen as replicating royal functions, as being single or collective political actors, each concerned with the common aim of maintaining and upholding *dharma* [moral order].[52]

Evidence from historical, political, and anthropological writing increasingly suggests that, contrary to earlier analysis, the achievement of superior personal rank, apart from one's caste position, has traditionally been and remains a major preoccupation in Indian society. In a society where domains are still conceived apart from territorial boundaries and bureaucratic offices, life for the politically motivated is a continuous struggle to protect one's status from challenges from rivals. In scholarly literature political factions are the domain form most familiar to students of Indian society, though recent work on Bengal points to other conceptions in indigenous sociopolitical perceptions. It is well known that factions are a characteristic of all levels of Indian political life. While some factional development can be seen as an organic element of non-traditional political change, we can understand the forms and values of lead-

---

52. M. Davis, *Rank and Rivalry: the Politics of Inequality in Rural West Bengal* (Cambridge, 1983), 112–13.

ership in much factional activity as a continued, if much evolved, expression of the indigenous ideology of ruling authority.

In writing about the nature of factional leadership in the village, Davis describes a political position which is continually open to challenge and which requires continual reaffirmation through success in status competition.[53]

> And even in the absence of open challenge, the achieved nature of factional leadership requires, periodically, the demonstration of those qualities by which leadership is generated. . . . Continued membership in a faction . . . depends on a return for support given. It is because factions are voluntary teams based largely on transactional ties that their membership is so variable. Simply, individuals can switch their loyalties and support at will.[54]

What are the implications of this political culture for people's use of the external legal system? The courtroom is not simply another arena where one can harass one's enemies, though such has been the dominating interpretation of Indian litigation since the beginning of the nineteenth century. Considered in the general context of the aspects of Indian political culture discussed here, courtrooms are yet another opportunity for the performance of status competitions between rivals for authority and control in a domain, be that domain a kin group, a village, a district, or an urban ward. Courtrooms are sites for the challenge of the unstable status of one's rivals. In a study published in 1974 Robert Kidder wrote that a "caste leader," the leader of an association devoted to the interests of a particular caste, did not define himself and his political career in terms of his association with the caste or its organization. Caste leaders were men of many activities, all of which were organized around the establishment of a general sphere of influence.[55] Litigation was just one of these activities. He notes:

> Lawsuits may be nothing more than strategies of pressure designed to yield temporary advantage within caste association, political party, financial institution, extended family, or business sector. It may affect all of these simultaneously depending on the nature of the suit and the pattern of relationships among the litigants.[56]

53 *Ibid.*, 162.
54. *Ibid.*, 162.
55. R. Kidder, "Litigation as a strategy for personal mobility: the case of urban caste association leaders," *Journal of Asian Studies* 23 (1974) 2, 189.
56. *Ibid.*, 186.

I do not mean to suggest that all litigation in the modern legal system has been or is the expression of status competition over authority and control in domains. However, I do assert that much that has seemed perverse about the nature of litigation activities in India can be understood through this cultural history approach. Here, for example, we do not need to interpret litigation activity as, in major part, the work of malcontents daring to break with local authorities. The courts provide another arena, another opportunity, in the round of activities of influence building and the challenging of status which characterize the lives of the politically aggressive.

Conclusion

Scholarly examination of the Anglo-Indian legal encounter has shifted in the postwar period from a focus on the special incidents of legal history to the relationship between legal and societal transformations. With the increasing acceptance in the social sciences and humanities of cultural studies, it is not surprising that the attempt to find basic structures of societal form and meaning appears in works examining the development of legal institutions and activities in India. The challenge of understanding and explaining the encounter does not of course end here. Another trend in postwar scholarship focusses on the relationship of legal development to objective shifts in the control of material resources and attending changes in political structures and values. Recent work in this direction includes an important article by David Washbrook, which places Anglo-Indian legal history in the framework of an interpretation of the changing goals of imperial policy.[57] A very different type of study, but one which is integrally related to issues of changes in resource control, is Marc Galanter's monumental examination of the law of compensatory discrimination in Independent India.[58] It is my hope, as work continues in legal studies, that a great divide does not develop between the concerns of cultural history and a focus on objective inequalities in resource control. Interest in combining the two approaches appears in Peter Robb's work on tenancy legislation in late nineteenth century Bihar[59] and

57. D.A. Washbrook, "Law, state and agrarian society in colonial India," *Modern Asian Studies* 15 (1981) 3, 649–721.
58. M. Galanter, *Competing Equalities: Law and the Backward Classes in India* (Berkeley, 1984).
59. P. Robb, "Law and agrarian society in India: the case of Bihar and the

Oliver Mendelsohn's discussion of litigation over land.[60] The connecting link, and one not to lose sight of, is that authority (a preoccupation of cultural historians) and power (a common fascination of students of inequalities) are best understood and explained in relation to each other. Obviously, notions of what is or is not legitimate control over resources inspire individual and group approaches to redistribution and appropriation, as well as approaches to social value and political competition.

APPENDIX

The number of persons per lawyer in selected countries:

United States (1960)	728
Canada (1961)	1,366
Italy (1957)	1,601
Great Britain (1959)	2,105
West Germany (1958)	3,012
India (1952)	4,920
Egypt (1964)	5,768
France (1958)	5,769
Japan (1960)	14,354
Nigeria (1964)	22,765
Indonesia (c. 1964)	c. 100,000

Taken from Galanter, "Displacement", 77.

---

nineteenth century tenancy debate," *Modern Asian Studies* 22 (1988) 2, 319–54.

60. O. Mendelsohn, "The pathology of the Indian legal system," *Modern Asian Studies* 15 (1981) 4, 823–63.

10

The Indian and the British Law Machines: Some Remarks on Law and Society in British India

D.H.A. KOLFF

The Indian and the British Law Machines

When, in 1960, Attorney-General Setalvad of India was called upon to explain Indian law in a series of lectures to an Anglo-Saxon audience, the pervading theme of his lectures was the fidelity of Indian law to British models. Though many questions can be asked about this resemblance, the phenomenon itself is obvious and striking. English public law, criminal law, law of torts, contract law generally, and procedure were in their essentials almost imported wholesale into the British Indian empire. Was this a superficial and alien layer of law superimposed on Indian society, but condemned to remain a foreign anomaly? Some authors have suggested that, at a deeper level of analysis, this was the case. They have argued, for instance, that Western legal thinking developed on the basis of an opposition between right and wrong, which required the determination of wrongs to be punished or put right, whereas Indian civilization emphasized settlement and compromise on the basis of equity. On the other hand, an American professor of law who gained much experience as a lawyer in the courts of post-independence South Asia, denied that such niceties were observable in practice. He did not consider that India managed its disputes in a very distinct manner: "the ratio of litigation to settlement was greater than in my own practice [in the USA]; the proportionate cost of litigation was higher; the minuteness of legal detail at issue was greater; the insistence on vindication of legal 'rights' was comparable." In short, he "felt completely at home with the bench and bar of India and South Asia generally."[1]

---

1. M.C. Setalvad, *The Common Law in India* (London, 1960). Harrop A. Freeman,

Yet, it would not be correct to ascribe these characteristics to a particularly harsh imposition of English law on Indian society during the colonial period. Protests were few. Although there were, during the years of most fervent nationalist initiative, the 1920s and 1930s, some attempts to replace the official courts of justice by "truly Indian tribunals which would work by conciliation, relying on moral suasion rather than coercive sanctions," the Constitution of independent India (1950) would generally endorse the existing legal system, especially the substantive law (i.e. the rules concerning society rather than the judicial system), but also to a large extent adjective law (i.e. mainly court procedure and evidence). Marc Galanter, on these grounds, has concluded that Anglo-Indian law appears thoroughly domesticated in India, having become "indigenous" on the operational level. Even so-called Hindu law as it now applies in India – largely family law for Hindus – is rationalized and transformed into something very different from the *dharmashastra* of ancien régime India: as administered in India now, the "Hindu Code" (1955–56), a system that regulates a large section of Indian society, cannot according to morality or judicial logic be opposed to, or even distinguished from, those parts of the legal system that are more immediately traceable as originally English. Indeed, to Indian lawyers nowadays, the system seems to present a consistent and fully Indian whole. Not surprisingly, Setalvad, the Delhi Attorney-General, concluded his lectures in the same vein. "So has been built up," he said, "on the basis of the principles of English law the fabric of modern Indian law which notwithstanding its foreign roots and origin is unmistakably Indian in its outlook and operation."[2]

Should the historian and the sociologist also simply accept that the history of Indian law during the last two centuries is tantamount to the story of the introduction and domestication of English law in the country? If this were all there is to the theme of colonial law in British India, it would appear to be quite an unexciting subject of study. But it is not. It is of considerable historical interest. The reason for this is partly that demonstrating the undoubtedly dominant impact of British law on South Asia still leaves unanswered a large number of questions. In a short review of Setalvad's book, Marc Galanter has, many years ago, listed a fair number of them.

"An introduction to hindu jurisprudence," *The American Journal of Comparative Law* 8 (1959), 29.

2. Marc Galanter, "The aborted restoration of 'indigenous' law in India," *Comparative Studies in Society and History* XIV (1972), 55, 63. M.C. Setalvad, *Common Law*, 225.

We can do no better than to rearrange them, to suit our purpose, in two areas of enquiry.

Firstly, though perhaps this appears the least interesting issue, in England English law was largely case law: the only three genuine codifying measures of nineteenth century England were passed by Parliament only as late as in 1882, 1890, and 1893. Neither English judge-made law nor piecemeal English statutes could be simply transplanted to India without first digesting and shaping them into some kind of systematized order. And this is in fact what happened. It was a vast effort of codification on the basis, though not exclusively, of English "common law," and the inevitable result was a considerable difference between the old English system "in which the major strands of the law are woven by the slow accretion of judicial precedent," and the Indian one "in which the judge and lawyer operate in the interstices of a detailed legislative (or constitutional) framework."[3] The Indian lawyer, therefore, thinks in terms of statutes, not, as does his English colleague, in terms of the judicial interpretation and articulation of legal concepts. In this respect, the similarity is between India and "Napoleonic" Europe rather than between colony and colonizer.

To understand present-day India it is indispensable to trace the origin of the Indian codes, and to consider the legal culture that resulted from them and is reflected in the Indian legal profession. Fortunately, the history of Indian codification has been fairly well researched. But it should be admitted from the very beginning that to describe the policies and arguments that gave birth to the laws and regulations of British India, though necessary, would provide us with a partial view of the Indian legal scene, a view from the top. It is unavoidable to venture out of the legislative chamber and the learned lawyer's study. In particular, one feels the need to know whether the system does truly fit Indian conditions in all respects, as argued by the 1960 Attorney-General whose views we have quoted, and, if it does, how this is to be explained. What, if any, has been the impact on it of Indian cultural demands, social structure and dynamics? If the Indian legal system, as it presents itself in the statute-book and the Supreme Court law reports, looks familiar to the student of Anglo-Saxon and European law, how does it function in the magistrate's court, how is it administered or used by the police, and what is its role in conflict management at the village level?

---

3. Marc Galanter, review of M.C. Setalvad, *Common Law*, in *The American Journal of Comparative Law* 10 (1961), 293.

The lawyer's view we should like to escape from tends to be satisfied with a legal positivist study of a system that, in his eyes, inevitably assumes a certain autonomy, a world of its own consisting of statutes, appeals, and the bustle of the superior courts. The student of comparative law on the other hand, is constrained to wonder whether, even if the systems he scrutinizes look remarkably similar at first sight, they play the same role in social control, in regulating the lives of individuals and the transactions between them, in the different societies where they prevail. If the Indian legal system, as seems probable given its largely alien origin (though it cannot be taken as proven without further enquiry), fits Indian conditions less well than the English system fits the English, to what extent does executive discretion make up for the deficiency? Does it explain, to add just one more possible issue, why in India "the separation of executive and judiciary has remained a persistent though not completely fulfilled aspiration?"[4]

Already these are more questions than we shall be capable of answering. But if we choose to try and do justice to the legal anthropology side of the subject, it is important to distinguish, at the lower reaches of the British Indian administration, three departments of the law. Family law, whether Hindu or Muslim, land law (proprietary, tenancy, fiscal, etc.), and adjective law were in agrarian India the most visible aspects of colonial law. The latter subject, consisting of procedure and the law of evidence, though necessarily rather dull to a historian when analyzed as positive law, appears to me crucial, even more than the other two, for an understanding of the contrasts between what I shall call the Indian and British law machines.[5] It is not that English procedure was thrust upon Indian agrarian society as the land revenue system was or, in some regions, Hindu family law was. British procedures were confined to the colonial judiciary, whereas the vast majority of village disputes were managed locally. Yet, precisely because they tended not to directly affect village and caste procedure, and because they built an all-India superstructure lacking organic links with "local law-ways," the impact of the courts was immense. Something like a dual procedural system was the result, though it consisted by no means two watertight compartments. That this was a typically nasty colonial phenomenon is not at all clear. Dualism after all

4. *Ibid.*, 292.
5. On this term, denoting the workings of adjective law, see Marcel Berlings and Clare Dyer, *The Law Machine*, 2nd ed. (Harmondsworth, 1986).

seems a healthy feature of any well-balanced relationship between law and society. Is it not a necessary, even a desirable asset of all legal systems of dispute settlement to be able to depend at the lowest levels on the capacity of antagonists to "settle out of court"?

Though the judges of the colonial state sometimes could, when called upon to do so, declare as unlawful decisions of village or caste tribunals (*panchayats*), there was no formal appeal from these decisions to the colonial court system, nor could the *panchayats* invoke the sanctions of the state to sustain their authority. This was a factor weakening local and regional political systems, and it was a formal break with the past. In the precolonial era, at least ideally, rajas and other rulers, taking their cue both from traditions of political expediency and equity and from legal systems such as the Muslim *shari'a* and Hindu legal discourse (*dharma*) as expounded and continually added to by brahmin jurists, could and sometimes did uphold local decisions and "law-ways." The latter term is used to denote different authorities (councils, individuals) presiding over different sets or relations, mainly within the village or the endogamous group, and using different sanctions: down-to-earth ones like fining, beating, and public shaming; and supernatural ones such as ritual expiation or, perhaps most effectively, as it entails a stoppage to a family's marriage prospects, outcasting.

Colonial administrators held different views on the question whether the local law-ways had always been an autonomous and self-sufficient system or whether Mughal and British rule had deprived the Indian legal system of its superstructure of appellate royal courts and dharmic positive law. Those who supported the first theory saw that in the villages, tribunals and headmen in giving their verdicts either referred to the customary law of the caste in which the dispute arose or gave an opinion on the basis of equity, as found after an examination of the history and circumstances of the case. On this level written law hardly had a role to play, especially not in a province like the Panjab where the brahmins didn't know the *shastras*, nor the mollas the *shari'a*.[6] The second opinion was represented well among the early Company servants in Bengal, who were struck by the lively tradition of *dharmashastra* studies there as well as in nearby Benares, and who decided to stick to the most authoritative Hindu legal texts they could find. Both views,

---

6. Alan Gledhill, "The compilation of customary law in the Punjab in the nineteenth century," in *La rédaction des coutumes dans le passé et dans le présent (Etudes d'histoire et d'ethnologie juridiques)*, ed. John Gilissen (Brussels, 1962), 137.

however, did not grasp the real nature of the ancient and medieval Indian law machine. Let me explain.

The real nature of *dharmashastra* or Hindu law was only gradually realized, viz. that it was not positive law, promulgated by a state beholden to enforce it, but an ideal picture of what in the brahminical view the law ought to be. As such, throughout the colonial period it enjoyed, as it still enjoys, great prestige. In this sense, J.D. Mayne, writing in 1878, was right in believing that "at this day it governs races of men, extending from Cashmere to Cape Comorin, who agree in nothing else except their submission to it." He knew very well that the South Indians were hardly aware of the fact that they were following the *Mitakshara*, one of the widespread *dharmashastra* texts. But "nor has an Englishman any conscious belief that his life is guided by Lord Coke and Lord Mansfield. . . . It is quite possible that these races may be trying unconsciously to follow the course of life which is adopted by the most respectable, the most intellectual, and the best educated among their neighbours. The result would be exactly the same as if they studied the *Mitakshara* for themselves. That this really is the case is an opinion which I arrived at, after fifteen years acquaintance with the litigation of every part of the Madras Presidency. Even in Malabar I have witnessed continued efforts on the part of the natives to cast off their own customs, and to deal with their property by partition, alienation, and devise, as if it were governed by the ordinary Hindu law."[7] It was a kind of legal "Sanskritisation," to use a modern anthropological term, an awareness of the source of which was not necessary, because that source was not positive law but an ideal of righteousness.

The authority of *dharma* was moral and non-legal. One could say it was Indian natural law, or, perhaps better still, a literary genre akin to Biblical and ancient Near-Eastern wisdom-literature, kept alive by the class of Indian literati and jurists, the brahmins. But though it was not positive law, the king, who was the patron of *dharmashastra* studies, could translate it into law. Wisdom literature could turn into statute by ordinance, which in its turn could, in time, contribute to local or caste custom. Conversely, the brahmin *pandits* could recognize custom and receive it into their scriptures. The ideal and the actual were not uncompromisingly opposed, but informed each other. This was the essence of the Indian law machine: the

---

7. John D. Mayne, *A Treatise on Hindu Law and Usage*, 3rd ed. (Madras-London, 1883), IX, XI, XII.

dynamic interaction of "wisdom-law," positive royal decrees, and customary local law-ways.[8]

They can best be compared to the three levels of the "weather machine."[9] First, there is the jet stream high in the air, unseen by those without special knowledge, yet influencing in a decisive way the general type of weather as ordinary mortals experience it; at the same time, though the jet streams do not change their course for months on end, they reflect the broad changes in ocean temperature and biotype on the earth's surface. Below this, and mediating between it and the daily incidence of rainfall, sunshine and gusts of wind, are the systems of high and low pressure and the fronts between regions of air of different origin, a knowledge of which allows us to predict some days ahead what will befall us. At the ground level reigns the endless vicissitude of local micro-climates and unpredictability: a hailstorm or a period of drought for one valley and a lucky escape for another. The weather machine comprises all three of these levels. In a largely similar way, the Indian law machine was a tripartite yet organically whole system.

The British conquerors could not, administratively or conceptually, hold together these three interconnected planes. It was their inevitable task to establish the rule of a unified, positive legal system. So the continuum of the Indian law machine was broken not into two but into three systems, each governed by a discipline of its own. We shall use Roman numerals to refer to them. The top part (I) no longer looked up to by administrators as the repository of final legal authority, was left to the learned theologians and Brahmins of Indian traditional scholarship and increasingly also to the austere and "orientalist" discipline of philology, mostly manned by Europeans. The central part, that of the positive colonial law (II), was a mixed selection of English common law, *dharmashastra*, *shari'a*, and compiled customary law. The latter three were subjected to uniform English court procedures and, therefore, duly distorted in the process. Thirdly, there was the ever-present, diffuse world of local law-ways now largely deprived of communication with other planes of judicial organization (III).

---

8. Bernard S. Jackson, "From dharma to law," *The American Journal of Comparative Law* 23 (1973), 490–512. See also, for the points made here, Robert Lingat, *The Classical Law of India*, ed. J.D.M. Derrett (Berkeley, 1973).

9. Nigel Calder, *The Weather Machine* (London, 1974).

Conflict Management and the Dichotomy of Law and Society (The On-going Entrepreneurship as Between Levels II and III)

The historian may well wonder whether the colonial regime took any steps to integrate these levels; whether, in other words, a British Indian law machine emerged that reconciled these different layers, thus lending support to the claims of its being Indian in spirit in spite of its largely English origin. Let us turn, for a moment, to Indian agrarian society and to the legal history of its local law-ways of conflict management.

In colonial India, just as during the ancien régimes and even in independent India, notions of the several schools of *dharmashastra* legal thinking continued to percolate in local ideas of equity or "custom," just as custom could still be received in shastric discourse. A mediating, middle layer of royal decrees was not indispensable for this process to continue. Also, when, in the colonial era, the state officially ignored local procedures and ways of conflict management, this did not bring about any radical change. Arbitration and justice were still meted out by those controlling the land, by village and caste *panchayats*, and by individuals with a reputation of being good arbitrators. Politically, the power of the state continued to be felt and, judicially, it was not irrelevant, though largely indirect. For instance, the superior landlord's recognition or grant of land ownership or the colonial administration's registration of lords of the land could still make and unmake political and judicial power. But the state was only one of many *loci* of power to reckon with, and generally, it was not the most important one. A diffuse world of multiple kinds and levels of authority and security had always allowed more than one legal or political option to the hopeful or the aggrieved, provided he invested regularly to maintain his stake in them. These were ingrained, immemorial patterns of conflict management. In ancien régime, precolonial India, where no state or state-like structure ever achieved a monopoly of the use of arms, power centers came and went in great variety and fluidity; they were unevenly scattered about the political and ethnographic map; some were ephemeral, others longer lived. Conflict in a world so constituted was not an aberration, a regrettable departure from a "normal" state of harmony, but a necessary, structural principle complementing solidarity and, more important, necessary for the periodical revival of solidarity. Perceived through time, it takes different shapes and, as villages went through periods of authority and confusion, a development cycle of conflict is often discernible: in times of weak village leadership, villagers became "litigants" resorting to outside clan or royal arbitration, reverting to village dispute settlement as it reasserted itself.[10]

After the arrival of the British, as the colonial government acquired in its territories a monopoly of large scale violence, but not of conflict management, such patterns continued unabated at the local level. So two very different legal worlds emerged. True, with the periodicity of conflict just described, the frontier between them was often crossed. Characteristic was the continuous litigious entrepreneurship on the sharp edge of the dichotomy, as soon as it came about with the conquest of Bengal. After independence also "litigants do not expect a settlement that will end the dispute to eventuate from recourse to the state courts." The lower courts could and still can, for example, be used to ruin an adversary, if one knows he will not be able in the long run to bear the costs of litigation. But such action used to be one of many skirmishes, and only a move in a wide-ranging strategy of conflict management; if resorted to, the court would only have before it part of the total, often quite ancient, dispute. Even the most inquisitive judge would not be able to penetrate agrarian society to the extent that afforded him a total view of a conflict; and if he tried, the law of evidence of his own court would have prevented him from officially taking cognizance of most of what he found out.[11] There is no Montaillou in British Indian legal history. The procedural gap between "out of court" agrarian conflict management and the colonial judiciary was indeed almost complete: though cases that had been before traditional tribunals might be referred to the state legal system, no traditional courts were incorporated in the British-Indian law machine or even recognized as judicial authority. Only a limited and diminishing number of big landlords in British territory were given the powers of a magistrate. On the whole, the sanctions of the state could not officially be invoked to back up "local law-ways," though, as indicated above, it is true that at the local level judicial and political power could in practice not be kept in different hands, and many a British-

---

10. Bernard S. Cohn, "Anthropological notes on disputes and law in India," *American Anthropologist* LXVII (1965), 97.

11. *Ibid.*, 105. The actual functioning of the colonial lower courts is hardly studied; fiction and memoirs afford the best impression of them. See, e.g. Robert Carstairs, *The Little World of an Indian District Officer* (London, 1912); Penderel Moon, *Strangers in India* (New York, 1945); Philip Woodruff, *Call the Next Witness* (London, 1948). See also D.A. Washbrook, "Law, state and agrarian society in colonial India," *Modern Asian Studies* XV (1981), 658ff.

supported landowner used his relationship with the police to sustain his power game.

It is difficult to say whether the domain of conflict that remained removed from adjudication by the state courts in British India was more extensive than, say, in early modern Europe. It probably was. The gap anyway was almost totally dichotomous, the two systems very dissimilar. According to Marc Galanter the "unresolved tension" between national and popular law even characterizes India as "a dualistic or colonial-style legal system." At the top, the reception of foreign law in India was "unprecedented in scope," even when compared to the reception of Roman law in medieval Europe, and was reinforced by "a post-Independence wave of reform and rationalisation." Yet, this did not mean the demise of traditional society, of local law-ways, or of the dynamic multiplicity of alliances, threats, and risk management connected with them. On the contrary, "traditional society is not passively regulated by the modern system; it uses the system for its own ends. . . . Traditional interests and expectations are . . . translated into suitable legal garb, into nationally intelligible terms."[12] The point here appears to be not that there is a gap between law and society that has to be bridged, or that duality is the essence of any country's law machine, but that the magnitude of the ongoing translation process put undue stress on India, and that this problem has its roots in India's colonial past. While it may seem alright to blame colonialism for the problem, it can probably not easily be ascertained whether the problem is greater in India than, for example, in modern Turkey, to mention a society that was never colonized. We, therefore, prefer the more simple question of how the British and Indian members of the colonial civil service approached the problem, whether for instance they attempted to diminish it by digesting and absorbing local law, or by attentively and repeatedly amending the codes imposed from above.

The British Search for Finality
(The Relationship of Levels I and II)

From the beginning, the British system was characterized by procedural and judiciary unity. There were no special courts for Mus-

12. Marc Galanter, "The displacement of traditional law in modern India," *Journal of Social Issues* XXIV (1968), 83–85. See on the genesis of this dichotomy especially J.D.M. Derrett, "The administration of Hindu law by the British," *Comparative Studies in Society and History* IV (1962), 14ff.

lims or Hindus and, in 1861, the three Presidency Supreme Courts for which Europeans had been accountable at law were merged with the provincial superior courts. Judges took cognizance of all kinds of cases. There was, in other words, no dual legal system in the sense of "different legal mechanisms applied to identical situations,"[13] though there were, for persons of different communities, differences in the substantive laws resorted to. Compared to the Muslim administration that preceded the British, this was revolutionary, as became apparent immediately after the East India Company took over the administration of Bengal, Bihar, and Orissa. In those first years of British rule there were still a number of officials of the old régime who continued in their profession. One of them in 1772, strongly remonstrated

> against allowing a Brahmin to be called in to the decision of any matters of inheritance or other dispute of Gentoos [i.e. hindus], saying that since the establishment of the Mahomedan dominion in Hindostan the Brahmins had never been admitted to any such jurisdiction; that to order a magistrate of the [muslim] faith to decide in conjunction with a Brahmin would be repugnant to the rules of the faith, and an innovation peculiarly improper in a country under the dominion of a Musselman Emperor. That where the matter in dispute can be decided by a reference to Brahmins, no interruption had ever been given to that mode of decision; but that where they (*sc.* Gentoos) think fit to resort to the established judicatures of the country, they must submit to a decision according to the rules and principles of that law by which alone these Courts were authorized to judge. That there would be the greatest absurdity in such an association of judicature, because the Brahmin would determine according to the precepts and usages of his caste and the magistrates must decide according to those of the Mahomedan law.[14]

The Mughal judicial system had clearly been a plural one: Brahminical procedure and substantive law had not been integrated in it, though they had been continued, perhaps even upheld, and occasionally sustained with the sanctions of the state. This legal pluralism was sharply reduced by the East India Company. The secular and uniform judiciary introduced by the E.I.C. applied both Hindu (*dharmashastra*) and Muslim (*shari'a*) law in cases regarding "inheritance, succession, marriage and caste and other religious usages and institutions," i.e. in family and religious suits. But British judges

13. See Filip Reyntjens' article in this volume.
14. G.C. Rankin, *Background to Indian Law* (Cambridge, 1946), 4–5.

were not legally trained; throughout the colonial period European
barristers would remain few in number in India. Moreover, the
Calcutta government was from the beginning of Company rule fully
aware of their ignorance of oriental law. To improve this, which was
urgent if anything like steady government was to be established,
learned brahmins, so-called *pandits*, were commissioned to produce a
digest of Hindu law. This was then translated from Sanskrit into
Persian, then in English and published in 1775. Many treatises were
to follow. Sir William Jones in particular, "obsessed with the need
for certainty and consistency," was instrumental in the process. He
and a number of his colleagues were in search of something similar
to Justinian's Corpus Juris; they were "persuaded that hindu law
was immemorially old and that it was possible to 'fix' it at any given
moment without doing it any harm."[15]

But this search for an authoritative, final version of the Hindu law
was foreign to its spirit. Later, thanks to the results of philological
researches, the British became embarrassingly aware of the immense body of texts, commentaries, and learned wisdom that once
had represented the top part of the Indian law machine. Modern
scholarship, as we saw, realizes that during the ancien régime this
body of legal learning by its nature was constantly, though slowly,
growing and shifting in relation to changing conditions without ever
acquiring the positive quality of legislation. The activities of the
pandits, India's legal *literati*, were at the center of this process. They
were not only the repositories of eternal legal principle, but also the
sophisticated and sensitive interpreters of changing legal opinion. As
a group, they were the soul of the traditional Indian or brahmin law
machine; they were the lawyer-intellectuals who rearticulated "hindu" values that derived from classical tradition and pronounced
new norms and idioms of behavior to suit new circumstances. This
process of law-finding was in the last analysis informed by the full
length of a continuum between the centers of Sanskrit learning and
the world of local equity and group custom. But in Warren Hasting's time this could not yet be grasped. Yet, the representatives of
ancien régime learned reflection were called to the Company's
assistance. To this phenomenon we now turn.

Apart from the ascertainment and publication of Hindu law in
digested form – codification strictly speaking it was not, because
these legal treatises were manuals for judges, not positive legislation

15. J.D.M. Derrett, "Sanskrit legal treatises compiled at the instance of the
British," *Zeitschrift für Vergleichende Rechtswissenschaft* 66 (1961), 72–117.

promulgated by the state – there was another method by which the East India Company endeavored to root its judicial decisions in traditional legal culture and to make up for the ignorance of its judges. From 1772 onward, Hindu *pandits* and Muslim *maulvis* began to act as "law officers" with the courts. They did not sit on the bench as assessors, but as experts, gave legal opinions on individual cases to enable judges to come to a verdict. Their office would be abolished only in 1864. Indeed, Warren Hastings (Governor and Governor-General, 1772–1785) realized the system would not work without a steady supply of learned *pandits*. So, in order to further shastric education, he established the Sanskrit Colleges at Benares and Calcutta. The compilation of digests would then see to it that they would speak with one voice. But in fact, of course, it was their tradition not to speak with one voice, but to rephrase and update the many-sided richness of old wisdom.

A fixed, institutionalized link between what we have called levels I and II could not therefore be established. Even the two devices to ascertain the Hindu law were at odds and competed with each other, because the more uniform and accurate the translated and printed Hindu law became, the more the responsiveness of the *pandits'* law-finding art would be stifled, the last revolutions of the ancien régime's law machine put a stop to. The logical end of this road was reached, as we saw, in 1864, when the courts declared themselves independent of the *pandits'* and *maulvis'* opinions and assumed full judicial knowledge of the Hindu and Muslim law.

Long before that, however, their influence had greatly diminished. Almost from the beginning, they had been under the suspicion of venality and prejudice, probably without much reason. More important is that they could not be made subservient to British procedures and to the colonial state's obsession with consistency and certainty without giving up much of what they stood for. The celebrated orientalist and judge Sir William Jones wrote in 1786 to a friend about his efforts to gear the Indian law machine to the cog-wheels of Calcutta rule: "One point I have already attained; I made the pundit of our court read and correct a copy of Halhed's book [the translation of 1775, mentioned above] in the original Sanscrit, and I then obliged him to attest it as good law, so that he never now can give corrupt opinions, without certain detection."[16] A single incorruptible printed book in the hands of some selected Indian lawyers was pronounced superior to the dynamics of dharmic

16. Cited in Derrett, "Sanskrit legal treatises," 94.

tradition, once participated in by all who had studied the texts.

A similar tendency to employ rather than respect ancien règime learning is discernible in the development of criminal law. Fisch has analyzed the British struggle for law and order during the first half-century of their rule in Bengal. The Company, after their take-over, continued the Muslim *shari'a* as the criminal *lex terrae* (except for British subjects), as it had been under the Mughals and their successors. It was explained by Muslim law officers or *maulvis*. As the *shari'a* partook of the revealed character of the Quran, it could not be amended or even codified. Yet, in a series of regulations, Muslim criminal law in Bengal was adapted to English susceptibilities and to the principles of an impersonal, centrally controlled government that required the equality of its subjects before the law and the strengthening of public, as opposed to private (e.g. the right of the relations of a murdered person to grant pardon to the murderer), criminal justice. The *maulvis*, however, could in good conscience not do otherwise than give their *fatwas* (opinions) on the basis of unadulterated *shari'a* learning, though the British might try to draw their attention to Muslim authors whose position differed to a certain extent from orthodoxy.

A device frequently resorted to was asking the *maulvis* to give an opinion on fictional cases that covered up the legislative innovations introduced by the government:

> they left the islamic law as a system unchanged and simply altered rules of procedure. If, for instance, the relations granted pardon, or if the witness was a hindu, or the victim the child of the murderer [in which case the *shari'a* did not consider retaliation as justified, though in most other cases of murder it did], the law officers had to prepare their *fatwas* under the assumption that pardon had not been granted, or that the witness was a Muslim, or a victim not the murderer's child. Thus, from a formal point of view not a new system of law was built up, but a system of fictions which transformed real cases in fictitious ones, so that the outcome, the *fatwa* of the law officers, although given according to the traditional islamic law, corresponded to the expectations and wishes of the British. Because the laws could not be changed, the facts to which they applied were changed – the outcome was the same.[17]

It is clear that under these circumstances with *pandits* and *maulvis* harnessed into the service of a legal system vastly different from the

---

17. Jörg Fisch, *Cheap Lives and Dear Limbs: the British Transformation of the Bengal Criminal Law 1769–1817* (Wiesbaden, 1983), 45–46.

dharma and *shari'a* traditions they represented, there was no question of a fusion of legal cultures. It is to be noted that both the Hindu and the Muslim systems clashed with the colonial state in terms of procedure in a way that posed an insoluble problem. This is not surprising, as the essence of a legal culture, whether Hindu, European, Muslim, or customary, is expressed in its "adjective" – the term, for our purposes, is clearly a misnomer – elements.

To Fisch, however, the supersession of the *maulvis* and the *shari'a* they were supposed to expound seemed to reflect the harshness of a colonial state that needed, mainly for purposes of law and order, a more severe criminal law. In the new regulations was incorporated a good deal of what under the ancien régime was dealt with under the head of "extraordinary justice," that is, in actual practice, political expediency, an analysis of the harshness of which is sorely needed before one could agree with Fisch on this particular issue. Surely, a British "colonialist" mentality may have contributed to the suspicion with which the Indian law officers were often regarded. Fundamentally, however, the dichotomy between precolonial and colonial justice is basically just another form of the difference between any ancien régime and the modern state.

The main reason why Indian law, either in the form of digests or piecemeal, as the Indian law officers' opinions on individual cases, could only very imperfectly – and to the British very unsatisfactorily – inform and contribute to the colonial legal system is to be found in the vast difference of the British and Indian (both Muslim and Hindu) systems of jurisprudence. The East India Company demanded certainty above all: a commodity that in the old political cultures, with their multiple centers of power, their informal management of risks, and open procedural patterns, simply had not made sense. In the 1820s, in practice though not yet in principle, British dependence on *pandits* and *maulvis* greatly diminished, whereas Bengal criminal law was gradually overgrown with legislation that changed its *shari'a* basis almost beyond recognition. In 1818, the British acquired full imperialist control over the subcontinent and this may well have further contributed to the increased feelings of responsibility and impatience that so often characterize colonialist, but not only colonialist, rulers. Intentions had not been bad. Sir William Jones, impatient, as we saw, with the Indian law machine as personified in the *pandits* of his court, had fully sympathized with Hindu and Muslim substantive civil law. In 1788, he had written: "Nothing could be more obviously just than to determine private contests according to those laws which the parties themselves had

ever considered as the rules of their conduct and engagements in
civil life."[18] Yet, as indicated above, radical change would come
soon. The reason, we suggest, was that the Company's state could
tolerate foreign conduct, foreign engagements and foreign laws, but
not foreign procedures that were in tune with the unpredictable flux
of medieval social change.

Among the modern legal historians of India who have described
the British law machine's handling of Indian legalist learning, Derrett is the most eminent. He deeply regrets that shastric learning,
especially after the middle of the nineteenth century, fell into the
hands of antiquarians and philologists. In his view, it deserved
better and he even suggests that "it is just conceivable that under
British pressure a working compromise between the two very different jurisprudential techniques might have arisen not too far from
stare decisis." The British insistence upon "clarity, certainty and
finality in terms foreign to Hindu tradition" prevented this.[19] Certainly, the comparison between the *pandits*' methods of finding justice on the basis of dharma and equity, in close touch with precedent
and changing political and social circumstances on the one hand,
and the English common law system of judge-made law based on
precedent (*stare decisis*: to stick to the court decisions arrived at in
earlier cases) on the other, is not far-fetched. Yet, even a strict
adherence to *stare decisis* must be considered too rigid a rule, incompatible with the freedom of Indian equity, because Indian equity
refers to *dharma* and textual wisdom, not to case-law. So when, by
the 1820s, the principle of *stare decisis* began to dominate the courts,
rendering the *pandits* largely superfluous in the process, a new system, now commonly called Anglo-Hindu Law, took over. The procedures of the old tripartite system could not be incorporated in the
modern state and that was the end of it as a living system, though as
a body of substantive rules it survived and even continued to grow.
The British set out to go it alone.

The Autonomous Development of the British Law Machine in India (Level II Only)

There would indeed be no way back. Yet, it was a long time before
something like a British law machine would get moving at full speed

18. Cited in Rankin, *Background*, 60, 61.
19. Derrett, "Sanskrit legal treatises," 111–12.

in India, and even then, as we showed, much of India's conflict domain would escape from its purview. In 1833, the new Charter Act passed at Westminster established one legislature at Calcutta with power of legislation over the whole of British India, and with authority not only over Indians, but also over Europeans. Though the dispatch drafted by James Mill which accompanied the Act advised caution, the aim in the long run was a radical one: a code of laws common, as far as possible, to all Indian ethnic and religious identities.

In the words of the dispatch, the Act contemplated "a period of inquiry, of consideration, of preparation, in some degree even of experiment." That would enable the legislative council "to embody the abstract and essential principles of good government in regulations adapted to the peculiar habits, character and institutions of the vast and infinitely diversified people under their sway."[20] The word "adapted," used here, disguised what was in reality a Benthamite, radical program. Even so, though the influence of the utilitarians was pervasive in the Indian administration and would remain so for decades, nothing like a utilitarian code was enacted in India until the late 1850s. An amended version of Macaulay's 1837 draft of a Penal Code would not be on the Indian statute book until 1860. During these decades, the ideas about codification evolved gradually from idealist to pragmatic. In 1840, the Law Commission in India proposed to proclaim the substantive law of England as the territorial law of India (i.e. outside the Presidency cities), and to apply it to all persons except Hindus and Muslims. Government had long ago realized that India contained many more communities than those of Hindus and Muslims, whom the regulations of Warren Hastings' time had left under their own personal law. The number of such people was daily increasing and was, at that time, expected to grow much further: Indian Christians, Anglo-Indians of mixed descent, Parsis and Armenians, whose laws were not available in written form or even impossible to ascertain. Then, there were large numbers of Portuguese, Jews, and an increasing number of European British subjects whom an act of 1836 had made amenable in civil cases to up-country courts along with Indians.

It was not that there was no rule that guided the courts in cases concerning these people: the point was that judges, in all matters not concerning Hindu and Muslim family and religious law, were to go by "justice, equity and good conscience," as the celebrated phrase

20. Cited in Rankin, *Background*, 60, 61.

ran. This allowed wide discretion to the country courts. Outside
Calcutta, Bombay, and Madras, as Rankin put it, "justice, equity
and good conscience were at large."[21] Often, especially in cases of
contract, it was possible to do justice on commonsense lines, but in
suits concerning family inheritance – a department of the law which
is by definition non-rational and in which what is conscientious in
one community is unconscientious in another – there was general
lack of system, and the decisions of courts in similar cases could vary
greatly, some judges following "custom," others the law of England
or their own idea of what was just.

The Indian Law Commission was well aware of the opinion of
those who asserted that "to the Oriental mind a personal law is
more familiar and appears more natural than a territorial law." But
even if one left Hindus and Muslims under their personal laws, they
argued, "there is probably no country in the world which contains
so many people who, if there is no law of the place [i.e. no *lex terrae*],
have no law whatever." Perhaps this was going a little too far, but it
is certain that without a law of the land, the British courts would not
be able to adjudicate great numbers of family law suits, many of
them brought by members of important urban business communities such as the Parsis and the Armenians. Something, in other
words, had to be done. Yet, "the introduction of the general law of
England as applicable in default of special law or custom to everyone and everything," which among other things involved a fusion of
English law and equity even before this was achieved in England
itself, was open to many objections. One of these was that English
judges and magistrates in India were amateurs as ill-equipped to
master the technicalities of English common and statutory law as
they had been with regard to Hindu and Muslim law seventy years
earlier. Even if the endless series of relevant British law reports and
statutes would have been made available in India, it is doubtful
whether the officers of the Indian Civil Service could be induced to
study them. Moreover, as pointed out earlier, there were in India
hardly any barristers to assist them. By 1845, no practical solution
to these problems had been found, though at an early stage the
suggestion had been made to digest, i.e. to systematize and, therefore, to simplify, English common and statute law to make it accessible to Indian courts. This suggestion would prove to be an important
one, because eventually this is, by and large, what happened, even
though the process would never cover the whole of English law and

21. *Ibid.*, 24.

would in the end produce codes rather than mere digests.

The Charter Act of 1853 – which would turn out to be the East India Company's last charter, as, in 1858, the Crown would take over the Indian administration – authorized the Queen to appoint a Law Commission in England which would, within a period of three years, propose enactments. This took the initiative away from Calcutta, and for several years it seemed as if the Secretary of State for India had assumed the character of the main legislator for India and would convert the Legislative Council in Calcutta into "a mere instrument" of his policies.[22] But this tendency would not continue. In 1870, the Secretary of State sided with the London Law Commissioners over a clause in the proposed contract legislation , and "expressed his views in terms which were objected to by the Government of India as derogatory to the independence of the Indian Legislature, and thus a difference of opinion about a technical point of law was elevated to the dignity of a grave constitutional controversy." The result was that the Law Commissioners resigned their commission and that the Indian government was allowed to take their own course again in legislation.[23]

But the London Law Commission had produced some results. Duly appointed as desired by the new Charter Act, it had in its report of 1855 launched its own plans for codification. Merely digesting English law would not have the advantages of unequivocal legislation. From now on much work was done on a body of substantive civil law of which English law was the basis, but which was to be enacted in a simplified, even modified form to suit Indian conditions. Certain categories of the population would remain under their own personal family or religious law, which would remain uncodified, whereas some subject matter of civil law would not be included in the codes at all. Yet, these codes became the law of the land. Macaulay's draft of a Penal Code was taken up, revised, and passed into law in 1860. In 1859 and 1861 respectively, a Code of Civil Procedure and a Code of Criminal Procedure passed into the Indian statute book; they were, in the opinion of Ilbert, the Law Member of the Indian Government in the early 1880s, "doubtless rough and capable of much improvement, but they constituted an enormous advance on the chaotic and incomplete regulations by which they had been preceded."[24] The Succession Act of 1865 was

22. *Ibid.*, 35–45, 84.
23. Courtenay Ilbert, *Legislative Methods and Forms* (Oxford, 1901), 133–35.
24. Ilbert, *Legislative Methods*, 131. The word "regulation" is in India, except in a loose sense, used for the enactments of the three Presidencies (Calcutta, Madras,

the first of the codes of civil substantive law; the Contract Act of
1872 was the second. Many less important new acts and amend-
ments were passed during these years – it was estimated that 211
enactments issued from the legislature during Henry Maine's seven
years (1862–69) as Law Member in Calcutta alone[25] – which on
several occasions led to complaints of "overlegislation." All this was
achieved before anything similar was tried in England. After 1872,
much work continued to be done along the governing principles laid
down in the Law commission's 1855 report. Yet, by that year, the
Benthamite era in Indian legal history, officially announced by the
Charter Act of 1833 and inaugurated by Macaulay's tenure as first
Law Member of the Governor-General's Council (1834–38), may be
considered as over. Another tendency, by then already of long
standing and of great influence especially outside Bengal and Madras, came to the forefront.

The Bombay Scheme of Gradual Transition

The provinces of British India, indeed, were too autonomous in
many respects, from a legislative as well as from an executive point
of view, not to develop a distinct administrative style of their own
that owed its character both to the incidents of colonial history and
to the cultures and social dynamics of the regional populations. The
result was considerable legal diversity. If Bentham, the inventor of
the word "codification," had his adherents in London and Calcutta,
the partisans of his great German antagonist Savigny, who had
warned against following foreign models, preferring to keep the law
in close organic relation with custom and common law, could be
found in Bombay and Lahore.[26]

Mountstuart Elphinstone, who as Governor of Bombay from 1819
to 1827 presided over the administrative integration of the Dekkan,
conquered in 1818, into British India, represented the tradition of
Warren Hastings and Sir William Jones. Hastings' position, as

---

Bombay) before 1834. See for the several kinds of enactments which together form the
Indian Statute-Book: C.D. Field, *Chronological Table of and Index to the Indian Statute
Book from the Year 1834 with a General Introduction to the Statute Law of India* (London,
1870).

25. Rankin, *Background*, 74.

26. See on Bentham's influence Eric Stokes, *The English Utilitarians and India*
(Oxford, 1959). Also see F.C. von Savigny, *Vom Beruf unsrer Zeit für Gesetzgebung und
Rechtswissenschaft* (Heidelberg, 1814).

formulated in 1774, had been that "the people of this country do not
require our aid to furnish them with a rule for their conduct, or a
standard for their property," and that, therefore, no essential change
was to be made in "the ancient constitution" of the British territories in India; it was enough to bring it "back to its original principles." Yet, even before Warren Hastings wrote these words a
conscious beginning had been made with the introduction of English
principles in the Company's possessions. Lord North's Regulating
Act of 1773 had instituted the Calcutta Supreme Court, which
would soon attempt to extend the authority of English law over the
administration of civil justice in Bengal. The "Battle of the Two
Philosophies," to use Eric Stokes's words, would, though assuming
different forms, remain central to official consciousness in India until
the days of the nationalist controversy. Fifty years after Hastings'
clash with the Supreme Court, the battle was still on: Romantic
paternalism versus Benthamite utilitarianism; the rule of men versus
the rule of impersonal laws and regulations; the indigenous system,
with its customs and privileges, versus egalitarianism and
anglicization.[27]

Emotional prejudice, as well as the different experiences of men
employed for decades either in personal negotiations with Indian
princes or as judges administering the Bengal Regulations of the
Cornwallis Code, shaped the officials' attitudes towards colonial
"expediency." Elphinstone was not an extreme example of the
"Romantic" generation in British Indian history. He knew that the
executive discretion that had characterized the first years of British
rule after the conquest of 1818 would have to give way to proceedings authorized by statute. The officers who had taken over the
government of the Dekkan had, as diplomats in the preceding years,
seen the Maratha administrative system at work under a Maratha
government, but, as Elphinstone told the Governor-General, "the
plan of proceeding on native customs without precise Regulations
cannot I am persuaded be kept up after the first set of public officers
shall have passed away, and it will then be necessary to introduce as
in other places a system depending less on personal character and
requiring less experience and knowledge of the people." Or, as
Ballhatchet, the perceptive historian of Elphinstone's "Deccan System," has put it: "Regulations were essential to preserve a system of
which the essence was the relative absence of Regulations."[28]

27. Stokes, *English Utilitarians*, 1, 3.
28. Kenneth Ballhatchet, *Social Policy and Social Change in Western India 1817–1830*
(London, 1957), 246.

What then were these regulations or, in other words, how did Elphinstone plan to take cognizance of Indian tradition and custom and be guided by it? He emphasized that there was a discrepancy between the ancient Hindu texts hitherto resorted to – especially in Bengal – on the presumption that these contained the law in its pristine purity, and modern practice as it was found in the Maratha states. In an often cited minute of July 22, 1823, he described the *dharmashastra* as "a collection of ancient treatises, neither clear nor consistent in themselves, and now buried under a heap of more modern commentaries; the whole beyond the knowledge of perhaps the most learned Pundits, and every part wholly unknown to the people who live under it." In many cases, what did work in practice were "known customs, founded indeed on the Dhurm Shaster, but modified by the convenience of different castes or communities, and no longer deriving authority from any written text." Elphinstone was interested in both written and unwritten law and looked forward to the compilation of a complete and consistent code in which contradictions and deficiencies in the material collected would be determined and supplied on "general principles of jurisprudence." The plan even today commands admiration in that it avoids the extremes of both imposed foreign-inspired codification and an over-religious veneration for indigenous customary improvisation. The procedure was to ascertain – again this unavoidable word – in each district whether there was "any book of acknowledged authority" for the whole of for part of the Hindu law, whereupon it could be found out what exceptions were practiced and what customs existed independent of these books or commentaries.[29]

There were two ways to achieve this; both intended to do justice to all the three levels of the old Indian law machine. The first was to interview the Hindu lawyers, *shastris*, heads of castes, and others familiar with the law, with custom, and with public opinion regarding the authority attached to these sources of law. In some of the Dekkan districts such investigations were set on foot; the result was published in 1827 as Arthur Steel's *Summary of the Law and Custom of Hindoo Castes within the Dekhun etc.*[30] The second method was "to

---

29. Rankin, *Background*, 7, 147.
30. Arthur Steel, *The Law and Custom of Hindoo Castes within the Dekhun Provinces subject to the Presidency of Bombay, chiefly affecting Civil Suits*, new ed. (London, 1868), iii–v. This edition is identical to the original one: Arthur Steel, *Summary of the Law and Custom of Hindoo Castes within the Dekhun Provinces subject to the Presidency of Bombay, chiefly affecting Civil Suits, ordered by the Honourable the Governor in Council to be printed, July 29, 1826* (Bombay, 1827). Van Vollenhoven therefore was wrong in supposing that these

extract from the courts of justice the information already obtained on these subjects in the course of judicial investigation." In the Bombay Presidency, the court records could be a rich source of usage, as the judges there, according to the wording of the 1799 regulation, were expected to enquire whether there was not "an unwritten yet ascertained common law" or "customary rule of the country" and whether this was not usually applied in cases like the one before him.[31] This was indeed a system very different from the Bengal one, where in all cases the same textbooks were to be consulted. In the Gujarat part of Bombay Presidency, where it had been in force since 1803, the second method of enquiry recommended itself, whereas in the Dekkan, a recent acquisition, it could not be tried until a body of records from which to abstract general rules would have accumulated. The resulting selection of Gujarati cases was published in two volumes in 1825, and fascinating cases they often are: about the jurisdiction of caste panchayats, for instance, and the efforts of the English judges, all the time following their own light as to "justice, equity and good conscience," to maintain the principle of equality before the law, and to withhold the sanctions of the state from the decisions of these tribunals.[32]

Elphinstone's plan had been to combine the result of the two kinds of enquiry in a digest to be "circulated for a certain time as a book of information, though not of authority." In this way – and of course the English system of judge-made common law proceeding by precedent would be a help here – it might "ultimately be improved by the decision of all doubtful questions, the removal of all glaring blemishes, and the filling up of all great deficiencies, until it forms a complete code of laws sanctioned by Government, and accessible in their vernacular language to all classes of its subjects."[33] Perhaps Elphinstone himself gave the best description of this program when in 1819 he told a colleague to consider himself happy to have only war and politics on his hands; he would not

---

customary laws were not published until 1868. See C. van Vollenhoven, "Aspects of the controversy on customary law in India," *The Asiatic Review* xxiii (1927), 118.

31. Rankin, *Background*, 14.

32. Harry Borradaile, *Reports of Civil Causes adjudged by the Court of Sudur Udalut for the Presidency of Bombay between the Years A.D. 1800 and A.D. 1824*, Vol. I (1800–1820) and Vol. II (1821–1824) (Bombay, 1825). See also, for some examples, the first cases in Marc Galanter, ed., *Introduction to the civilisation of India; legal materials for the study of modern India* (cyclost. Chicago, 1965); and Erskine Perry, *Cases Illustrative of Oriental Life and the Application of English Law to India in H.M. Supreme Court at Bombay* (London, 1853).

33. Cited in Steel, *Law and Custom*, xviii.

know what difficulty was until he came to reconcile "efficiency with economy and Maratha *Maamool* [custom] with Jeremy Bentham."[34]

After Elphinstone's departure and the loss of legislative autonomy under the Charter Act of 1833 which created a central legislature in Calcutta, the plan for a Bombay code based on Indian legal traditions lay dormant for forty years. What was already achieved, however, would not be lost. The Elphinstone Code – really a collection of twenty-seven Bombay Regulations – of 1827 provided that for all suits, in the absence of an Act of Parliament or a Regulation, the law to be observed should be "the usage of the country in which the suit arose"; if none such was discernible, the law of the defendant would be applied and in the absence of specific law and usage, "justice, equity and good conscience alone." Even where the general Hindu law was consulted, it was subject to modification not only by custom but also by later commentaries recognized as a result of Elphinstone's enquiries. His efforts had aimed to take cognizance of, and preserve as far as possible, the Indian law machine, the dynamic interplay of Brahminical Great Tradition as represented by the *dharmashastra* texts and the *ordre vécu* – or perhaps we should say the *droit vécu* – of custom, village conflict, and compromise. He knew that the Indian law-finding process had to be geared to the cogs of British procedures and perhaps gradually give way to their expanding logic. But he had realized that, in order to slow down this process to a speed that was no longer destructive but allowed for natural growth, it was imperative to keep Hindu and customary law together, so that they formed an organic whole, and he recognized that indeed something like an Indian law machine did exist and should be kept going at least for the time being.

Taking Cognizance of Custom (Level III): J.H. Nelson and Madras

The issue of customary law is a crucial one and was much discussed elsewhere as well, in particular in Madras. It seems useful, if only because of its importance from the point of view of comparative colonial legal history, to briefly consider the debate in that province. I am referring to the rigorous attacks of J.H. Nelson on the Madras Government's approach to Hindu and customary law. Nelson was a member of the covenanted Indian Civil Service and a district judge.

---

34. Cited in Ballhatchet, *Social Policy*, 36.

He was also the British Indian Van Vollenhoven, though he was
first and foremost a man of practical Indian experience and fought
his battles against the imposition of "foreign" law on South India
fifty years before the Leiden professor did the same for the Indonesian Archipelago.[35] As the inhabitants of Madras were no Hindu
Aryans, he argued, shastric law did not apply to them. His view was
that shastric studies even in Bengal were artificially revived, even
invented, by Sir William Jones and other orientalist enthusiasts.
Ancient Indian texts, such as the *Mitakshara*, as translated towards
the end of the eighteenth and the beginning of the nineteenth centuries, were completely foreign to the population of Madras. The
conduct of an ordinary South Indian, he wrote, "unless indeed he
happens to come into our Courts as a litigant, is no more affected by
precepts contained in the *Mitakshara* than it is by precepts contained
in the Psalms of David." He disputed the existence of schools of law
in different parts of India and argued that there was no proof of
authoritative modern Sanskrit commentaries, such as Elphinstone
had been in search of in Bombay, that could bridge the gap between
the rule of ancient Hindu (i.e., in his eyes, North Indian) law and
the order of South Indian custom. He, therefore, denied the validity
of the Hindu Great Tradition in the Madras province. He saw, in
other words, no traces of the complete Indian law machine as we
have defined it:

Things in his view were infinitely more simple. And so it was only
logical for him to suggest a short enabling act to fill the legal
vacuum; such an act "should recognize and proclaim the general
right of the Indian to consult his own inclination in all matters of
marriage, adoption, alienation, testation and the like."[36] Government should refrain from all interference with substantive law and
stand in awe before the genius of society. The model, suggested out
of pure love for Indian tradition, is further removed from it than
almost any other produced by the British. It can be represented as
follows:

35. See the article of C. Fasseur in this volume.
36. Cited in Rankin, *Background*, 153, 157, J.D.M. Derrett, "J.H. Nelson: a forgotten administrator-historian of India," in J.D.M. Derrett, *Essays in Classical and Modern
Hindu Law*, vol. 2 (Leiden, 1977), 404–23.

(II)
|
III

whereas the Bengal and Madras system could be shown as:

(I)
|
II

Van Vollenhoven, though less blunt than Nelson, would in the end come to a conclusion not very different from Nelson's. He clearly saw an ally in this English judge who, half a century before him, had swum so bravely against the current in a manner so similar to his. Though Elphinstone, he explained rather pedantically to the readers of *The Asiatic Review* of 1927, had done much good in Bombay, his plan to record the legal usages of the province had failed because he had "not clearly grasped . . . the theory of the problem of the relation of indigenous law to religious law." The gap between the two could never be bridged, and a choice had to be made for either of them. He was of the opinion, wrongly as we have seen, that Elphinstone had made the choice: "it is to him that we are indebted for the legal principle that the judge must put indigenous, not religious law into application." Others in the Bombay administration were to be blamed for the "entirely superfluous" search for Hindu law in the Presidency. Van Vollenhoven explained Elphinstone's "correct" attitude by pointing out that he "was on intimate terms with Indians (a hundred years ago), loved the land and the people, and had high hopes of them." This made him a good legislator unlike Macaulay who felt an exile in India and "pitted" for England.[37] It is interesting to note the sentimental psychology that seems to be the moving force behind Van Vollenhoven's message here. Nelson, he found, was right to "explode with wrath" at the idea that Hindu law could be considered the customary law of the Madras population. Van Vollenhoven's own recipe is not to lose touch with living society in the way that transcendent and abstract religion, whether Islam or Hinduism, inevitably does. And he quotes with approval Thomas Munro, Governor of Madras from 1819 to 1827, who had said: "It is not necessary to go to Arabia, or even to Hindostan, to discover the usage of the Carnatic [i.e.

37. Van Vollenhoven, "Aspects," 118–21.

Madras]; we ought to search for it on the spot."[38]

There was, of course, something in what Nelson had so uncompromisingly brought forward. J.D. Mayne, whose *Hindu Law and Usage* ran into nine editions between 1878 and 1922, admitted so much. For too long the Madras Government had accepted the *Mitakshara* as the last word on Hindu law. "The consequence was a state of arrested progress, in which no voices were heard unless they came from the tomb. It was as if a German were to administer English law from the resources of a library furnished with Fleta, Glanville and Bracton [twelfth and thirteenth century judges] and terminating with Lord Coke [died 1634]." On the other hand, many parts of the Brahminical laws were, historically speaking, based upon usage, whereas in their turn they had for centuries moulded to their own model the usages of even the speakers of non-Indo-Aryan languages.[39] We must conclude, therefore, that Nelson and Van Vollenhoven both erred in defining "Hindu" as "religious" and, therefore, "foreign" to agrarian liberties and common sense. It was also wrong to label the shastras as "religious." But, most importantly, medieval Brahmin jurists, as Derrett has shown, were not out to impose dharmic orthodoxy, but "thought that local and caste customs were always to be applied in practice and . . . denied, except in special instances, that any one law was to be applied to the whole population of any single desha [i.e. region or, perhaps better, German Land]." It is true, however, that in Bengal, as Derrett remarks, "the tradition of study of Sanskrit legal texts was in the 1780s stronger than anywhere else" in India and "was a much more genuinely integral part of the people's heritage." Madras was "sanskritised" to a much lesser extent. Yet, legislation in that province had since 1802 followed the example of the Bengal regulations in not expressly providing for custom, and "thus dozens of customs were, from the legal standpoint, steamrollered out of existence." In 1873, at last, the Madras High Court Act made it plain that customs were to be given effect, but even then the High Court judges remained reluctant to permit customs to be proved in derogation of Hindu law as they saw it. Indeed without statutory support they could hardly have freed themselves from judge-made Anglo-Hindu law. Much in consequence depended on the legislature and it was increasingly clear that public opinion, i.e. the new Hindu intelligentsia, supported the old policy of "gradual judicial reform in favor of

38. *Ibid.*, 125–27. Hindostan is, roughly, North India.
39. Mayne, *Hindu Law and Usage*, 34; Rankin, *Background*, 154, xi.

uniformity and 'better' morality." This tendency towards all-India
unity would democratically culminate after independence in the
Hindu Code of 1955–1956.[40]

The Dream of Anglo-Indian Nationhood in the Panjab

In the cities of the Panjab, the wealthy and influential Hindus and
Muslims followed their own personal laws, but it was some years
after the final conquest of 1849 before the British discovered that the
agricultural population was generally governed by rules of customary law. Outside the cities, it was only with regard to marriage and
divorce that any great difference was found between Hindus and
Muslims. In all other matters concerning personal relationships and
in cases relating to land tenures, Panjab custom, though often
resembling rules of Hindu law, operated independently and in complete ignorance of shastric learning of any description. Even before
this was recognized, it was decided not to extend the Bengal Acts and
Regulations to the newly conquered border province. The country
was "primitive" and required a strong executive with wide discretionary authority: the complex niceties of the Cornwallis system of
1793 would make little sense so far "up country." Panjab, in other
words, became non-regulation territory to be ruled by executive
order rather than by legislation.

Fasseur and I have argued elsewhere that, from a comparative
point of view, the regulation versus non-regulation dichotomy in
directly-ruled British India is a crucial one. Heuristically speaking,
it seems to me to be at least as fruitful as the direct versus indirect
rule dichotomy. The Dutch administrative system on Java, for instance, shows a much closer resemblance to non-regulation Panjab
than to a "normal" British-Indian province like regulation
Bengal.[41] That is why, in a volume on comparative colonial law, this
Indian province deserves at least as much attention as the three
"Presidencies" so far dealt with.

Only toward the end of the century would the personal laws of the
Hindus and Muslims of the Panjab gradually assume a greater
importance in public opinion and, as a consequence, in the courts.
For many decades, however, the province was allowed a legal person-

40. Derrett, "J.H. Nelson," 367ff.
41. C. Fasseur and D.H.A. Kolff, "Some remarks on the development of colonial
bureaucracies in India and Indonesia," *Itinerario* 10 (1986), 31–34.

ality of its own.[42] In 1854, this found expression in a manual circulated for the information and guidance of civil servants: even patriarchal rule could not mean that every judicial officer should be a law unto himself. It comprised rules drawn from the Regulations and from Hindu, Muslim, English and French law, as well as from provincial usage. As this little book was administered without question by the civil courts for a period of eighteen years, people came generally to refer to it as to the "Punjab Civil Code." In cases relating to succession, family law, and the transfer of landed property, it prevented by the strength it gave to custom the importation of the intricate rules and case-law – English, Hindu, and Muslim – of Bengal.[43]

The Punjab Laws Bill of 1872 seemed for a while to herald the end of this practice. The Law Member at that time, J. Fitzjames Stephen, intended to fill the gap in the written law of the province. An amendment, however, of George Campbell, an old Panjab hand who wanted to prevent the importation of the complicated rules of the regulation provinces into the Northwest, marked the more critical attitude that had by then been building up for some time toward the imposition of codes from above. In the Panjab, custom would be the primary rule of decision in questions regarding succession, special property of females, betrothal, marriage, divorce, dower, adoption, guardianship, minority, bastardy, family relations, wills, legacies, gifts, partitions, or any religious usage or institution. Muslim and Hindu law, in so far as it was not already altered or abolished by the legislature, would come only secondarily. Fitzjames Stephen accepted Campbell's amendment, because for twenty years already, customs had been "most scrupulously registered" during the land settlements, i.e. the administrative operations during which the fiscal responsibility to pay the land revenue was "settled" on individuals or groups of land owners.[44] With the help of these settlement records, the vacuum in the civil law could be filled.

The plan seems logical enough. For many years before 1872, during the land revenue settlements, the practice had been followed of collectively interrogating villagers of the same tribe or part of the district, and of recording their joint answers. C.L. Tupper, a

42. Gledhill, *Compilation*, 138, 144, 150. See on the Panjab administrative system P.H.M. van den Dungen, *The Punjab Tradition: Influence and Authority in Nineteenth-Century India* (London, 1972).

43. C.L. Tupper, ed., *A Selection from the Records of the Punjab Government (Punjab Customary Law, Vol. I)* (Calcutta, 1881), 5, 7.

44. Rankin, *Background*, 16.

member of the Indian Civil Service, who in the 1880s published a
series of volumes on the customary law of the Panjab based on these
records, was confident that Government would before long possess
tribal codes in the vernacular for almost every district in the province. But, as in Bombay Presidency, there was another way to
discover system in the genius of agrarian society. This was the
Gujarat method, mentioned above: to compile and condense the
decisions of the courts on point of customary law in order in the end
to produce a precise codification of custom as judicially recognized
in the province. Two barristers, Boulnois and Rattigan, attempted
to do this in the 1870s.[45] It is not at all clear that either of these two
approaches in itself would have yielded good results. In Bombay, as
we saw, Elphinstone had planned to combine both methods, though
each of them was recognized as primarily suited to a different part of
the provinces. In the Panjab, on the other hand, they presented
themselves as rivals for the same territory. To leave the actual task
of ascertaining custom to the courts would have left the door open to
the exceedingly intricate learning of Hindu case-law as it emerged
from individual suits, in which often no clear proof of custom would
be found. Surely, the court could again and again begin a fresh
investigation into local usage, but the information gathered in this
way would be piecemeal, haphazard, and extremely slow to yield
anything approaching coherence. The law of evidence did, moreover, not always allow custom to be established. In short, it could well
be argued that usage should be molded in accordance with some
"comprehensive and consistent scheme of policy."[46] Tupper, for
one, thought that not the Boulnois and Rattigan method, but only
his kind of work, based on the settlement records and on continued
enquiries along such lines, could guarantee the comprehensiveness
and consistency required.

There is not much point in going any further into the history of
this debate unless one realizes what the impact on society is of any
systematic collection of custom, whether through the judiciary process of judge-made case law, or with the help of questionnaires used
by the settlement officers of the executive branch of the administration. In one respect, the phrase "customary law" is a contradiction
in terms. The village elders, once having given evidence as witnesses
in court, or having explained village equity at the time of the

45. Ch. Boulnois and W.H. Rattigan, *Notes on Customary law as administered in the
Courts of the Punjab, with an Introduction to the Study of Customary Law in India by W.H.
Rattigan* (London, 1876; 2nd rev. ed. Lahore, 1878).

46. Tupper, *Selection*, 11–13.

drawing up of the *rivaj-i-am* as required at settlement, find their opinions are then divorced from the particular context in which they were given and that an impersonal authority is bestowed on them. From then on, the village has lost its old position as guardian of customary behavior to the employees of government interpreting the newly sanctioned customary laws. It is clear that, once evidence of "custom" was digested into manuals and the like, once it was proclaimed as something very much approaching "law," the village or tribe thus treated became an object rather than a subject of judiciary procedures. "Customary law" now operated out of the context of circumstantial knowledge and evidence, deprived of the quality of village equity as weighed and articulated by men who were daily subjected to it themselves. Custom, therefore, ceased to reflect the *droit vécu* of agrarian society. It is true, as is often said, that custom was first preserved, then upgraded and "frozen" out of relevance to the flux of village life. The important fact, however, is not that it was written down. Traditional society had always drawn inspiration from its written *shastras*, and these had absorbed much of what had once been custom. Crucial was the novel authority of a supralocal procedural code capable of taking cognizance implicitly, as well as explicitly, of only a fragment of what used to be taken into account as relevant evidence by the village law – ways of dispute management.

Only men like Nelson and Van Vollenhoven seem, in their final analysis of the colonial predicament, to have realized this. Their advice would be not to collect custom at all if it could be avoided, but to leave everything to local independence. But this impeccable logic was incompatible with colonial rule, and with any kind of modern rule, for that matter. And so the vast majority of British civil servants in the Indian Empire would envisage a totally different kind of future for Indian society. The Panjab Lieutenant-Governor, and, at his suggestion, the Government of India, did not support the idea of codifying and thus sanctioning customary law; to do this would perpetuate tribal organization and custom. "Tribal" customs should only be enforced so long as they were suited to the expectations and views of justice of the members of the societies to which they applied: "But the tendency of our administration is to dissolve the tribal bond and to give free scope to individual energy . . . The process is gradual, but sure; and though the Lieutenant-Governor does not desire to hasten the decay, he would not propose any measure which would prolong the existence of a custom for a longer time than is necessary to prevent the dislocation of the society which

has been governed by it."[47] Therefore, instead of allowing the
executive to use customary law as an instrument of social construction, Government preferred to leave the enforcement of it to the
courts until such time as it would, by a natural process of degeneration, have survived itself.

Against this, Tupper's vision for the Panjab was one of nation
building and Anglo-Indian Partnership. To go only by judicially
recognized custom, i.e. "to leave the work of reconstruction to the
necessarily motionless, machine-like action of the Courts," would
not be politic, because it would mean to forgo the direction of a
guiding principle: "The question, what is the state of society which
the Government would wish to see established in the Punjab, is still
an open one. The political solution of the question mainly, I think,
depends on the way in which it is resolved to deal with customary
law." It could not be said more clearly: to Tupper and many of his
colleagues in the Panjab, this was not a debate to be left to lawyers,
it was a crucial political dilemma. It had been the tendency so far to
uphold the core "native institutions" of the Panjab, that is to say the
tribe, the clan, and the village community. Indeed, as Tupper
admitted, the latter "has been in some places constructed where it
did not before exist." But how could these institutions withstand
"the disintegrating influences of the severalty of interest which the
course of justice undesignedly promotes?" This could only be done
on the basis of a firm vision of the future. Quoting from Tacitus'
Germania, Tupper presented his political credo: through tribe, clan,
and village community, Government could "gain its firmest hold on
the inclinations and motives of the people. The people can be led by
their own leaders. It is much easier for a foreign Government to deal
with organized bodies of men, through those who can be trusted on
both sides, than with miscellaneous hordes of individuals. Native
society will, I believe, be the happier, so long as it can still be held
together by the bonds of consanguinity."

I have no doubt in my mind that a program like this – as well as
other aspects of official thinking in the colonies – cannot be fully
understood without a touch of psychohistory. Like Nelson's and
Van Vollenhoven's, Tupper's was a vision of happiness, built on an
intimacy shaped by eighteen years of executive sympathy in the
province under the Punjab Civil Code and by a host of anthropological material carefully collected during the land settlements. At-
tentive colonial care to him was an indispensable political asset. It

47. *Ibid.*, 221.

filled a vacuum that it would be dangerous to leave to others to fill: "You cannot expect to find in this country the closeness of those ties which hold men together in Europe. You cannot have the extensive political co-operation which springs in part from representative government, and in part from the sentiment of common territorial nationality." Anglo-Indian nationhood could never be cemented by a transcendent faith. Tupper's attitude towards Indian religion was as negative as that of Nelson or Van Vollenhoven: "If you weaken the sense of tribal fellowship the only thing that could be put in its room would be religion, not a polytheistic indifferentism or a contemplative philosophy, but a religion like those of the Sikhs or Muhammadans, that by inspiring enthusiasm would generate a sense of brotherhood: and here the British Government could take no part." The "motionless" and "machine-like" courts would not be able to avoid this, but the Panjab administrative tradition, as it had grown since 1849, could. "A tribe", Tupper felt sure in his heart, "recognized and lifted into the system of British administration, has, in the guardianship of the governing body, the best possible chance of disusing savagery and learning the wisdom of civilized men."[48] It is the tale of Prospero and Caliban over again.[49] Customary law would be the central instrument of this policy, or, as Tupper put it, "the view I had been led to form of the character of customary law in great part suggested to me the feasibility of using it for public or political ends."[50]

Conclusion

This discussion, as it took place in the Panjab, was another form of "The Battle of the Two Philosophies," in which the essential colonial dilemma was reflected: the choice between good government, based on just and universal principles on the one hand, and equally well-intentioned government that took its cue from the "genius" of the people as experienced and invented by caring foreign amateurs. The difference is that the first approach could achieve a number of results on the road to modernization, and was adopted by the Indian elites in the period of nationalism, whereas the latter was continually

48. *Ibid.*, 16–21.
49. Cf. O. Mannoni, *Prospero and Caliban, the psychology of colonization* (New York-Washington, 1964).
50. Tupper, *Selection*, 22.

on the defensive and would, at the most, contribute a measure of wholesome delay. This is most clear in the fate of the old Indian law machine as we have described it. Its procedures were totally at odds with those required by the modern state. Even the great debate of the two philosophies, in spite of all rhetorics, really was concerned only with the question how best to replace the old Indian legal system. The 1833 Charter Act had called for experiments which in the long run would lead to the creation of a British law machine for India, a scientific model based on universal legal reflection. These experiments, which lasted throughout the century, assumed different forms in the different provinces of the Indian empire. If a typology would have to be invented, province by province, of colonial legal policies in India, the Bombay experiments should perhaps be characterized as closest to the traditional Indian law machine, i.e. as Hindu-customary law, the Bengal and Madras systems as Anglo-Hindu law, and the Panjab school of administration as Anglo-customary law. Together they form the three varieties of the British Indian law apparatus. All three of them were in one essential respect at odds with the Indian ancien régime's law machine: the procedures of the judiciary were, practically from the very beginning, those of the modern state, i.e. they aimed at certainty and finality. Thus pushed ahead, India inexorably moved to legal unity, until in 1955–1956 a Hindu Code was enacted, which was almost the fulfillment of the radical program of 1833. Only the Indian Muslims partly escaped from this legal unity, just as, in 1947, most of their coreligionists had escaped from Indian territory itself.

The old Indian law machine partly survived in decapitated form in agrarian India, where modern rule obtains at times imperfectly. Also, some of the legal problems we have touched upon in this paper have found no solution yet. The Indian legal scene, historical as well as contemporary, presents a range of issues extremely rich as a source of comparative legal studies. This applies not least to the continuities of the old Indian law machine. Perhaps it is not often realized that Hindu law, as Derrett remarked, "was the oldest continuous system of law, and that its materials were, in their richness and diversity, superior to Roman law, while the longevity of its institutions altogether exceeded anything which any other system could proffer."[51] Together with India's size and the comparatively long span of its colonial history, this explains the exceptional diversity and intricacy of its legal history.

51. Lingat, *Classical Law*, ix.

As for the present, if the law of evidence, the organization of the judiciary and legal procedure, show a remarkable similarity to those of England, the old Indian law machine, always a vital part of Indian civilization, is more than just a memory. Time and again, it reasserts itself in political ideals, in religion and in substantive law. This is a dialogue that will not end as long as India remains what it has always enjoyed being: a land of lawyers. So we find neither the unitary system pronounced in force by the lawyers we quoted in the beginning of this essay, nor a dualist system composed of foreign and indigenous elements that ill adapt to each other. What obtains is the old tripartite law machine, seemingly irretrievably broken into independent parts and straining itself to digest the chunks of European law it was forced to swallow in the colonial era, yet struggling to refind its former organic wholeness.

11

Colonial Dilemma: Van Vollenhoven and the Struggle Between Adat Law and Western Law in Indonesia

C. FASSEUR

Introduction

The main feature of the legal system in Indonesia during the colonial era was its dualistic character. This dual legal system had been in existence since the eighteenth century, when the Dutch gained control of the interior of Java. It was solidly anchored in the Government Regulation (*Regeringsreglement*) for the Netherlands Indies of 1854.[1] According to article 75 of this "Indian constitution," jurisdiction, legislation, and legal procedures for Dutchmen and other "Europeans" (an expression that after 1899 also covered the Japanese) had to be based on regulations and ordinances as much as possible in conformity with the laws and procedures that existed in The Netherlands (the so-called principle of concordance). "Natives" on the other hand, i.e. Indonesians, including the Chinese minority who were especially important in Indonesian business life, were subjected to their own "religious laws, institutions and customs" – so far as they were "not in conflict with generally recognized

1. I will not try to describe in detail here the very complicated and judicial dualistic situation that existed in the Netherlands Indies during the last century of colonial rule, the period before 1848 having been admirably summarized by John Ball in his *Indonesian Legal History 1602–1848* (Sydney, 1982). Such an elaborate survey would burden the general argument of this essay and be a very tedious affair indeed. It may suffice here to mention some authors who have presented (in English) useful surveys of this complex matter. M.B. Hooker, in *Legal Pluralism. An Introduction to Colonial and Neo-colonial Laws* (Oxford, 1975), has written an informative chapter on "Dutch colonial law and the legal systems of Indonesia," 250–300. See further Daniel S. Lev, "Judicial unification in post-colonial Indonesia," *Indonesia* 16 (1973), 1–37; "Colonial law and the genesis of the Indonesian state," *Indonesia* 40 (1985), 57–74; and several other publications. See also the succinct introduction written by H.W.J. Sonius in *Van Vollenhoven on Indonesian Adat Law*, ed. J.F. Holleman (The Hague, 1981).

principles of equity and justice" – except where "natives" or those equated with them had voluntarily accepted European (Dutch) law either generally (which only happened in the case of "mixed" marriages) or specifically for certain transactions. Furthermore, the colonial administration could declare – and did so many times – the applicability of certain regulations and ordinances to the Indonesian population or part of it (for instance the Chinese minority).[2] Finally, there were two separate court systems, for Europeans and non-Europeans, although in "native" cases appeals went to the European courts and Dutchmen – either civil servants or professional judges – ordinarily presided over the non-European courts.

At the turn of the twentieth century the dual legal system came under fire. The plural and judicial organization in the Netherlands Indies was seriously challenged by government proposals for a unified legal system. By way of argument for such a reform reference was made to other colonial territories, in particular British India. A fierce discussion about the advantages and disadvantages of the introduction of modern and uniform European law concepts into native societies and of the suppression or conservation of indigenous customary law in Indonesia (or *adat* law) flared up in The Netherlands and went on for many years. This debate was to dominate any further developments in the Indonesian legal field during the last four decades of colonial rule. Finally, the day was won, perhaps somewhat surprisingly, by the so-called Leiden *adat* law school, which had its champion and most outstanding representative in Cornelis van Vollenhoven (1874–1933). The debate and its outcome will be discussed in more detail in the next pages.

2. Ball, *Indonesian Legal History*, 224. The Government Regulation of 1854 (article 109) made a distinction between Europeans and those equated with them (native Christians) on the one hand, and "natives" and those equated with them (Chinese, Arabs, and other "Orientals," until 1899 including Japanese) on the other hand. Each of these categories was subjected to its own system of public (administrative, penal) and private (family, civil, commercial) law. The question of who belonged to the European and who to the native group was not decided by the law. The criterion was an ethnological one and did not cause many difficulties in practice. Not until 1920 were the inhabitants of the Netherlands Indies given the right to ask for a judicial decision about their classification if they wished so.

By a law of December 31, 1906 (but not operative until January 1, 1920) a new legal division was made between: 1. Europeans (including Japanese, Siamese, and other non-European nations with a European system of family law); 2. Natives (Indonesians including Indonesian Christians); and 3. Foreign Orientals (Chinese, Arabs, and other Asiatic nations not covered by 1).

This mainly racial classification, however, was not definitive for the private law that was applied to the different categories and subcategories. Indonesian Christians, for instance, had the same marriage law as the European group; after 1855 the commercial law was the same for Europeans, Chinese, and Arabs.

An Architect of *Adat* Law

It was the famous Leiden Orientalist Christiaan Snouck Hurgronje (1857–1936) who coined the expression *adat* law and used it for the first time in his book *De Atjehers* (*The Acehnese*) published in 1893. To a certain degree this was symptomatic of the slow discovery and appreciation of native customary law in Indonesia. Even the phrase "religious laws, institutions and customs" that had been used in the Government Regulation of 1854 was characteristic of the many misunderstandings to which the notion of indigenous law had given birth, as *adat* law was erroneously identified with religious, i.e. Islamic law.[3]

The "discovery of *adat* law" – to quote the title of one of Van Vollenhoven's almost innumerable publications in this field – did not start before the 1880s, thus about a century ago. Until the middle of the nineteenth century the Dutch knew next to nothing about the *adat* law of the Javanese and other Indonesians whom they had been ruling for such a long time. A systematic description and analysis of Indonesian *adat* law only really got under way after the appointment of Van Vollenhoven to the Leiden chair of *adat* law of the Netherlands Indies in 1901. This was in more than one sense a freshman's start, as he was at that moment only twenty-seven years old.[4]

For more than three decades, until his early death in 1933, the forceful, albeit somewhat unbalanced, personality of Van Vollenhoven was the nucleus of the *adat* movement in The Netherlands, which also had, as we shall see, certain political connotations. He founded a real "school" of *adat* law disciples. His students wrote more than 20 doctoral dissertations on this subject. Not a few of them later reached high positions in the colonial bureaucracy since, from 1902 on, Leiden University had the monopoly of the training and education of future Dutch civil servants for the East Indian administration. But Van Vollenhoven himself easily carries off the palm. It was on him and his tireless work that the labor of others, his pupils, admirers, and even his opponents, was centered.[5] With his

3. C. van Vollenhoven, *De Ontdekking van het Adatrecht* (Leiden, 1928), 108–09.

4. See Sonius in Holleman (ed.), *Van Vollenhoven*, xxxi 4.seq.; F.D.E. van Ossenbruggen, "Prof. Mr. Cornelis van Vollenhoven als ontdekker van het adatrecht," in *Honderd Jaar Studie van Indonesië 1850–1950*, ed. H.J.M. Maier and A. Teeuw (The Hague, 1976), 59–100.

5. V.E. Korn, "Adat law" in *Report of the Scientific Work done in the Netherlands on behalf of the Dutch Overseas Territories* (Amsterdam, 1948), 157; see also 257–59.

great work *Het adatrecht van Nederlandsch-Indië* (*Adat law in the Nether-lands Indies*) – the first volume (of three) was published in 1918, but the first installments had already been appearing since 1906 – he set his seal forever upon the scientific study of this subject. In 1909 he also took the initiative in establishing the Commission for *Adat* law (*Adatrecht-commissie*), of which he was to remain secretary until the end of his life; in setting in motion the publication of the many volumes on *adat* law published by this body; in founding in 1917 the *Adat* Law Foundation (*Adatrecht-stichting*), with its magnificent li-brary still present in Leiden; and finally in being the fountainhead in many other activities in the interest of the study of the customary law of Indonesia. Without any exaggeration, in writing Van Vol-lenhoven's obituary, one of his admirers, F.D.E. van Ossenbruggen, could proclaim that he had been the man "who elevated *adat* law to a science" and who had made the denial of such a science impossible once and for all.[6] Dutch legal language adopted the word "*adatrecht*" for the first time in 1910; Dutch dictionaries did so in 1914.

A Reluctant Administration

After 1900, the growing interest in the "new science" of *adat* law presented a very different picture from the preceding ages of official neglect of indigenous law in Indonesia. With the exception of one or two compilations of old Javanese laws in the eighteenth century, literature and research had been virtually nonexistent until 1848. In that year a whole system of new legislation for Europeans was introduced: a civil code; a commercial code; a code of civil procedure (for civil suits against Europeans); a code of criminal procedure; and a new ordinance on the judiciary. A penal code for Europeans followed in 1866. Apart from new rules on native judiciary (com-bined with the regulation on court organization for Europeans) and only one ordinance on indigenous civil and criminal procedures, the Indonesians were left to themselves and to their own, also unknown, *adat* law. A rather hasty proposal to apply the European civil code partially to them was stranded by Governor General J.J. Rochussen in 1848/49. He was of the opinion that such a radical measure would play havoc with Javanese society and, for that reason, was "hazar-dous" and "impolitic" as long as no other social order was there to take the place of the original one (for instance an order based on

6. Ossenbruggen, "Van Vollenhoven," 59.

Christianity instead of Islam).[7] He was also afraid of the impact of such a far reaching proposal on the cultivation system in Java that was pouring huge profits into the Dutch treasury at that time. It was possible, he argued, to base a similar system of forced crop cultivation on native traditions and customs, but impossible to do so on Western judicial concepts.

John Ball in his study on Indonesian legal history concludes from these and other observations that European self-interest and indifference to the indigenous legal order contributed most to the evolution of dualism in the colonial legal system, in particular in a country like Indonesia.[8] Daniel S. Lev also suggests that colonial law and especially plural law, plurally administered, was intended primarily to make exploitation efficient. Nevertheless even Lev has to acknowledge that different courts and different laws were only "equitable"; otherwise people denied their own law might rebel.[9] The Dutch indeed faced an insoluble dilemma. The adoption of Western law for the Indonesians would have meant that Indonesian society was turned upside down. At the very least it was a big leap in the dark, nobody being able to foretell the consequences of the abolition of *adat* law, as nobody knew anything about it. For this reason – insufficient knowledge of indigenous land rights – in 1866 a majority of the Second Chamber of the Dutch Parliament rejected a bill proposed by the Minister for the Colonies, I.D. Fransen van de Putte, to confer the proprietary rights over the cultivated land to the Javanese cultivators, at the same time granting an award of the ownership of the uncultivated land to the government. This rejection led to a temporary schism in the liberal party and the fall of the liberal government.

The Dutch were neither fools nor angels. They were, however, severely handicapped by their lack of knowledge of the indigenous languages, in particular Javanese. How could they have studied *adat* without sufficient knowledge of native vocabulary and customs? Only in 1842 – almost forty years after the foundation of the East Indian College at Haileybury (in 1806), where the future officials for the British Indian Civil Service were trained – was the instruction and education of young officials for the Dutch East Indian administration begun at the Royal Academy for Engineers in Delft. The Minister for the Colonies, J.C. Baud, who was instrumental in

7. Ball, *Indonesian Legal History*, 220–22.
8. Ball, *Indonesian Legal History*, 236.
9. Lev, "Colonial law," 57, 60.

achieving this decision, thought that it was "a manifest truth that a subjected people can not, in the long run, be kept in subjection without violence unless the foreign ruler was determined to govern this people with fairness and justice and, above all, in deference to native attitudes, customs and bias."[10] To achieve this latter, knowledge of the Javanese language in particular would be a prerequisite; language instruction thus became the core of the education bestowed on the future Dutch East Indian officials, first in Delft and, after the liquidation of the institute in 1900, in Leiden. Baud's well-known penchant for the Javanese language also had other antecedents: as a Governor General he had once had to decide on the execution of the death sentence on three Javanese who had been accused of robbery and murder. On reading the judicial documents Baud was assailed by the uneasy feeling that the Dutch official who had presided over the native court had, because of his poor command of Javanese, condemned three innocent people. Baud decided to permit them to request a reprieve from the death sentence. Before a decision had been reached on their petition another, similar crime was committed in the same region. The offenders were caught and subsequently confessed to being guilty of the previous robbery as well. These events had not failed to make a deep impression on him.[11]

After 1850, with their better command of indigenous languages, some Dutch officials – certainly not all of them – became more interested in the customs and attitudes of the people they had to administer. The "discovery" of *adat* law had begun in reality. The first scientific works were published by civil servants such as G.A. Wilken (1847–1891) on the Central Moluccas, the Minahasa in Northern Sulawesi, and Sumatra, and F.A. Liefrinck (1853–1927) on Bali and Lombok. Both were ardent self-taught anthropologists and ethnologists (Wilken ended his short life as a professor of ethnology in Leiden).[12] Their shrewd observations on native customs and traditions, the rights to the soil, family law, and other topics provided many useful bricks for Van Vollenhoven's monumental edifice on *adat* law in Indonesia. The missionaries, too, acquitted themselves well, although they were sometimes more

10. *Historische Nota over het Vraagstuk van de Opleiding en Benoembaarheid voor den Administratieven Dienst* (Batavia, 1900), 23.

11. See C. Fasseur, "Leiden and empire: university and colonial office 1825–1925," in *Leiden-Oriental Connections, 1850–1940*, ed. W. Otterspeer (Leiden, 1989), 187–203.

12. Van Vollenhoven, *Ontdekking Adatrecht*, 99–106.

skeptical of all these "pagan" institutions or traditions obscured by "the darkness of Islam." On the other hand, the Dutch lawyers who served in the judicial functions in Indonesia were often less enthusiastic, convinced as they were of the superiority of Western concepts of law to those of "primitive" societies. Their attitude to native law was broadly the same as that of the physician who runs into the tribal health services of the local medicine man.[13] Their judicial training and the terminology they were used to, molded on Roman and Dutch law, were moreover a serious handicap to a better understanding and appreciation of the specific identity and essence of *adat* law institutions. In this respect civil servants like Liefrinck and Wilken, not burdened by a judicial education, were often less inclined to torture *adat* law concepts on the Procrustes-bed of Western terminology and definitions.

The rather condescending way in which the Dutch lawyers during the second half of the nineteenth century used to look upon the *adat* law institutions with which they were confronted had, at least for the time being, more impact on the shaping of government policy in this field than the interest shown in native law by some civil servants who lacked the prestige of the professionals. We should also be aware of the enormous influence of Western ethnocentricism and feelings of superiority in that imperialistic age with regard to – I quote Rudyard Kipling – "the lesser breeds without the law." Questions could arise not only about the intrinsic value of *adat* law but also about the feasibility of its implementation. First, *adat* law was by definition unwritten and for that reason difficult to get to know or to understand. According to article 7 of the Regulation on court organization and administration of justice of 1848, the judge had in all civil and penal cases against "native" defendants to interrogate their "priests" (sic) and chiefs on the relevant customs and institutions – a time-consuming and usually not very satisfactory occupation. Secondly, *adat* law, as even a cursory glance at it could show, was very multiform and regionally different. For instance, in his writings, Van Vollenhoven distinguished no fewer that nineteen *adat* law "circles" in the Indonesian area. This marked local and regional differentiation was an evil in the eyes of Dutch lawyers nurtured in the cradle of centralistic Napoleonic law concepts. It also presented a rather mournful spectacle to the sympathizers of native law.

Finally, and here the Dutch looked to the example set by the

13. Ibid., 114.

British in India, time did not seem to be on the side of *adat* law. Did not progress demand the introduction of a uniform and "higher" law than these native institutions and curious customs which were so badly equipped for the modern epoch? The legal policy of the British government in India in the footsteps of Macaulay – the adoption of a penal code in 1860 and a code of criminal procedure in 1861 which were applicable to all groups of the population, not to mention the more or less simultaneous enactment of a complete code of civil procedure, the Succession Act of 1865 and the law of contracts introduced in 1872 – appeared to be worthy of imitation.[14] How these feelings influenced government policy in colonial Indonesia can best be shown by means of the penal law system that was introduced after 1848, pluralistic in name but not in fact.

Dualistic Penal Law: Unity Under a Multiform Cloak

Penal law had not been covered by the wave of codification that hit the colony, at least the European segment of it, in 1848. Holland did not then possess a proper national penal code of its own and was still applying the French penal code (*Code Pénal*) imposed by Napoleon after his short-lived annexation of the country in 1810. After 1848, therefore, the Dutch had no other choice but to maintain the "old-Dutch" and "Roman" penal law that went as far back as 1642. After the largely futile efforts of three drafting committees in both Indonesia and in Holland, a penal code for Europeans in the Netherlands Indies could finally be promulgated in 1866; it took effect on January 1, 1867.[15] The newly adopted penal code was a faithful copy of the French code that remained valid in The Netherlands until 1886. But what policy should be followed toward the native Indonesian population? *Adat* penal law was virtually unknown and the cruel and inhuman penalties inflicted by Islamic courts (e.g. amputation of the hands) had already been abolished at the beginning of the nineteenth century. As a rule Dutch judges applied Dutch penal law concepts in cases which were brought to trial (as they did in civil cases).

The Dutch government therefore decided to frame a penal code for natives and other non-Europeans that in its turn would be a

14. Cf. C. van Vollenhoven, *Koloniale Studiën* 9 (1925) I, 313; John Strachey, *India. Its Administration and Progress* (London, 1911), 99–118.
15. See C. Fasseur, "Een vergeten strafwetboek," in *Handhaving van de Rechtsorde. Bundel aangeboden aan Albert Mulder*, ed. W.C. van Binsbergen (Zwolle, 1988), 37–53.

faithful copy of the European one adopted in 1866. Later on a commentator jokingly compared this decision to the course of events in a parsimonious Dutch middle-class household. After many years of loyal service the threadbare coat of the master of the house was not thrown away but cut up into a jacket for the oldest son, subsequently into a cap for the second one and so forth.[16] In 1866, F.F.L.U. Last, member of the Supreme Court in Batavia, was given a commission for the drafting of a native penal code modelled on the European counterpart. Last, however, did not appear to be entirely convinced of the wisdom of his mandate. In a letter to the Governor General in 1868 he argued that such "a servile imitation" could be rendered just as well by "the humblest of all clerks," but that the result of such an imitation would be totally unintelligible to even the cleverest native chief. In Last's opinion, moreover, the French penal code "written for a turbulent French nation more than half a century ago" was completely unsuitable for implementation in the "peaceful" Javanese society.[17] These were interesting, if not very constructive, remarks, which had a predictable effect. A few months after he had lodged his complaints Last was discharged as a government commissioner. His successor was the ambitious director of the new Department of Justice in Batavia, T.H. der Kinderen, who wasted no love whatsoever on *adat* law. His penal code for natives that came into force in 1873 was an almost perfect copy of the European edition. From that time on *adat* penal law was a thing of the past, mourned only by a handful of ethnologists. Some of them afterward stated, not very convincingly, that the introduction of Western penal law had stimulated the almost suppressed tradition of headhunting by Dayak tribes in Borneo as; unlike the old *adat* institutions, the new penal code did not recognize the possibility of a compensation order and so had rekindled the practice of vendetta![18]

When a really national penal code was introduced in The Netherlands in 1886, history seemed to repeat itself. A new penal code for Europeans in the Netherlands Indies, again a copy of the code then valid in the mother country, was promulgated in 1898 but did not obtain statutory force as the Minister for the Colonies preferred to wait for the framing of its "native sister" before adopting both codes

16. M.C. Piepers, quoted in *De Indische Gids* 1888, I, 776.
17. Last to Governor General, February 2, 1868 in *Archief Ministerie van Koloniën 1850–1900* (Algemeen Rijksarchief), exhibitum May 20, 1868, portfolio 2081.
18. H.H. van Kol, *Handelingen Tweede Kamer der Staten-Generaal* October 10, 1906, 40 (Van Kol referred to the so-called *bangun* or compensation money for manslaughter in *adat* penal law).

at the same moment. That moment, however, as we shall see, was never to come.

The Drive Toward Unification

The trend for unification in the field of penal law might be explained with the argument that an efficient enforcement of "law and order" – in any colonial territory always an important asset, and certainly so in the eyes of a small power like the Dutch – required a legislation which was in principle the same for all inhabitants. On the other hand, differentiation could be accepted more easily in private and commercial law, as long as the economic ties between different groups of the population (not only between the tiny Western and the huge non-Western part of it, but also between the native population of different regions) were weak or even nonexistent. Difficulties arose, however, as soon as cases were regularly submitted to the courts in which the litigants belonged to different cultural and ethnic groups with different systems of law. Which law should be applied, and how was the judge to be cognizant with the particular branch of *adat* law of the parties involved in the conflict that he had to solve?

These questions became more and more urgent in the 1890s as a result of the improvement of communications in the Indies during the last quarter of the nineteenth century, the increased mobility of the population, and the upsurge of the economy after a long period of depression. The first railways in Java were constructed around 1870, and the first extensive network of shipping routes in the Archipelago had been organized by a government-licensed shipping company around 1890. There was another pressing motive for a fundamental reconsideration of the necessity for judicial reforms in the Indies, too. The legal status of the small but fast growing segment of the indigenous population who had been converted to Christianity was completely unclear. According to the letter of the Government Regulation of 1854 (article 75), they were subjected to the "religious laws, institutions and customs," marriage law excepted, on the same basis as their Mohammedan countrymen. But what did this expression mean exactly? Had one to think of Islamic laws or of a sort of Christian substitute, and how could one clarify such a non-denominational Christian *adat* law? Moreover, in the eyes of the missionaries, Indonesian Christians were certainly discriminated against, as they had to perform forced labor on Sundays and Christian holidays, but had to rest on Islamic feasts.

In 1890, the Dutch scholar L.W.C. van den Berg (1845–1927), a former adviser to the Dutch colonial government on Oriental languages and Islamic law, wrote an alarming article in the influential Dutch political monthly *De Gids*, in which he painted the legal status of the Indonesian Christians in the darkest colors. His conclusion was that the cause of Christianity could not be expected to make much progress in the Indies unless the legal status of its Indonesian converts was greatly improved. "As a result of his lack of legal certainty," Van den Berg wrote, "the native Christian is a creature that can hardly take any step on his path of life without stumbling over judicial questions."[19] This harsh sentence could not fail to make a considerable impact on the powerful Christian political parties in The Netherlands. The improvement of the legal status of their Indonesian co-religionists, in order to expedite the spreading of the Gospel, became one of the main issues of their colonial program in the years that followed. The Liberal Party, entrenched on the government benches, until 1901, when a coalition of Protestant and Roman Catholic parties took over, also felt somewhat disturbed. In 1892, a state commission was established for the revision of the colonial legislation in the field of private law, with Van den Berg as its secretary.[20] It drafted an ambitious program of action for judicial reform that did not, however, prove to be very effective in the years that followed. Legislation, certainly when it is prepared by a commission, is always a long-winded affair!

After 1897, a second line of approach was followed by the liberal Minister for the Colonies, J.Th. Cremer. Van Vollenhoven, then a young official at the Colonial Office, was his private secretary. Probably Van Vollenhoven inspired Cremer's decision to embark on a new course. This new policy aimed at a codification of local *adat* law, taking the compilation of *adats* in the Christian regions of the Archipelago (the Minahasa and the Moluccas) first. J.H. Carpentier Alting (1864–1929), president of the native court (*landraad*) in the Minahasa, later on a Leiden professor, prepared a compilation in two volumes of certain *adats* in that area (inter alia adoption and matrimonial law).[21] But this tree also failed to bear fruit. The

19. Cf. L.W.C. van den Berg, "Het kruis tegenover de halve maan," *De Gids* 1890, 4, 97. A short biography of this interesting scholar is in *Encyclopaedie van Nederlandsch Indië* 6 (The Hague, 1932), 31.
20. See Royal Decree of July 30, 1892 for the establishment of this not very well-known state commission (it was not even mentioned by Van Vollenhoven in his work on the discovery of adat law!), in *Archief Kabinet van de Koningin* (Algemeen Rijksarchief), portfolio 3117.
21. See my article on J.H. Carpentier Alting in *Biografisch Woordenboek van Nederland*,

original intention was, of course, to afford more certainty to both the local population and the government officials. In this respect we should be aware of the Dutch judicial axiom, one of the cornerstones of the Dutch civil code, that custom does not bind (does not give any rights) unless the law refers explicitly to it. Therefore, compared to Anglo-Saxon legal culture, the Dutch legal system allows very little room for any unwritten customary law contribution which does not have a basis in the written law. But the recording of *adats* threatened to amount to the simultaneous fossilization of native law, as it could then no longer accommodate itself to changing circumstances and local needs. Besides, the work proved to be of gigantic proportions and therefore a timeconsuming affair. Not only was a prior local enquiry an absolute condition even an expert like Carpentier Alting took almost four years to complete the first chapters of his compilation on the Minahasa – but as Van Vollenhoven himself rightly guessed, no fewer than nineteen or twenty of such local codifications would be needed to chart the complex and highly diverse legal situation in the whole of Indonesia. This vision of a multiplication of overlapping codifications, prepared by an army of eager *adat* experts, taking half a century or longer, did not appeal much to government officials or to practicing lawyers who were looking for an immediate solution to their many questions. The Batavian "desklords," as Van Vollenhoven called them, were even less pleased with his ideas when he suggested that each *adat* codification would be abrogated automatically after ten or fifteen years in order to force the administration continuously to adapt the *adat* regulations to new developments and changed circumstances in native society.[22]

After the fall of the Liberal government in 1901, however, the judicial policy of the Dutch took a new turn. The Christian Minister for the Colonies, A.W.F. Idenburg, commissioned Van den Berg to prepare a radical modification of the much discussed article 75 of the Government Regulation of 1854. This resulted in a bill that was sent to the Dutch Parliament in 1904. It was Idenburg's successor, the liberal D. Fock, who took upon himself the task of defending this proposal in Parliament at the end of 1906 (the legislative process in

3 (The Hague, 1989). Van Vollenhoven's warm support for Cremer's approach (he later changed his mind, however) appears from his publications, mentioned in note 22.

22. Cf. C. van Vollenhoven, "Geen juristenrecht voor den inlander," *De XXe Eeuw* (March 1905), 1–42; esp. 38–39. See also *Verslagen Indisch Genootschap* December 2, 1905, 19–22.

The Netherlands had, and still has, a lamentable reputation for tardiness).

The fact that Fock did not have any objections to endorsing a bill which was originally drafted under the responsibility of his political opponent and predecessor demonstrated that the main political parties in Holland had been able to come to terms with each other in the field of judicial reform in Indonesia. This coalition was indicative of a new era, that of the so-called ethical policy. This policy was aimed at the emancipation or elevation of the indigenous population. Welfare, modernization and "good government" were its catchwords. But how could these lofty aims be realized under the poor, obscure, and backward *adat* law system Indonesian society was subjected to? One of the leading liberal politicians of his days, C.Th. van Deventer, the man who had actually inaugurated the ethical policy some years before, even saw a direct link between unification of law and common prosperity; the latter was not really possible without the former. Only Western law could ensure judicial certainty for the indigenous people, and industry and commerce would follow in its footsteps and flourish. In his words – and we should not forget that Van Deventer, like Fock, had been a professional advocate in Java for many years – "one must recognize that the natural development for Orientals in a colony administered by a Western power is that they, albeit slowly, will have to conform to Western law." And in quoting Macaulay he assured his fellow members of parliament: "Uniformity when you can have it, diversity when you must have it, but in all cases certainty."[23]

The comparison with other colonial territories, in particular British India – elaborated upon in the numerous appendices of the explanatory memorandum to the bill – strengthened Van Deventer and like-minded M.P.'s in their belief that unification would win the day and that time would soon overtake dualism.

The obvious tenor of the government proposal was to pave the way for a general application of European law in native society. European law – concordant with the laws existing in Holland – would be the rule. *Adat* law would be the exception, only being relevant if "the different needs" of the indigenous population made any such deviation necessary. This would mean that *adat* law would

23. D. Fock, *Handelingen Tweede Kamer der Staten-Generaal* October 11, 1906, 59–65; C.Th. van Deventer, *Handelingen*, October 10, 1906, 35–36. Van Deventer, who wrote in 1899 a famous article in *De Gids* on Holland's "debt of honour" to Indonesia, was also the author of a long article on "Rechtshervorming in Indië," which had Macaulay's saying as a motto, in *De Gids* in January 1905.

be banished to the outskirts of civilized society; only in certain limited fields – for instance family law and intestate law – might it continue to play an important role, provided that the European law referred expressly to the use of *adat* law. In this way – and that was of course the great attraction of the government bill for many M.P.'s of the Christian parties in the Second Chamber – the problems surrounding the legal system of the Indonesian Christians would have been solved as well.[24]

Success seemed to be within reach, but the outcome of the parliamentary debate was, after all, a bitter disappointment to Fock and Van Deventer. The bill was amended by a dissident majority in the Second Chamber and in its final version – promulgated on the last day of 1906 – an unworkable instrument for the government.[25] It was never put into force and was finally replaced by a new regulation in 1919. The failure was the direct result of the one man crusade waged by Van Vollenhoven against the government proposals. In a very eloquent manner the young Leiden professor had managed to warn Parliament against the far-reaching consequences of such a rash decision as the abolition of *adat* law without any prior enquiry.[26] His admonition that Parliament must be wiser than the government had a marked effect. A majority of wavering liberals and Calvinist M.P.'s (who were less convinced of the blessings of Western judicial civilization than the former lawyers Fock and Van Deventer) backed an amendment to the bill which turned its main intention upside down. Not *adat* law but European law would be the exception to the rule. Only when the needs of native society required it, declared the new article 75, could European law be declared applicable. The burden of proof was thus actually turned 180 degrees. The old axiom that the colonial government should be cautious about native institutions and customs had carried the day. As one speaker in Parliament ironically summarized the debate: the amendment had been a lifeboat for the Minister when his ship was sinking, but it had brought him to the wrong shore, that is to say it had brought him back to the same shore of the river which he had wished to cross![27] And so it was.

24. This appears from the lengthy debates in Parliament, see *Handelingen Tweede Kamer der Staten-Generaal* October 10–16, 1906, 30–109.

25. For a concise summary of the debate see J. de Louter, "De wijziging van het Regerings-Reglement van Nederlandsch-Indië," *De Gids* 1907, I, 331–49.

26. See his publications mentioned in note 22.

27. The prominent Christian politician A.F. de Savornin Lohman, cf. De Louter, "De wijziging," 344.

Stalemate

In the light of hindsight the long discussions on the bill of 1904 were the decisive moment in the drive towards unification of law in Indonesia during the last decades of colonial rule. Not unification as such but legal certainty had been the ultimate goal of the supporters of judicial reforms. If legal diversity did not obstruct this ideal it might then have been acceptable after all. After 1906, therefore, the movement for unification thus gradually lost its momentum and finally petered out. The "unifiers" were satisfied when a new law, adopted in 1919 and giving article 75 its definite form, declared that private and public law must be regulated by government ordinance, which implied that *adat* law should be codified.[28] So, as the years passed by, Van Vollenhoven was able to reap the fruits of his campaign against the expansion of Western law in the Archipelago. His students obtained important positions in the colonial administration and his ideas received a more general acceptance as time went by. The only lasting achievement of the unification lobby was the adoption of a unified penal code for the Netherlands Indies in 1918, in which the separate codes for Europeans and natives were amalgamated.[29] But this was more a question of form than of substance, as both penal codes had been more or less identical already. The penal code of 1918 – almost identical with the Dutch one, with some special provisions for the implementation of punishments meted out to Indonesian offenders – is still valid in present-day Indonesia. But proposals for the introduction of a uniform code of criminal procedure for all groups of the population – Indonesians, Chinese, and Europeans – broke down in 1919, and such was also the fate of the draft of a unified code of civil law published in 1923. This code, which numbered 2220 articles (!), was safely locked up in a desk after a blistering attack by Van Vollenhoven on this odious specimen of a "ready-made judicial product: a unified private law for the Indies."[30]

European law for everyone would from then on be a thing of the

---

28. Cf. *Indisch Tijdschrift van het Recht*, 114 (1922), 227–308; Ph. Kleintjes, *Staatsinstellingen van Nederlandsch-Indië*, 5th ed. (Amsterdam, 1929), 2, 242–54.

29. The work on this unified code started in 1911 and was finished in 1915. It was carried out by a subcommittee of the state commission of 1892. The work on the code of criminal procedure came to grief as the Dutch were unwilling to confer equal procedural guarantees upon the Indonesians.

30. "Juridisch confectiewerk; eenheidsprivaatrecht voor Indië," *Koloniale Studiën* 9 (1925), 293–318.

past. And Van Vollenhoven did not miss the opportunity to stress the point that even in India – for such a long time held up as a striking example to all "unifiers," i.e. lawyers, mission friends, and radical liberal politicians – a debate was going on about the advantages of the codification of *adat* law. He was also very effective in his fight against a government proposal that would, if successful, have compelled the Indonesians to the full acceptance of European legal principles with regard to the ownership of land, for the sake of the large-scale agrarian development from which Western enterprises would have profited most. This bill threatened to become a repetition of the history of 1866. In 1919, it inspired Van Vollenhoven to write a bellicose pamphlet, *The Indonesian and his land (De Indonesiër en zijn grond)*, whereafter the bill was withdrawn by the Minister for the Colonies.[31]

On the other hand, Van Vollenhoven was less successful in the promotion of a real *adat* alternative that could respond to the needs of modern society. In 1910, he made a courageous attempt to draft *A specimen code of Indonesian adat law (Een adatwetboekje voor heel Indië)*. In only 111 articles a whole set of coordinated *adat* law principles, ready for immediate use by the judge, was presented to the reader. But the booklet proved to be too rudimentary an edifice to give a satisfying answer to the question of how *adat* law could be made operational in practice. For instance, in the chapter on *adat* penal law (Van Vollenhoven's draft covered not only private law but also public law), punishable offenses were defined as facts that conflicted with *adat* law and/or facts that violated the good faith required in society, unless the judge was of the opinion that this behavior had been justified by the demands of self-interest![32] Here and elsewhere legal certainty had been entirely lost sight of. This guideline for the judge was in reality the proclamation of his complete freedom to invent the law that, depending on the circumstances, suited people most. Thus it opened the door for judicial arbitrariness. In his later years Van Vollenhoven, though, proved himself to be a fierce opponent of any codification of *adat* law, for fear that it might stifle a harmonious

31. Other, less controversial legislative measures aimed at fostering a greater economic viability met with a lot of opposition from Van Vollenhoven whenever they took too little account of *adat*, for instance the 1908 ordinance on credit facilities, which provided for the encumbrance of land in cases of debt, thus avoiding the often onerous consequences of the *adat* way of handing over land in return for a loan. See Sonius in Holleman, ed., *Van Vollenhoven*, xxxviii, who gives several other examples, too.

32. Van Vollenhoven, *Adatwetboekje*, 31.

development of native customs and institutions. At most, all the study of *adat* law could in his opinion offer the judge a manual to assist him in making up his mind in any concrete case he might have to deal with.[33]

Perhaps this inability to present a workable alternative was not so much Van Vollenhoven's fault as that of *adat* law itself. Could it really be a useful instrument for responding to the needs of the individual and society in a rapidly changing and modernizing Indonesian world? Van Vollenhoven and his students might have been so busy in pursuing their enquiries and gathering data about *adat* law – a work that by definition could not ever be finished – that they never seriously got round to answering this crucial question. It was Professor J. de Louter, one of the few critical voices in the 1920s not silenced by the great master, who formulated the dilemma sharply. Is it enough, he asked, to judge the policy of a colonial government according to the degree to which it respects native institutions and *adat* law, or should the criterion be that such a government must give the law that best suits the needs of modern society, thus preventing Indonesia from turning into an open-air *adat* museum? For De Louter himself the answer to this question was not difficult. He considered the judgement of a colonial administration solely by the yard-stick of respect for native customs and *adats* "not only one-sided and unfair but moreover shortsighted and dangerous."[34] Although it would be unfair to postulate that Van Vollenhoven had entirely shut his eyes to these dangers, the question may nevertheless be posed as to whether he was entirely aware of the risk that his protectionist policy could deny Indonesia many opportunities for further development.[35]

An alternative might have been the introduction of an intermediate system of law that tried to combine elements of both Western and *adat* law in a delicate equilibrium. The concept of such a "mixed" law for all groups of the population, Europeans and Indonesians alike, had for instance found a stout defender in the prominent Dutch East Indian official I.A. Nederburgh, who also

33. Cf. Van Vollenhoven's opinion (September 1931), in the translation by Holleman, ed., *Van Vollenhoven*, 260: "The problem cannot be solved by codification, or replacement, or unification, or partial retention of *adat* law, nor by such revision or publication of it as jurisprudents or policy makers see fit to make, but only by the people's own will to maintain, expand and rejuvenate their law."

34. J. de Louter, "De ontdekking van het adatrecht," *De Indische Gids* 51 (1929) 1, 666–67.

35. Compare Lev's critical remarks on Van Vollenhoven and his work in "Colonial law," 63–67.

edited a magazine *Wet en Adat* (*Law and Adat*) for some years at the turn of the century.[36] But there were severe doubts about the feasibility of this approach, i.e. the many years it would take to finish the job and the final result. Would the outcome not be – to draw a modern parallel – like a Javanese gamelan orchestra conducted by Herbert von Karajan or vice versa the Berliner Philharmoniker conducted by a Javanese *dalang*, the presenter of the Javanese shadow play, wayang?

As in other respects – for instance in their attitude towards the Indonesian nationalist movement – the colonial policy of the Dutch in the field of legal and judicial reforms, so hopefully inaugurated at the very outset of the twentieth century, ended in the last decade before the Second World War in a deadlock, in which there was hardly any room for maneuver. Although the pride of the Dutch in their achievements in the field of *adat* law studies might have been justified, seen from a scientific point of view and in an international perspective, here too they were unable to find an adequate solution to the many problems which a rapidly modernizing colonial Indonesia had to face.

Aftermath

What did the Indonesians themselves think of the judicial reforms and the *adat* law policy of the Dutch? As is usual in a colonial situation, their opinion was never asked. Moreover, in the colonial era there were hardly any Indonesian lawyers to give an opinion. Rudimentary legal training for Indonesians was not introduced until 1909. A complete law faculty was opened in Batavia (Jakarta) only in 1924. This faculty would become the cornerstone of the first full-fledged university in Indonesia, founded in 1940 after the German occupation of The Netherlands. One of the most prominent professors in this law faculty was Bernard ter Haar, who taught *adat* law. This pupil of Van Vollenhoven was also the author of a well-known work on Indonesian customary law, the first full treatise on this subject to be translated into English: *Beginselen en stelsel van adatrecht* (*translated as Adat Law in Indonesia*).[37] In 1942, on the eve of

36. I.A. Nederburgh, "Rechtshervorming in Nederlandsch Indië," *Verslagen Indisch Genootschap* December 2, 1905, 1–19 and Sonius in Holleman, ed., *Van Vollenhoven*, xxxvi–xxxviii.

37. This was also the first time (1948) that a major work on *adat* law was made accessible to readers who did not understand Dutch! Ter Haar died during the

the Japanese invasion of Indonesia, the colony numbered 194 professional advocates in all, of whom 122 were Dutch, thirty-six ethnic Chinese and only thirty-six ethnic Indonesian. Moreover, in 1939, there were around thirty academically trained Indonesian judges, all of them, with one exception, sitting in native courts, although Dutch judges were still in the majority in this branch of the judiciary as well.[38]

Many of these Indonesian lawyers had received their university training in Holland, in particular at the university of Leiden, for want of an Indonesian academic alternative. The first Indonesian who submitted his doctoral dissertation to Van Vollenhoven was Moestapa in 1913 (on the *adat* of the Sundanese in West Java). He was followed by seven other fellow countrymen who wrote their theses under the supervision of Van Vollenhoven or his close colleagues. The best-known and most influential of them was Supomo, who became Ter Haar's successor to the chair of *adat* law at Jakarta University and the first republican Minister of Justice in independent Indonesia after 1945.[39] It was he who drafted the constitution of the new state. Supomo's attitude towards *adat* law was highly ambiguous. Although the writer of two books on *adat* law before the war and a well-known expert, he turned coat after 1945. And so did the large majority of influential Indonesian lawyers.[40]

The choice presented to independent Indonesia between the unifying Western legal tradition and *adat* law has thus been resolved in favor of the former. The European codes on both private and penal law have retained their validity, although their applicability in practice is limited to the rather small upper strata of Indonesian society and economic life that require the intervention of professional judicial institutions. *Adat* or unwritten law is usually reserved for

Second World War. See for the role of Ter Haar in the intellectual life of colonial Indonesia and his impact on his Indonesian students (three of them wrote a doctoral dissertation on *adat* law under his supervision): G.J. Resink, "Rechtshoogeschool, Jongereneed, 'Stuw' en Gestuwden" in *Bijdragen tot de Taal-, Land- en Volkenkunde* 130 (1974), 428–49.

38. Lev, "Colonial law," 60, 68 (note 19).
39. See Holleman, ed., *Van Vollenhoven*, xxxix, lxv (note 23).
40. Lev, "Colonial law," 69, stresses the point that most Indonesian advocates who practiced in both the courts for Europeans and the native courts were contemptuous of local *adat* and *adat* institutions; being nationalists they preferred "modern" legal institutions and procedures even if they were of European origin. For a summary of Supomo's own view on the future of *adat* law, see his short biography of his predecessor Prof. B. ter Haar in *Gedenkboek uitgegeven ter Gelegenheid van het Vijf en Twintigjarig Bestaan van het Rechtswetenschappelijk Hoger Onderwijs in Indonesië* (Groningen-Jakarta, 1949), 38–52.

the lower classes, mainly rural Indonesians, at the village level. *Adat* judiciary courts, the position of which was strengthened by the Dutch in the last decade of colonial rule, especially in the islands outside Java, were abolished during the war and during the years of revolution that followed. Only Islamic courts survived. In the words of Lev (who is evidently overstating his case) "the substantive law of post-1945 Indonesia remained almost exactly the same as it was in 1941."[41]

M.B. Hooker thinks it ironic that the views of opponents of Van Vollenhoven, who were in his opinion the real colonialists, have come to prevail in modern Indonesia after all.[42] This should come as no surprise to us. In 1928, an influential Indonesian member of the Dutch East Indies Volksraad (People's Council, a sort of representative assembly, constituted in 1918, with mainly advisory powers) had already observed that "the admiration of *adat* law is to be found more among Europeans than among Indonesians."[43] And Van Vollenhoven himself thought it necessary to warn the Indonesian protagonists of unified law that their aspirations were wrong, as legal differences between Europeans and Indonesians could be justified because of the different conditions prevailing in native society.[44] This reproach was indicative of the suspicion with which Indonesian intellectuals and nationalists before the war viewed the Leiden *adat* school. "Unification" was their slogan, not the endless judicial and ethnic fragmentation and differentiation which seemed to be the inseparable sisters of the protectionist *adat* law policy.[45] How could a unified and independent country survive without a unified regime of law? How could a "primitive" *adat* law be a suitable vehicle for modernization? In spite of Van Vollenhoven's honest intentions, *adat* and all that he had stood for were seen as an impediment to further development, *adat* chiefs as tools of the Dutch (which indeed they often were), and *adat* law as fundamentally a Dutch, not an Indonesian, creation.[46] This proved to be a bad omen for the position of *adat* law in post-war independent Indonesia.

41. Lev, "Colonial law," 69.
42. Hooker, "Dutch colonial law," 283.
43. Is. H. Cassutto, *Het Adatrecht van Nederlandsch-Indië, zijn Waarde voor het Heden en voor de Toekomst* (Groningen-Batavia, 1935), 29 (note 29).
44. Cassutto, *Adatrecht*, 29 (note 30).
45. Lev, "Judicial unification," 4–5.
46. Lev, "Colonial law," 64.

12

Jurisdiction as Politics: The Gold Coast During the Colonial Period

JARLE SIMENSEN

> How were men tried? There is no better touchstone for a social
> system than this question.
>
> —Marc Bloch[1]

Problem and Background[2]

In the tradition of colonial studies British policy-making in the area
of local jurisdiction has generally been handled as a separate com-
partment ("native affairs") determined mainly by administrative
considerations.[3] The aim of this article is, by taking the Gold Coast
Colony and the district of Akim Abuakwa as a case, to discuss how
the development of the judicial system at the local level must be seen
as part of a total *political process*. On the British side it is clear that
legislation in this field was closely tied up with constitutional policy
at the central level, with the overriding aim of securing colonial
control by manipulating local alliances. On the African side we can
see how the traditional elite, with the paramount chief of Akim
Abuakwa, Ofori Atta, as their leading representative, were able to
use their political platform to influence legislation governing local
jurisdiction in their own favor and exploit the system of customary
law to secure their material interests. The substantive content of this

---

1. Marc Bloch, *Feudal Society* (London, 1961), 359.
2. This paper is largely based on material from J. Simensen, *Commoners, Chiefs and
Colonial Government. British Policy and Local Politics in Akim Abuakwa, Ghana, under
Colonial Rule* (Ph.D. dissertation, Department of History, University of Trondheim,
1975). References to the original material in the National Archives of Ghana will only
be given at quotations. Page number in Simensen will be given at the end of the
reference.
3. Lord Hailey, *Native Administration in the British African Territories, I–IV* (London,
1951); Margery Perham, *Native Administration in Nigeria* (London, 1937).

257

process is particularly clear in the area of land control, and some special attention will therefore be paid to this issue in the district of Akim Abuakwa for the sake of exemplification.

Generalization to the rest of British West Africa must be hedged with reservations; the Gold Coast was not a typical British colony. Economic and educational development was much advanced. Already by 1914, it was the world's leading exporter of cocoa, and modern gold mining by European firms had started in the 1880s.[4] In 1928, the Colony had sixty practicing African lawyers and about twelve thousand clerks.[5] By 1940, half of the children at school age received some primary education. A vital dynamic of British-African political interaction was therefore to be expected. Nor was Ofori Atta of Akim a typical paramount chief. Akim Abuakwa, with 150,000 inhabitants in 1931 and 235,000 in 1945,[6] was one of the most populous of the about fifty paramount districts (petty king-doms of the pre-colonial area) of the Gold Coast, and in terms of cocoa production and gold and diamond mining it was the richest. Ofori Atta himself was an outstanding personality, the son of a Presbyterian minister, Paramount chief from 1912 to his death in 1943, member of the Legislative Council from 1916 and one of the two first Africans to be appointed to the Governor's Executive Council in 1942, a regular subscriber to *Hansard* and *The Times*, and a Knight of the British Empire from 1928. However, it is a safe contention that the framing of the judicial system in the other British West African dependencies was influenced by a similar political dynamic, although to a lesser degree. This was also the case in Nigeria when the model system of indirect rule was developed under Lord Lugard.[7]

It was a special feature of the Gold Coast that the legal platform of British authority was disputed throughout the colonial period.[8] From the beginning it was based on treaty, first the military alliance against Ashanti in 1821 and then the "Bond" of 1844, whereby the British could interfere in the affairs of the local kingdoms to secure peace, "the protection of individuals and property," and "the

---

4. Standard accounts of economic and educational change are R. Szereszewski, *Structural Changes in the Economy of Ghana 1891–1911* (London, 1965) and P. Foster, *Education and Social Change in Ghana* (London, 1965).

5. Figures taken from R. Buell, *The Native Problem in Africa* (New York, 1928).

6. Gold Coast Census Report 1948, 62.

7. J. Simensen, *Lord Lugard og Indirekte Styre. Nord-Nigeria 1900–1918* (Cand. philol. thesis., Department of History, University of Oslo, 1966).

8. A standard account is W. Harvey, *Law and Social Change in Ghana* (Princeton, 1966).

moulding of the customs of the country to the general principles of British law."[9] Crown colony rule was established over the coastal areas in 1874, and through the military conquest of Ashanti in 1901 the British in fact had achieved a monopoly of force. This was not, however, followed by a declaration of unrestricted British legal sovereignty over the Colony area between Ashanti and the coast. The chiefs of the Colony continued to use the principle of inherent rights, as opposed to derived rights, as a defense against British efforts at closer regulation of their tribunals. The educated African elite on their side defended the principle of inherent rights as a platform for democratic political reform and ultimately devolution of British authority.

The substantive importance of this legal issue appeared when the Governor in 1897 introduced a Land Bill, whereby he aimed to take public control of "unused" lands in order to put an end to wild speculation during the mining concession boom of the 1890s, and to secure that income from land would be used for public development and not squandered on litigation by irresponsible chiefs. The chiefs and lawyers now joined forces in the Aborigines' Rights Protection Society, and a delegation to London in 1897 achieved recognition by the Colonial Office of the principle that the inherent rights of land control rested with the local "stools" – the symbols of chiefly power. Thus a large part of the fruits of modernization continued to come to the traditional elite and, through their land litigation, into the hand of the lawyers, in both cases with obvious consequences for their political strength.

Law Making: The Native Jurisdiction Ordinance of 1910

Traditional tribunals of the inland districts had been recognized under the Native Jurisdiction Ordinance of 1883, which set a limit to tribunal authority both in civil and criminal matters. The Native Prisons Ordinance of 1888 then practically took away their effective power of punishment by imprisonment. Of even greater consequence was the rapid expansion of the British Supreme Court system, to which anybody had open access. Important cases, particularly land matters and stool disputes (election and deposition of chiefs),

9. The text of the "Bond" in J.J. Crooks, *Records Relating to Gold Coast Settlements: from 1750 to 1874* (Dublin, 1923).

were increasingly taken directly to the Supreme Court. The authority and income of the traditional tribunals suffered accordingly and
the chiefs had a growing problem controlling internal conflicts, both
between chiefs and commoners and between paramount and divisional chiefs.

After 1901, when the Colony area was finally delimited, it became
clear that a principal decision had to be taken on the future of the
traditional tribunals. The solution chosen by the Native Jurisdiction
Ordinance of 1910 was to strengthen the position of the tribunals by
making them into compulsory courts of first instance in smaller
criminal cases, in all land matters, and in other civil suits up to a
certain limit. But the District Commissioner had weak powers of
control and unclear powers of enforcement if the findings of the
tribunals were contested. And plans to declare the principle of
derived rights were dropped after protests from leading chiefs. Still,
in retrospect, the 1910 Ordinance has been regarded as a first step in
the direction of orthodox indirect rule.

It may therefore come as a surprise to find that the decision to
strengthen the traditional tribunals was hotly contested within the
British establishment. The Chief Justice, Brandford-Griffith, held
that "forcing the natives back on themselves" by excluding the
Supreme Court from the great bulk of the jurisdiction of the Colony
would inevitably lead to a deterioration in the quality of justice.[10]
The Supreme Court acting on appeal would have to rely on "the
confusing and often incomprehensible documents from the native
tribunals." There were numerous warnings against the extortion
and "unmentionable abominations" of the traditional tribunals.
The critics argued that the Ordinance represented a betrayal of the
British trust on the Gold Coast to secure basic human rights: "liberty of person, liberty of consciousness and justice."[11]

The alternative recommended by the critics was to graft the
native tribunals directly onto the Supreme Court system and start
employing educated Africans in their service, or more radically, to
drop the chiefs altogether and extend the town model with Magistrate's courts to the inland districts as well. Both alternatives would
indicate a shift of political alliance toward the educated elite, a
development which the Colonial Secretary, Major Bryan, consi-

---

10. Brandford-Griffith's minority report (n.d.) is found in Ghana National Archives (GNA) Adm. 11–1138; Simensen, *Commoners*, 83.
11. Major Bryan's memo, September 13, 1909, enclosed in Rodger to SS, October
19, 1909, Colonial Office (CO) 96–486; Simensen, *Commoners*, 85.

dered to be in accordance with the economic and social development of the country: "If it be sound policy to educate . . . the natives generally on European lines, then it cannot be sound policy to govern through the native chiefs under the present conditions. We should not have two policies of which the former is destructive of the latter." In an exercise of counter-factual argument he held that without the Colonial Government "there would probably have been minor revolutions all over the Colony" because of the effect of money and education.

To the majority of the administrative officers, however, the expansion of European law was not a primary concern. We can even notice a certain resentment towards the Supreme Court system, which represented a check on autocracy. To be useful administrative agents, the chiefs needed to be strengthened in their judicial capacity, a standard argument in the development of indirect rule in the colonial territories. But in the Gold Coast this argument was of less relevance because an educated class of Africans was available who could have manned an alternative local administrative and judicial system on a European model. The main cause for the choice of policy in the realm of "native affairs," including jurisdiction, was the political antagonism and cultural prejudice of the British toward the African educated elite, who by their very existence represented, if not an actual, then a potential threat to the colonial system as an alternative governing elite. This became even clearer in the next phase of legislation.

Law Making: The Native Administration Ordinance of 1927

World War I gave a boost to the political ambitions of the educated Africans. In 1920, the West African National Congress demanded a monopoly of representation for the educated elite and a majority in the Legislative Council in financial matters. This was a challenge both to the Colonial Government and the chiefs, and for the British the maim aim of constitutional reform now became to mobilize the chiefs as a barrier against the claims of the educated elite. In this Ofori Atta played a key role. Rallying a number of paramount chiefs behind him, he successfully destroyed the credentials of the 1920 Congress delegation to London. A period of bitter constitutional wrangling followed, ending in 1926 with the creation of three Provincial Councils of chiefs, who each elected two representatives to the Legislative Council, none of whom must be an educated person! The number of directly elected educated representatives from the major towns remained at three. Thus the Gold Coast Colony, the most advanced of the British West African territories, was equipped with the least democratic constitution.

Simultaneously preparations went on for a reform of local juris- diction in the direction of orthodox indirect rule, based on the principles of derived rights, rationalization and central control. The chiefs naturally stuck to their arguments for inherent rights and freedom from control, and because of their key role in the constitu- tional conflict the Government could not afford to put on pressure which might antagonize the traditional rulers. To get out of the deadlock the British took the extraordinary step of asking Ofori Atta to consult with the paramount chiefs, come up with a compromise proposal, and introduce a new Native Jurisdiction Bill in the Legis- lative Council. It must be the only time in British colonial history that the initiative in a major piece of legislation was left to a traditional chief. We will now see how the new Native Administra- tion Ordinance of 1927 was framed so as to suit the interest of the paramount chiefs, particularly Ofori Atta.

Ofori Atta's general ambition can be summarized as maximum local autonomy combined with increasing centralization under pa- ramount authority. The term "native state" was now substituted for "paramount district," and the degree of autonomy granted – on paper – was astonishing. The State Councils of the various native states were recognized as tribunals in political disputes, and took over from the Governor and the Supreme Court the right to adjudi- cate matters concerning elections and depositions. They could take preventive measures against political opposition and were even granted the right to deport recalcitrant subchiefs, a clause framed with direct reference to Ofori Atta's conflict with the division of Asamankese. The Ordinance also extended the by-law-making powers of the State Councils in a manner that Ofori Atta interpreted as a delegation of legislative authority.

The argument for the Ordinance in these questions was to con- solidate customary authority, but there could be no doubt that the new powers of the paramount authorities went beyond what custom prescribed. In Akim Abuakwa this was revealed by the controversies created when the State Council in accordance with the Ordinance tried to codify customary law with regard to such matters as the composition of the State Council, proper procedure in elections and depositions, and the political rights of groups that provided a check on the power of the paramount chief (the commoner *asafo* companies and the separate council of the Amantoo-mmiensa group of villages immediately surrounding the state capital of Kibbi). Let us now consider in some more detail how Ofori Atta tried to exploit the new powers in the question of land control and jurisdiction over immigrants.

Law in Action: Ofori Atta and the Immigrants

The large influx of cocoa farmers into Akim Abuakwa from the neighboring districts to the east and south raised the crucial question of tribal versus territorial jurisdiction. The immigrants continued to take their cases to the paramount chiefs of their home states of Akwapim, Krobo and Ga, and in some cases established their own tribunals independent of Akim authority. The immigrant share of the population was increasing and had reached about sixty percent in 1948. Judicial control was therefore a matter of utmost importance to secure both the policy of the state and the tribunal income to the Akim chiefs.

Ofori Atta had started his offensive to bring the immigrants under Akim jurisdiction already in 1915. The problem was that the custom was on the side of the immigrants. Mensah Sarbah's and Caseley Hayford's learned treatises on Akan law were quite definite that political allegiance was personal and tribal.[12] Ofori Atta's answer in this situation was that custom was changing: since the time of migration and wars of the eighteenth century the political system had been consolidated, and the reach of the tribal oath (the means of summons before the traditional tribunals) had become more and more coterminous with the territorial extent of the stool land. However, when it came to political rights in the form of representation of the local councils and tribunals Ofori Atta stuck to the tribal principle. With territorial political rights the immigrants would soon have swamped the native Akims! Thus the use of custom varied according to the purpose of the argument.

In principle Ofori Atta had the Government's support in this matter; territorial authority was central to any effort at rationalization of local administration. A special problem in the eastern parts of Akim was, however, that the Akwapim an Krobo farmers had

---

12. J. Mensah Sarbah, *Fanti National Constitution* (London, 1906); J.E. Caseley Hayford, *Gold Coast Native Institutions* (London, 1903).

moved in large groups into sparsely populated areas contiguous to
their home states, and had purchased their land without any political conditions. The result of two Government enquiries was to
distinguish between group purchases, where continued tribal
allegiance was recognized, and individual purchases, which had to
lead to territorial allegiance. But the distinction between the two
was difficult to define, and the matter deadlocked.

The Native Administration Ordinance of 1927 was supposed to
provide a new start in that the principle of territorial jurisdiction
was now explicitly declared. Still, enforcement was difficult, as the
immigrants could settle disputes through secret arbitration and even
continue to take cases to their home state without report. The
deadlock therefore continued after 1927, and cases that came out in
the open had to be solved in the District Commissioner's court. The
outcome in this matter thus showed that the formal declarations of
the Native Administration Ordinance did not automatically materialize in practice.[13]

A new test for Ofori Atta's ambition toward autonomous regulation of the affairs of his state arose when he claimed the right to
legislate in land matters. The economic relationship to the immigrants was now the central issue, but crucial questions concerning the
basis of political and judicial authority again came to the surface.
Purchase contracts and rent agreements with immigrants varied
greatly and were often vague in nature without written documents;
there was reason to argue that Akim's interests had been grossly
neglected. Ofori Atta's dissatisfaction centered particularly on the
New Juabens, who had come to Akim already in the 1870s, had
settled interspersedly with the Akim native population, and often
paid no land rent at all. In 1918, the Akim State Council issued a
declaration that the New Juabens would pay a yearly due of £1 per
head to the local Akim chief, one third which would be passed onto
the paramount chief. This was based on the customary claim of a
one third contribution to the landowner (*abusa*). The Attorney
General, however, declared that the State Council declaration repre-

---

13. The anthropologist Margarethe Field wrote a rather partial evaluation of the
Akim-Krobo conflict in which she was categorical that custom prescribed tribal
jurisdiction. She condemned Ofori Atta's "Gestapo"-tactics, which she saw as a sign
of panic: " . . . the Akims have mounted a horse which will one day kick them off."
British support of Ofori Atta was predictable: "A large, cohesive state with a strong
central authority is at all times Heavens' richest gift to the Indirect Ruler." Report by
Margareth Field, nr. 12, December 26, 1941, in GNA, CSO 0381-SF 15; Simensen,
Commoners, 210.

sented an effort at local taxation, which was *ultra vires* of the existing Native Jurisdiction Ordinance, all the more so since it was discriminative, aiming at one particular tribal group. He drew a sharp distinction between public law and private contract, and suggested that Ofori Atta should rather aim for voluntary adjustments of existing rent agreements. The distinction was not immediately clear to Ofori Atta, but he proceeded as advised, and got his pound of flesh from the New Juabens, with some help from the District Commissioner.

The Native Administration Ordinance of 1927 (section 40) formally extended the by-law-making powers of Native Authorities beyond declaration of custom to matters concerning "good government and the welfare of the inhabitants." On this basis the Akim State Council now announced a general progressive taxation (1d per tree) on all non-Akim cocoa growers, aiming particularly at the New Juabens. This time Ofori Atta acted with great assurance. He claimed that the State Council must be free to determine "the fiscal policy" of the state, only with the duty to inform the Government.[14] To his great consternation, however, the Government took the same stand as in 1918, and held that the by-law powers of the 1927 Ordinance did not give a right to direct taxation. That right belonged solely to the central Government, and no local taxation could in any case be approved before regular stool treasuries had been established – which meant increased central intervention, not more local autonomy! Ofori Atta was again reduced to a revision of private rent agreements and he pursued his course with such militancy that violent clashes with the New Juabens occurred and Government police intervention was needed.

Throughout the dispute both Ofori Atta and the New Juabens continued to have problems distinguishing between taxation and rent, between political authority and land ownership, and between the tribal and territorial principle. When Ofori Atta justified taxation by reference to traditional contribution he did not distinguish between the territorial, compulsory nature of the first and the tribal, voluntary nature of the second. And he saw no problem in using territorial legislative authority to impose a discriminate tax on a tribal group. At the same time he also justified the New Juabens levy on the basis of ultimate land ownership, and maintained that Government refusal implied a violation of property rights. The

14. Ofori Atta to District Commissioner, January 25, 1928, GNA, Adm. 11–184; Simensen, *Commoners*, 201.

New Juabens on their side could not understand that the British allowed Ofori Atta to continue his pressure for rent increase after the tax effort had been stopped; after all, the intentions and effects were largely the same. The New Juabens also manipulated the arguments of tribal and territorial rights to suit their interest. They continued to pay allegiance to their tribal head, the paramount chief of New Juaben, while in an effort to avoid the tax, they claimed to be "naturalised" Akims who could not be singled out for special treatment![15]

The most important outcome of the dispute, however, was to disclose a wide difference of views between Ofori Atta and the British as to the autonomy of the "native state" within the colonial framework. In the interest of state-building the British had refused to recognize local legislative powers in the vital area of finance. The Native Administration Ordinance had not made a significant difference in this respect, in spite of its wider by-law clauses.

Law in Action: Ofori Atta and Asamankese

The most important legal question to Ofori Atta concerned the paramount rights over land under divisional chiefs and the paramount share of proceeds from land sales and rents in the divisions. In Akim this question was all the more important, since little land came directly under the paramount stool, and since land sales and mining concessions brought large incomes to the divisions. This was particularly the case in Asamankese, where diamonds were discovered in 1919, and the chief collected yearly rents of about £10.000 from the African Selection Trust alone.[16] The legal contest in this matter became the outstanding case in the Gold Coast during the interwar period, and the repercussions reached right up to the Privy Council and Parliament in London. This was partly because of the money involved, but also because African lawyers had a direct interest in the case, both as agents and land owners and as politicians out to take revenge on Ofori Atta for his role in the constitutional struggle.

Ofori Atta started his offensive through a State Council declaration in 1915 which claimed that no land transfers could take place in

15. Ofori Atta to DC, April 10, 1928, *ibid.*; Simensen, *Commoners*, 203.
16. Maclennon note August 31, 1935, CO 96–721, 31039; Simensen, *Commoners*, 231.

Akim without the consent of the paramount chief. His case for a tightening of control was a strong one: between one quarter and one third of all Akim land had by then been alienated. Reckless chiefs sold off land to capitalize on their time on the stool. An examination of the mining concession register showed that the area formally leased in Akim Abuakwa – because of overlapping leases and double granting – exceeded the total area of the state! "Mother Akim Abuakwa" was in danger of being erased from the map.[17] The material claim of the paramount stool had in 1902 been defined by the State Council as one quarter of sales and lease money and it was increased to one third in 1920.

In the years that followed, Ofori Atta repeatedly took deposition action against divisional chiefs who disregarded his land policy, at times with the support of the District Commissioner. The Governor was in do doubt that this represented a centralization "beyond the precepts of pure custom," but he accepted it as being in harmony with British policy in native affairs.[18] Most of the chiefs of the State Council were brought into line, but the chief of Asamankese broke away and declared his independence of Akim paramount authority in 1921.

Custom in the matter was vague and was directly tied up with concepts concerning the nature and origin of the Akim state. Mensah Sarbah and Caseley Hayford were quite definite that the inherent rights of land ownership rested in the divisions, and that the "native states" were only federations for judicial purposes. The chief of Asamankese, Kwaku Amoah, naturally stuck to the same view. He described Akim political organization according to a family model, where his own relationship to the paramount chief was one of "friendship based on marriage" and the chiefs were like elder and younger brothers to one another.[19] In his eyes Ofori Atta's claims and deposition actions with British support represented an effort to impose "autocracy" and "a reign of terror," to extort money from the divisions. Yet Kwaku Amoah admitted that he sometimes had asked paramount permission to sell land to cover stool debts, and also on occasions had brought contributions from land sales to Kibbi.[20] Some sort of loose paramount overlordship thus seems to have been recognized.

17. Ofori Atta to Commissioner of the Eastern Province (CEP) February 16, 1926, GNA, Adm. January 11, 1453; Simensen, *Commoners*, 110.
18. Conf. to SS, March 31, 1923, CO 96–638; Simensen, *Commoners*, 124.
19. Note of interview with SNA, March 3, 1922, GNA, Adm. 11–1105; Simensen, *Commoners*, 131.
20. Ofori Atta maintained that it was on record that the chief of Asamankese had

Ofori Atta maintained on his side that the Akim state was built on a feudal model, more like Ashante and different from the Fante states which Mensah Sarbah and Caseley Hayford described.[21] The Akim royal dynasty had migrated from Ashante and led the Akim divisional chiefs in defense against neighboring states, and thus established their authority and ultimate land control on the basis of conquest. The modern land hunters resembled ancient invaders, and the duty of the paramount chief was again to take the lead in defense of the true interests of the people. But Ofori Atta also admitted that in this case he was out to change custom: he talked of the need for "gradual improvement to meet the need of modern times."[22]

The Government's problem was that they were unsure of their legal powers in political disputes between paramount and divisional chiefs. The Native Jurisdiction Ordinance of 1910 was not clear on this point. In practice District Commissioners often took summary administrative action to support paramount chiefs, and chiefs themselves no doubt used force extensively to intimidate political opponents. But it was another matter in the Asamankese dispute, where capable lawyers were lying in wait to catch the British or Ofori Atta acting *ultra vires*. The crucial question therefore became the legitimate use of force – the ultimate sanction of political authority – to back up a settlement in the Asamankese dispute.

The moment the lawyers were waiting for came in 1922, when a sub-chief of Asamankese was arrested for running away from a Government mediation meeting in Accra. Action was now brought in the Supreme Court against the Secretary of Native Affairs and the Provincial and District Commissioners concerned for wrongful application of threat of force, false imprisonment and, "conspiracy" with Ofori Atta against Asamankese.[23] The trial was an extraordinary and embarrassing affair; the examination of the British District Commissioner by the African council for Asamankese, Kobina Sekyi, took up fifty pages in the report. The "conspiracy" action was

---

stated before the Kibbi tribunal that a share of proceeds from Asamankese land usually was given to the paramount chief. Ofori Atta's answer to Asamankese petition, November 4, 1921. GNA. Adm. 11–1105; Simensen, *Commoners*, 132.

21. Ofori Atta to CEP, February 16, 1926, Adm. January 11, 1453; Simensen, *Commoners*, 120.

22. Ofori Atta to the chief of Taffo, April 7, 1917, *Quarterly Report*, Sept. 1917; Simensen, *Commoners*, 120.

23. Reports on the Asamankese case and the "conspiracy" action in GNA, Adm. 11–1105, *Quarterly Report*, and in conf. to SS. March 31, 1923, CO 96–638; Simensen, *Commoners*, 129.

dismissed, but the arrest of the sub-chief was pronounced *ultra vires* without basis in law or court order. The judge took care to specify the legal limitations of British administrative authority, including that of the Governor.[24] This was an example of how the British tradition of "rule of law" and independence of the judiciary gave room of maneuver for African political opposition. When the Government in 1924 planned to act against Asamankese on the basis of a special Deportation Ordinance, the lawyers successfully blocked this action by appealing the conspiracy judgement and continually keeping the dispute *sub judice*, thus precluding political action.

The Asamankese problem was no doubt foremost on Ofori Atta's mind when he produced the draft for the Native Administration Ordinance of 1927. As we have seen, the authority to settle political disputes in the native states, including the right to order deportation, was now transferred to the State Council. However, when the Asamankese chief continued to refuse to appear in Kibbi before the State Council, the problem of enforcement arose again. Arrest action was finally taken in May 1929, but it ended in a failure, due to a combination of bad luck, British hesitancy, and Kibbi blunder. The Asamankese ringleaders got away to Accra, which under the Native Administration Ordinance meant that the consent of the Ga paramount chief was needed for their arrest. In Ofori Atta's absence the situation in Kibbi now got out of control. Two lorry-loads of armed people crossed the border into the Ga state without arrest warrant and got hold of some twenty Asamankese people, who were brought to Kibbi and maltreated in a traditional manner: human excrements and women's menstruation cloth were forced into their mouths and they were made to parade the town carrying brimful latrine pans on their heads. The lawyers naturally jumped in and achieved the release of the prisoners under writs of *habeas corpus*. Sizable compensation was later awarded to those involved.

To Ofori Atta those were days of desperation. The crisis had revealed that he lacked the force to match his wide authority under the Ordinance of 1927, and that the British were reluctant to act as a cat's paw. The arrests and maltreatment also seriously affected his

24. "The Governor of a Crown Colony can only exercise sovereign powers within the limits of his commission (and) it is equally clear that the members of the political staff have no authority to intervene with the liberty or property of a member of the public whether a chief or otherwise, unless such interference is legal, in other words authorized by legislation or Common Law, and further that the order of the Governor does not in itself apart from legislation make an act legal which would otherwise have been illegal." Judgement in January 29, 1923, GNA, Amd. 11–1105; Simensen, *Commoners*, vol. II, note section, 31.

moral and political standing with the British. The Governor's harsh comment was that they "greatly impeded my desire to uphold the authority of his state."[25] In the Colonial Office in London the Maltreatment episode created "indignation and disgust," with the comment that such instances as these cannot but cast doubt on the fitness of the Gold Coast people to administer the internal affairs of the various native communities.[26]

An effort at arbitration was now made through a judge of the Supreme Court, Justice Hall. His award in 1929 struck a compromise: Ofori Atta's right to a one third share of land proceeds was recognized, but the inherent land ownership of the divisions was upheld, and no prior paramount assent to sales was demanded.[27] However, Asamankese appealed the award, the lawyers probably acting both to retain their fees and to continue to bleed their political opponent, Ofori Atta. The case slowly crept its way through the Divisional Court, the Full Court, the West African Court of Appeal, and to the Privy Council in London, where the appeal was finally dismissed in 1932. However, new legal action was planned by the inventive Asamankese lawyers. In 1933, it was calculated that each of the two parties has spent about £100.000 on the case.[28] The court cases in Accra demanded long stays in the capital by sizeable delegations from the two parties. Ofori Atta might fret at the outlay, but there is evidence that the Asamankese people thoroughly enjoyed the excursions. Was this a sense of traditional political battle carried into a new and more pleasant forum than the thorny bush?

In spite of the Hall award the British hesitated to enforce paramount authority. Instead they moved in the opposite way of increasing Government intervention. By the Asamankese Division Regulation Ordinance of 1935 they took control of Asamankese finance through the establishment of a "stool treasury" under Government direction. The arguments were largely the same as those used in connection with the Land Bill of 1897: to secure that land income

25. Governor's minute May 30, 1929. GNA, Adm. 11–1105; Simensen, *Commoners*, 216.

26. CO despatch January 10, 1930, transmitted to Ofori Atta, in Colonial Secretary to CEP April 8, 1930; GNA, Adm. January 29, 1939; Simensen, *Commoners*, 216.

27. The Hall award in Slater to SS, October 23, 1929, CO 96–691, 6531, nr. 792. The one third paramount share was defined by Ward as one third of the whole of the concession money paid by the diamond company to the Asamankese sub-stool of Akwatia. The Asamankese claim was that by custom the maximum paramount share was one third of the one third due to Asamankese from the Akwatia sub-stool. See Simensen, *Commoners*, 216.

28. Conf. to SS. December 19, 1933, Co 96–713, 216143–II; Simensen, *Commoners*, 133.

was used for public development. By the middle of the 1930s, senior British officers had for some time been convinced that the wide powers granted to the native states under the Ordinance of 1927 was a "grave mistake."[29] In the Colonial Office comments were made about the "strange spell" that Ofori Atta for some years had exercised over the Gold Coast Government.[30] Thus Asamankese had become the nail in the coffin of Ofori Atta's policy of maximum local autonomy, revealing the need for reform in the direction of increased central control.

Judicial Reform in the 1930s: The Traditional Oath

Reform first took the shape of an effort in 1931–32 to transfer the Nigerian indirect rule-model, in the form of the Nigerian Native Authorities Ordinance of 1916 and the Nigerian Native Courts Ordinance of 1918, more or less wholesale to the Gold Coast. The immediate motive was to strengthen Colony finance, which had been weakened by the depression, through a "native revenue measure" on the Nigerian model. In African eyes this was of course a highly suspicious motive, and a tactical blunder was made when the urban population was first singled out for direct taxation. This mobilized the educated elite, and when a scheme for general local taxation through the native authorities was launched, the country was up in protest. Ofori Atta had again been a key collaborator, this time together with his divisional chiefs, who also stood to benefit from the scheme. Five leading Akim chiefs were deposed by their people, and Government forces had to be called out to Kibbi to save the paramount chief from a similar fate. Lawyer politicians were again active in aid of Akim opposition. After this fiasco any thought of wholesale indirect rule legislation had to be put on ice.

There was general agreement, however, that something must be done to strengthen central control of the local tribunals. As comments were invited from the District Commissioners, reports of grave abuse came in.[31] Stories were told of young men seeking the protection of the District Commissioner because they had money and were afraid to be fleeced by the chiefs and elders in the tribunals on trumped-up charges. Tribunal police and clerks were rarely well

29. CEP diary January 13, 1931 and January 31, 1931 with Governor's comments; also Slater to SS, October 13, 1931, CO 96–697; Simensen, *Commoners*, 223.
30. Bushe min. April 18, 1934, CO 96–713, 216113–II; Simensen, *Commoners*, 224.
31. Quoted in Simensen, *Commoners*, 265–66.

qualified or well paid, and sometimes added to the extortion by selling their favors to the highest bidder. People were afraid to appealing for fear of local sanctions. All this confirmed the forecasts of those who had opposed giving the chiefs exclusive jurisdiction during the 1906–1910 debate, and it was a matter of painful self-criticism that the eyes of the Government had been closed to such judicial malpractice for political reasons. Governor Slater's conclusion in 1931 was: "We must legislate to stop this scandal even if (which I am afraid I doubt) it is comparatively rare."[32] Popular respect for the tribunals was also at stake. The Eastern Provincial Commissioner lecturing the chiefs on the subject in 1935 declared: "I do not think your judicial system will be able to survive many more shocks if I am right in judging enlightened opinion."[33]

Ofori Atta led the campaign of defense against increased District Commissioner control, and maintained that any regularization of the tribunals must take place on a voluntary basis, without infringing the principle of inherent judicial rights. The Government had a bait, however: with more control they would recognize more tribunals. So agreement was achieved in 1935 on an amendment to the Native Administration Ordinance which gave the District Commissioner the right to intervene in the tribunals and review criminal cases and costs in civil cases without waiting for appeal. Any idea of using qualified educated people or Government pensioners as paid local magistrates was, however, firmly turned down by Ofori Atta: the judicial functions were essential to chieftaincy. He referred to the Akan saying that "it was to prevent greed and cheating that *ohene* (the chief) was made."[34]

The uncontrolled powers of the native tribunals were dramatically revealed during the cocoa hold-ups of 1931 and 1937. In both cases the chiefs were persuaded by militant farmers to use their traditional oath to strengthen discipline. Any breach of the boycott would then lead to action in the local tribunal. The African lawyers this time supported the chiefs, and argued they were only using their inherent right to legislate for the welfare of the people! A judgement in the Supreme Court in 1931 made it clear, however, that the oath could only be legally used in areas defined by the Native Adminis-

32. *Quarterly Report*, Akwamu, Dec. 1931, with min. by Slater, December 2, 1931, GNA, Adm. 11-1048.

33. Eastern Provincial Council Report, September 18, 1935, not classified; Accession nr. 803/1956; Simensen, *Commoners*, 282.

34. Ofori Atta to Joint Provincial Council meeting July 23, 1936. CSO 212/232; Simensen, *Commoners*, 283–84.

tration Ordinance. But the problem was that its illegitimate use could not easily be controlled.

The oath problem was another example of the practical political importance of the question of inherent v. derived judicial rights. To the Government the boycott use of the oath was an intolerable provocation; it seriously taxed their confidence in the tribunals. Law officers were of the opinion that the oath should be abolished altogether. But a familiar dilemma of indirect rule then again came to the fore. The point of ruling through the chiefs was that their traditional authority could be mobilized for Government purpose. If this authority were destroyed by abolition of the oath, the chiefs would be entirely dependent on Government enforcement, and the rationale for their function as administrative agents would thus largely disappear. In the words of *the Kumasihene*: "If it were not for the oath I should be left alone here tomorrow."[35] It was also clear that because of its religious nature the oath could not simply be legislated away: "The oath cannot die."[36] Its effective, but secret use during the 1937 hold-ups again proved that it was very much alive.

During the cocoa boycott of 1937 Ofori Atta's brother, J.B. Danquah, made an ingenuous effort to justify the use of the oath with reference to European legal concepts.[37] He argued that the boycott use of the oath could be compared to British trade union action against strike breakers. By doing so he conveniently disregarded the fact that the oath had a general and compulsory public function in local community. Equally dubious but not less interesting was his argument that the oath represented the principle of a *volonté générale* which justified social action against deviants from the will of the majority! Both arguments were probably more motivated by tactics than by a genuine attempt to reconcile European and African legal concepts.

The Rise and Fall of Indirect Rule

Orthodox indirect rule was finally established in the Gold Coast in 1944 in the form of a Native Courts and a Native Authority Ordinance based on an explicit proclamation of derived rights, and with central control of tribunal competence, personnel, and function

---

35. Reported in SNA to CEP, May 13,1935, GNA. Adm. June 29, 1911; Simensen, *Commoners*, 286.
36. DC to CEP, September 20, 1935, *ibid.*
37. J.B. Danquah, *The Liberty of the Subject* (Kibbi, 1938).

according to Lugard's formula: "there are not two sets of rulers – the British and the Natives – working either separately or in cooperation, but a single government in which the chiefs have clearly defined duties."[38] Even persons other than the chief could now be appointed as head of a native court. This legislation might seem to be the logical result of a long-term local development. It therefore comes as a surprise to discover that it was preceded by an open-ended debate with clearly formulated alternatives, just like the debate preceding the Native Jurisdiction Ordinance of 1910.

A number of observers and political officers during the late 1930s concluded that the days of rule through the chiefs in the Gold Coast was at an end, and must be superseded by a system of local government based on a European model. As early as 1926 the Government anthropologist R.S. Rattray, the great Ashante specialist who was a wholehearted adherent of indirect rule, declared that is was too late to try this system in the Colony where developments were "based on European lines."[39] Secretary of Natives Affairs W.J.A. Jones, who had tried to introduce the Nigerian model in the early 1930s, and later created a model system of indirect rule in the Northern Territories, stated in 1936 that he was firmly convinced that the days of the chief in the Colony had gone and that a rural council system admitting educated people to authority should be introduced.[40] Even Donald Cameron, who had been governor both of Tanganyika and Nigeria, stated in 1936 that indirect rule was an impossibility in the Gold Coast, where "authority comes from below and not from above as in Nigeria."[41] Officers of the technical departments like agriculture and sanitation reported that it was impossible any longer to work through the chiefs, and argued the need for local committees where educated people could be represented. The leading law officer of the Colonial Office, Sir Grattan Bushe, had returned from West Africa in 1933 with a flat denunciation of the native tribunals: "One of the more striking facts of our Colonial administration is the tolerance shown in the past to the persecution of the natives by their chiefs."[42] His remedy was to extend the area of the British Magis-

38. F.D. Lugard, *Instructions to Political Officers* (London, 1906).

39. Rattray memo, on Ashante for Ormsby-Gore's visit in 1926; CO 96–662; Simensen, *Commoners*, 298.

40. Jones to Creasy June 11, 1936, CO 96–730, and Jones opinion in conf. to SS December 3, 1936; CO 96–725; Simensen, *Commoners*, 298.

41. Cameron in Colonial Office interview October 20, 1936, CO 96–730, 31228; Simensen, *Commoners*, 298.

42. Bushe note November 9, 1938, on Annual Reports, Eastern Province, 1937–38; Simensen, *Commoners*, 299.

trates' courts in the town. This sounded like an echo of Chief Justice Brandford-Griffith's criticism of the Native Jurisdiction Ordinance of 1910.

Given this background the problem becomes rather to explain why the British did not change to a local judicial and administrative system more in accordance with economic and educational developments, but instead continued to push through an orthodox system of indirect rule. The answer lies partly in the low quality and lack of drive at the top level of the Gold Coast Government, but mainly in the intervention of the Colonial Office, who after some initial doubt decided that the Gold Coast must be brought into line. The driving force behind this push was Lord Hailey, the venerated Indian administrator who later established himself as the expert on African "native administration." He was brought in as advisor on Gold Coast affairs, visited the Colony in 1936 and again on an official enquiry in 1940. Hailey's overriding concern was to preserve the colonial system and to use the chiefs to shore up the advance of the educated elite. He considered that the time had now come for the British to face the opposition and steer such a program through with a firm hand.[43]

Governor Burns was sent out in 1942 to effect the Colonial Office policy, and again we can see how legislation in the field of native affairs was closely tied up with constitutional policy. The aim was to devolve power in such a manner as to preserve maximum control, and the instruments for this purpose were the chiefs. This was the moment when Ofori Atta was appointed a member of the Governor Executive Council, and from this position he supported the new legislation. The chiefs were given a decisive influence in the new Legislative Assembly through an indirect system of election, but the precondition was that they accepted the principles of derived rights and central control in the new Native Courts and Native Authority Ordinances. In Governor Burns' words: "the boys will have a price if they behave."[44]

But Indirect Rule (with capital letters) was shortlived on the Gold Coast. After the riots of 1948, the brutal conclusion of the Watson commission was that nothing had impressed them so much as the intense unpopularity of the chiefs, and that nothing less than modern local government institutions would do to satisfy the commoners.

43. Hailey at Colonial Office meeting December 14, 1936, CO 06–730, 31228; Simensen, *Commoners*, 301.
44. Burns to Creasy, September 4, 1944, CO 96–781, 31499; Simensen, *Commoners*, 311.

Among Nkrumah's first legislative measures was the Local Government Ordinances of 1951, which introduced elected local councils on a European model. In the same year the Korsah commission recommended the total replacement of native tribunals by professional Magistrates' courts. This was effected through the Local Courts Act of 1956.

The element of power struggle continued to be prominent. The royal dynasty of Akim Abuakwa was a conservative bastion against Nkrumah's policy, and mobilized the resources of the state in the struggle. However, Ofori Atta's old enemies, the immigrants and Asamankese, linked up with the new regime, and on the basis of territorial political rights the old establishment was outvoted at the elections. Land control again became a crucial issue, and by the Akim Abuakwa Stool Revenue Ordinance of 1958 the Nkrumah Government took direct public control of all Akin stool land – in the manner desired by the British in the 1897 Land Bill and partly realized through the Asamankese Ordinance of 1935. Five hundred Government police occupied Kibbi and removed Ofori Atta II from his stool.

Conclusion

The purpose of this paper has been to sketch the main stages of the development of local jurisdiction in the Gold Coast under colonial rule. In retrospect we can see that the long term trend of British policy was the rationalization of the traditional African system and incorporation of it into the modern state under central control. However, "indirect rule" was a wide term used with at least three distinct variations: the protectorate system of the pre-1901 period with vague British overrule; the system of the 1927 Ordinance, with considerable judicial autonomy for the native states, based on the principle of inherent rights; and finally the Indirect Rule (with capital letters) system of 1944, based on derived rights, defined duties, and central control.

The development toward Indirect Rule in the Gold Coast cannot be explained simply as a diffusion of European law and influence. Legislation in this field resulted from a complex process of political interaction between the British, the traditional chiefs, and the educated elite. The judicial autonomy of the 1927 Ordinance went against British aims and interests, and was achieved because the constitutional conflict between the British and the educated elite put the chiefs in an exceptionally strong political position.

Nor was the development toward Indirect Rule in the Gold Coast heavily determined. An alternative existed and was proposed by leading British officers from the beginning of the century: namely local law courts on a European model, largely manned by educated Africans. In the Gold Coast, with its advanced economic and educational development and large African middle class, this was a realistic alternative. The primary aim of the colonial establishment was not, however, the expansion of European law but the consolidation of administrative control, and in this perspective the chiefs were preferable partners. When the system of rule through the chiefs approached a standstill in the 1930s, and the time seemed ripe for radical change, the Colonial Office intervened to push through orthodox Indirect Rule. At this point diffusion replaced interaction.

By concentrating on the traditional petty kingdom and colonial administrative district of Akim Abuakwa we have been able to follow "law in action" in some selected cases. Here we can observe the features of modern state-building duplicated at local level. Ofori Atta's aim as a resourceful paramount chief was to utilize British legislation and manipulate local custom to create a territorial (as opposed to tribal) system of rule based on centralization and a degree of rationalization. His ambition toward autonomy was, however, a lost cause. It is at this level that we best can see European and African legal concepts clashing and intermingling, and follow native tribunals both in their judicial and political functions – a distinction scarcely relevant in the precolonial system. A host of questions arise from the observation of this legal arena, and there can be little doubt that the court records of a place like Akim Abuakwa represent exciting potential for research.

13

The Law Market: The Legal Encounter in British East and Central Africa

MARTIN CHANOCK

> British administration in overseas countries has conferred no
> greater benefit than English law and justice.
> —Sir Kenneth Roberts-Wray
>
> This was Law Market as that Slave Market.
> —G.S. Mwase[1]

Introduction

The legal colonization of large parts of the non-European world as a
result of the expansion of Europe has been one of the most thorough,
and most durable, of the effects of imperialism. The imposed legal
forms of Europe have survived decolonization, and continue to be
used by the post-colonial states in Africa. No significant attempts
have been made to indigenize their legal systems. The comprehension of this process of legal colonization has been dominated by a
model of explanation which has emphasized legal dualism, in which
the legal systems of the colonial territories were considered to have
been comprised of both the law of the colonizers and that of the
colonized.[2] Yet it may be that this model of comprehension, which
emphasizes dual or plural systems based on imported foreign law,
and indigenous law, is not best suited to explaining the development
of the legal systems of British colonial Africa. I shall suggest that it is
more appropriate to base the analysis of the historical process of the

---

1. Sir Kenneth Roberts-Wray, "The adaptation of imported law in Africa," *Journal
of African Law* 4 (1960). G.S. Mwase, *Strike a Blow and Die*, ed. R. Rotberg (Cambridge, MA 1967), 83.
2. See e.g. M.B. Hooker, *Legal Pluralism* (Oxford, 1975).

interaction of indigenous custom and colonial law on a different model. This model considers the legal system as one in which the colonial law, itself a specific creation rather than an import, and the new state and economy continually fashion African custom from the materials proffered by the colonized societies. In this perspective both foreign and indigenous laws are products of the colonial situation, continually being formed in response to new historical circumstances.

The legal mission of the imperial lawgivers is an important part of the understanding of both the cultural history of imperialism and the nature of the colonial states which were established. The claim to have brought a civilizing law and order has been an important part of the justification of colonialism. It has been answered with an indignant refutation, an insistence that legal systems of customary law expressing the African genius already existed in Africa.[3] When the colonial period ended, the customary law, its indigenous and historical character already asserted, was looked to as being the natural heart of the law of the new African states. A questioning, therefore, of this version of the nature of customary law has important political implications, for it questions the legitimacy of those parts of the legal systems of the modern states based on the neo-traditional customary law.[4] But the reformulation allows a greater understanding of the developing nature and content of the customary law.

We must also reformulate our ideas about the imported law. It is misleading, at least in the British case with which I am dealing, to leave relatively unexamined the notion that the law of the colonial state was imported from the metropolis. If we accept that law is not, in the well known words of Oliver Wendell Holmes, "a brooding omnipresence in the sky," and that it is continually created and re-created in specific situations, the result will be an emphasis instead on the specificity of the colonial situation in creating the law of the colonial state. Those elements which were imported deteriorated on the long journey; and, in reality, much of the non-African

3. M.L. Chanock, *Law, Custom and Social Order* (Cambridge, 1985) chapter 1. Many highflown thoughts were expressed on either side of this issue. Few have been concerned with the "drab cruelties," to use Thurmon Arnold's phrase, of law in action, whether it be imported or African.

4. This point will be considered below in relation to both land tenure and marriage. M.L. Chanock, "Neither customary nor legal. Customary law in an era of family law reform," *International Journal of Law and the Family* (1989), and "Paradigms, policies and property. A review of the customary law of land tenure," *Law in Colonial Africa*, ed. K. Mann and R. Roberts (London, 1991).

law was colonial and imperial law devised specifically for the Empire. Clearly we must understand the imposition of non-African legal forms on Africa, but the preliminary distinction must be made between the law of England and the "English" elements of the legal systems of the colonial states. And we must be aware that not only was the statute law in its most important parts law specifically enacted for imperial purposes and colonial situations, but also that the common law of England was invoked in legal situations very different from those of the metropole. In colonial courts and villages the white administrators and judges confronted a subject population. This political and ethnic context can never be absent from a consideration of the legal encounter.

In the article that follows, which is a general overview based on syntheses of my own work and that of others, I shall analyze both the imposed legal system and the customary laws that it creates. The latter are partly created by the state in accordance with its views about the nature of African societies. But, more importantly, customary law is a continuing political response to the colonial state, and to the new economy, a prime mode of inserting the interests of sections of the African population into colonial policies. I shall outline how colonial governments lent support to some versions of customary law in areas like land tenure and marriage: the "creation" of customary law being made not with imported materials, but by choices from those locally available. The reasons for the choices on the colonizers' side were essentially administrative and political, and generally underwrote their alliances with those upon whom colonial rule depended. This leads to another preliminary point to be made about legal pluralism, or legal dualism. These fruitful analytical devices have enabled a greater understanding of legal systems both by exposing the partial nature of the state's regulatory order, and by illuminating the African situation in which the State validated more than one legal system. But I suggest that if we ask ourselves from whose perspective the systems appear as plural or dual, a different emphasis emerges. Analyses of the colonial economy used to be based upon the notion of the dual economy, with cash subsistence sectors, and African workers and peasants were depicted as magically passing from one sector to the other at different phases in their economic activities. This kind of analysis is, rightly, no longer fashionable. We understand instead that all parts of the colonial economy were linked together and that, from the point of view of the colonized, if not the economist, the struggle for survival took place in one world, not two. Likewise, living in the world of law might be better understood if the connections between the parts are emphasized.

Law and Order

Approaches to the question of criminal law in colonial situations have been affected both by the development of new ways of comprehending crime in general, and by the writing of the history of African resistance to colonial rule. Both of these bodies of knowledge serve to create a new definition of colonial criminality. Crime appears less as moral transgression, and more as created by the definitions of the political power. The offender is perceived to be both a victim and a rebel. With criminality created by definition from above, criminal acts appear to be either acts of desperation committed by the oppressed, or to be more positive acts of revolt against systems of property law and labor discipline.[5] New definitions of criminality were imposed by the colonial state, which was from the first also utterly determined to claim a monopoly over criminal punishment, which was considered to be an essential part of the exercise of the authority of the state. Part of the Imperial legal mission was to impose a sense of the criminal act as an offense against the public. Primitive men, as one judge put it, made no distinction between "the civil wrong which is compensated by damages to the individual, and the criminal wrong which is compensated by fine or forced labour exacted by the community."[6] The broad strategy of the colonial governments was, as Hailey wrote, one of "endeavouring to introduce to the African the conception of the public offence ... and punishment ... instead of ... compensation and other forms of arbitral adjustment."[7] Customary criminal law was,

5. See in general C. Sumner, ed., *Crime, Justice and Underdevelopment* (London, 1982); D. Crummey, ed., *Banditry, Rebellion and Social Protest in Africa* (London, 1986); and *Africa* 56 (1986) 4, "Crime and Colonialism in Africa."

6. J. Macdonnell, then legal adviser to the N.E. Rhodesian administration; Chanock, *Law, Custom and Social Order*, 75.

7. Baron Hailey, *Native Administration and Political Development in Tropical Africa 1900-42* (Nendeln, 1979), ed. A. Kirk-Greene, 285. Cf the view of Sir Bernard Bourdillon, the Governor of Uganda, quoted in H. Morris and J. Read, *Indirect Rule and the Search for Justice* (Oxford, 1972), 298-299. "We have ... imposed upon the natives of Uganda an alien system of justice. Our object in doing so was ... to inculcate more satisfactory ideas of right and wrong; to teach the native that crime is, in the main, to be regarded as an offence against society and not as an offence against the individual; and gradually to teach him to appreciate that European methods of administering justice are both more effective and equitable than the rough and ready method to which he was accustomed."

unlike customary family law, neither recognized nor given scope to develop. As the Nyasaland High Court said in 1940, the state could not allow "a haphazard development of native criminal law by primitive courts operating seperately."[8]

Colonial criminal law was severe and authoritarian. It relied far more heavily on corporal punishment than the criminal courts of Britain. Powers of arbitrary arrest, deportation, collective punishment, and control of movement existed and were used especially where the authority of the state was felt to be challenged.[9] Wide discretions were given to District Officials. We might note the provision in Northern Rhodesia which gave the power to punish, as criminal, disobedience to any "reasonable order," which was defined as "any order which the circumstances may make necessary but which is not actually provided for in this or some other law."[10] Long before the Labour Ordinances were passed in Nyasaland, the local courts were advised that even in the absence of a law "it is a recognised factor in the administration of the country that natives must be made to comply with the provisions of reasonable agreements" for otherwise the authority of the government would be undermined.[11]

Yet it should also be emphasized that the oppressive law was not systematically omnipresent. Colonial officials were very thin on the ground, and policing was irregular. African police were usually former soldiers and untrained: "each man became a policeman on being issued with a uniform and equipment."[12] Large parts of colonial territories outside of the towns and areas of white settlement went unpoliced until the increase in security forces after the second world war.[13] When police forces were strengthened during this period the emphasis was on riot control and political policing, rather than on the protection of the African populations of the rapidly

8. *Joseph Lumbandi v Rex*, Nyasaland Reports 1940.

9. See e.g. Y.P. Ghai and J.P. Mcauslan, *Public Law and Political Change in Kenya*, (London, 1970), chapter 9.

10. Zambia National Archives. Proclamation 8, 1916. Law Department Circular no. 8, 1917.

11. Chanock, *Law, Custom and Social Order*, 104. Colonial Governments were not constrained by legal niceties. One of the better known examples is, in the absence of a legal color bar on the Kenyan highlands, Lord Elgin's instruction that "as a matter of administrative convenience" grants of land should not be made to Asians. Cmnd 4117, 1908.

12. Malawi National Archives. Judicial Department, Short Administrative History.

13. D. Killingray, "The maintenance of law and order in British Colonial Africa," *African Affairs* 85 (1986), 340.

growing towns. Law and order in the rural areas was essentially
dependent on the chiefs and headmen who were the foundation of
colonial administration. Headmen were legally required to report
and investigate crimes and detain wrongdoers, and were usually the
Administration's chief witnesses at criminal trials. This provides one
of the many fundamental links between the State's law and that of
the villages. For great new powers were in the hands of the headmen, and this is part of the context in which their judgment of local
disputes of all sorts, both civil and criminal, henceforth took place.
Not only were African tribunals transformed in this way by being
incorporated into the colonial system and by being made responsible
for the administration of coercive colonial regulations, they also had
at their command the unwritten customary criminal law, which
could be used to punish conduct which they disliked which was not
against any written law.[14]

The selective nature of law enforcement and the priority given to
administrative goals must also be considered. In both urban and
rural areas the numbers of convictions for common law crimes like
assault and larceny, the two largest categories, were well below
those for infractions of laws specific to colonial control. Of these,
offenses against the tax and employment laws were the most significant, and these varied widely from year to year and district to
district, depending on the enthusiasm and priorities of the local
district officer. The colonial statute book illustrates the possible
range and nature of legal interventions into local life. Ordinances
controled in great detail the methods of cultivation, and sale of
foodstuffs and cash crops; use of forests and vacant lands; hunting;
brewing; animal husbandry; marriage, movement, and residence.[15]
Neither the basic nor the detailed laws of the territories of East and
Central Africa were available in any language other than English, in
spite of repeated requests for translations. The picture is one of a
population subject to extensive regulation imposed by laws, the
content of which they did not know, and randomly administered by

14. See e.g. Ghai and Mcauslan, *Public Law*, chapter 4, especially 153–54. See too
S.F. Moore, *Social Facts and Fabrications. Customary Law on Kilimanjaro 1880–1980*
(Cambridge, 1986), 152. "The chiefs obviously used their authority to require the
obedience of their subjects. Their power over the court must have been a significant
part of this authority." In 1941 Lord Hailey was still able to write, "In their
administrative capacity, Native Authorities have power to make local bye-laws, and
to issue legal orders, a breach of which is punishable in the native courts. . . . The
position regarding issue of legal 'orders' by native authorities . . . is still somewhat
indeterminate."

15. For one list see Chanock, *Law, Custom and Social order*, 269–70.

officials, both white and African, who combined administrative and judicial roles. The laws codified for administrators the huge extent of their powers. This was the essential reality of the coming of the British rule of law to colonial Africa. Beyond this level of legality there were the High Courts of the territories. Appeals from ordinary accused or litigants very rarely reached them, and, indeed, were actively discouraged, because of the view that the reversal of judgments given at any level undermined the authority of the local headmen or officials. There were occasions, arising usually out of provisions for the review of criminal sentencing, in which the High Courts took the opportunity to correct and castigate, in the name of a lawyer's rather than an administrator's view of legality, the verdicts of the administrators' courts.[16] But this was a remote level of law which rarely intruded into the lives of colonial subjects:[17] its legalistic style was irrelevant to them, and was also regarded with hostility by the district officers. Another legal style dominated the colonial courts at the lower level. While one need not romanticize the mediated and consensual nature of pre-colonial disputing, there was a clearly felt contrast between indigenous methods of hearing and arbitration and the summary authoritarianism of the colonial courts.[18]

The colonial criminal justice system not only defined criminality in ways far from congruent with indigenous definitions, it also took away control over the combatting of wrong from Africans. The result was widespread dissatisfaction with colonial justice among the African population, not simply because of its routine oppressions, but because of its omissions. Economic disruptions, the strains of redefining kinship obligations, new ways of appropriating property, and the loss of legitimate African authority at all levels produced a high level of anxiety and anger in local societies. Fierce and vital disputes involving accusations of sorcery and witchcraft, which were rife in colonial society, could not legally be dealt with by Africans, as the colonial governments outlawed both witchcraft accusations and ordealing, and the accusations were ignored by the state's courts, which were, indeed, obliged to punish the accusers rather than investigate the accused.[19] The abolition of ordealing threw a great weight onto the system of criminal justice, which it declined to bear.

16. Morris and Read, *Indirect Rule and the Search for Justice*, chapter 9.
17. Moore, *Social Facts and Fabrications*, 151 on the absence of knowledge of higher court rulings in the local courts and of the effect on their workings.
18. See for example Chanock, *Law, Custom and Social Order*, 132–33.
19. See e.g. Chanock, *Law, Custom and Social Order*, chapter 5.

The state's criminal courts thus appeared to many to have a perverted set of values. Harsh punishments were handed out for infractions of regulations, or for incidents of violence arising out of events
like drunken brawling, while truly intended evil was unpunishable.
The result of the legal misencounter in this domain was continual
anger.

Land and Property

Much of the discourse about the difference between British and
African concepts of land law has revolved around a simple dichotomy: African customary law is a system which is considered to be
based upon variations on the theme of communal tenure, while
British law enshrines the private ownership of land. The story of the
colonial period is therefore basically seen as one in which communal
tenure – the existing customary law – fights a defensive battle
against the imposition of a legal regime which increasingly legalizes
private ownership and the commodification of land.[20] Yet I would
argue that the ideas about communal tenure which came to be
embodied in both British and African assertions about the customary law cannot be taken as given, but that they must be understood
as developing in response to the colonial situation. The customary
law of tenure is constructed partly out of British ideas about property in African societies, and partly from the successful assertion of
interests by some sections of the African rural population. Its
character can be better understood as an historical product of colonialism than as an indigenous expression pre-dating and running
alongside colonial land law. Indeed had the colonial state not endorsed the production of a system of communal tenure, the commodification of land could well have emerged far more quickly.[21]

An evolutionary framework of understanding dominated the colonial period, and lay behind thinking about land law, which was

20. The common framework of comprehension in the British literature can be
summed up by quoting Lord Lugard. "In the earliest stage the land and its produce is
shared by the community as a whole; . . . later the control of the land is vested in the
head of the family. When the tribal state is reached, the control passes to the chief,
who allots unoccupied lands at will, but is not justified in dispossessing any family or
person who is using the land. Later still, especially when the pressure of population
has given land an exchange value the conception of proprietary rights in it
emerges. . . . These processes of natural evolution, leading up to individual ownership, may . . . be traced in every civilisation known to history." *The Dual Mandate in
British Tropical Africa* (London, 1922), 280–81.
21. Chanock, "Paradigms, policies and property. A review of the customary law of
land tenure" in Mann and Roberts, eds., *Law and Colonial Africa*.

continually concerned with diagnosing the state to which Africans could be said to have evolved, in order to prescribe the appropriate dose of chiefly control or individual rights. It was also the version that was formally endorsed by the Imperial legal system. Three important Privy Council cases described and imposed the British legal version of African tenure. In *Re Southern Rhodesia 1919 A.C.* [22] the Privy Council specifically adopted the evolutionary framework and found that Africans had no individual rights in land, and that such concepts were "foreign to their ideas." Two years later in *Amodu Tijani v Southern Nigeria (Secretary) 1921 A.C.* the phrase appears again. Lord Haldane quoted with approval the view in an 1898 report that "individual ownership of land is foreign to native ideas. Land belongs to the community, the village and the family, never to the individual." In "every case" it was controlled or allocated by the chief or headman. Thus, to the legal endorsement of communal ownership was added a sweeping legitimation of the rights of the polity, in the person of the chiefs, over the individual. These rights, as Haldane said, had been recognized "as the outcome of deliberate policy."[23] In *Sobuzha v Miller and others 1926 A.C.* Haldane, adopting "foreign to native ideas" as his own phrase, declared "the true character of native title to land throughout the Empire" to be "a uniform one."[24] All "natives" henceforth were trapped within what was supposed to be their own idea of communal ownership, but made subject to overriding political rights of allocation, which was also declared to be their idea as a matter of "deliberate policy."

It is to the question of policy that we must turn. For we need to analyze not only the rights of the chiefs in this light, but also the denial of individual tenure. Neither can simply be accepted as a timeless, natural, and uniform aspect of ideas about tenure which were not "foreign to native ideas." Both are promoted during the colonial period as "native ideas," partly by the colonial polity, and partly by interested "natives." It is clear when we look at the development of the regime of land allocation, which came to be both perceived and presented as part of a customary law of tenure, that it represented the combination of interests of the colonial governments and African local authorities. Analysis of the development of the institution of chieftaincy in colonial Africa has long concluded that

22. Especially 215–16 and 233–34.
23. 404–05.
24. 525.

indigenous rulers were in many ways endowed with powers which they had not had before. In this case the British perception, derived from their own law, that land rights flowed downward from the sovereign, meshed with their understanding of primitive societies, in which the rights did not lie with the individual users. Clearly they had, then, to flow downward from the chiefs, a model which fit well with the insertion of the Crown as the overall source of rights over African land. On the ground, this became an essential part of the preservation and promotion of the powers of the Chiefs, who were rapidly developed into a key element of British rule. And the chiefs themselves were not slow to assert these rights to a receptive official audience. While the claims of the Crown meant that the chiefs would not be recognized as owners, the imperatives of administration granted to them rights as allocators. As Meek explains, "The grant to individuals of absolute rights of ownership, would tend to disrupt the native polity. . . . The control of alienation of land has been in consequence one of the main planks of the British system of 'Indirect Rule.'"[25] The authority of the chiefs was to be maintained by the promotion of their role as the allocators of land, and so was the dependence of their subjects. Exploitation was to be curbed by not allowing the Chiefs the right to sell the land they supposedly held in trust, and by the same denial of the appropriateness of ownership for Africans, curbs were put on the freedom of the subjects. Also, because the allocatory regime was a system of hierarchies flowing down from the Crown, through chiefs, sub-chiefs, clan heads, and family heads, and because land could be acquired in no other way, access to land remained dependent on family and marital status. Only by being and behaving as the subject of a chief, a dutiful son or son-in-law, or an obedient wife, was access to the means of existence acquired. This, as I shall suggest below, had important implications for the creation of a customary law of kinship.

One of the striking features of any examination of African land tenure in the colonial period is the strength and variety of the assertion by Africans of a right to individual ownership not accorded to them in the colonial version of African customary law. It rapidly became apparent that, whatever theories there might exist about the absence of individual tenure, land usage was "individual" (broadly speaking, that is, members of "individual" households). There is no shortage of analyses of the rights of land users based on observation

25. C.K. Meek, *Land Law and Custom in the Colonies* (London, 1946), 10.

of what actually happened rather than on evolutionary schemes.[26] Gluckman's overall survey of the use of land found that it was "highly individualistic," and that every system was reducible to the ownership of specific rights by individuals.[27] And while Gluckman linked these rights to membership of a political community, and thus to a regime of allocation, White, for example, in his description of Central African tenure systems, found this unnecessary. The rights were, he found, "essentially individual, acquired by the individual, enjoyed by him, and disposed of by him."[28]

Many Africans had been saying this for more than half a century. From the first years of cash cropping, i.e. as soon as it made sense to assert individual rights, and as soon as it became feasible to record and defend them, there was much vocal rejection of communal title. These ambitions received scant sympathy at the time from the majority of colonial officials, and perhaps even less later from historians. Meek can be taken as representative of the colonial view when he wrote that over much of Africa the holders of customary titles were trying to convert them into "indefeasible titles," and were "arming themselves with bogus deeds often obtained from bogus lawyers."[29] Much is revealed by his choice of words: what was bogus to him was also the ambitions of the claimants. Boahen's summary is typical of the historians' approach: "the commercialisation of land . . . led to the illegal sale of communal land by unscrupulous family heads."[30] Hostility to the assertion of individual title, especially to the attempts to claim a right to buy and sell, has been common to both ends of the political spectrum: it was shared by colonial rulers and radical African opponents of colonialism. We shall need to consider the reasons for this unusual area of agreement between opponents.

26. Chanock, "Paradigms, policies and property"; E. Colson, "The impact of the colonial period on the definition of land rights," in *Colonialism in Africa* vol. 3, ed. by V. Turner (Cambridge, 1971); R.W. James, *Land Tenure and Policy in Tanzania* (Toronto, 1971); A. Munro, "Land Law in Kenya," *Wisconsin Law Review* (1966); M.P. Mvunga, *Land Law and Policy in Zambia* (Lusaka, 1982).
27. M. Gluckman, "African land tenure," *Human Problems in British Central Africa* 3, 1945.
28. C.M.N. White, "Terminological confusion in African land tenure," in *Readings in African Law*, ed. E. Cotran and N. Rubin (London, 1970), 257. The "him" is important here, as we shall see below. The rights of "hers" proved even more difficult for colonial officials to recognize.
29. Meek, *Land Law and Custom in the Colonies*, 2nd edition, 1968, 5.
30. A. Adu Boahen, "Colonialism in Africa: its impact and significance," in *Africa Under Colonial Domination 1880–1935* (Paris/London, 1985), 794. Unesco General History of Africa 7.

There was also, of course, within African societies, intense opposition to the assertion of individual title, particularly to the right to sell land.[31] The point that must be stressed here is that there was, from the beginning of the colonial period, not one system of African tenure, but widespread and continuing conflict about rights in land among Africans. These conflicts took place in a context of increasing population pressure on land; of new types of economic opportunity; and of the widespread early seizure of land by European companies and settlers, with a feeling of continuing threat to African land as a result. The conflicting assertions were made within the context of a political system in which, for a version of customary claims to gain authenticity, it had to be "heard" by and recognized as such by the institutions of the ruling power. What would be heard depended not only on the ideological map of African societies which had been etched in imperial legal institutions, but on the necessities of colonial domination.[32] To admit that African titles were comparable to European titles would have called into question the original expropriations of land on which much of the colonial economy rested, and undermined the legitimacy of a reserves system. Only by the quarantining of African tenure systems, could the European claims be validated.

Overall, we can see that we cannot continue to think about the gradual corrupting of systems of communal tenure by foreign notions of individual title. To understand the "customary law" of land tenure we must situate the explanation fundamentally in the realm of political assertions, by both rulers and ruled, as they unfold within the context of the colonial political economy. Ultimately, as the colonial period drew to an end, the ruling paradigm became not what rights Africans had in land, but what legal regime would best promote development. In some places individual rights were pro-

---

31. The complexities of who (in economic, gender and generational terms) asserted or denied individual tenure, and when (in terms of life cycle, marriage and death, as well as economic cycles) it was asserted is analyzed in Chanock, "Paradigms, policies and property: a review of the customary law of land tenure."

32. Policy, and therefore law-making, also varied widely from place to place. Sir Arthur Philips noted of Kenya in 1945 that "In one district we see customary law being re-shaped by public opinion and powerful interests without either encouragement or hindrance: . . . and the result seems invariably to be a trend towards individualism. In another district we find a policy in force which seeks neither to accelerate nor retard the spontaneous individualistic movement, but which does attempt to guide and regularize it. . . . In yet another district we see a policy which . . . is based on the deliberate aim of applying a brake to what are regarded as . . . dangerous individualistic tendencies. In each of these cases law is, conciously or unconciously, being made." Quoted in Munro, "Land Law in Kenya," 1084.

moted to increase production. In others the state retained control over allocation with the same end in view. Administrative and economic policies, not questions about rights, framed the new customary law in this area. Another question which must be raised is the extent to which the colonial land regime really affected practices on the ground. District officers consistently complained about "illegal" transfers of land, an indication of the limits of the state's law.[33] And in the increasingly crowded urban areas, although the land regime of the colonial state accorded no new rights of ownership in most cities that were either "traditional" or "new", an active "illegal" trade in plots, buildings, and rooms soon became a feature of urban life.[34]

Economic transformation also brought a multitude of new economic relationships which eventually found expression in changing legal forms.[35] In many parts of Africa markets developed for goods which had not been alienable in any ways behond kin groups before. Opportunities to sell food, for example, forced a different kind of definition of rights of ownership. In places where the control of food had been in women's hands, the development of a market led to the assertion of proprietal rights by men. The question of the ownership of cattle also brought complex problems of definition. Here we must point our understanding two ways. There was the need to define ownership in relation to the outside buyers, but a different set of problems remained for the members of a group who might still be asserting a multitude of rights in the now marketable goods. How far did, (and what is the process by which), the external definitions of the market place become those of the local groups? And what was the effect on the status relationships upon which the local claims were based? Here we can see plainly that we cannot separate the problems of property law and ownership from those of status and kinship in describing and explaining the process of legal colonization. Obligations and expectations arising out of relationships in communities were not easily eradicated when those who could do so

33. This problem was behind much of Hailey's unease about the uncontrolled development of African law in general and in particular in the economic field. See Chanock, *Law, Custom and Social Order*, 231 and Baron Hailey, *African Survey* (Oxford, 1938), 830–833 and 868–875.

34. See, for example, L. White, "A Colonial State and an African petit-bourgeoisie. Prostitution, property and class struggle in Nairobi 1936–1940," in *Struggle for the City: Migrant Labour, Capital and State in Urban Africa*, ed F. Cooper (London, 1983).

35. See the discussion (in relation to West Africa) in F. Snyder, *Capitalism and Legal Change* (London, 1981).

adopted the "outside" definitions of ownership. This legal frontier, that on which the separation of rights in things from questions of status is taking place, is one on which conflict is particularly fierce. It involved the reinterpretation and narrowing of the circle of kinship obligations, and an attack upon the idealized moral economy of African life. Legal colonization in this area has particularly divisive effects, because the economically aggressive could use the State's courts to impose new property and contractual relationships on others. Unlike the areas of land and family, little legitimacy was given to African legal ideas in areas like debt, contract and rights to new forms of property.

As migrant labor developed, the labor which had previously been controlled by household and family heads could be sold on the market for money. Whose was the money? Inasmuch as the colonial legal systems recognized customary law, they endorsed the patriarchal control of family estates. But this could not fit easily with an overall ideological endorsement of the rights to private property. And nor could it survive the pressures of an economy in which both sons and fathers were dealing with outsiders. Could the assets of the father be seized to pay the debts of the son, or the son's wages attached to meet his father's obligations? Similar and even more divisive problems of separation occurred as households shrank and consumption and accumulation centered upon spouse and children. Where debts owing to "strangers" were involved, the colonial legal system was supportive of an individualization of ownership, but there was no clear map to guide in the realms of family property. Succession on death, when many disputes arose, remained governed by customary law. And while the state's law recognized wages as belonging to the individual, this did not reduce claims, resentments, feelings of obligation and guilt, and bitter disputes, often taking the form of accusations of witchcraft, when money income was not handed to, or shared with, the appropriate elders. The fundamental point is that the coming of Western property law to Africa has a complex and attenuated effect changing different realms of life in different ways.[36]

African ideas in the realm of commercial law were accorded little respect in the colonial system. Over much of rural Africa, Africans were regarded as children in the ways of the market place. The

---

36. See Chanock, "A peculiar sharpness: an essay on property in the history of customary law in Colonial Africa," in *Journal of African History* 32 (1991), 65–88.

customary law was consequently seen as a collection of unusable ideas that incorporated the collective responsibility for debt, lacking ways of enforcing contracts or bringing disputes to an end, and innocent of claims for the imposition of damages for breach of contract. District officers commented widely on the ways in which societies were honeycombed by debts which were never paid, and over which there was endless and apparently inconclusive litigation. The weakness of, or even absence of, a customary law in this area was considered to be a hindrance to the development of African commerce.[37]

Labor

There appear to be three major and interlocking themes in the legal colonization of Africa in this realm. The first concerns the effects of the legal non-recognition of slavery and its effects on African society; the second the imposition of British forms of individual labor contract, and the use of the tax system and other statutory forms of levying forced labor; and the third the changes in the customary control of the labor of the young and of women, in peasant society, resulting from the spread of the cash economy and the development of a labor-market. Forced labor and the labor contract provided the new means for the coercion of labor beyond the villages in the wake of slavery, while the abolition of slavery had widespread effects on the development of new ways of legitimating the control of the labor in the village economy. It has often been pointed out that the Master and Servant legislation introduced into British Africa was built around the principle of criminal sanction for breach of contract, and that the criminal punishing of defaulting workers was one of the major occupations of the colonial courts.[38] East and Central African

37. Ghai noted that damages were neither claimed nor awarded for breach of contract and that, as a result, African commerce was being ruined by unpaid debts. He also pointed to the feature that had stood out for so many commentators, that there was a "certain lack of finality about transactions." See "Customary contracts and transactions in Kenya" in *Ideas and Procedures in African Customary Law*, ed. M. Gluckman (London, 1969), 338–44. On litigation regarding loans and other cash transactions see Moore, *Social Facts and Fabrications*, 187–90. Taking about half the time of the courts studied, these cases were settled outside of either of the formally recognized legal "systems": "they usually do not state rules at all, but rather hand down rulings." (190).

38. Sumner, ed., *Crime Justice and Underdevelopment*. It should be noted that the legislation was not peculiar to colonialism, and that it was only in the 1870s that breach of a contract of employment ceased to be treated as criminal in English law.

legislation was based upon statutes from the Cape Colony and not only provided substantial criminal penalties for desertion, but made similarly punishable neglect of duties, negligence, and refusal to work. Offenses of this nature, vivid testimony to relations between employers and employees, occupied time in the colonial courts, which functioned as instruments of labor discipline. In Kenya and parts of Nyasaland people resident on land that had been taken by white settlers were obliged to enter into labor tenancy agreements which subjected them to the same criminal sanctions. Coercive control of labor was clearly central to the large scale mobilization of labour for colonial enterprises in mining and agriculture, in conditions where the proletarians in the making had alternative modes of support. It survived even the attempts by the Labour Government in Britain between 1929 and 1931 to abolish it, as the colonial governments of East and Central Africa insisted that criminal sanction remained essential to the securing of a labor supply. In addition, the taxation system was used to force labor out of the villages; this also survived the weak protest of the Labour Colonial Secretary.[39] Controversy also raged over the levying of forced labor by the colonial governments.[40] This too was legitimated by colonial governments, by the contrivance of a "customary" right on the part of chiefs to levy labor for communal purposes. Hailey remarks ingenuously of state compulsion that it was "necessary to consider the native custom under which those in management of tribal or group affairs could call for communal labour, for, as will be seen, the existence of this custom has facilitated the exaction by the administrations of labour for public purposes."[41]

We should note also the use of compulsion not only over agri-

---

Colonial law simply continued the sanctions abandoned as a mode of control in metropolitan law.

39. See Lord Passfield's reminder to the Northern Rhodesian Governor in 1930 that it was contrary to the policy of the British Government "that any taxation levied upon the natives should be such that . . . it obliges them to labour for wages as the only practical means of obtaining the money to pay their taxes." Quoted in E. Berger, *Labour, Race and Colonial Rule* (Oxford, 1974), 37.

40. On this, and on labor law and policy generally see Lord Hailey, *African Survey*, chapter 11.

41. Baron Hailey, *African Survey*, 605–06. See also 608–11. Like other forms of forced labor this area was to fall under the Geneva Convention of 1930, which was ratified by the British Government in 1931. This introduced a new tier of law to the legal encounter. But, with greater realism, Hailey wrote, "It would be difficult, and it would also be unsafe, to generalise as to the extent to which the restrictions placed by legislation on the use of forced labour are observed in practice. Here, as elsewhere, the spirit of the administration, and the traditions of its personnel, count for much." (629).

cultural methods,[42] but to force the growing of particular crops, because this gives an insight into the nature of colonial legality. As Hailey points out, British administrations in East Africa relied not on legal powers but on "moral pressure." He quotes a Tanganyika government circular of 1925 to the effect that if an administrative officer found that "a particular community turns a deaf ear to his exhortation to them to adopt some form of active work, it will be his duty to use every legitimate means at his command to induce them to take up the cultivation of economic crops."[43] We must bear in mind when looking at the gaps in the colonial statute book that they do not necessarily indicate an absence of the application of state power to the lives of colonial subjects.

It was not only colonial employers who had to evolve and legalize means of controlling labor. African agriculturalists, especially those responding to the new opportunities in marketable crops, also had problems in coercing labor in the aftermath of slavery. As the colonial governments tended to take over the rights claimed by chiefs to levy communal labor, they had increasing resort to the idiom of kinship. This idiom was also employable to emphasize rights over the labor of both women and children, while control over access to land was also usable to limit the options of dependents. Audrey Richards remarked of Bemba hierarchies in 1939 that "All relationships between an inferior and his superior involve the former in giving some kind of labour." And she wrote, "the aim of every Bemba was to secure rights over the services of others, whether slaves, relatives, fellow villagers or subjects."[44] Competition for labor resources among the colonized is not only an essential part of the story of the development of labor law in the colonial period, but also a part of the story of the making of customary law in the realms of land and family. Labor law covers not just state compulsion and contractual relationships rewarded by money, but also claims upon labor made by the manipulation of customary resources.

Family

We can usefully bridge the discussions of labor and kinship by underlining the importance of the control of labor as new markets

42. See Chanock, "Agricultural change and continuity in Malawi," in *The Roots of Rural Poverty*, ed. R. Palmer and N. Parsons (London, 1979).
43. *African Survey*, 631–32.
44. A. Richards, *Land, Labour and Diet in Northern Rhodesia* (London, 1939), 142.

emerge, and also as alternatives to a traditional way of life in the form of labor migrancy develop for young men and women. It is for this reason, among others, that a "customary law" of marriage develops, which brings the enforcement of familial obligations into the realm of the state's courts. The new value of labor in the new economy provides a backdrop for many other important struggles. One of the effects of the legal non-recognition of slavery is the development of a "family law," the rationale of which is to repair the legitimacy of the control of this class of dependents. The abolition of slavery is not to be understood as a conclusive wiping out of a sort of social excrescence, but must be situated in the context of the arrangements affecting the control of dependents as a whole. Not only do conflicts about slave status remain important in the villages in disputes about both land and family, but the claims put forward by the rulers of society about the nature of the customary family law are substantially affected by the need to control those women who had previously been secured in other ways. The importance of slavery to the labor systems of many societies seems plain, and a particularly high value was placed on female slaves, for both their labor and reproductive capacities, which could be acquired without any of the payments or reciprocal duties involved in non-slave marriages. In attacking slavery the colonial state was threatening an important part of the bonds attaching women to men. Overall, in relation to these bonds, we need to consider the effects of legal colonization on the status of women: the assault on polygamous marriage; the weakening of matriliny; and the efforts of both colonizers and colonized to construct and control a moral universe appropriate to the new conditions.

The frontier between the new law and legal institutions and African systems of marriage was a particularly active one. From the earliest period of colonial rule, colonial courts were actively involved in judging marital disputes brought to them by African litigants. An immediate question is why this should have been so.[45] (There is the further question of how to classify the disputes of this sort brought to the colonial courts. While it seemed natural to the British administrators to think of them in terms of a law of marriage, the substance of the disputes was often the recovery of bride – wealth payments made, labor dues or other payments owing, and other proprietal

---

45. In general see Chanock, *Law, Custom and Social Order*, Chapters 8 to 11; and A. Hastings and A. Philips, *Survey of African Marriage and Family Life* (London, 1953). On marriage laws in East Africa see Morris and Read, *Indirect Rule and the Search for Justice* (Oxford, 1972), chapter 7.

matters. Access to and use of land also depended on marriages. In matrilineal areas where men could, on divorce, lose their right to the land they had been cultivating, more than morality was at stake.) It seems possible to divide the early phase of colonial rule in this respect from later ones. Early colonial judicial officers were scornful of and hostile to African marital institutions, which they characterized as a whole world of immoralities, featuring: the pawning of young girls; the perpetual minority status of women, and their absence of property rights; polygamy; the purchase of wives; sexual laxity; and the oppression of women. A virtual reign of terror was supposed to cement the marital relationship. They were initially ready to take an active role in bringing such marriages to an end, particularly when they appeared to be liberating women from them. An African woman's "position in life, from her childhood to her grave," wrote one early British observer was "one of gloom, discouragement and disgrace."[46]

And indeed it was women, or their families, who learned quickly to seek relief in the colonial courts. Many of these cases were related to the ending of legal recognition of slavery, and many slave wives sought the judgment of the district courts in their efforts to return to their kin. District officers puzzled as to how to separate the law of marriage from the status of slavery. It should not surprise us that this early sensitivity toward the rights of African women in the colonial courts did not last. Slave wives were soon held to be bound to their marriages unless redemption was paid. Beyond the surface of a bourgeois chivalry (if such a concept is permissible), the colonial officials came from a legal system and culture which did not accord equality to women, nor allow them easy escape from marriage. The voices that were increasingly heard asserting an African marriage law were the voices of the outraged men. British law, wrote Charles Dundas, by giving rights to sons and to women, "falls like a thunderbolt into the midst of native society. All precedent and custom are cast aside, and the controllers of society are disabled." The British had "loosened the ties of matrimony" by too freely granting divorces to "frivolous girls."[47] Judges soon came round to the view that African men should be given every assistance in the maintenance of the security of their "domestic rights." "If divorce were made too easy," said one, "tribal rule would break up and

46. T.M. Thomas, *Eleven Years in Central Africa* (London, 1872), 259.
47. C. Dundas, "The organisation and laws of some Bantu tribes of East Africa," in *Journal of the Royal Anthropological Institute* 45 (1915), 305; and "Native laws of some Bantu tribes of East Africa," *JRAI* 51 (1921), 266.

disappear."[48] The kind of marriage law which would be allowed to develop, like the kind of land law, depended on the necessities of rule through indigenous local authorities. As I have said, alternative versions of the land law were not "heard" by the colonial state, and neither were the women's nor the young men's versions of the marriage law.

The retreat of the colonial states from reformism to a support for what they deemed to be customary marriage had its counterpart on the missionary side, in spite of the sharp conflict between state and church over the question of polygamy. "What is the one supreme difficulty?," asked one missionary, "The marriage question: that is the rock." There can be, proclaimed the *Church in the Mission Field* "no question of polygamy. It is simply one of the gross evils of heathen society which, like habitual murder and slavery, must at all costs be ended."[49] Initially the churches welcomed with open arms the female fugitives from polygamous marriages, but soon they found that male voices were being raised on a sensitive point: the churches were undermining the significance and indissolubility of marriage in general. Gradually defense of indissolubility came to take precedence. The clergy, like the district officers, began to condemn the women who sought relief in their courts, and their emphasis too swung around to support of marital stability, which meant in effect that they too "heard" the voices of the male elders, and not the alternative versions.

Clearly a part of the story of the impact of British law in this field is to be found in the thicket of marriage ordinances which sprung up in the colonial territories. The first point to be made here applies as well to the protective efforts of the colonial state in the matters of slavery and women's status. An early question must be, what difference does the state's law make? There are areas of life from which the colonial state remained distant, in which the clear and present powers continued to be exercised by family and male elders. The formal law of the marriage ordinances, while it did shape the overall legal environment, was effectively absent from most lives. The Western law which was of greater importance was the Churches' version, with its hostility to divorce. But while the law in the sense of the

---

48. Chanock, *Law, Custom and Social Order*, 149.
49. Chanock, *Law, Custom and Social Order*, 150; and generally 150–59. We should not limit our consideration of legal colonization to the State's law. The churches had their own courts and their own law and these became an important part of the legal environment. Monogamy became the law for the adherents to the mission churches while opposition to it fuelled the growth of independent Christianity.

Marriage Ordinances had little effect on African law, the way in which the colonial courts administered "customary" law had a considerable impact, and in this sense African family law was transformed by the colonial legal system. In the first place marriage was drawn from the realm of inter-familial relations into that of the State and its law and courts, and customary law was changed in this process. In dealing with the relationship between the state's legal order and customary regimes in the realm of kinship in Africa, it is necessary to remind ourselves that this is not only a colonial question. The extension of state regulation of the family is a part of Western legal history, much of it contemporaneous with the colonial period, and it is a history which is increasingly understood in terms of the politics of gender. In looking at the impact of British family law on Africa, therefore, one must ask, about both its impositions and interventions, how they were related to the designs of colonial rule. We may soon discover the dominance of the administrative agenda on the government's side. And what can be said about the African side? The male rulers of African societies were able to insert their social agenda into the colonial legal process because the outrage which they felt about developments in relations between genders and generations, which flowed from the colonial conquest, struck a sympathetic cord with British officials. The strains of labor migrancy, the development of the money economy, urbanization, and poverty and disruption resulting from loss of land, were all producing fundamental changes in behavior in the realm of the family.

As in the case of the systemization of land tenure, the impact of colonial law on family law was to systematize the varying and often competing patterns of practice in local societies. Colonial social anthropology, as produced by professional anthropologists, and, under their influence, by government officers responsible for administering and judging, determinedly ironed out the variable and contested nature of marital institutions.[50] Most importantly, in the area under consideration, was the production of the models of patrilineal and matrilineal societies. Government officers did not use these models in the way that social scientists might. They were treated as real, and acted upon in a way that contributed to the shaping of the systems that they purported to describe. The model became the legal regime. In matrilineal societies it was said that little bridewealth was paid; labor service to the matrikin was required; residence was matrilocal; the

50. For an extended critique see Chanock, *Law, Custom and Social Order,* chapter 2.

descendents were part of the matrikin; and the maternal uncle was the legal guardian. Patrilineal societies were seen as a mirror image with high bridewealth; patrilocal residence; and full rights over wife, children, and property belonging to the patrikin. The systems were perceived as being tribally bound. Indeed the notion of the tribe was fundamental to this process of systemization. All Africans were conceived of as having a definite and immutable tribal identity, and each "tribe" as having a definite and immutable system of customs. In their "recognition," therefore, of African customary law, the district officers applied the rules appropriate to the perceived system to those deemed to belong to it. Before "customary" marriages could be recognized (and this was increasingly necessary for taxation purposes, as well as permission to reside in urban areas and on white estates), colonial courts insisted that the system's appropriate rules regarding matters like bridewealth and consent had been applied by the parties. Marriage was bureaucratized by state application and underwent a process of legalization not simply by being defined and systematized, but by including the world of inter-familial relations in the realm of the state and its laws. Variants and alternative versions of "custom" were marginalized and rendered extra-legal.

It is clear, looking back over the colonial period as a whole, that the position of women was not substantially improved. By the end of the colonial period in East and Central Africa unmarried women remained legal minors on the basis of the fiction that this was their status in customary law. While it had been established in law, if not in fact, that the consent of women was necessary to a valid marriage, it still remained the case that the consent of a woman was not sufficient, and required the endorsement of her male guardian. If we place this in the context of a steady inflation of bridewealth payments (and the substitution of labor service by such payments) we can see a narrowing of effective choice, a shift in advantage towards older over younger men, and increasing difficulties in the way of women leaving marriages where substantial payments, which would have to be returned by their male kin, had been made. In the urban areas in particular this produced widespread avoidance of "legal" customary marriage, which in turn fuelled the insistence on it by the older generation, supported by the officials. Urban "customary" marriage continued to be regarded as beyond the law by the colonial state.[51] Nor did the impact of British law secure property rights for

51. See in general A.L. Epstein, *Urbanisation and Kinship. The Domestic Domain on the*

African women. As minors, unmarried women remained unable to hold property of their own. With the increasing nucleation of households and monetization of the economy, the effective expectations of married women with respect to property were separated from their wider kin and subordinated to husbands. Colonial law was increasingly impatient with and intolerant of lack of definition in property rights. In the conditions of rural life, property like land and cattle could be the subject of many competing and overlapping claims, depending on the changing status of the claimants. But legalization rendered women's claims unrecognizable. Land, which as we have seen was subject to a regime of administrative allocation, became scarcer for women. As cash cropping spread through rural areas women were separated from the products of agricultural labor, which were appropriated by men. In addition women whose husbands depended on wage labor were left, on divorce or the death of a husband, without a share in the estate. On divorce for many the option of returning to their families of origin and exercising claims to land and support was no longer available. And on the death of a spouse the state-endorsed version of "custom" legitimated the seizure of his property, which included home and household goods, by his relatives.[52] This was clearly not "customary law" in the sense of received practice because the situations to which it applied were new. It provides further illustration of the way in which claims which were congenial to the British view of property and gender relations could establish themselves as legitimated custom.

Conclusions

There is a definite trend away from analyzing metropolitan legal systems in terms of one legal system emanating from the state. The centralized paradigm is breaking down as efforts are made to uncover the multiple centers of power, regulation, disputing, and rule making. In the light of the "discovery" of the diffuse nature of power and of legal pluralism at the center it may seem quixotic to question the importance of pluralism at the periphery, where it appears on the face of it obvious that many culturally distinct and historically

---

Copperbelt of Zambia 1950–56 (London, 1981); and A. Philips, *A Survey of African Marriage and Family Life* (London, 1953).

52. See on this "property grabbing" C.M. Himonga, "Family Property Disputes: The Predicament of Women and Children in a Zambian Urban Community" (Ph.d diss., London, 1985).

validated systems of regulation have contended with the introduced
Western law of the colonial states. Nonetheless I would want to
argue that the concept of legal pluralism, as it has been usually
employed in the African context in the sense of the co-existence of
relatively discreet systems, can be damaging to attempts to understand the process of legal colonization. Analysis of pluralism in the
immediate pre- and post-independence periods assumed that the
plural parts were imported law and the customary law. Perhaps it
might also be enlightening to see the colonial legal system – an
amalgam of two new types of law – as one system.[53] We must look
first at the transformation of both customary legal concepts and
imported ones by the dialogue they conducted in the colonial situation. Customary law, in order to be heard, must speak the language
of the colonizers' law. Even in order to resist, it must insert itself into
the state's system and institutions. The result is one language,
perhaps spoken with many different accents, rather than a plurality
of tongues. Plural centers of power were not commonly welcomed or
recognized in the colonial states, and are not in the post-colonial
states, either. Legal pluralism is more likely to be found in conditions of relative political consensus and a confident state. Where the
political center is relatively weaker, so perhaps legal pluralism, the
product of the state's confidence, becomes weaker too.

One fundamental change which remains to be mentioned is that
of the imposition of written upon oral forms. It is closely related to
another question, which is how far the laws of the colonial state
actually reached. The arbitration of civil and criminal cases continued in the villages, witchcaft cases were still judged and heard,
slavery was slow to disappear, and land transactions not sanctioned
by law took place. Written law had little influence here, and, as I
have suggested, often not much in the official "Native Courts,"
given that official rules of law were very rarely cited. Colonial
lawyers and administrators feared that writing would freeze the
development of custom, and resisted its codification. I do not think
that the written versions of customary law, eventually produced by
government anthropologists, had this effect. A written law is far
from frozen, as familiarity with judicial interpretation in European

53. It is affected by other regulatory orders: the legal system of Britain, the rules of
the churches and of economic organizations like mines and agricultural estates, and
the regulatory orders of African societies. I am attracted by the possibilities of the
analysis of interlegality as suggested in B. de Sousa, Santos, "Law: a map of
misreading. Toward a postmodern conception of law," in *Journal of Law and Society* 14,
(1987), 3.

and British systems shows. It was rather the unwritten law which tended to be stridently "frozen" in its assertions. Overall the real effect of writing was not to arrest change, but to contribute to the primacy of the state's law, not only in substance, but in form. Writing is the tool of administration. It facilitates the application of principles over the negotiation of substantive positions. In this sense it contributes to the legalization of customary law.

It should by now be plain that in considering the impact of British law on the African colonies and on African law we must unpack with care the contents of both British and customary laws. The British legal system was not exported to Africa, in spite of the formulae in the various founding Orders-in-Council which proclaimed the laws of England at a certain date to be applicable to the newly annexed territory. For legal rules are not real until they are applied or invoked by particular people in particular institutional and societal settings. In Africa, as elsewhere in the Empire, the British legal system underwent a transformation into an Anglo-colonial system. The colonial judiciary was not drawn from the same pool as the metropolitan judges, but from a professional colonial legal service. Typically these men served in large numbers of colonial territories in the course of their careers, which usually combined both administrative and judicial posts.[54] This interchangeability underlines the existence of a colonial legal culture, separate from the metropolitan one. One of the most marked features of East and Central Africa's experience is that the legal profession was simply absent from the legal experiences of most Africans in the colonial system. Lawyers were specifically excluded from the "native" courts operating under indirect rule and very rarely available to those charged in the higher courts.[55] The codes of criminal law and procedure were adapted from other parts of the Empire and were constructed to fit the imposition of law by alien and authoritarian rule, in which the element of force perforated the threadbare legal fabric far more obviously than in Britain. In the absence of juries, a strong profession, and a politically influential public audience, the style of judging and punishing in both

54. E.g. Sir Charles Griffin, who was Chief Justice of Uganda from 1921–32, had been Attorney General of Gibralter and Chief Justice of the Leeward Islands. Sir Walter Huggard was a magistrate in Nigeria; Attorney-General in Trinidad and Tobago, Kenya, and the Straits Settlements; the Chief Justice of the Straits; and a High Court Judge of the High Commission Territories in South Africa. Sir John Ainley, Chief Justice of Kenya from 1963, served on the Bench in the Gold Coast, Uganda, Eastern Nigeria, Sarawak, North Borneo, and Brunei.
55. See e.g. Ghai and Mcauslan, *Public Law*, 353.

civil and criminal cases was less restrained than that in Britain. There
was, below the level of the highest courts, no separation of powers.
Legal and administrative work were done by the same officials. Apart
from the confusion of goals which this entailed, it had a distinct impact
on the content of British law as it actually reached Africa. For not only
did the rules of the colonial statute book impose an extensive and
different control of daily life, but the rules of English common law,
when invoked, were simplified and misconstrued by officials with little
more than rudimentary recollections of textbooks. The failings of the
system in this respect were evident to metropolitan lawyers. The commission of enquiry into the administration of justice in East Africa
concluded simply that the machinery for the administration of justice as
apparently set up by law in these territories did not work, and, as it was
then constituted, could not work. Colonial High Courts also had ample
opportunities to express their horror at the lawgiving style of the
administrators. But these condemnations in the name of legal ideal-
ism were of little effect, because of the close connections between law
and the imperatives of administration.[56] Ultimately if one wants to
understand the transplanting of British law, one needs to focus not
on the idea of law embodied in the lawyers' view of the metropolitan
legal system, but instead to situate the account in the administrative
necessities of the colonial state. The verbiage and rhetoric of the
common law have proved infinitely adaptable. That they are to be
found decorating colonial legal systems should not lead us to believe
that it was in any sense transplanted to Africa. The substance of the
common law is not found in the law in the books in colonial Africa,
and the law in action was no more than ineffectively haunted by its
spirit. The administrative paradigm of law, in which law consists of
the directives of the state and is a prime means of securing its goals
and exercising its powers, has been the major legacy to the postcolonial states. The colonial period provided no foundation for the use
of law by citizens in defense of their rights.

While the Africanization of the legal system has not taken place,
there has been much manipulation of custom, which has had the
effect of masking the continuing colonial nature of the state and its
law. Land law, which gives the state and its agencies control over
allocation in countries like Tanzania, Zambia, and Malawi, which
preserves the colonial estates and farms, and which cannot deliver

---

56. For an excellent account of the lawyers' view of officials' justice see Morris and
Read, *Indirect Rule and the Search for Justice*, 98–103 and 295–308. See also Ghai and
Mcauslan, *Public Law*, chapter 13.

meaningful access to land to all who want it, is legitimated in the name of customary tenure. Similarly, where women's effective political representation has been weak, a customary family law has been used to reconcile male and traditionalist support to the state. The orchestration of custom, rather than its preservation, has given the appearance of the form of customary/modern dualism to the postcolonial systems. The experience of people living with the colonial legal systems of their legacies has been more fundamentally shaped by other factors. The economic changes brought the possibility of individualizing rights in property, while the state continued to frustrate the assertion of these rights in many ways. The institutional processes of disputing in the colonial state separated individuals from communities while giving them no remedies against the state's powers.[57] The language of the state was legalizing and regularizing, its operations capricious. If we look at the total picture of the effects on the regulation of personal and property relations among Africans, and the subjection of Africans to the legal regime of the state, we can sum up the consequences of the legal encounter as being individualization without rights, and bureaucratization without the rule of law.

---

57. Cf Moore's remark that "The *individualisation and decontextualising of disputes* . . . is a central social fact" characterizing the courts (her italics). *Social Facts and Fabrications*, 168.

14

Symbiosis of Indigenous and Western Law in Africa and Asia: An Essay in Legal Pluralism

FRANZ VON BENDA-BECKMANN

Introduction

It is not the objective of this paper to give a comprehensive overview of the forms of symbiosis of indigenous and Western law in African and Asian states. We all are more or less aware of the general structure of legal systems in the former colonial and contemporary independent states, those grand schemes in which different legal systems are distinguished, their spheres of validity defined, and the organizations and procedures for their application demarcated. These spheres of operation are distinct, usually linked to the legal status of persons, objects, or relationships. It is only when subjects belonging to different categories having their own laws come into contact that problems arise. Choices have to be made, and the proper solutions are again prescribed by legal science, by the law of conflicts or *intergentiel recht*, as it was called in the Netherlands East Indies.[1] Aspects of these rules are described in several contributions in this volume. So in order not to be unnecessarily repetitive, I shall be more selective, and I shall take up the metaphor of *legal symbiosis* which the editors of this volume have asked me to write about.

The metaphor is fitting in that it stresses life. It points to dynamic and historical interrelationships between different laws in the thought and practice of people. It directs us to look into the ways in which laws are involved in human agency. It also reminds us that we should not look at the different legal systems in isolation, but at

---

1. See for the Netherlands East Indies, R.D. Kollewijn, *Intergentiel Recht* (The Hague, 1955); for British colonies, see A.N. Allott, *Essays in African Law* (London, 1970); see also M.B. Hooker, *A Concise Legal History of Southeast Asia* (Oxford, 1975) and F. Reyntjes in this volume.

their interrelatedness through human agency. And it leads us to adopt as point of departure the idea that life is different in time and space. These seem to be simple, nearly banal guidelines for an inquiry into historical and contemporary legal pluralism in developing countries.[2] But in the practice of research and scholarly writing, they are not commonly adhered to. More often than not, the coexistence of legal subsystems is abstracted from their life-contexts or selectively reduced to some specific contexts. To a large extent description and analysis are confined to a reconstruction of legislative history, of public argumentations in legal political debates, and to court practices. They rarely move beyond them, since they are the "proper" legal contexts as defined through legalistic thinking and legal ideology.

For legal ideology negates time and space (except in its own terms). This is, in a way, inherent in the normativity of general rules which claim validity here and there, now and in the future. But an additional, ideological element comes into being through the further claim to an existence or nonexistence of legal rules here and there, now and in the future, on the basis of the assertion of normative validity. The maintenance of this ideological claim is largely made possible through the way in which "legal reality" is conceived in legal science and conventional legal sociology. This view – the "gap-approach" – is premised upon the distinction between the "ought" and the "is," between ideal and practice. Real law is only that law which corresponds, in terms of behavior and sanctioning decision making, to the ideal of the rules. Thus this reality is construed by its relation to the normative claims of the legal system. It is measured in terms of a smaller or greater disparity between the actual behavior of people and the normative claims of law with respect to this behavior. Through this reduction of the reality of legal rules, other forms of their empirical existence, for instance in the knowledge of populations, are obfuscated and are presumed on the basis of normative assertions.

This view has also been extended to plural legal systems. As a consequence, two (or more) of such law-behavior spheres are constructed, the "legal reality" of government law, and of traditional law. These separate spheres are defined by the normative claims of

---

2. For approaches to legal pluralism see J. Vanderlinden, "Le pluralisme juridique," in *Le Pluralisme Juridique*, J. Gillissen ed., (Brussels, 1971); M.B. Hooker, *Legal Pluralism: an Introduction to Colonial and Neo-Colonial Law* (Oxford, 1978); M. Galanter, "Justice in many rooms," *Journal of Legal Pluralism* 19 (1981) 1; J. Griffiths, "What is legal pluralism," *Journal of Legal Pluralism* 24 (1986) 1.

the respective subsystems. Behavior which, in legal terms, is "subject to," or "governed by" a specific legal subsystem, is related to that subsystem. Since the "reality" of law or legal pluralism is looked for in those forms of practice which are relevant in terms of legalistic doctrines, other possible forms of "life" of law or legal symbiosis are obscured, defined out of existence. In particular, the question of whether behavior is simultaneously influenced by both legal systems, irrespective of the normative claims of these systems, cannot be systematically posed.

This perspective has heavily influenced the analysis of law/legal pluralism and social and economic change in developing countries, where causes for "underdevelopment" have been ascribed to legal subsystems on the basis of such normative presumptions.[3] Economic behavior, which was subject to *adat* law according to the state legal system, was explained by reference to this law only. Possible influences of government law or local law, which normatively did not govern these activities, therefore tended to be ignored.

In this article I shall first try to develop a perspective on legal symbiosis free of such legalistic ideology. I shall then use this perspective in order to throw some more light on the relationships between law, or rather legal symbiosis, and economic development, a field of theorizing, speculation, and political rhetoric which has been and still is pervaded by legal ideology. I shall focus in particular upon contexts in which legal symbiosis with respect to matters of land and labor plays a role, the spheres of agricultural production and the distribution of and trade with agricultural products.[4] This perspective forces us to take a closer look at the laws coexisting in these spheres, the so-called customary and the so-called Western law. As is also apparent from Chanock's contribution in this volume, we shall encounter much law made by "Western" people in these contexts, but these laws are often different from the Western law we usually think of, the laws originating from Europe made to fit European circumstances. And it will also appear that the customary

3. This has been done by both by critics of state and of traditional laws. See Merryman, "Comparative law and social change: on the origins, style, decline and revival of the law and development movement," *American Journal of Comparative Law* 25 (1977), 457–91; D.N. Greenberg, "Law and development in the light of dependency theory," *Research in Law and Sociology*, vol. 3, S. Spitzer ed. (1980), 129–59; and H.W.O. Okoth-Ogendo, *The Political Economy of Law: An Essay in the Legal Organization of Underdevelopment in Kenya, 1895–1974* (J.S. Dissertation, Yale Law School, 1978 [unpublished]).

4. See on the same problem the contribution of Chanock in this volume; also M. Chanock, *Law, Custom and Social Order* (Cambridge, 1985).

laws we come across to a large extent are not very customary, and certainly not purely indigenous.[5] And it is when we think of these contexts that it appears that the metaphor of legal symbiosis may be a misleading one. For symbiosis, the consorting together, or partnership, of dissimilar organisms, ordinarily connotes an association which is mutually advantageous. And however we may evaluate the coexistence of different legal systems in the former colonies in Africa and Asia, it will be difficult to maintain an image of mutual advantage. To speak of parasitism would probably be more appropriate.

A Methodological Perspective

Let me first try to explain what I mean with an emphasis on time, space, and human agency. In order not to be stranded in too abstract jargon, I shall take for illustration a type of legal symbiosis which has occurred, and continues to occur in most developing countries: the situation in which customary law, or *adat*(law) as it is called in Indonesia, is applied in government courts.[6] Take a case as was common in West Sumatran courts in the middle of this century. In a dispute about the inheritance to a person's self-earned property one party argues that the property should devolve according to Minangkabau *adat* to himself, the deceased's sister's son. The other party argues that the deceased had made a donation of the property to him, the deceased's son, and that such donation is valid according to Islamic law. The judge decides that the valid law in question is Minangkabau *adat* law which, however, has adapted itself to the changing social and economic circumstances so as to recognize a property holder's right to dispose free of any legal restraints over his self-earned property, since this is his individual ownership. During the court hearings, the testimony of the plaintiff's lineage head, his brother, who had been present when the testament had been drawn up, is not admitted because he is too closely related to the party. Such a simple case shows a multitude of encounters between legal systems and various forms of legal symbiosis. The dispute process takes place under the condition of legal pluralism. Besides, we see

5. These points are also very clearly illustrated by the contribution of Chanock in this volume; see also the articles by Price and Kolff on India in this volume.
6. For a more detailed description see K. von Benda-Beckmann, *The Broken Stairways to Consensus: Village Justice and State Courts in Minangkabau* (Dordrecht, 1984); F. von Benda-Beckmann, *Property in Social Continuity. Continuity and Change in the Maintenance of Property Relationships in Minangkabau, West Sumatra* (The Hague, 1979).

legal symbiosis in the process of interaction: one party uses Islamic law, the other one *adat*, in order to justify their claims to the inheritance. In the court room interaction, the judge reasons in Dutch legal terms, the villagers in *adat* terms. Finally, such decisions are a particular form of legal symbiosis, perhaps the most perfect one imaginable, since both government and *adat* law are involved in the judgement. In addition, we have to consider that the context of the court is just one of many contexts in which different forms of legal symbiosis play a role. I shall illustrate this in some more detail.

Legal Symbiosis in Different Contexts

In principle, general rules or concrete decisions, (re)statements of laws or of the relations between normative systems, do not exist outside the contexts in which they have been produced. Whether they "exist," and whatever their form of existence may be as condition and influence for further behavior, depends on the ways in which such statements and decisions are known, maintained, and used in different, later contexts. Law, and forms of legal symbiosis, thus can have different forms and contents in different contexts, and the context-specific forms of legal symbiosis may have their specific consequences in other contexts. Let me illustrate this briefly, again with examples taken from field research in Minangkabau.

a) In the state courts the system maintained as the valid one is presented as *adat* law. However, in some crucial respects it is different from decisions taken in a similar dispute in procedures in village *adat* councils. Just let me note three important aspects:

1. The introduction of the legal notion of individual ownership is different from the *adat* notion of self-earned property (*harato pancaharian*). If taken seriously and systematically, it would mean that the property objects would maintain their ownership status also after the holder's death and would be subject to the same rules concerning disposition and inheritance as before. In *adat*, on the other hand, self-earned property would become inherited property (*harato pusako*) and subject to different rules with respect to transactions, notably inheritance.

2. Elements of the Dutch laws of evidence, also different from *adat* ideas, are made part of the judgement (the brother should have been heard as lineage head; the clan head's testimony should have had more weight than other testimonies). This is quite an

important point, since in West Sumatra, as elsewhere,[7] the crucial problem is not so much what "rules" to apply to a given set of "facts," but how and with the help of which rules to establish what the relevants facts are.

3. The interactive element of joint decision making, essential in *adat*, has been eliminated in the court procedure. In *adat*, what we distinguish and formalize separately as procedural and substantive law is hardly distinguishable. In *adat* thinking a substantively just decision, as an interpretation of general *adat* rules and principles with respect to a concrete problematic situation, cannot be taken in a process in which the situation is subsumed under the rule. It must be arrived at through a process of joint deliberation leading to a consensus. This process is not, and cannot be, reproduced in the court, which results in the process of decision making and rule interpretation being quite different, often leading to different results as well.[8]

b) In the villages, the greater part of the villagers maintain the inheritance rule according to which "children inherit self-earned property from their father" as changed *adat* law. Proponents of pure Islam, on the other hand, maintain that Islamic law is applied.

c) In actual inheritance cases, it is usually *adat* which is used as the normative orientation for the classification and division of property, though the use of Islamic principles to divide inheritances is tolerated if nobody objects to it.

d) In the provincial political scene, inheritance law has become a cartelized sphere of activities: family property should devolve according to *adat*, self-earned property according to Islam. These conclusions of conferences of *adat* leaders, Islamic leaders, and local politicians and lawyers held in 1952 and 1968 has also been ratified by the association of judges. But in the context of court decision making, the judges continued to apply what they consider to be *adat* law.

e) In legal science and politics among the national elite, the relationship between *adat* and other subsystems, and of the content of *adat*, to some extent is different again.

---

7. These procedural elements are also emphasised in the contributions of Kolff and Reyntjens.

8. See also the contributions of Kolff and Reyntjens.

Different Consequences in Different Contexts

Different forms and contents of laws and legal symbiosis thus exist in different contexts. And what goes on in these contexts can have consequences in, may be interdependent with, what goes on in other contexts, and these consequences and interdependencies can vary, too. The following is just a brief illustration of what this means in the Minangkabau example.

a) More often than not, the decision and its motivation are retranslated into *adat* in later village interactions. In their reinterpreted form, the decision and the rules embodied in it become an element for the continuing dispute about the property in the village. Some villagers redefine the property status again as self-earned, with the consequence that after the next inheritance it would become inherited property, subject to matrilineal rules of inheritance. Others insist on maintaining the ownership status of the property after the present holder's death.

b) At the same time, and later, other judges in other courts may remain unaware of the decision laying down the new *adat* law having been taken, and continue their decision making in a different form. But the case may also be reported and become a guideline for other judges, influencing their decisions in inheritance disputes. The decision may be taken up by the Supreme Court and declared to be "the new *adat* inheritance law of Minangkabau."

c) Dissertations may be written about the new inheritance rule in which much intellectual energy is spent on the analysis of the interaction of Islamic law, *adat*, and government law. Through its incorporation into the works of legal science, the decision may become a standard element in the training in law for a generation of law students and administrators and determine their view about contemporary Minangkabau *adat* law, although it is different from local inheritance rules and/or court practices.

d) It may also happen that the decision does not become part of legal science, but is not forgotten in the villages. There, people may maintain it as the "court's *adat* law," a different rule system besides their own village *adat*. It may be this interpretation of *adat*, not the village version of it, which may influence later villagers to bring their dispute to a court rather than have it decided by *adat* authorities in the village.

The Involvement of Law in Human Agency

When analyzing these different forms of legal symbiosis in different contexts, we must, however, distinguish the different ways in which legal rules and procedures are involved in human agency.

a) Law, or rather legal pluralism, is part of the conditions under which parties, witnesses and judges, but also villagers, *adat* authorities, legal scientists and local politicians, act. It constitutes an important part of the normative and institutional environment. *Adat*, Islamic law, and government law together constitute the normative repertoire, in terms of which the participants can rationalize and justify their claims, behavior, and decisions. These conditions are historically constituted, and are communicated to the participants in different forms of learning processes. This pluralistic legal repertoire forms a part of the (possible) influences on the behavior of the participants in this process. It may give their behavior a certain direction by way of motivation, shaping the objectives of behavior; it may also structure the instrumental alternatives, the participants' means of attaining certain objectives, such as the alternatives of transferring property or of attaining a decision in a dispute.

b) If the whole legal repertoire here functions as a source of guidance and direction for behavior, and comes close to what we use to call "causes" for behavior, in the behavioral process itself legal rules or subsystems may be selectively used as a resource. Law may be used instrumentally in the sense of the use of a legally structured mode of action or transaction. For instance we can think of the use made of rights, the making of a donation, or the use of a government court procedure. Disputants and decision makers may be engaged in "forum shopping."[9]

Law may also be used as "reason" for behavior, as a means to account for the rational and legitimate character of one's own or others' behavior, whatever the actual driving forces behind the behavior may have been.

c) Thus in the courts the symbiosis of different forms of law is a condition under which parties, witnesses, and judges use elements of

9. For the analysis of patterns of differential uses of dispute settlement institutions see also L. Nader and H. Todd, eds., *The Disputing Process – Law in Ten Societies* (New York, 1978); F. von Benda-Beckmann, 'Some comparative generalizations about the differential use of state and folk institutions of dispute settlement," in *People's Law and State Law*, ed A.N. Allott and G.R. Woodman (Dordrecht, 1985), 187–205. See also the contributions of Price and Simensen in this volume.

the legal symbiosis in their actions. At the same time, the courts are also the place in which this condition is being changed. The judgements resulting from the court procedures become part of the, now changed, conditions of legal symbiosis that play a role in future behavior, in and perhaps outside the court context.

When speaking of legal symbiosis we thus can think in terms of conditions of behavior, which are the result of human agency in other time- and space-bound interaction settings, and which have consequences in new interaction settings, which then become conditions for further interaction processes themselves.

Legal Pluralism

The behavioral processes which I have described imply choices. Such choices between different legal instrumentalities (e.g. between donations, testaments or intestate inheritance) and between legal and non-legal means to attain certain objectives are already possible within a single legal system. But the repertoire of legal instrumentalities, of institutions which take decisions in terms of law, and of rationalization and justification schemes is widely enlarged by legal pluralism.

Such choices usually are not free but constrained by a variety of political, economic, social, and also legal factors, on the level of structures, institutions, interpersonal relations, and individual personality. I cannot go deeply into the literature which attempts to explain the patterns of differential use of normative systems and dispute institutions. Here, I only wish to emphasize two points.

a) In situations of legal pluralism, the choice for one of the available systems may go far beyond the concrete problem at hand, such as the regulation of an inheritance, the transfer of property, or the settlement of a dispute. The choice of the proper law or legal procedure is often seen as a choice between *Weltanschauungen*, between normative systems as a whole. As has been suggested by several scholars, the relationship between legal systems cannot be understood without consideration of the sociopolitical setting in which they are embedded. In societies which have plural legal systems the relationship is largely determined by the relationships between the persons and institutions who teach, preach, interpret, and apply them. In the case of normative systems with universalistic pretensions in particular, the systems provide legitimate bases for the exercise of authority through general regimentation and decision

making. The interpretation of the relationships between the systems
is a question of who can make his interpretation stick and exercise
power through interpreting and applying it. Asserting that one's
own system should govern a particular field of social life, like inheritance or access to land, implies the assertion of one's own legitimate
power basis. This is why specific issues like inheritance become
subject to the general question of which normative system is the
dominant one. Thus in the case of Minangkabau inheritance of
self-earned property in the 1970s, it made no more difference
whether village *adat*, court *adat*, or the Minangkabau version of
Islamic law were applied: they all led to the same result. But there
still were serious legal political struggles going on about which law
should be applied in inheritance matters.

b) But however the choice options may be restricted through differences in power and socioeconomic position between individuals and
institutions, it is always the totality of the normative and institutional
repertoire which is a possible factor influencing people's behavior. It
is not just the law or legal subsystem they are "subject to" or
"governed by."

Obviously, the way in which legal symbiosis and legal pluralism
are structured by state law will be one of the constraining factors.
However, the state's definition of legal pluralism (or centralism) will
never be the only one in which the system for proper choices is laid
down. The other systems, like *adat* or Islamic law, have their own
rules about "legal symbiosis," whether or not they are recognized by
the state system. There are plural images and interpretations of legal
pluralism. The picture drawn by government politicians, lawmakers, judges, and legal scientists is just one of them. Other people,
representatives of their own system like local or religious leaders,
may hold other perspectives of the relationships between the normative subsystems, define legal pluralism, also normatively and ideo-
logically, quite differently. And such non-state perceptions or claims
to legal pluralism may have their own, independent consequences
for people's actions. Whatever colonial legislators and legal scientists wrote, for instance, on the relationship between government
law, Islamic law, and *adat* or *adat* law, the Minangkabau certainly
had their own ideas about these relationships, and it was their own
ideas, more than those of Dutch or Indonesian lawyers, which
influenced their actions.

We must always assume under conditions of legal pluralism,
people will take into account what they think and experience to be

the whole range of the normative and institutional world, and this totality may, more or less, influence people's behavior, and make them make choices, voluntarily or under constraint. Thus even when people make the choice to conform to one normative system, let us say *adat*, to which they are subject according to the state legal system, the dominant motivation may be a conscious rejection of the other system, the state system, due to factors inherent to that system or its operation. From the fact that people conform to *adat*, use *adat* transaction forms, use *adat* maxims to rationalize or justify their behavior, we cannot deduce that this behavior would have been motivated, or caused, by *adat*. The same holds true, the other way round, when people use state law or state courts.

Legal Symbiosis and Economic Development

Let me look now with this perspective at the relationship between law, or legal symbiosis, and economic development. The thinking about this relationship is also overshadowed by legalistic and ideological assumptions. A seemingly inextinguishable prejudice holds that Western laws are favorable to economic development and modernization, while traditional, customary laws are not; on the contrary, it is held that such customary laws hinder or prevent development. This is believed although it has been repeatedly shown that a) Western law, if applied to local populations at large, rarely fulfilled its promises, and that b) local normative systems were quite adaptable to social and economic changes.[10] The *prima facie* evidence adduced is the economic development in Europe, but also in the colonies. Did not the European sector in the dual economy, governed by Western law, flourish, and did not the native sector, subject to customary laws, stagnate, or underdevelop? Was the recognition of customary laws, of *adat* laws in Indonesia, not ultimately harmful for the Indonesians themselves? And was this not realized by Indonesian and African leaders after Independence since

---

10. See Merryman, "Comparative law"; Greenberg, "Law and development"; Okoth-Ogendo, *Political Economy*; F. Snyder, "Colonialism and legal form; the creation of customary law in Senegal," *Journal of Legal Pluralism* 19 (1981), 49–90. For the discussion about *adat* law policy in the Netherlands see the contribution of Fasseur in this volume. I have discussed some mechanisms through which these assumptions are maintained also through local populations in F. von Benda-Beckmann," Scapegoat and Magic charm: Law in Development Theory and Practice," *Journal of Legal Pluralism* 28 (1989), 129–148.

they increased the speed with which all possible spheres of social, economic, and political life were codified in the name of nation building, legal certainty, and economic modernization?

These assumptions are largely based upon the legalistic conceptualization I have talked about earlier. Activities subject to, or governed by, one legal subsystem are held to be influenced/caused by this subsystem. Thus we get a near equation of the dual economy with the dual legal system as it is laid down in state and legal science structures of legal pluralism. Besides, there is an exaggerated concern with nation-wide legislation and with the great fields of law which are distinguished in Western legal systems, like criminal and civil law, family law, inheritance law, commercial law, etc. Such perspectives tend to ignore or underestimate "legal symbiosis" in the fields of social practice which they analyze. And they tend to use the terms of customary and Western law too easily for different laws and law-related practices in different contexts.

Let us therefore look more closely at the laws coexisting in the spheres of land and labor, of production, distribution and trade, which are relevant for the economic activities of the indigenous populations.

Western Law

What is Western law? When we speak of Western law, we must keep separate two distinct sets of legal regulations which in colonial times were both made by "Western" people. On the one hand we have the law which had evolved in Europe for European societies. Some elements of this law, French, English, or Dutch, were received in the colonies. In the first place these laws were to serve as the law governing the social relations between the Europeans in the colonies. In the second place, some of these laws were extended to other population groups. Little of this law applied to indigenous populations, and irrespective of what the state system decreed, indigenous populations made hardly any use of them.

But besides this Western law, other laws were made to regulate the relationships between the immigrant European and the indigenous population. Such laws had to be made in order to structure and to legitimate the relations of political domination and economic exploitation of the natural and human resources in the colonies. In the first place, this meant a new constitutional system in which essential political functions, among them the making of normative regulations and decision making, were transferred to nonindigenous political functionaries. In the second place, the new laws had to make possible what the whole colonial venture was all about. It had to create a basis for a new economic order in the politically dominated regions. Primarily, it meant the legitimation and control of trade and the internal distribution of produce, and the criminalization of any competition from indigenous or other European traders. Secondly, it meant that the new laws had to structure and legitimate access to the productive resources of land and labor. Thirdly, it meant the securing of a surplus from indigenous forms of production.

In order to achieve these aims, a multitude of laws and regulations were made and changed in accordance with economic and political priorities. They included the establishment of trade and marketing monopolies and prohibitions, the imposition of taxes, the expropriation from land under indigenous control, the introduction of forced labor, the imposition of systems of forced cultivation and delivery to state or private enterprises, and the prohibition of economic activities for indigenous peoples.[11]

As is also shown clearly in Chanock's contribution in this volume, these laws were in many respects different from the laws valid in Europe, the Western laws we usually think of. We have of course to beware of anachronisms and too undifferentiated generalizations. The legal regulation of the distribution of political power, the control of production and distribution of economic resources in Europe, at the different historical periods we have to think of, were of course quite different from what now is Western law. Political rights for all citizens, including poor and female ones, were not common then in Europe either. The separation of powers, in particularly the emergence of an independent judiciary, also was a relatively new development in Europe. Labor relations were also rather cruel in Europe, and access to land and markets was also restricted. Yet there certainly was no equivalent to the legal structure of the new regimes of

---

11. See also Chanock, *Law, Custom and Social Order*. One of the most detailed studies is that of Okoth-Ogendo on Kenyan agrarian laws: Okoth-Ogendo, *Political Economy*, and "Development and the legal process in Kenya: an analysis of the role of law in rural development administration," *International Journal of the Sociology of Law* 12 (1984). Okoth-Ogendo documents how the spheres of agricultural production and distribution and marketing were "plastered" with European law. One of the few legal histories to bring this out clearly is J. Ball, *Indonesian Legal History 1602–1848* (Sydney, 1982). See also P. Fitzpatrick, *Law and State in Papua New Guinea* (New York, 1980); J. Breman, *Control of Land and Labour in Colonial Java* (Dordrecht, 1983), and J. Breman, *Koelies, Planters en Koloniale Politiek* (Dordrecht, 1987); R.S. Elson, *Javenese Peasants and the Colonial Sugar Industry* (Singapore, 1984).

direct or indirect rule which were established in the colonies, and
which transferred considerable political powers to the new levels of
political integration. And although political and judicial corruption
was also quite widespread in long periods of Western history, it
probably never reached the degree which characterized the actual
processes of government and judicial action in many phases of
colonial and post colonial history.

Customary Law

Obviously, to a large extent economic activities of the indigenous
populations were also regulated by customary legal forms. But we
can note that there was no question of indigenous economic activity
being solely or predominantly subject to their own law. In the
spheres of production, distribution, and trade there were many
"Western laws" which were in symbiosis with customary law.

However, these local normative systems, their procedures, and their
social, economic, political, and religious significance had changed.
In particular, the introduction and expansion of the political and
administrative institutions and forms of economic production had
affected their scope and quality of operation. The customary laws
were probably as much the product of tradition as of their adaptations to the new external influences. The recent discussions about
the "creation of tradition" and traditional law in colonial society
have made quite clear that the local normative systems in the
colonial period were certainly not the same as before the presence of
the colonial system.[12]

12. See also Chanock, "Neo-traditionalism and customary law in Malawi," *African
Law Journal* 18 (1978), and *Law, Custom and Social Order*, and in this volume. In these
discussions it is asserted that what went under the name of "tradition," traditional or
customary law, essentially was a creation of political, economic, and legal-
administrative measures of the colonial political and economic elites. The discussion
revolves around matters legal and non-legal (see F. Snyder, "Law and development
in the light of dependency theory," *Law and Society Review* 19 (1980), 723–804, and the
special number of the *Journal of African Law* 1984). I shall briefly mention some of the
themes, foci, of the discussions. In the first place, it pertains to the period before
colonial rule. There is the (re)creation of the governed people's past, their customs
and traditions. They are seen as relatively static, unchanging, immutable; they
involve the negation of a dynamic history prior to the advent of colonial rule. In the
second place, there is the construction of contemporary custom and tradition, and its
retrojection into the past, or vice versa, the identification of present day custom. The
creation of "the village," desa, in other parts of Indonesia, notably on Java, has
received much attention by scholars of Javanese history (see Breman, *Control*, and *Het
Dorp in Azië als Koloniale Schijngestalte* (Amsterdam, 1987); C. Holtzappel, *Het Verband
tussen Desa en Rijksorganisatie in prekoloniaal Java* (Leiden, 1986).

Besides, there was not just "the" or "one" customary law. I have already alluded to the variety of life-forms, existences of what is called customary law. Apart from being adapted by indigenous populations themselves in response to the changing political and economic conditions, these laws, like in the court decision from West Sumatra, were transformed by colonial administrators and scientists. This pertains to the following aspects in particular:

- the translation of indigenous normative systems into "law" at all, in order to have it at least recognized in the contexts of the state government system;
- the imposition of Western legal logic into indigenous concepts;
- the transformation of indigenous rules and principles into Western "rules" and the dissection of the procedural from the substantive elements in indigenous laws;[13]
- the translation of property relationships into the Western ideas of public and private legal domains, the assimilation of indigenous property forms to the notions of individual and communal ownership, and derivative rights (use rights etc.).[14]

This is not just a historical phenomenon: it goes on; just think of the readjustments of "*adat* law" in Indonesia, particularly in the domain of inheritance.

There is, I think, one aspect to these transformations which has a certain inevitability. It comes about through the translation of one's own cognitive and normative system into the terms of the other. On the methodological level – can non-Western folk systems be

13. See also Kolff and Reyntjens in this volume. For Minangkabau see K. von Benda-Beckmann, "Traditional law in a nontraditional context," *Indonesia Circle* 27 (1982) 39–50; idem., *The Broken Stairways*.

14. This discussion is closely related to the one mentioned earlier (see note 4). It has extensively been argued that the characteristics of the traditional local systems were distorted by their transformation in Western legal and bureaucratic thought and legal forms. More specifically, instances of invention of "communality" have been reported from Fiji; my wife and I have described such transformations in detail for the way in which Minangkabau forms of property were assimilated to Western legal forms of individual and communal ownership. See already C. van Vollenhoven, *Miskenningen van het Adatrecht* (Leiden, 1909). See further the already quoted titles by F. and K. von Benda-Beckmann, Snyder, Chanock, and Fitzpatrick. See also the recent special number of the *Journal of African Law* (1984) devoted to this discussion. A weakness of these discussions, however, is that they tend to generalize a customary law created in specific contexts into the customary law; see F. von Benda-Beckmann, "Law out of context: a comment on the creation of traditional law discussion," *Journal of African Law* 28 (1984).

adequately described in terms of Western legal categories?[15] – the idea of a comparative analytical system in which both indigenous and Western concepts can be analyzed could bring some comfort. But on the level of legal policy and law application, it could not. Policy and decision makers could not afford the non-committal attitude made possible by, or even required for, the use of a comparative analytical framework. Decisions had to be made, indigenous law had to be applied. If it was one essential element of an indigenous legal system that just and right decisions and interpretations of indigenous norms could only be arrived at through a process of communal deliberation leading to a consensual decision by local leaders legitimated to participate in this process – and if on the other hand the decision had to be taken by a single judge working within a different procedural context – then the right decision could, in no way, be reached.

There was, of course, great variety in the extent of, and the motivations behind, such transformations. Besides ignorance and the inability to take distance from one's own legal logic, overt policy considerations played a role, such as a stronger emphasis on autonomy in social and economic affairs by individual and nuclear families, and an inclination toward reducing obligations of individuals with respect to the community (the clan, tribe, or village). Depending on priorities in economic policy, we also find a stronger communalization of supra-individual relationships (the family property, the clan property, the village as corporate economic and political unit). A true "fit" between the systems was not possible. While champions of *adat* in Indonesia, like Van Vollenhoven, stressed the political and economic rights of local populations, others stressed the obligations and tried to fabricate a legitimate basis for the political oppression and economic exploitation of the local population largely in the name of *adat*. Though phrased in legal terms, the solutions found were ultimately and inevitably political.[16]

---

15. See already Van Vollenhoven, *Miskenningen*; see further the Bohannan-Gluckman controversy, the consensus for a comparative analytical system, etc. See L. Nader, ed., *Law in Culture and Society* (Chicago, 1969), and the parallel discussion around emic and etic approaches in general social and cultural anthropology.

16. The history of land rights on Java for instance shows such perversions of *adat*. By treating the native chiefs as the "owner of the country" – land and people – one could take over sovereignty and the jurisdiction over productive resources and labor (see the already quoted titles by Okoth-Ogendo, Snyder, Ball and Breman).

Legal Symbiosis and Economic Development

In the contexts of economic activities, there thus coexisted a multitude of different normative systems, different kinds of "Western" and of "customary" law. The question to which degree the economic conditions of the rural populations can be mainly attributed to any single subsystem is difficult to answer even for one region, and it is even more difficult to give general answers to this question.

But it is rather obvious that the expansion of economic activities of indigenous populations was much more inhibited by the "Western" laws and the political and economic practices legitimated by reference of these laws than by their adherence to the mutilated and transformed indigenous normative systems.

It makes a difference whether you have relatively free access to land, or whether you are driven off into crowded native reserves; or whether the state claims all not yet cultivated land, and withdraws it from your future exploitation by handing it out to European farmers or entrepreneurs.

It makes a difference whether you have to give tribute to patrons, clan leaders or nobilities, or whether you have to deliver two fifths of the produce as "land rent" or have to pay similar amounts in the form of taxes.

It makes a difference whether you can plan your economic activities according to your own priorities, favorable trade prospects, for example, or whether you are forbidden to produce certain crops, or forced to produce certain crops.

It makes a difference whether you can earn a profit by sale or trade, or whether you have to deliver your products compulsorily to representatives of state or private enterprises who want the surplus for themselves.

It makes a difference whether you have control over your own labor even if subject to local, and often traditional, demands by indigenous leaders – or whether part of your labor time is expropriated by the state or private enterprises, such as plantation owners.

It makes a difference whether you can withdraw from inhumane labor conditions or whether you cannot.

Most of these laws and regulations, often on sub-national levels, were used quite effectively. Besides, the political and economic practices, while legitimated by reference to these laws, often deviated considerably from the normative regulations, rarely to the benefit of local farmers and laborers. And it was these laws which established and maintained the political, economic, and social superiority of a small elite, which allowed this elite to obtain an impressive level of welfare. It was not the imported "modern" Western laws, the Dutch civil law, the English law of sales, or the commercial codes, the rational courts, or the legal certainty often associated with Western laws and courts which enabled the colonial minorities to prosper. Given the above political and economic restrictions, it would probably not have made much difference whether "the rest" of the economic activities among the indigenous populations would have been governed by "Western" law, for example the civil or commercial code, or not.

Conclusions

The pictures of legal symbiosis which I have tried to evoke are rather complex. Yet they are only glimpses at legal symbiosis in Minangkabau in a short historical period, and a very general view on legal symbiosis in the spheres of economic activity. In other historical periods we would get different pictures, and looking at other spheres of social life, marriage relations for instance, we would get a different picture again. Evidently, it will be nearly impossible to bring into picture all forms of legal symbiosis in all time and space contexts in the former colonial states. We shall have to reduce this complexity, look for new categories of data and theoretical problems about which to generalize.

Our research will profit if we can distance ourselves from the often ideological assumptions embedded in legalistic thinking. Their generation and maintenance through time should form part of our research;[17] they should not, implicitly or explicitly, form the point of departure for our research and thus guide, and misform, our research interests and perceptions of historical and contemporary conditions. It seems to be more important to start new research by delineating contexts of interaction, and interdependences between specified contexts. In particular, we should go beyond those contexts about which there is already a wealth of historical and recent material;[18] we should move to legal history, which has taken place in the various regions of the states we study. We should give more attention to forms of legal symbiosis in which people construct their

17. See the contribution by C. Fasseur in this volume.
18. See for some recent interesting collections Allott and Woodman, *People's Law*; M. Chiba, ed., *Asian Indigenous Law in Interaction with Received Law* (London, 1986); S. Burman and B.E. Harrell-Bond, eds., *The Imposition of Law* (New York, 1979).

own innovative law out of traditional indigenous, Western, and religious normative systems. We should study the interaction of legal systems in the interaction of people, and not as a comparison of abstract normative schemes which are correlated to behavior according to legalistic guidelines. We should ask to which degree people's behavior has been influenced by law and what use they made of law and administrative institutions, and look for the factors which seem to lead to certain normative influences and law-use patterns.[19] If we are interested in more than recording legislative and court histories, if we are interested in the actual life of legal systems, we must have some basic idea about the possible relations between normative systems and human agency, whether we are engaged in micro- or in macro-studies. The ideas provided by the normativity and ideology of lawyers, by the political rhetoric of politicians and development experts, are not very useful.[20]

19. See e.g. the attempts of S.F. Moore, "Law and social change: the semi-autonomous social field as an appropriate field of study," *Law and Society Review* 7 (1973), 719ff; idem, *Social Facts and Fabrications: "Customary" Law on Kilimanjaro, 1880–1980* (Cambridge, 1986); R. Kidder, "Towards an integrated theory of imposed law," in Burman and Harrell-Bond, eds., *The Imposition of Law*. See also our own efforts: F. von Benda-Beckmann, "Some comments on the problems of comparing the relationship between traditional and state systems of administration of justice in Africa and Indonesia," *Journal of Legal Pluralism* 19 (1981), 165–75 (on the question to which degree characteristics of traditional political organizations influenced the relative resistance of local forms of decision making to the imposition of the state administrative and judicial system); F. von Benda-Beckmann, "Leegstaande lucht-kastelen: over de pathologie van grondrechtshervormingen in ontwikkelingslanden," in *Recht in ontwikkeling-Tien agrarisch-rechtelijke opstellen*, ed. W. Brussaard et al. (Deventer, 1986) (on the significance of the socio-spatial relations of state institutions to indigenous forms of political-judicial jurisdictions); and F. and K. von Benda-Beckmann, "Adat and religion in Minangkabau and Ambon," in *Time Past, Time Present, Time Future*, ed. H. Claessen and D. Moyer, (Dordrecht, 1988) (on the explanation of the differences in the relationships between adat, religion, and government system in West Sumatra and Christian and Islamic Ambon).

20. For a critical analysis of the normative construction of past and present conditions, and the resultant distorted image of social and economic change in Minangkabau, see F. and K. von Benda-Beckmann, "Transformation and change in Minangkabau adat," in *Change and Continuity in Minangkabau: Local, Regional and Historical Perspectives*, ed. L.L. Thomas and F. von Benda-Beckmann (Athens, 1985).

Notes on the Contributors

Franz von Benda-Beckmann is professor in the law of developing countries at the Agricultural University in Wageningen. He is the author of *Property in Social Continuity* (The Hague, 1979); co-editor with L.L. Thomas of *Change and Continuity in Minangkabau* (Athens, 1985); and co-editor with M. van der Velde of *Law as a Resource in Agrarian Struggles* (Wageningen, 1992).

Martin Chanock is reader in legal studies at La Trobe University, Bundoora. His publications include *Unconsummated Union. Britain, Rhodesia, and South Africa, 1900–1945* (Manchester, 1977) and *Law, Custom and Social Order. The Colonial Experience in Malawi and Zambia* (Cambridge, 1985).

Paul H. Ch'en is professor of comparative law at the University of Tokyo and the author of *Chinese Legal Tradition under the Mongols* (Princeton, 1979) and *The Formation of the Early Meiji Legal Order* (Oxford, 1981).

Dagmar Engels is director at the *Volkshochschule* in Ulm (Germany). She is the author of *Beyond Purdah? Women in Bengal, 1890–1930* (Oxford, 1992).

C. Fasseur is professor of Southeast Asian history at the University of Leiden and author of *The Politics of Colonial Exploitation: Java, the Dutch and the Cultivation System* (Ithaca, 1992).

Jörg Fisch is professor of modern history at the University of Zürich. Among his books are *Cheap Lives and Dear Limbs. The British Transformation of the Bengal Criminal Law, 1769–1817* (Wiesbaden, 1983); *Die europäische Expansion und das Völkerrecht* (Stuttgart, 1984).

D.H.A. Kolff is professor of South Asian history at the University of

Leiden and the author of *Naukar, Rajput and Sepoy. The Ethnohistory of the Military Labour Market in Hindustan, 1450-1850* (Cambridge, 1990).

H.-J. Leue (University of Heidelberg) is the author of *Britische Indien-Politik, 1926-1932: Motive, Methoden und Misserfolg imperialer Politik am Vorabend der Dekolonisation* (Wiesbaden, 1981) and several articles in the field of overseas history.

J.-L. Miège is retired professor of history at the *Université de Provence* and former director of the *Institut d'Histoire des Pays d'Outre-Mer* at Aix-en-Provence. His publications include *Maroc et l'Europe* (Paris, 1961-1964, 4 vols.) and *Expansion européenne et décolonisation de 1870 à nos jours* (Paris, 1973).

Esin Örücü is professor of comparative law at the Erasmus University, Rotterdam, and head of the Department of Jurisprudence, Glasgow University. She is author of *A Public Law Approach to Real Property - Restraints on Property Rights* (in Turkish) (Istanbul, 1976) and co-author with M. Aitkenhead, N. Burrows, and R. Jagtenberg of *Law and Lawyers in European Integration. A Comparative Analysis of the Education, Attitudes, and Specialisation of Scottish and Dutch Lawyers* (Rotterdam, 1988).

Pamela Price is associate professor of history at the University of Oslo. She published *Resources and Rule in Zamindari South India, 1802-1903: Sivagangai and Ramnad as Kingdoms under the Raj* (Madison, 1979) and articles in *Modern Asian Studies, South Asia*, and other scholarly journals.

Filip Reyntjens is senior lecturer in law and politics at the University of Antwerp and director of the Africa Institute in Brussels. Among his books are *Pouvoir et Droit au Rwanda* (Tervuren, 1985); *Burundi 1972-1988. Continuité et Changement* (Brussels, 1989) and *Rechtsvergelijking* (Brussels, 1991).

Eric Seizelet is assistant professor at the *Institut de Recherches Comparatives sur les Institutions et le Droit (Section Corée-Japon)* of the *Centre National de la Recherche Scientifique* in Paris. Among his recent publications are *Les Petits-fils du Soleil: la Jeunesse japonaise et le Patriotisme* (Paris, 1988) and *Monarchie et Démocratie dans le Japon d'après-guerre* (Paris, 1990).

Jarle Simensen is professor of modern history at the University of Trondheim. Among his publications are *Commoners, Chiefs and Colonial Government. Akim Abuakwa, Ghana, under British Rule* (Trondheim, 1975); *Norwegian missions in African history*, vol. I (*South Africa*) and vol. II (Madagascar), (Oslo/Oxford, 1986); and *Education as Development Aid. NORAD and Trawling Education at Ghana Nautical College, 1964–1980* (Oslo, 1991).

Index

331

338

Pondicherry, 142, 144, 155 n. 87
Portugal, Portuguese, 132 n. 9, 135 n.
21, 136, 138, 156, 217
Positive law, 112; in India, 204, 205,
206, 207, 212
Pottinger, Sir Henry, 86
Private law: in Japan, 71; in Maghrib,
103; in Congo, 115
Privy Council, 180, 266, 270
Procedural law, 30, 31
Property, 149
Protégé's, 5, 6
Provincial Court in China, British, 90,
91, 94, 96, 97, 99
Prussianisation of state (Japan), 71, 72
Public law (in India), 160, 161, 178,
201

Quran, 101, 106, 180, 214

Rabbinical courts in Maghrib, 105
Racial discrimination, 124
Rammohan Roy, 162, 163
Rattigan, 230
Rattray, R.S., 274
Recorder's Courts (in India), 147, 152
Regulations on Commercial Court
Procedures in Ottoman Empire, 47
Regulations for the Conduct of Judicial
Processes (Japan), 71
Religious law/ecclesiastical law (in
India), 112, 160, 182
Religious practices, 160, 182, 211
Rights over land (Gold Coast), 264-71
Robbery, 181
Rochussen, J.J., 240
Roessler, 68
Roman law, 22, 55, 210, 243, 244
Roman-Dutch law, 43
"Roman" penal law, 244
Royal Commissioner (in Rwanda and
Burundi), 113
Royal courts (in India), 180
Rudolf, 68
Rwanda (Ruanda), 111, 112, 113, 117,
125, 126
Ryukyu archipelago, 68

Samurai, 68, 69, 70, 76
Sanskritisation, 160
Sati. See widow burning
Satsuma clan, 66, 68
Savigny, F.C. von, 220
Scotland, 174
Separation of powers, 204, 304, 319

Sexual control, 162
Seitaisho (Instrument of Government),
69
Sekyi, Kobina, 268
Setalvad, 201, 202
Settlers, colonies of settlement, 16, 20,
21-22, 27-28
Seydel, Max von, 69
Shanghai, international settlement, 94,
95
Shari'a (Islamic law), 41, 46, 47, 52,
101, 180, 205, 207, 211, 214, 215
Shastra, 159, 161, 180, 181, 182, 183,
184, 205
Sheriat. See Shari'a
Shibata mission, 68
Shinto state ideology, 79
Ships' councils, 130
Shogunate, 78
Sino-Japanese War, 66
Slater, Governor, 272
Slavery, slave trade, 16, 22, 26, 34
Snouck Hurgronje, Christiaan, 239
Sorcery, 285
Southwest Africa, 4
Spain, colonial rule of, 3, 4, 17, 18
Special Marriage Act (India), 167
Standing Counsel and Attorney (of
EIC), 143
State law: in Zaire, 112, 123; in Africa,
127
States-General, 130
Statute law (in Africa), 126
Storres, Charles B., 69
St. Thomé, 136
Stridhan, 164, 168
Substantive law: in Congo, 114; in
Zaire, 125; India, 148, 154, 181,
202, 211, 215
Succession, inheritance, 115, 122, 144,
146, 182, 195, 211
Succession Act of 1865 (India), 219,
244
Sudra, 166
Suicide, 34
Süleyman the Magnificent, 39
Su Ming-kang (Bencon), 131
Sundanese, 255
Supomo, 255
Supreme Court: in India, 152, 182,
203, 211; in Gold Coast, 260, 261,
262, 268, 270, 272
Surat, 138, 139, 143
Surayi Devlet (Council of State), 47
Superintendent of Trade (China), 85,